THE ARROGANCE OF THE MODERN

*Historical Theology
Held in Contempt*

David W. Hall

The Calvin Institute
Oak Ridge, TN 37830

© 1997
The Covenant Foundation
190 Manhattan Ave.
Oak Ridge, TN 37830
(covpca@usit.net)

The publisher gratefully acknowledges permission granted by The Kuyper Institute for permission to reprint, "Revolutionary Pulpits" which originally appeared in *Election Day Sermons* (1996).

Library of Congress Cataloging-in-Publication Data: 96-93140

Hall, David W.
The Arrogance of the Modern

1. Church History; 2. Theology; 3. Ethics;
4. Biblical Studies; 5. Reformation Thought.

Includes Bibliographical References and Index

ISBN: 0-9650367-4-x

First Edition 1997
Printed in the United States of America

Cover Design: *Jobe Design*, Memphis, TN

To order copies, write:
The Calvin Institute,
190 Manhattan Ave.
Oak Ridge, TN 37830

THE ARROGANCE
OF THE MODERN

Table of Contents

Preface

For Shakespeare, "The past is prologue." Many Christians are rediscovering that same truth concerning most issues of our day. The past is actually an excellent introduction to many current issues. Regrettably, many Christians stand upon the stage of history with virtually no idea of what has preceded. Besides being placed at a distinct disadvantage with such tardy stage entrance, Christians are finding that forsaking the best of prior thought is an extremely imprudent *modus operandi*. The seduction of the superiority of modernity blindfolds many to the past.

Many act as though their chief desire is to run away from their spiritual predecessors as far and as fast as possible. Not only do many people forsake their spiritual parents, moreover, some contemporaries seem to suffer from repressed memories—a dubious syndrome that allows children to slander their parents *ex post facto;* all the while, such vilification denies these deceased ancestors the opportunity to speak for themselves. If they could speak, maybe Christians would find that their spiritual parents were not as barbaric as once suspected.

This book is written in the hope that the next generation will be wiser in its admiration of history than recent generations have been. Specifically, I hope that future Christians will embrace the good from their spiritual forebears rather than despise it before they even become acquainted with it. When the apostle Paul spoke of "forgetting those things which lie behind," he certainly was not advocating that Christians should become mindless about the past; yet, that is all too often the case.

One may wish to view this work as an apology for the usefulness of history. Indeed, it is a defense of what has gone before. Perhaps as in the words of Woody Allen: "History has to repeat itself. For no one listens the first time." If the reiteration of some of the lessons of history will inform and equip present and future Christians, this writer will be pleased.

Another way to see this collection of ideas is to view it as an attempt to vindicate—to vindicate some exemplary Christians who may have known and lived in far more conformity to God's will than many of us ever will. If they are our betters—despite massive maligning by modern skepticism—then it may be time to rehabilitate their reputations. I will be glad to be known as a vindicator of past saints as long as they were as exemplary as the ones discussed herein.

This work is also a very lengthy footnote on a singular text with enormous epistemological ramification. Nearly every essay contained returns at some point to the *leitmotif* enunciated by Solomon: "There is nothing new under the sun." These essays are many variations that support and elaborate upon that central theme. These discussions include some of my various meanderings to see if Solomon was accurate or not. Not to worry, his assertion remains unfalsified.

C. S. Lewis reflected a hearty perspective similar to the one in this work. In *God in the Dock*, he found himself highly skeptical of several modernistic notions. In "Dogma and the Universe," he spoke to a common scandal in the words below.

> It is a common reproach against Christianity that its dogmas are unchanging, while human knowledge is in continual growth. Hence, to unbelievers, we seem to be always engaged in the hopeless task of trying to force the new knowledge into molds which it has outgrown. I think this feeling alienates the outsider much more than any particular discrepancy . . . For it seems to him clear that, if our ancestors had known what we know about the universe, Christianity would never have existed at all.[1]

Lewis found that a historical perspective helpfully diagnosed a number of philosophical assumptions when applied to, say, certain areas of science. On the specific issue of the size of the earth in relation to the universe, Lewis noted: "There is no question here of knowledge having grown . . . The real question is why the spatial insignificance of the earth, after being known for centuries, should suddenly in the last century have become an argument against Christianity. I do not know why this has happened; but I am sure it does not mark an increased clarity of thought . . ."[2] Thus, he suggested that a knowledge of the history of science could help analyze a modern issue. Lewis believed that neither the facts nor the attempts to refute Christianity had been radically altered over immense stretches of time.

In his chapter "On the Reading of Old Books," he made a number of key observations. Decrying the habit of initially turning to secondary sources rather than primary sources, Lewis thought it was "topsy-turvy" to maintain a "preference for the modern books and this shyness of the old ones."[3] Yet, he noted the great prevalence of this modernophilia in theological circles. Whereas, Lewis preferred to have the reader first attend to the direct sources (with whatever guidance was necessary), he found a trend that substituted rumor for primary sources. He noted: "Where you find a little study circle of Christian laity you can be almost certain that they are studying not St. Luke or St. Paul or St. Augustine or Thomas Aquinas or Hooker or Butler, but Nicolas Berdyaev, Jacques Maritain, Reinhold Niebuhr, or Dorothy Sayers or even myself."[4]

---

[1] C. S. Lewis, *God in the Dock* (Grand Rapids: Eerdmans, 1970), p. 38.

[2] Ibid., p. 39.

[3] Lewis, op. cit., p. 201.

[4] Idem. Today's evangelical circles may be studying Schaeffer, Swindoll, Lucado, or Dobson, but probably not myself.

Lewis recommended this remedy: "But if he must read only the new or only the old, I would advise him to read the old. And I would give him this advice precisely because he is an amateur and therefore much less protected than the expert against the dangers of an exclusive contemporary diet. A new book is still on its trial and the amateur is not in a position to judge it. It has to be tested against the great body of Christian thought down the ages, and all its hidden implications . . . have to be brought to light."[5]

Lewis continued with a metaphor similar to the one I have used above about entering the play after intermission. He asserted that if one enters a discussion group at 11:00, without knowing what has gone on from 8:00-11:00, one may interpret many things out of context. Inside jokes, laughter, references, and other nuances will not be appreciated. In the same way, Lewis continued, "you may be led to accept what you would have indignantly rejected if you knew its real significance."[6] The "only safety," according to Lewis, was to hold to the standard of plain ("mere" as the puritan Richard Baxter called it) Christianity "which puts the controversies of the moment in their proper perspective." This approach preserves a crucial perspective that is often wanting amidst today's ideological forays.

Lewis recommended the classics, the great books of Christianity. Among these he recommended Augustine, Aquinas, Boethius, Bunyan, Hooker, Pascal, Spenser, Butler, and others. The essays in this volume attempt to acquaint the reader with a few other greats, mainly from the Christian tradition with which I am most familiar. No doubt others could add to the debate by reviewing their own tradition.

Lewis warned that "[e]very age has its own outlook. It is specially good at seeing certain truths and specially liable to make certain mistakes. We all, therefore, need the books that will correct the characteristic mistakes of our own period. And that means the old books. All contemporary writers share to some extent the contemporary outlook—even those, like myself, who seem most opposed to it."[7] Lewis, more clearly than many moderns, observed "the characteristic blindness of the twentieth century. . . . None of us can fully escape this blindness, but we shall certainly increase it, and weaken our guard against it, if we read only modern books. Where they are true they will give us truths which we half knew already. Where they are false they will aggravate the error with which we are already dangerously ill."[8]

Lewis correctly saw the danger of holding the past in contempt and called for a fresh acquaintance with the best of the past. As these essays suggest, those who love C. S. Lewis may want to imitate his appreciation for the *paleo*.

I, too, want to concur with Lewis and others who have realized this. The theology of an earlier day has much to teach us. We might begin by admitting that

---

[5] Idem.
[6] Idem.
[7] Ibid., p. 202.
[8] Idem.

there is a beam in our own eye—our presumption that we have superior insight. Part I of this book illustrates of what happens when we forsake historic theology by "forgetting what is past." Part II, then, is an attempt to remove the log and accept healing salve from earlier spiritual opthamologists.

This modest attempt is, of course, far short of comprehensive. Although certainly not an exhaustive catalogue of issues, I do offer this volume as a primer on the use of church history to solve select ills. Many other issues can and will be considered by other works and other authors. While this volume cannot address every issue in detail, I do hope that as an introduction to portions of church history it will engender a greater appreciation for the longevity of superb thought.

I am glad to acknowledge the expert help given to me by friends and editors Bill Thiessen and Anne Jaeger. Tim Rake contributed immense help in all stages of this book's development. I am thankful for a brother like this with such rare insight coupled with giftedness. I also want to take this opportunity to thank Brenda Jobe (who enjoyed too much the calls to discuss my "arrogance" with me) for her excellent cover design. I gladly thank the Covenant Foundation for their judgment and unfailing support. Together we wish to dedicate this volume to our spiritual parents, particularly to our mothers. This book is affectionately dedicated to:

Florence Dotson McClain, in whose memory the Covenant Foundation was begun and who reared one of the most principled men in the world;

Martha Buckner, who gave us one of the great theologian-physicists of the twenty-first century;

Kathryn Prater, who instilled class and conservativism in her son who is one of the finest stewards and physicians alive;

Virginia Lynch, who gave her son an analytic gift, a sharp wit, and love for the important things;

Joyce Hall, who attempted to teach her son to read and write, and who has endured much from him.

Remembering the Past for the Present and Future

Just as loss of memory in an individual is a psychiatric defect calling for a medical treatment, so too any community which has no social memory is suffering from an illness.[1]

Many Christians treat the past like a dead, and therefore irrelevant, ancestor. As a result, memory has little place in an age that has little vision. Rather than repressing memories about our predecessors and their virtue, remembering may be an undetected aid "for the living of these days"—unless, of course, we have definitively judged that our spiritual parents were so feeble, inferior, cowardly, or unenlightened as to be prevented from communing at the same table as we. That is the arrogance of the modern.

Agreeing with Solomon that "there is nothing new under the sun" (Eccl. 1:9), Christians in all ages can instruct those who live later. We, in turn, can learn much by standing on the shoulders of those who have preceded us. After all, if the "faith was handed down once and for all" (Jude 3), one may expect little change in core biblical truths over the centuries. Since the faith is essentially the same in all centuries, surely we can learn from other brothers and sisters in Christ. We will find some agreement with Chesterton who called the church a "democracy of the dead," meaning that (for those who love popular referenda) if we truly understand the unity of the church—both militant and triumphant—we will not deliberately disenfranchise those who have gone home to be with the Lord. They, too, have much to say in the referenda of today; though they are dead, they still speak (Heb. 11:4)—and we need to learn to listen. Perhaps fewer mistakes would be made if we returned free expression to those spiritual pioneers who have preceded us.

Most young adults only develop a deep appreciation for their parents when they are tested. That may be true in spiritual things as well. As one is tested by a

---

[1] Lord Acton, cited in John Briggs, "God, Time and History," *Eerdmans Handbook to the History of Christianity*, Tim Dowley, ed. (Grand Rapids: Eerdmans, 1977), p. 2.

very modern and often perplexing world, the Christian not only wants to know God's Word and will, but also on many occasions would like to ask his parents a few questions like: "What did you do when such and such happened? How did you handle a particular situation? What resources are available in regard to the following issues?"

The good news is that God has not left us totally without helpful advisors. Yet, frequently we do not even know they exist or where to turn for help. Much of that is our own fault or due to our over-confident unwillingness to receive advice. Often modern Christians shut themselves off from helpful sources of direction by deciding from the outset that the knowledge of previous generations is of little or no value. Although the similarity is unintended, that is not altogether different from the 1960s slogan: "Don't trust anyone over thirty."

Funny that when most of us became "Thirtysomething," things changed. Similarly, it may be time to admit that we can trust some earlier Christians and beliefs—those that were well thought-out and scriptural—that are centuries old. Many earlier episodes of spiritual history may benefit evangelicals, if we can merely be healed of our phobia of anything older than thirty years old.

The Value of Testimonies from History

One contemporary thinker recently questioned whether there was value in knowing a medieval Christian thinker. Phrasing the important question this way, he queried: "But can a seven-hundred-year-old thinker still be relevant today? Students of logic will recognize the implication of the question as the fallacy of 'chronological snobbery.' 'New is true' and 'old is mold,' we are told. Logic informs us, however, that time has no necessary connection with truth. Or at least, if there were any kind of connection, then the time-honored thought ought to have the edge."[2]

An appropriate assessment of the motive and utility of remembering was summarized well by Scotsman William Symington a century and a half ago:

> The disposition to commemorate events, whether of public or private interest, springs from a law of our nature. It is true, the law has been abused,—grossly abused, for purposes of a superstitious character, . . . Nevertheless, the law is good, if men use it lawfully. . . . Matters of great and permanent utility, the due consideration of which is fitted to exert a continued beneficial influence on society, are thus held forth to the view of the community, and prevented from passing into oblivion. The very act of reminiscence itself is calculated to call into operation, and consequently to improve by exercising, some of the higher moral principles of the heart, such as gratitude for benefits received, veneration for departed worth, and imitation of praiseworthy excellence.[3]

---

[2] Norman Geisler, *Thomas Aquinas: An Evangelical Appraisal* (Grand Rapids: Baker, 1991), p. 11.

[3] William Symington, "Historical Sketch of the Westminster Assembly of Divines," *Commemoration of the Bicentenary of the Westminster Assembly of Divines* (Glasgow, 1843), pp. 31-32.

Lord Acton spoke of the past as capable of teaching by illuminating "the instructions derived from the errors of great men."[4] He also noted: "The value of history is its certainty—against which opinion is broken." If we find that our parents were on to some things that we have not realized, or if perhaps their insights were deeper than the average paperback Christian book, then we should not be so arrogant as to cling to an uncritical bias for the modern. Jeremiah spoke of the "ancient paths" (Jer. 6:16)—those tried and trusted ruts of life that rebels sought to re-fill because they were routine. We may even find, as C. S. Lewis did, that some of the ancient Christian examples are preferable to many unproven modern ones. As Lewis advised of a newer book or work, "It has to be tested against the great body of Christian thought down the ages, and all its hidden implications (often unsuspected by the author himself) have to be brought to light . . . The only safety is to have a standard of plain, central Christianity . . . which puts the controversies of the moment in their proper perspective. Such a standard can be acquired only from the old books. It is a good rule, after reading a new book, never to allow yourself another new one till you have read an old one in between."[5]

Lewis exhorted: "The only palliative is to keep the clean sea breeze of the centuries blowing through our minds, and this can be done only by reading old books. Not, of course, that there is any magic about the past. People were no cleverer then than they are now; they made as many mistakes as we. But not the same mistakes . . ."[6]

Nearly a century ago, G. K. Chesterton gave testimony about the value of rediscovering our past Christian heritage, when he found that the best truths had already been mined:

> I did, like all other solemn little boys, try to be in advance of the age. Like them I tried to be some ten minutes in advance of the truth. And I found that I was eighteen hundred years behind it . . . When I fancied that I stood alone I was really in the ridiculous position of being backed up by all Christendom. It may be, Heaven forgive me, that I did try to be original; but I only succeeded in inventing all by myself an inferior copy of the existing traditions of civilized religion . . . It might amuse a friend or an enemy to read how I gradually learnt from the truth of some stray legend or from the falsehood of some dominant philosophy, things that I might have learnt from my catechism—if I had ever learnt it . . . I found at last what I might have found in the nearest parish church.[7]

Lord Acton could have been helpful once again. He asked, "How is man superior to prejudice, passion, and interest?" His answer was: "By the study of History and the pursuit of the required character."[8] Moreover, he recommended an

---

[4] J. Rufus Fears, ed., *Selected Writings of Lord Action: Essays in Religion, Politics, and Morality* (Indianapolis: Liberty Press, 1988), p. 623.

[5] C. S. Lewis, *God in the Dock* (Grand Rapids: Eerdmans, 1970), p. 201.

[6] Idem.

[7] G. K. Chesterton, *Orthodoxy* (London: Lane, 1909), pp. 16-17.

[8] J. Rufus Fears, op. cit., p. 620.

option that is often ignored: "Resist your time—take a foothold outside it—see other times and ask yourself whether the time of our ancestors is fit for us."[9]

A Theology of and Worth Remembering

Before proceeding, a few preliminary questions deserve to be answered: Does God want us to remember the past and be encouraged by it? Why should we remember any event in a past age? Why remember? Is it helpful, or is it automatically idolatry that is wrongly focused?

A biblical study of the role of remembering in the Christian life might be helpful for many contemporaries because most people are so routinely negative about the value of history. Memory and its beneficial effect is often taken for granted; yet nearly 300 variations of the word "remember" appear in the Bible. Notwithstanding the present arrogance toward the past, we find that remembering is not only commanded, but furthermore is a distinctively helpful tool for Christian living. Many times the great saints in the Scripture were told to remember how God had worked faithfully in their lives in an earlier day. The purpose of this memory was to remind them that God "in whom there is no shadow of turning" (Jas. 1:17) will remain faithful in the present and the future just as he was in the past. The biblical logic is that *if* God was so faithful in the past (and does not change; he is "immutable"), *then* remembering his unchanging faithfulness will spur us on to trust him in our own lives and struggles.

One indication of the special importance of spiritual remembering is the regularity with which this activity is ascribed to God. In the earliest books of the Bible, God selects this word to emphasize his whole-hearted care and providence for his people. God "remembered" Noah (Gen. 8:1; 9:15), Abraham (Gen. 19:29), and Rachel (Gen. 30:22). God specifically "remembers" his covenant with Abraham (Ex. 2:24 and 6:5) as a means of covenant renewal and inspiring Moses to be obedient.

God also remembers Hannah's yearning for maternity (1 Sam. 1:19); when he remembers, he does something about it, indicating that spiritual remembering is not merely a cognitive activity devoid of application. God and his people act differently if they remember. God remembers his covenant with Abraham, Isaac, and Jacob (Ex. 32:13); he also remembers the land, covenant, and ancestors who covenanted with him on earlier occasions (Lev. 26:42, 45). In David's time, God remembered his covenant (Ps. 105:8) as he did with Ezekiel (Ez. 16:60). Even at the birth of Jesus, Zechariah praises God who shows "mercy to our fathers and remembers his holy covenant" (Lk. 1:72). God himself models a lofty role for remembrance.

The Psalter has the greatest concentration of verses calling for remembrance. Several titles of Psalms are even classified as "remembering" Psalms (Ps. 38, 70). Imagine, a genre of inspired poetry whose focus was to bring to remembrance! In

---

[9] Idem.

several instances the phrase "Praise his holy name" can be translated "Give thanks at the remembrance of his holiness" (Ps. 30:4; 97:12). God's righteousness is an enduring remembrance throughout all generations (Ps. 102:12).

Nearly all of Psalm 78 is a retrospective of what God has already done in history. Either this is a pedantic history lesson—of little comfort or applicability to the struggling believer—or else it is a pattern of sanctified response. It is clearly the latter. One means of sanctification or personal encouragement is to recollect or to remember. Harking back to the Exodus wandering, Psalm 78 states that Israel "remembered that God was their Rock" (Ps. 78:35) following God's chastisement and renewed their trust in him. God also "remembered that they were but flesh, a passing breeze that does not return" (Ps. 78:39) and he extended mercy to them. Nevertheless, in their lapses, "They did not remember his power—the day he redeemed them from the oppressor" (Ps. 78:42).

God remembers his love and faithfulness (Ps. 98:3), his holy promise (Ps. 105:42), his covenant (Ps. 106:45), and his wonderful works (Ps. 111:4), while the people often fail to remember God's many kindnesses (Ps. 106:7). The Psalmist asked to be remembered by God when he shows mercy (Ps. 107:4), and David remembers God's ancient judgments or laws (Ps. 119:52). As a devotional staple, the Psalmist meditated: "In the night I remember your name [and all that it stands for], O Lord" (Ps. 119:55). When the people of God remembered better days, they wept (Ps. 137:1), and the forever-enduring love of God is associated with the "One who remembered us in our low estate" (Ps. 136:23). Remembering God and his dealings with people in history must be important in light of its prominence; at least it was for the saints in biblical ages who surpass many moderns in spirituality. If it was good enough for them, it surely is for us, too.

The Prophet Isaiah, in a time of national and spiritual decline, seemed to value remembering highly. It may even be that in those times of spiritual declension, mindful commemorations are most needed. In Isaiah 63:11, as a means of revival, God's "people remembered the days of old, the days of Moses and his people . . ." Could it be that revival might be hastened by the covenant people of God re-acquainting themselves with God's history? Though some may see mental recollection as merely an academic exercise, the biblical pages reveal an uncanny association between revival and remembering.

Later in biblical history, God called on Jacob and Israel to "remember these things" (Is. 44:21), and to rebels God said, "Remember this, fix it in mind . . . Remember the former things, those of long ago; I am God, and there is no other . . . I make known the end from the beginning, from ancient times, what is still to come" (Is. 46:8-9). Isaiah is in continuity with Moses who had sung, "Remember the days of old; consider the generations long past. Ask your father and he will tell you, your elders, and they will explain to you" (Dt. 32:7).

God even provides concrete aids to help his people remember. The tassels with Scripture verses (not dissimilar to a Scripture Memory Packet) were "so you will remember all the commands of the Lord, that you may obey them . . . Then you will remember to obey all my commands" (Num. 15:39-40). In the belly of the fish, Jonah found remembering to be vital: "When my life was ebbing away, I remembered you, O Lord" (Jon. 2:7). Perhaps we should have more of this 'memorializing.' On the last page of the NT, as the remnant is revived, they found a written memorial to be helpful: "Then those who feared the Lord talked with each other, and the Lord listened and heard. A scroll of remembrance was written in his presence concerning those who feared the Lord and honored his name" (Mal. 3:16).

Perhaps the OT advice is not outdated: "Remember how the Lord your God led you. . . . remember the Lord your God, for it is he who gives you the ability to produce wealth, and so confirms his covenant, which he swore to your forefathers . . . Remember this and never forget how you provoked the Lord to anger. . . . do not be afraid of them; remember well what the Lord your God did . . ." (Dt. 8:2; 8:18; 9:7; and 7:18). To remember, therefore, is to benefit from the past.

In the NT, Peter remembers the words of the Lord (Mt. 26:7) and is cut to the heart. The disciples also remember the Lord's teaching (Lk. 24:8) and thereby grow in discipleship. Hebrews 10:32 shows the relationship between memory and courage when the Christians are told to "[r]emember those earlier days after you had received the light, when you stood your ground in great contest in the face of suffering." The aim of that remembering is to "not throw away your confidence; it will be richly rewarded" (Heb. 10:35). Thus memory aids in perseverance (10:36).

Peter's epistles seem especially appreciative of the value of remembering how God has acted in the past. In fact the very purpose of Peter's second epistle is to use remembering "to stimulate you to wholesome thinking" (2 Pet. 3:1), a worthy virtue in any age. He reminds his readers of already established truths (2 Pet. 1:12), thinks "it is right to refresh your memory as long as I live in the tent of this body" (2 Pet. 1:13), and commits himself to "every effort to see that . . . you will always be able to remember these things" (2 Pet. 1:15). The presbyter knew the value of remembering in regard to spiritual growth.

The same can be said of the Apostle John. When he wrote to the faltering church at Ephesus, which was in danger of forsaking her first love, he did not tell her to forget about the past and set her sights only on current or futuristic perspectives. On the contrary the Apostle of Love urged the people to remember "the height from which you have fallen! Repent and do the things you did at first" (Rev. 2:5). Remembering is positive and necessary. Also, he called for the church at Sardis, the church that was in the terminal ward, to strengthen any remaining vital signs of spirituality. Specifically he said, "Remember, therefore, what you have received and heard; obey it, and repent" (Rev. 3:3).

In Scripture, memory is reserved for important things; it has a very important function for Christians. Specifically Christians are to:

- Remember their Creator in the days of their youth (Eccl. 12:1)—as a means of calling covenant children to faithfulness amidst the hormonal revolution.

- Remember the Sabbath (Ex. 20:8) and keep it holy—as a means of spiritual renewal.
- Remember specific days—in Exodus 13:3, the people are instructed to "Commemorate this day" (Passover), and later in Esther 9:28 the deliverance of the Jews in Xerxes' time (The Feast of Purim) is to be "remembered and observed in every generation."
- Remember the Lord—in Nehemiah 4:14, as Nehemiah exhorted the people to faithfulness, he said to the nobles and officials: "Don't be afraid of them. Remember the Lord, who is great and awesome."
- "Remember Jesus Christ, raised from the dead, descended from David," Paul urged Timothy (2 Tim 2:8).
- "Remember those in prison" (Heb. 13:3); "remember the poor" (Gal. 2:10); and "Remember your leaders, who spoke the word of God to you. Consider the outcome of their way of life and imitate their faith. Jesus Christ is the same yesterday and today and forever" (Heb. 13:7).
- "Remember Me as often as you do this," said our Lord of the sacrament (Lk. 22:19).

Remembering is frequently advised; it is a thoughtful reflection on the things of God; it unites the historical past and the ethical present (Gal. 2:10; Heb. 13:3), and is a part of the renewing of our minds (Rom. 12:2). For our spiritual ancestors, remembering was a potent incentive to regain faithfulness to the Lord. Do not our churches, homes, and nations need this kind of revival—a faithful recollection of God's mighty deeds? Are we above this? If done properly with focus on God, memory of the past has great value.

If the scriptural principles of our predecessors were correct, then a remembering of those is indeed promising. Yet one must constantly preserve the balance between respecting the past and worshiping the past. As long as ancestor-worship is avoided, remembering has great promise, for in so doing, one studies the providence of God, his handiwork in a particular epoch of history. Since all history is God's history, we have nothing to fear and much to gain from remembering the past as a guide for the present and the future. His-Story is useful to God's children in the church and in daily living.

The history of any church, spiritual moment, or person is a worthwhile guide. Church history is our friend not an opposing fiend. Only the arrogance of self-centered modernism would induce Christians to despise the lessons of the past. The history of earlier episodes in church history can sound strikingly modern and have great value to guide Christians in the twenty-first century. One contemporary author, George Grant, summarized: "Remembrance and forgetfulness are the measuring rods of faithfulness throughout the entire canon of Scripture."

To fail to profit from our own history is also one of the surest paths to demise. Alexander Solzhenitsyn put it very well: "To destroy a people you must first sever their roots." This study is our commitment to avoid destroying ourselves and our children; instead, we seek to be renewed in our roots.

William Symington once helped capture the significance of remembering:

> We would not be chargeable with the enormous wickedness of forgetting that men are only what God makes them, and that to him all the glory . . . is to be ascribed. But we are, at the same time, unable to see wherein the bestowment of a due meed of praise on the memory of such . . . contravenes any maxim of sound morality, or any dictate of inspiration. We . . . have no hesitation in attempting to awaken, in the men of the present generation, sentiments of admiration and gratitude for the memory of worthies to whom all are so deeply indebted. . . . While we claim and exercise the right of bringing these, like all other human productions, to the infallible touchstone of Revelation.[10]

Of the value of re-applying the past, Moses D. Hoge wrote:

> Sometimes it is good to get free from the narrow environments of the immediate present and ascend some eminence which commands a view of ways long since trodden, and then, from what is taught in the review, learn to forecast the ever-widening way of the future. It is only by such studies that we catch the spirit of the great historic eras which have been potent in shaping the institutions of our own times. It is only when we can transport ourselves to the distant past and evoke from its obscurity the forms of its heroic men; it is only when we acquaint ourselves with the errors they combated, the difficulties they surmounted, the hardships they endured, that we can fully comprehend the character of the men who thus toiled and suffered, or appreciate the value.[11]

As observed a century ago, we would do well to affirm: "Ah, the past is never dead! All history is God's mighty electric battery charged to the full with slumbering forces which have subdued kingdoms, overturned thrones, and shaken the world to its center."[12]

In his *City of God*, St. Augustine defended the Christian church against allegations that it was the cause of the decay of the once-great Empire. Rather, Augustine placed the blame for societal decay in the eclipse of virtue in the Roman era. Specifically, he alleged that forgetting the past contributed to the downfall of an empire: "[T]he good old customs have been lost, and for so great an evil not only are we responsible but we should face judgment, like culprits fearing the

---

[10] "Historical Sketch of the Westminster Assembly of Divines" by William Symington in *Commemoration of the Bicentenary of the Westminster Assembly of Divines* (Glasgow, 1843), pp. 69, 71.

[11] Francis Beattie *et al, Memorial Volume of the Westminster Assembly, 1647-1897,* (Richmond: The Presbyterian Committee of Publication, 1897), p. 189.

[12] William Henry Roberts, ed., *Addresses at the Celebration of the Two-Hundred and Fiftieth Anniversary of the Westminster Assembly* (Philadelphia: Presbyterian Board of Publication, 1898), p. 273 (hereafter cited as *Anniversary Addresses*).

penalty of death. By our own vices, not by chance, we have lost the republic, though we retain the name."[13] We would do well to recall his diagnosis in our own day.

Since this essay began with a quotation from Lord Acton, it might be fitting to allow him the last word as well. Opposed to a determinism by caprice, Acton advised that "knowledge of history means choice of ancestors."[14] He differentiated between being governed by the past as opposed to a liberating knowledge gained from the past. He recommended: "Live both in the future and the past. Who does not live in the past does not live in the future." Acton, who spoke of progress as "the religion of those who have none,"[15] also noted that history "gives us the line of progress, the condition of progress, the demonstration of error."[16] Of this historical perspective, Acton cheered: "If it enables us to govern the future . . . by disclosing the secret of progress and the course sailed, the nation that knows the course best and possesses the most perfect chart will have an advantage over others in shaping the destiny of man."[17]

---

[13] Augustine, *The City of God* (New York: Doubleday, 1958), p. 75.

[14] J. Rufus Fears, op. cit., p. 620.

[15] Ibid., p. 636.

[16] Ibid., p. 634.

[17] Idem.

Orthodoxy and Strategy:
On Not Having a Strategy for
the New Decade or Millennium

The premier evangelical guild in the United States recently invited papers discussing strategy for the upcoming decade for its 44th annual meeting. Following a now familiar pattern, the evangelical strategizers docketed their symposium three years after the decade had already begun. Participants of the Evangelical Theological Society were invited to address the subject of "The Strategy for the Church in the 90s." The invitation urged participants to give their best thought regarding strategic implementation for church ministry to a rapidly changing world. At that meeting, I offered a slightly contrarian view explaining why that topic itself may not only be unnecessary but, in fact, inadvisable. I attempted to accomplish three things. First, I provided four reasons why it may be unwise to provide a strategy custom-fitted to respond to the latest trends of a decade. Second, I presented a collage of five studies from different fields that argue such rapid change in the ecology of ministry makes it nearly impossible to tailor a strategy for one decade. Third, I briefly sketched a biblical alternative suggesting a return to a more classical strategy rather than one that is unduly attentive to the tides of modernity.

As a practicing pastor, let me say that I extend my hand to any who recognize that much of the demographic demon foisted on the church by growth experts has been monumentally foolish and magnificently ineffectual. The last thing a parish minister needs to hear is another "Vision 2000 Plan," "Megavangelical Trends for the Nineties," or "Successful Assimilation of Generations X, Y, Z, L, and T." I am prepared to regurgitate any more strategizing sessions that merely relay the demographic atoms to us that any competent chamber of commerce or trendy magazine can report. A little more insight, yea even criticism, would be more helpful to this pastor than the sum total of strategy books. To the academics, I want to testify that my life and ministry are more strengthened by one sinewy theological text than a decade's worth of pop plannings. Pastors are not helped by avoiding meat. That is, in fact, what we need. Other pastors of integrity (non-Pythagoreans, I call them, in that they are usually characterized more by deep spiritual insight than by mathematical models disguised as "Vision Documents") need support in seeking to overturn the *ersatz* maxim of American Church Growth that appears to me to be: Demographical correctness is the ecclesiastical version of political correctness. Please help us overturn the unbiblical idea that to be demographically correct in church planting is somehow to function as political correctness (shorthand for bias and non-reasoning) does in the liberal academy.

Along that line, if I have to endure another testimonial to the *need to be relevant*, i.e., another of the faddish appeals to be sensitive to gender movements (as if the 80s discovered a novel category of ontology in gender), or pleas for churches to be cognizant of pending enviro-catastrophes, I think I may break into a fit of quoting the OT prophets that would sound glossalalic. Do we really have to be so perennially relevant? This pastor asks, "Do we? Who says so? On what authority? Is it helping?" We could do with a little less hipsterism and a little more substance. It is my abiding conviction that any attractiveness the Christian church can offer to our society in the 90s (or beyond) will be related to those *mores* and truths of unchanging substance rather than the shifting sands of cultural sculpting.

Who is it that really thinks the following, e. g., is helpful for the actual (not the theoretical or bureaucratic) ministry of the church? The AP reported that 41 US denominations announced their plans to establish more than 46,000 new churches in the next 8 years. Incredible—in the truest sense of the word, unbelievable—to be sure. Not including the largest church in the US even, this group boasts of creating in 8 years about 20% of what it took over 300 years to develop—in eight years! At least two denominations plan to double their size in that time; if 46,000 churches were really planted in 8 years that would yield an aggregate greater than all the (1) Southern Baptists or (2) United Methodists or (3) the Presbyterians, Episcopalians and United Church of Christ combined. Is this strategy? More like foolishness or *hubris*. Isn't there a better way to plan for the future?

Do we help the church with such colloquiums or possibly damage the testimony and credibility of the church, even running the risk of having the Lord's name blasphemed among the nations due to our (of late) "name-it-claim-it" church growth strategies? It is time for a return to valuing orthodoxy over strategy. It will not begin a moment too soon. In fact, strategy not only has many limitations, but may even be impossible if the sense is that churches can strategize like other businesses. Below are several reasons to support this thesis.

Four Good Reasons Not to Have a Strategy for the 90s

1. First of all it might be helpful for us to *challenge the very assumption of progress* (or change).[1] Underlying a specified strategy for one particular decade is the premise that from decade to decade there are such large-scale changes in

---

[1] In the nineteenth century, Acton called "progress" the religion of those who have none.

society or in the church that it becomes incumbent upon that church to change in order to keep pace. Most evangelicals of the 60s and 70s strongly dissented from the hyper-ecumenical aphorism of that time: "Let the World set the agenda for the Church." It is doubtful that things have changed much since then; however, it seems that some evangelicals have a short memory.

Most evangelicals have an eschatology or a view of the future that implies either a decidedly upward or downward trend in history. Premillennialists have, for example, believed that society is winding down, heading for greater catastrophe and consequently, if anything, a strategy for one particular decade should take that into account. On the other hand, postmillennialists believe there is a definite upward slope to world history. In both of these macro views of history and society, an assumption of some trend underlies each view. Hence underlying any strategy for change is an assumption of some directionality or progress in the gospel. Before much strategizing goes forward, someone should challenge the progress-presumption. Churches and societies can, and have, deteriorated or remained static.

Recently it was reported that U.S. church attendance was up slightly since 1950 to an all-time high[2] (thus partially discrediting the down-grade version of the secularization thesis). The overall percentages of church attendance are not greatly different over the span of five quite tumultuous decades. Several studies have challenged the assumption of change or progress. For example Andrew Greeley's study[3] challenged the secularization thesis, i.e., that our society was trending radically downward with uncontrollable momentum. Others have sought to characterize the times in which we live as hopelessly unredeemable, while still others have an unwarranted optimism, perhaps an example of Eric Voegelin's "Imminentization of the Eschaton." However, in both of these schemes there is an assumption that society is changing so rapidly (and its progress is either markedly up or down) that change is an inevitable part of life. Still others have sought to chronicle the macroscopic "restructuring" of modern American religion.[4]

Christians may want to question this emerging dogma, as even certain sociologists with data in hand are beginning to question it. Is it really the case that our society or the world around us has changed so much in the 90s that 80s strategies are outdated? Are good strategies outdated so quickly? Has there been that much change between the 60s and the 90s? With tie-die, bell-bottoms, and wire-rims making their way back, has society really changed by quantum levels? Or are we

---

[2] In Glenn Firebaugh and Brian Harley's "Trends in U.S. Church Attendance: Secularization and Revival, or Merely Lifecycle Effects?" (*The Journal for the Scientific Study of Religion*, vol. 30, no. 4, 1991), it is reported that in 1939, 40% of Protestants attended church regularly, while in 1984, 42% did. Other studies have confirmed average weekly attendance to be in the low-40% range as a constant for the last 50 years.

[3] See Andrew M. Greeley's *Religious Change in America* (Cambridge, MA: Harvard University Press, 1989).

[4] Cf. e.g., Robert Wuthnow's *The Restructuring of American Religion: Society and Faith since World War II* (Princeton, NJ: Princeton University Press, 1988).

recycling? Can't we also make a good case that indeed the underlying truths of anthropology, theology and sociology are indeed unchanged? In fact these are definitely more constant. If indeed they are constants, then strategy might not necessarily change from decade to decade. Instead, it should be purposefully crafted to be more decade-resistant.

2. The second very good reason for not tailoring a strategy for the 90s is that each new decennial strategy is *situation-specific* and at best short-term. To be sure, as the decades roll certain adjustments need to be made from time to time. However, as each new decade dawns, it must be candidly confessed that we have a habit of dealing with "hot button topics" and those factors that reflect recent concern. Normally these discussions are among scholars huddled in research faculties and other leaders with particular interests or turfs to protect. All of their suggestions are at best short-term remedies to the crisis *du jour*, and it should at least be asked whether or not a long-term strategy would be more worthy of our time. In fact a long-term strategy might be better. If one were to go back and review, for example, the papers of various associations and societies that suggested strategy for the 60s, for the 70s, for the 80s, and now for the 90s, would we really wish to devote our time and attention to strategizing for such a small slice of history in the likelihood that by the time we come to the next millennium much of it will be embarrassingly outdated?

3. The third very good reason for challenging the scientific-strategizing movement is because the vaunted rationality of science itself is being called into question. While many evangelicals may resort to such skepticism in an evolution/creation debate, it seems inconsistent to reverse field and address future strategy uncritically dependent upon the hidden dogma of the rationality of science. Specifically, insofar as demographics or mathematically measurable models are based on a Baconian model of objectivity-as-unskewed-by-the-observer (which quantum mechanics has now shown to be inaccurate), then for evangelicals to take into our walls the Trojan Horse of scientism, even if baptized into evangelistic strategies, is once again to sell part of our birthright. Paul Feyerabend has even had the temerity to suggest this very notion to the secular academic community in such works as *Against Method: Outline of Anarchy* (1975), *Farewell to Reason* (1987), and recently in *Beyond Reason* (1991). His thesis is that the enterprise of science is not only non-objective but downright subjective, contrary to pure rationality, and frequently driven more by emotional, personal, professional, and financial concerns, not to mention turf-wars. It is time for evangelical leaders who question the pure rationality of science in one stadium also to question its application in our own home field. Certain strategies are only valid if the underlying foundation of science is infallible. With secularists now admitting the sham of the Cartesian approach, shame on us if we take it up to enshrine our sacred bovine methodologies. Because the scientific endeavor is fraught with prejudice, emotion, and the skewing of evidence, we should be cautious in ushering the same assumptions into the church as an unexamined basis of a decade-strategy.

4. The fourth very good reason not to devote ourselves to a strategy for the 90s is that there is an inchoate but noticeable and substantial shift even among evangelicals in what appears to be a retrograde direction *returning to the classics.* Evangelicals, instead of moving forward "progressively," are in many ways moving "backwards" toward greater appreciation of fixed doctrine, discipline, liturgy, and leadership corporate culture. Evangelicals have made a detectable classic turn in doctrine, worship, discipline and emphasis on the local church over the last two decades. If indeed the trajectory of evangelicals is moving backwards rather than forward, then we might consider returning more to the classical, discovering more of those "old paths," instead of looking for new paths.

It was J. C. Ryle who, upon returning from his first church growth strategy conference, diagnosed the yen-for-hipness this way:

> There is an Athenian love of novelty abroad, and a morbid distaste for anything old and regular, and in the beaten paths of our forefathers. Thousands will crowd to hear a new voice and a new doctrine without considering for a moment whether what they hear is true. There is an incessant craving after any teaching which is sensational, and exciting, and rousing to the feelings. There is an unhealthy appetite for a sort of spasmodic and hysterical Christianity. . . . The whole tone of men's minds on what constitutes practical Christianity seems lowered. The old golden standard of the behavior which becomes a Christian man or woman appears debased and degenerated. The tendency of modern thought is to reject dogmas, creeds, and every kind of bounds in religion. It is thought grand and wise to condemn no opinion whatsoever, and to pronounce all earnest and clever teachers to be trustworthy . . . all these mighty foundation-stones are coolly tossed overboard like lumber, in order to lighten the ship of Christianity, and enable it to keep pace with modern science. Stand up for these great verities and you are called narrow, illiberal, old-fashioned, and a theological fossil![5]

A historical question must be asked, "Is it really the case that novel paths or new discoveries have strengthened evangelicals?" Or, to put it another way, "After 200 years of evangelicalism in America has such experimentation buttressed or diminished evangelicalism?" The question I pose at the outset is: "Might we not be wiser—instead of looking to the future and conforming our strategy to the world and to new dynamics around us in the world—might we not at this strategic juncture in our life return to a more God-centered approach that values the contributions of the community of faith for centuries prior to our decade to find strength in those old paths?" That, at least, is the slightly contrarian plea of this chapter.

Five Recent Studies of Enduring Import

This study, while not as systematic as some, is based on research from some of the best minds of Christendom. Several recent studies have caught my attention, and I

---

[5] J.C. Ryle, *The Church Today.*

would like to represent these as a collage, once again buttressing the argument that we need not come up with a new decennial or millennial strategy. In fact, the pace of change is so rapid in some fields that it is virtually impossible to print a manual before it is obsolete.

These five studies speak symphonically to dissuade us from following culture, summoning us, instead, to more basic and urgent tasks. Those more fundamental aspects are often obscured in strategy studies, and these macro-topics are also more deserving of our strategic attention than lesser trends. These five studies describe identifiable trends, each of which is far more extensive than a mere decade, and which also are more a part of the landscape to come than a short-term trend. Hence, these studies are summarized to focus our attention on massive issues not *minutiae*. It is the slightly contrarian plea of this essay that if we must strategize then we ought not merely respond to the microscopic issues of a small slice of history.

(1) One of those much larger trends that should be targeted by any strategic colloquium is one of our society's foundational myths that has in no small measure seeped into the church. Perhaps better than anyone else, Robert Bellah exposes the danger of John Locke's legacy.[6] In dealing with the question of the foundation a social thought and public policy Bellah notes,

> If there is one philosopher behind the American experiment it is Locke. Locke, as we know, begins with a state of nature in which individuals who have worked and gained a little property by the sweat of their brow, decide voluntarily to enter a social contract through which they will set up a limited government, . . . There are many peculiarities about this myth, which is one of the fundamental myths of origin of American society (461).

Bellah quizzically asks of these who voluntarily enter into social contract as if they are isolated atoms: "Where do these adults come from? Did they have no parents? Who took care of them when they were little? How did they learn to speak so they could make their social contract? Locke leaves us in the dark about all these matters" (462). Bellah further notes that it is "remarkable how much of our current understanding of social reality flows from the original institutionalization at the end of the 18th century . . . and how much of that was dependent on the thought of John Locke. Locke's teaching is one of the most powerful, if not *the* most powerful ideologies ever invented. Indeed, it is proving to be more enduring and influential which is not to say truer than Marxism." (462) As Bellah correctly surmises, government is created for the protection of property. Then individuals "freely consent" with their sole basis resting in voluntary agreement. Bellah says:

---

[6] For example, cf. his "Cultural Barriers to the Understanding of the Church and its Public Role" in *Missiology*, October, 1991, vol. xix, no. 4. Page references in parentheses, until the next footnote, are from this article.

In many respects this vision has turned out to be as utopian as Marx's realm of freedom. The Lockean myth conflicts with biblical religion in essential ways. It conflicts fundamentally with the Hebrew notion of covenant. The covenant is a relation between God and a people, but the parties to the covenant, unlike the parties in the Lockean contract, have a prior relation: the relation between Creator and created. And the covenant is not a limited relation based on self interest, but an unlimited commitment based on loyalty and trust. (462)

Further Bellah notes, "The Lockean myth conflicts profoundly with the Pauline understanding of the church as the body of Christ." (463) In addition he says, "The problem is that the Lockean notion of contract does not exist only in the economic and political spheres; it influences our understanding of all human relations, including both family and church. With respect to the family, a legal scholar has recently written, instead of the individual belonging to the family, it is the family which is coming to be at the service of the individual" (463). As Bellah applies this Lockean contract model to the church, he finds it to be a profound perversion, noting that "Consumer Christians shop for the best package deal they can get, and when they find a better deal, they have little hesitation about switching." (463) He goes on to add, "In a Lockean culture religion becomes radically subjective and privatized" (463) based on the subjective feeling of those for whom the social contract is in their own self interest. At any time later they may voluntarily bow out of that social contract, thus disrupting any long-term commitment to the church or its government.

Bellah says, "It seems to me the first problem is at the same time theological and sociological, how to communicate the deep social realism of biblical religion to an individualistic culture. To understand in our bones, so to speak, Paul's great organic metaphor of the body of Christ is to understand that there are many gifts ..." (463). Bellah is helpful to those who wish to formulate a durable ecclesiology when he comments as follows:

If religion is a purely private matter, and essentially a matter of subjective feeling, then one person's feelings are as valid as another, there is nothing subjective about which to test them. Thus there can be no such thing as authority in religion. Indeed, to individualistic Americans there is little sense of valid authority in any sphere, certainly not in politics or even in law. Perhaps the only exception is science ... (463)

Bellah is very helpful in reminding evangelicals to avoid this trap: "There are many churches today that see themselves as competing for market shares of believers and will try whatever seems to work to make sure that they compete successfully" (470). Bellah is right in warning of the danger of this Lockean view toward the public witness as well as the organization of the church. It strikes at the vitals of the church's proper view of authority. Further, he is wise in offering this caveat to neo-ecclesiology:

Thus in including the laity in the decision making process, the bishops do not dilute their authority, they enhance it. Yet unlike a democratic official, the bishops do not just represent the opinions of the people, whatever they happen to be. What is particularly difficult for an individualistic culture to understand, within the church or without it, is that the authority which the bishops speaks is not his own . . . [It is transcendental] (464).

Bellah bemoans the fact that the Lockean myth has unleashed such extra-ordinary energy and that it has caused the release of Pandora from her box onto the American church. He laments the "[e]xclusively self-interest maximizers" (468), and appropriately warns the church that the Lockean foundation, if it is the philosophical premise of a church, is perhaps as damaging as anything, unin-tentionally (albeit ultimately) elevating the human will above the covenant of God.

This study demands our attention and forcefully raises a seminal question: "Shouldn't the Christian church give more strategic attention to this macro-trend, than to the next wave of decennial demographics?" In some circles, John Locke is revered as a Christian, and it is often the case that he is uncritically accepted. Perhaps it is time for Christians to review not only his political writings, but more importantly his theological foundations to see if he is as orthodox as we think he is on the large questions.[7] The question may be asked, "Is a voluntary social contract in accord with a biblical view of the inner organic unity of the church?" A 90s strategy might be welcomed if it addressed this issue; yet merely strategizing to remediate short-term trends seems myopic in comparison. There is nothing wrong with strategy. Still, the concern of this essay is that the focus of such strategy should not be infatuated with short-term minor trends that effect the church's periphery but with the large trends at the heart of a culture in need of Christ.

Another leading evangelical has similarly demonstrated how damaging a pure egalitarianism can be if permitted to drive the strategy engine. Nathan Hatch has provided a critique of earlier evangelical preaching *sans* classical frame stemming from the "hermeneutics of populism" which demanded a simultaneous rejection of hierarchicalism and the elevation of the individual's conscience.[8] He observes that "American churches' profound commitment to audience in the early decades of the nineteenth century shaped the way religious thinking was organized and carried out . . . Insurgent religious leaders . . . considered people's common sense more

---

[7] One could also consult the recent study by Peter A. Schouls, "John Locke and the Rise of Western Fundamentalism: A Hypothesis" in *Religious Studies and Theology*, May-Sept. 1990, vol. 10, nos. 2-3, pp. 9 ff. Other critics of Lockean thought, e.g., Gary North in *Political Polytheism: The Myth of Pluralism* (Tyler, TX: Institute for Christian Economics, 1989), point out: "It was Locke's vision of religiously neutral politics that triumphed after 1690 . . . Newton and Locke by 1700 had triumphed philosophically over Aquinas and Calvin. The ultimate political victor (posthumously) was Roger Williams." (cited in *Westminster's Confession* [Tyler, TX: Institute for Christian Economics, 1991]), p. xvii.

[8] Nathan Hatch, *The Democratization of American Christianity* (New Haven, CT: Yale University Press, 1989). The page numbers in parentheses for the next page are from this work.

reliable, even in theology, than the judgment of an educated few . . . This shift involved a new faith in public opinion as an arbiter of truth" (162). Hatch illuminates the dominant ideology of American evangelicalism under the paradigm of populism, concluding that the driving force of this Christianity is not to be found so much in its organizational styles, nor even in sociological terms, nor in the quality of its leaders, nor ideas. Instead the "central force has been its democratic or populist orientation" (213).

Hatch warns that "[t]he American Revolution is the most crucial event in American History" (5). That claim is further substantiated as Hatch recites the invitation of one of the charismatic exemplars of the Revolutionary period (Elias Smith): "Let us be republicans indeed . . . Many are republicans as to government, and yet are but half republicans, being in matters of religion still bound to a catechism, creed, covenant, or a superstitious priest. Venture to be as independent in things of religion, as those which respect the government in which you live" (69). Hatch rightfully exposes this philosophic root. Recently many evangelicals have begun to recognize this extreme in their own mirror of experience. Part of Hatch's suggested replacement is a return to classic Christianity and a turn away from an overly-democratized faith. This sibling of Locke's social-contract-individualism may be far more worthy of the attention of strategic planners than short-term trends within the span of a single decade.

In this book and elsewhere, Hatch has effectively warned the sincere Christian of the dangers of an overly democratic approach to our Christianity. It is possible to elevate the political dynamic of democracy *per se* to a theological *a priori*. Such theological *a priori* makes democracy or independency as a religious commitment (not only political, but also theological) equally immune from revision so that it functions as an absolute with all other variables to be adjusted to it. Hatch and others are helpful of warning of the absolute democratic impulse.

Nathan Hatch, Robert Bellah, and others have done the church a service by exposing the extreme privatization that has occurred in our day. It might behoove us to deal with that large question rather than the particular social dynamics of the new decade, especially since this is a large presuppositional part of American Christendom. We would do well to give more of our attention to this macro-issue since this foundational cultural dynamic is of longer standing than the next census report. Its prospective remedy also offers more promise.

(2) A second such study has been provided by Craig Van Gelder.[9] In an excellent study, Van Gelder proposes the thesis that modern America, following centuries of Enlightenment-based culture, has collapsed at its center. One result is a large socio-religious shift which requires him to declare that America is now a mission field. This new secularization thesis is one that challenges the church. For those fabricating a strategy for the 90s—assuming we live in a post-modern culture

---

[9] Craig Van Gelder, "A great New Fact of Our Day: America as a Mission Field," *Missiology*, October, 1991, vol. xix, no. 4. Page references until next footnote are to this work.

—before we attempt to reach out to that society (with the evangelical techniques and assumptions native to our cultural context), perhaps our strategy should first be informed by Van Gelder's thesis.

Van Gelder suggests that something fundamental has shifted within our society, relegating the former mainline denominations now to the sideline. He reports one aspect of this shift: "The role of God was dethroned as a valid claim to authority. This role was replaced by an emphasis on objective facts." (411) Following upon that was the collapse of the project of modernity that has led America to be a post-modern culture. Along with the collapse of modernity has also come the repudiation of the assumptions of a Newtonian world view (412). Van Gelder sees us rapidly passing the modernist project, and even diagnoses our society as on the verge of rejection of post-modernism. He refers to this as a "second phase of disestablishment and pluralism (414) which occurred between the two World Wars, and warns that there is now on the horizon a "third disestablishment of the churches" (414) that began in the 1960s and 70s.[10] With the maturation of the baby boom and in light of a zealous secularism in our society, Van Gelder helpfully identifies these trends. He warns: "What will be interesting to watch is the style of the church which will develop in the 1990s and following to serve the emerging generation which is looking for relational acceptance."[11]

Once again a challenge to the "floating average" approach to strategic planning is in order. What leads any author to believe that words about the next "emerging generation" will not be dated two decades from hence, thus discouraging the allocation of much energy to developing a decennial approach? Moreover, if there is the large scale disestablishment that Hammond and Van Gelder seek to document, then it might be wise for the church to spend more time discussing that macroscopic social dynamic which endures for more than one decade than trying to tailor the church to micro distinctives merely for the 90s.

3. Another far-reaching dynamic in our society that must be dealt with is the repercussion of divorce and broken homes. In a 1992 issue of *Newsweek*, a series of articles substantiated (what the Scriptures have taught for centuries) that the children of broken marriages take the wounds of that cataclysm with them throughout their entire adult lives. That this has dramatic consequences in our society is an understatement to be sure. If indeed we wish to concentrate on the changing factors of society there are few, if any, more fundamental than the changes wrought on American homes due to divorce and broken homes in the post-1960 era. I suggest that more attention should be given to this large social dynamic rather than dealing with other "mega" trends that come and go as decades move on. In the *Newsweek* article some of the following are reported.[12]

---

[10] See also Phillip Hammond, *Religion and Personal Autonomy: The Third Disestablishment in America* and a 1991 Symposium on the subject in *The Journal for the Scientific Study of Religion*, vol. 30, no. 4, pp. 516 ff.

[11] Van Gelder, op. cit., p. 416.

[12] *Newsweek*, Jan. 13, 1992, pp. 49-53.

- "In 1965 the divorce rate was 2.5 per 1,000 population. By 1976 it had doubled to 5.0"
- "In a 1989 book *Second Chances*, a study of 60 divorced couples from California, Judith Wallerstein and Sandra Blakeslee wrote that almost half the children in these families "entered adulthood as worried, under-achieving, self-deprecating and sometimes angry young men and women."
- "In a 1987 study, University of Texas sociologists Norval Glenn and Kathryn Kramer found that white women who were younger than sixteen when their parents divorced or separated were 50% more likely to be divorced or separated themselves. The difference was less for white males (32%) and for blacks (15-16%), but all children of divorce appeared more prone to break-ups than children whose parents stayed married."
- Today's generation of young adults is the first to emerge from the period in which the number of divorces in America rose sharply, from about 400,000 in 1960 to roughly 1.1 million a year since the mid-70s."
- According to Larry Bumpass and Sara McClanahan, the adult children of divorced parents are more likely to break up than those whose parents who have stayed together. Bumpass projects that 60% of recent marriages will eventually end in divorce, 10 percentage higher than even the most dire predictions of the last few years."[13]

This and other articles are beginning to show the vast ramifications of divorce and failed marriages on our children. It is as yet unknown what repercussions these will have on American society or on the church. Thus the rise in divorce-related dynamics is something to which churchmen and women should be sensitive, but it is very difficult to predict its ramifications. Any number of studies could reach different conclusions for how the church strategizes to minister to this pressing need of society in the 90s. However, in the end it will probably be the case that any such studies that do strategize will come back to old paths in their approach to biblical remedies. These and other studies are helpful in anticipating the coming cycle of divorce. Still the critique must be careful not to view this single dynamic as the end-all of problems in American society. It is not the first and only important dynamic in our society, nor will it be the last. In the end, we will still find it tenuous to affirm, "After all, maybe there is something new under the sun." Instead, the critique and the strategies for the 90s should be careful to keep these in a longer eschatologico-historical perspective rather than affording these dynamics the preferred status of primacy.

4. A fourth study of recent note is a very excellent encouragement to orient more toward the old paths, emphasizing the heuristic of tradition rather than the strategies of modernity. Arthur Versluis argues that the battle front in our society today is not so much over which tradition or which trend is taking place, but instead the battle line is drawn in our society whether or not we will accept tradition or

---

[13] *Newsweek*, Jan. 13, 1992, pp. 48, 49, 50, and 52..

absolute truth at all. Versluis documents the bitter debate in academia over a canon of any sort.[14] Allen Bloom and others have documented the great attack on western classics. Versluis admits that "[b]oth sides have political agendas" (4), and that the left wing "Radicals' concern is primarily with tearing down. For him all works of art are merely manifestations of an oppressive societal order that must be subverted and overcome. He values the work of the critique far more than the work of literature which he is nominally studying" (4). Versluis draws the conclusion that,

> Cultural conservatism must be based above all on the recognition that there exist certain universal spiritual truths. And there is the crux of the matter: to the radical, indeed to virtually any modern, there are no universal truths. Modern man believes that all truths are merely 'cultural conditioning,' that mankind 'evolved' from lower species and retains 'an animal nature,' and that, compared to the fruits of contemporary 'progress,' the writing and traditions inherited from antiquity have only an occasional accidental validity (5).

Versluis reports that the issue at stake is the underlying question of canon. Is there absolute truth or is all relative? With clarity he says,

> For the battle today is not between one great tradition and another, but between all traditions on the one hand, and the anti-traditional modern world on the other . . . this battle between modernity and tradition is essentially a battle between the forces of destruction and those of preservation . . . today modernity is attacking the canon, the intellectual inheritance of mankind, through nihilistic theoreticism (6).

Versluis sees the battle as between any traditions upholding truth whatsoever, not between competing traditions of truth. He chronicles the grave impact of nihilism as he says,

> The fruit of this nihilism is not just an absence of morality and spirituality, but of mockery and a despising of all that wise men hold dearer than life itself. America's urban problems may also be seen as a battle in the ongoing conflict between modernity and tradition. How long will it be before we recognize the connection between modern anti-religiosity and the descent into barbarism in our cities? Can we really believe that man was meant to live without a spiritual center, without a culture? (7)

Versluis is at pains to make it clear that this debate is, "[n]ot in fact a squabble between hidebound reactionaries on the one hand and 'forward thinking,' 'open-minded' people on the other. Rather the real debate here is between those who recognize and embrace the vitality of our intellectual inheritance as human beings,

---

[14] Arthur Versluis, "The Canon Debate Solv'd, a Modest Solution," *The University Bookman* (1991) vol. xxi, no. 4, pp. 4-13. The page numbers in parentheses until the next footnote are from this essay.

and those who reject tradition in favor of the latest egotistical critical theory and are in favor of nothing at all" (7). Thus Versluis argues for a canon or a standard of judgment rather than the absence of such. His observations, along with the other documented trends in evangelicalism, may be harbingers of a return to the classic, even a return to mere traditional Christianity. One wonders if evangelicals will be on the cutting edge of this reshaping of modern American religion, or if evangelicals will preserve their now-traditional time lag behind cultural dynamics.

As Versluis concludes, he is helpful to point out: "For the essence of any traditional canon is the subordination of the artist to that which he is trying to convey or transmit. To one who arrogantly insists upon his 'originality,' the test of art is its divergence from the past, an attitude that produces the banality of virtually all contemporary art; but the traditional artist sees himself as a vehicle for greatness that far exceeds his own capacity or significance" (9). This may well apply to relevance in theology and decennial strategizings that seek to relate the Church's ministry forms to the latest trends. Versluis contends that this "is not a question just for Western tradition, but it is a battle for truth at all and in standing fast against the onslaught of the radical multi-culturalists" (10). Christians will want to be circumspect both in their embracing of tradition and also in their repudiation of it. Isn't the dynamic that Versluis identifies more foundational and important than decennial trends in the 90s?

5. Another far-reaching dynamic in our society that must be dealt with is the technological evolution documented by Neil Postman and others.[15] Neil Postman finishes his critique begun in 1985 (*Amusing Ourselves to Death*) with his latest book, appropriately sub-titled "The Surrender of Culture to Technology." In a learned style laced with parables, illuminating illustrations from little-known epochs of history, and citations from the world's leading thinkers, Postman has marshaled an impressive argument that all technologies bring with them curses as well as blessings.

Postman's proclamation is that along with new technologies also newly generated structures and problems invariably arise, to wit: "New technologies alter the structure of our interests . . . They alter the character of our symbols: the things we think with" (20). Whenever a new technology is added, "you are not left with the same environment . . . you have a new environment, and you have reconstituted the conditions of survival. . . . A new technology does not add or subtract something. It changes everything." (18) The introduction of any new technology also ushers in many unintended consequences.

He warns that technologies are not neutral and that once introduced the landscape is hardly the same. Drawing from sources as diverse as Freud, Marx, Wittgenstein, C. S. Lewis, Hillel, and Plato, Postman applies an old adage, viz.: "To a man with a hammer, everything looks like a nail. Without being too literal, we may extend the truism: To a man with a camera, everything looks like an image.

---

[15] Neil Postman, *Technopoly* (New York: Alfred Knopf, 1992).

To a man with a computer, everything looks like data. And to a man with a grade sheet, everything looks like a number." (14) Thus technology shapes our categories.

Another part of Postman's thesis is his contention that there are three distinct phases of technological evolution. He sees the emergence of technology *per se* as fitting a taxonomy of evolution from tool-users to technocracies, and finally to technopolies. Prior to the seventeenth century, a tool-using culture prevailed in which humans used tools, but did not allow them to undermine or alter basic ideologies. Then came the second stage, the technocracy, in which the technologies themselves began to rival certain basic belief patterns and rose toward positions of cultural prominence. Roughly from Newton to Henry Ford, this second phase of technical ascension was observed. Of this phase Postman says, "[T]heological assumptions served as a controlling ideology, and whatever tools were invented had ultimately to fit within that ideology. We may further say that all tool-using cultures . . . are theocratic or, if not that, unified by some metaphysical theory" (26). Following the rise of positivism, and other quantifiable scientific methods, the age of Technopoly commenced. Interestingly, Postman argues that theology, metaphysics, ideology, and other belief-systems were allowable in stages #1 or #2, but not in Technopoly (stage #3).

This third phase began in America (which Postman says is uniquely situated to become the first culture of Technopoly [48]) shortly after the mechanization processes in the time of Henry Ford, and has accelerated into our own times. In distinguishing between phases #2 and #3 Postman says, "Technocracy does not have as its aim a grand reductionism in which human life must find its meaning in machinery and technique. Technopoly does." (52) The definition of Technopoly as "the submission of all forms of cultural life to the sovereignty of technique and technology" (52) is further clarified as "the deification of technology, which means that the culture seeks its authorization in technology, finds it satisfactions in technology, and takes its orders from technology . . . [requiring] the development of a new kind of social order, and of necessity leads to the rapid dissolution of much that is associated with traditional beliefs" (71). Technopoly, to turn a phrase, "is a form of cultural AIDS . . . an acronym for Anti-Information Deficiency Syndrome. That is why it is possible to say almost anything without contradiction provided you begin your utterance with the words, 'A study has shown . . .' or 'Scientists now tell us that. . .' In a Technopoly there can be no transcendent sense of purpose or meaning, no cultural coherence" (63). He notes that, "Technopoly deprives us of the social, political, historical, metaphysical, logical, or spiritual bases for knowing what is beyond belief" (58). Further the new creed of the *technopolis* provides a replacement for all orthodoxies, viz.:

> To every Old World belief, habit, or tradition there was and still is a technological alternative. To prayer, the alternative is penicillin; to family roots, the alternative is mobility; to reading, the alternative is television; to restraint, the alternative is immediate gratification; to sin, the alternative is psychotherapy; to political

ideology, the alternative is popular appeal established through scientific polling. There is even an alternative to the painful riddle of death, as Freud called it. The riddle may be postponed through longer life, and then perhaps solved altogether by cryogenics. (54)

Of scientism as a leading by-product of Technopoly, Postman states, "It is the desperate hope, and wish, and ultimately the illusory belief that some standardized set of procedures called 'science' can provide us with an unimpeachable source of moral authority, a superhuman basis for answers to questions . . ." (162) Here, the Christian has an answer to "Technopoly's grand illusion" (162). Postman is also astute to sense where solutions will be found: "Our most serious problems are not technical, nor do they arise from inadequate information. If a nuclear catastrophe occurs, it shall not be because of inadequate information. Where people are dying of starvation, it does not occur because of inadequate information. If families, children are mistreated . . . the computer is useless in addressing them" (119).

Of the eclipse of religion amidst Technopoly, he laments that "our repertoire of significant national, religious, and mythological symbols has been seriously drained of its potency . . . all the once regnant world systems that have sustained (also distorted) Western intellectual life, from theologies to ideologies, are taken to be in severe collapse." We dwell in a "mood of skepticism, an agnosticism of judgment, sometimes a world-weary nihilism in which even the most conventional minds begin to question both distinctions of value and the value of distinctions" (179), with efficiency as an ubiquitous goal of Technopoly. Into this void comes the Technopoly story with its "emphasis on progress without limits, rights without responsibilities, and technology without cost" (179).

In view of the studies of Postman and others,[16] the impact of technology is certainly a large factor that should be included in any study of future strategy. My plea is that if we must strategize, let us be concerned with these matters rather than short-term trends. In reviewing these five excellent studies, one sees that indeed tradition can be of help and there is great reason to be hesitant before lock-stepping to the cadence of modernity. In fact, there may be more fodder for strategy for the 90s in some of the past studies than in some of the modern ones. It may also be realized that the common thread of these studies is the confrontation between the classic tradition and the modern preference of the individual.

There are, of course, numerous other current studies that help us identify surrounding trends. The plea of this article is certainly not a call to sociological obscurantism; neither is it a *desideratum* to be ignorant of imposing changes. To the contrary, that is the very petition: that the Church be aware of gigantic changes

---

[16] Cf. e. g., Jacques Ellul, *The Technological Society* (New York: Alfred A. Knopf, 1964); Albert H. Teich, ed., *Technology and Man's Future* (New York: St. Martin's Press, 1977); and Egbert Schuurman's monograph, *Technology and the Future* (Toronto: Wedge, 1980). Cf. also Schuurman's "A Confrontation with Technicism as the Spiritual Climate of the West," *Westminster Theological Journal*, vol. 58, no. 1 (Spring 1996), pp. 63-84.

which lie at the root of any society. However, a caveat is in order in that the recent past "strategy" rounds have largely missed the target, having been aimed more often than not at extremities or peripherals rather than at root issues. If a "strategy" is to identify the massive philosophic theaters in need of redress, then perhaps the five studies above can be considered. On the other hand, if only a ten-year period is being considered for strategy, then that very approach may stand in dire need of correction.

The point is that there may be no reason to fabricate a strategy for the 90s *qua* unique decade. In fact there is no charge in Scripture to formulate a strategy for a particular decade. On the contrary, there is an eternal strategy and a mandate which calls us to perpetual obedience. It might be appropriate to have a renewed vigor in our attention to the Great Commission—not only as it speaks of our need for evangelism. The Great Commission is also a timeless strategy for any decade or century. In its three-fold greatness, the Great Commission calls us not to focus in on one particular strategy by itself, but to be involved in a tri-partite extension of the gospel by discipling, by teaching, and by publicizing the sacraments.

Far from presenting a command to create a strategy for individual decades, this pastor finds it difficult to find any intimation by Scripture that the foundational apostles and prophets were interested in forming a strategy for a particular decade or millennium. Certainly it is the case that history was not moving as quickly (on a relative scale) then as now. Nonetheless, we see nothing in the New Testament Scriptures (nor in the Old Testament Scriptures) to indicate that we are to contrive contemporary strategies. On the contrary, the frequency of the words "eternal" and "forever" indicate that God's strategy is one for all ages. It must also be remembered that if we do indeed try to contrive strategy for one decade, we will always be playing the game of catch up. Evangelicals in America in this century have demonstrated that behavior time and time again, and it is hoped that we will resist the temptation to be laggards-trying-to-keep-up in yet another decade.

If our job is to receive the data of social change, then analyze it, and then re-enter it as new data for a new program, then we will by the very nature of the case always be lagging behind our cultural change. The world will be setting the agenda for the church. We yearn to reverse that and advance ahead of society for a change. Likely, the best possible way to do that is to have an inside source into eternal revealed truth to protect us from the winds of doctrine and the practice of change.

We may even find ourselves more appreciative of recycling the past than hurdling forward surrounded by so great a cloud of neo-pagan witnesses. We might find, as some disciplines are, that the past affords more heuristic value than many contemporary studies. In 1978, Robert Jastrow, one of America's foremost astronomers, concluded his *God and the Astronomers* with this parable.

> At this moment it seems as though science will never be able to raise the curtain on the mystery of creation. For the scientist who has lived by his faith in the power of reason, the story ends like a bad dream. He has scaled the mountains of

ignorance; he is about to conquer the highest peak; as he pulls himself over the final rock, he is greeted by a band of . . . theologians . . . who have been sitting there for centuries.

Such is Jastrow's analogy of the way that new scientists seem to be discovering old truths that have been there all along. He is skeptical about the prowess of modern methods. Perhaps the church considering a strategy for the 90s might benefit from this parable.

This parable could well be retold in terms of the modern church's own pursuit for innovative methods for growth. It often seems that the latest craze from the Church Strategy Scientists becomes the marching order for our church. And these may be as inferior as the sincere but deluded efforts of secular scientists to discover God by scaling the mountains of ignorance. One could almost retell Jastrow's parable as follows:

At this moment it seems as though the Church Strategy Scientists will never be able to raise the curtain on the mystery of church growth and future strategy. For the Church Strategy Scientist who has lived by his faith in the power of demographics and sure-fire growth techniques, the story ends like a bad dream, for churches cannot be made to adapt, nor thrive, merely by copying someone else's non-transferable strategy. The secret is God's alone to will and to work as he sovereignly pleases. Nonetheless, the Church Strategy Expert (often from a scientific committee from Headquarters) insists that he understands the intricacies and repeatability of quantitative strategies. So *he scales the mountains of ignorance and technique; he is about to conquer the final peak; as he pulls himself over the final rock*, seeking to make the church grow according to his will, denying the indubitable lack of success of his theories, but still clinging to his faulty strategy of accommodation, *he is greeted by a band of Old School Shepherds* who know better than to mock God's prerogatives. They had been sitting there for centuries, not too glamorous, and perhaps not succeeding as quickly as man-centered, demographically-informed strategies. Nonetheless, faithfully and with integrity, they have been there all along; and will be there, longer than the other fads of ministry. They will survive even the future trends of secular science, Church Quantification, and subsequent strategies. The Old School has been there all along. And it will be.

The Positive Program for the 90s and Beyond

Instead, in keeping with both the putative reversal (as in the classic turn), as well as in the questioning of the assumption of progress, and in light of the large social dynamics above, this discussion suggests that it would be better to find our strategy in the timeless exhortation of Scripture. Specifically I would plead instead that we adopt 2 Timothy 4:1-5 as our strategy for the 90s. This passage sketches large, broad, philosophical, and ministerial principles that should be pursued rather than an overly specific and trend-dominated approach to culture. In the first five verses of 2 Timothy 4, we have specific marching orders that are worthy of the attention of any generation. Rather than formulating a strategy for the 90s, we ought to go back and redouble our efforts in applying the *verbs* of 2 Timothy 4. Those verbs could serve as the emphases of ministerial action and strategy for the 90s. These age-old strategies are as follows.

1. *Preach the Word* (Homiletical Strategy). In order to bolster the prospects of strategic evangelicalism, a renewal of emphasis on preaching the Word of God in an unfettered manner will help the flocks weather any storms of change. Perhaps it has been too long since our seminaries and churches knew the power of preaching "not with persuasive words, but with a demonstration of the Spirit's power" (1 Cor. 2:4). If preaching the Word is one of the ordained means of grace, then shouldn't that take precedence in any biblical strategy? Too often we have resorted to manipulative techniques, worldly political methods, and gimmicks. An enduring strategy will elevate the role of preaching. As Richard Wentz has said,

> Until a generation ago, the theologians in Western Christianity were preachers. That is to say, whether they taught in theological faculties, religion departments, or served as pastors, they also preached. And they understood their intellectual assignments to be instrumental, a facilitation of the task of preaching the Word and opening the mind to the wisdom of Holy Tradition . . . It would not be difficult to demonstrate that American theology during the eighteenth and nineteenth centuries was composed by those who were primarily pastors. Their sermons were often homiletical models of theological discourse. Those who were not pastors were professors who preached to students, faculty, and the congregations within their circuits of influence. Jonathan Edwards, Horace Bushnell, or John Williamson Nevin are incomprehensible if we disregard the role of the pulpit in the development of their thinking . . . [17]

Preaching must be re-elevated. Paige Patterson recently commented on a part of this comprehensive future strategy, "Only through profound, consistent exposition of the Scriptures, particularly of the pivotal doctrinal passages which provide the framework for biblical Christianity, can the sheep of our be folds be prepared for the radical pluralism which looms before them in the 21st century."[18]

Preaching must be given a renewed place in the life of any church that hopes to reach our culture in the 90s, strategically or otherwise. Such preaching can scarcely afford to ignore the individualism, anti-traditionalism, post-modernism, and immorality illustrated by the studies above.

2. *Correct, rebuke and encourage* (Church Discipline Strategy). In 2 Timothy 4:2c, Paul enjoins the pastor to practice the ministry of correction or church discipline. In our generation of anything-goes-ism, we have too often fallen victim

---

[17] Richard Wentz, "Theologian as Preacher," *Anglican Theological Review,* Spring 1989, vol. lxxi, no. 2, pp. 4-7.

[18] Paige Patterson, "My Vision of the Twenty-First Century SBC," *Review and Expositor,* Winter 1991, vol. 88, no. 1, p. 39.

to the world's mindset that believes all is relative. The Church of Jesus Christ is, however, built on another epistemological and moral foundation. She, the "pillar and ground of truth" (1 Tim. 3:15), must prophetically denounce error and immorality as it occurs. Not only these declarations, but moreover, her actions of discipline need to be revived today. Any strategies aside, if the church has no moral credibility with her culture, she will obviously be a colossal strategic failure. A totally affirming evangelical church of the 90s, one lacking high internal standards and church discipline, will not only fail to reach the society of the 90s, but will likely be absorbed by it.

Church discipline, while certainly not a panacea, is, nonetheless, part of the enduring arsenal of the church in any decade. We can benefit from a leading Baptist spokesman, Paige Patterson, who pleads for a renewal in the practice of church discipline.

> [C]hurch discipline must be recovered as a practice of the local church. This proposal is especially hazardous in a litigious age. Furthermore, the abuses associated with church discipline in earlier eras leave little healthy precedent from the recent past. Radical pluralism and toleration of heresy or aberrant behavior of almost any variety are allowed, as the churches often shirk loving responsibility while hiding behind a misplaced sentimentalism masquerading as 'love' . . . Restoration of meaningful church membership through such discipline would curtail shallow evangelism, and it would also restore a measure of integrity to church membership.[19]

From Patterson's comments we the impact of the 80s in reviving discipline and church government as issues of perennial moment. The lost art and necessity of internal discipline forced some to review their own biblical convictions and governmental standards. It is imperative to retain the strategic ministry of correction in the 90s. No decade will alter the face of humanity so much as to render this tactic obsolete.

3. *Careful Instruction* (Christian Education Strategy) or the regularity of teaching. The church is to dispense careful teaching with patience. She is to be a teaching center. Perhaps it is fitting that many of the churches that have recently been most effective in reaching the lost have also been churches characterized by an excellent teaching ministry. "Teaching them all which I have commanded" may not be as glamorous as some newer high-tech forms of ministry, but it is clearly commanded and has for centuries proven effective. It may be time for a strategic educational plan to be made—one that emphasizes good biblical instruction more than gimmickry, the latest findings of one church growth school, or the most recent contemporary music style baptized with Christian text.

4. Next, in the departure strategy issued to Timothy by Paul, we plead for a long-overdue renewal in *Sound Doctrine* (Theological Strategy). It is also more

---

[19] Ibid., pp. 43-44.

than a coincidence that 2 Timothy 4:3-4 documents the tendency for an audience orientation to discourage such. It is as timely as ever to be reminded that members of our parishes will not naturally be disposed toward doctrinal soundness. They will invariably prefer teachings that affirm all lifestyles as they are, please the craving for self-righteousness, and in essence "suit their own desires."

The church members described in that scenario were more interested in myths, cutesy stories that soothe the conscience, and teachers who flatter their pleasure-addicted ears. In the midst of this distressing penchant, it is interesting that the church is not ordered to conform its doctrine to that cultural dynamic. On the contrary, the strategy for this situation (as in our own time) is for sound doctrine to be maintained in the face of this homiletical hedonism. A few pages later in the NT, Paul enjoins Titus: "You must teach what is in accord with sound doctrine" (Tit. 2:1). In the 90s and in the twenty-first century, it is imperative for any strategy that hopes to survive more than a decade to emphasize and promulgate sound doctrine.

Noting that "Doctrine determines attitudes," Alister McGrath has recently decried the elevation of relevance over truthfulness:

> The attractiveness of a belief is all too often inversely proportional to its truth . . . To allow relevance to be given greater weight than truth is a mark of intellectual shallowness and moral irresponsibility. The first and most fundamental of all questions must be this: Is it true? Is it worthy of belief and trust? Truth is certainly no guarantee of relevance, but no one can build his personal life around a lie. Christian doctrine is concerned to declare that Christian morality rests upon a secure foundation . . . To care about doctrines is to care about the reliability of the foundations of the Christian life. It is to be passionately concerned that our actions and attitudes, our hopes and fears, are a response to God and not to something or someone making claims to deity, which collapse upon closer inspection.[20]

5. *Evangelism and the full range of Pastoral Ministry* (Pastoral Strategy). In 2 Timothy 4:5, Paul exhorts, "Keep your head in all situations. Endure hardship. Do the work of an evangelist. Discharge all the duties of your ministry." These commands remind us of the comprehensive, balanced view of ministry. In all decades, we would do well to call on our people to endure hardship (the avoidance of difficulty may have been related to some of the health-and-wealth nonsense of the 80s), and keep a balanced perspective in all situations. Extremes are often dangerous warning signs. Moreover, the strategy for the 90s is not permitted to forget the great task of evangelism nor the lesser tasks of routine pastoral ministry. It may be time to challenge each church to re-examine its own ministry priorities to make sure that ongoing evangelism is a regular feature of each congregation, and also that pastoral care or "all the duties of the ministry" are maintained as well.

---

[20] Alister McGrath in *The Journal of the Evangelical Theological Society*, June 1991, vol. 34, no. 2, p. 150.

Finally, although listed second in this list, "Be prepared in season and out of season" (2 Tim. 4:2b). The Christian who wishes to strategize must recall that we are not only to prepare for one known moment, the particularities of a decade, or singular trends. On the contrary, we are called to persistent vigilance. Could it not be appropriately paraphrased that, "The price of evangelical strategy is eternal vigilance"? Indeed, our long-term strategy *is* to be prepared not for one season, decade, or an expected battle, but to be prepared for any eventuality that arises.

Conclusion

This is indeed a call to return to the local church with its emphasis and practice of ministry there. The five strategies extracted above from 2 Timothy 4—the (1) Homiletical Strategy, (2) Discipline Strategy, (3) Christian Education Strategy, (4) Theological Strategy, and (5) Pastoral-Evangelistic Strategy—do indeed focus on the church as change agent rather than the church as conforming agent. These internal adjustments are admittedly classic, non-decennial, and non-sociological. In short they are not very modern or 90s-ish. Yet we echo the comments that Thomas Oden made to a professional theological society not too long ago: "I am doggedly pledged to irrelevance insofar as relevance implies a corrupt indebtedness to modernity. What is deemed most relevant in theology is often moldy in a few days . . . I am pledged not to become fixated upon the ever-spawning species of current critical opinion but instead to focus single-mindedly upon early consensual assent to apostolic teaching . . ."[21]

Oden's caveat concerning creeping *modernitis* among evangelicals must have some place in a strategy for the 90s. Would we not be better off to pursue a strategy sensitive to the past rather than come up with a strategy uniquely designed for the 90s? It is admitted that these may not lead to novel or innovative techniques. But technique-ism has not shown itself superior to any of these classic strategies.

Whenever we consider strategy for the future, and that only if we must at that, we might do well to benefit from some advice from the past and give more attention to macro-foundational issues. As ecclesiological engineers gather for symposia on the coming millennia,[22] I wish they would allow Chesterton a seat at the table.

---

[21] Thomas Oden, "The Long Journey Home," *Journal of the Evangelical Theological Society*, Mar. 1991, vol. 34, no. 1. p. 80.

[22] Imagine a strategy conference in 999 AD whose purpose was to strategize for the Second Millennium. Who could have possibly predicted the massive changes ahead? When those 'visionaries' start calling for the "Strategy for the Third Millennium" Conferences, someone should ask if they can possibly predict the massive changes ahead, or do they assume that there will be fewer changes (or that they are brighter than the thinkers of the past)? As one small example, I recall that when I originally prepared this paper, I did not know a single member in the original audience who had email; now, a mere four years later virtually everyone does. A hundred years ago, no one had a fax, a telephone, a car, or a jet. Nor were they predicted. History will probably repeat itself in terms of the unpredictability of the future. Thus, we might batten down the hatches as the millennium approaches and keep doing what we have done for centuries. The best will last.

Nearly a century ago, G. K. Chesterton wrote with relevance to the question raised in this discussion. He confessed that although he confidently sought to be "some ten minutes in advance of the truth," all along he could have found many of life's enduring answers in his nearest parish church or in an earlier catechism, had he not been so enamored with the faddishness of the tactics of his day. Maybe, just maybe, a more appropriate strategy was revealed by the 90s (AD) . . . than in the 1990s.

The Brits Expose the Imbecile Habit

Several British thinkers in the twentieth century have underscored the value of retaining past ideological strengths. The voices of G. K. Chesterton, Dorothy Sayers, and Michael Oakeshott need to be heard again.

Even though many of us have become familiar with C. S. Lewis, we might not be acquainted with his ideological mentor, G. K. Chesterton. Gilbert Keith Chesterton was born in Kensington, England in May of 1874. He was a brilliant child who developed a habit of loyalty to certain ideals. His parents recognized his artistic ability, and enrolled him in the Slade School of Art. Upon completion of his work there, his earliest successes in life were as an illustrator. His teenage years coincided with the arrival of humanistic skepticism in England at the turn of the century. He was exposed to all the 'modern' notions associated with unbelief. In 1901, he married Frances Bogg who introduced him to the Anglican Church. His subsequent pilgrimage toward Orthodoxy was a colorful one.

He began writing at a young age, and soon was published as a novelist, a poet, a literary critic, a playwright, an editor, and eventually as a serious essayist. The topics he addressed were broad and he frequently exhibited a style that was refreshingly irreverent. The author of *The Napoleon of Notting Hill* (a book of political fiction), *Heretics* (an exposé of the errors of major philosophical schools of the time), and *What's Wrong with the World* (a social critique), he also wrote literary critiques of the works of Robert Browning and Charles Dickens. Chesterton was one of the most literary of Christians in the twentieth century. In addition, he would become known for his published studies on *St. Thomas Aquinas* and *St. Francis of Assisi*. Two of his most enduring works were: *The Everlasting Man* and his *Autobiography* that documented his trek into the Roman Catholic Church.

Chesterton reported this "odd effect of the great agnostics in arousing doubts deeper than their own might be illustrated in many ways. . . . As I read and re-read all the non-Christian or anti-Christian accounts of the faith, from Huxley to Bradlaugh, a slow and awful impression grew gradually but graphically upon my mind, the impression that Christianity must be a most extraordinary thing. For not only (as I understood) had Christianity the most flaming vices, but it had apparently a mystical talent for combining vices which seemed inconsistent with each other. It was attacked on all sides and for all contradictory reasons."[1]

In 1922, he was received into the Roman Catholic Church under the ministry of Father John O'Connor (the model for Father Brown in Chesterton's series of detective novels). His writings leave a trail of one who went from an ardent agnostic to a strong, quite traditional believer. His 1908 book *Orthodoxy* (a most eloquent book written when he was only 34) attempts to answer his critics who thought he was flirting with insanity for professing his faith. This book was intended to be a companion to his *Heretics*; in it, he sought to positively state what he believed in contrast to the critique contained in *Heretics*. In his Preface, Chesterton thought Orthodoxy was an explanation "not of whether the Christian faith can be believed, but of how [he] personally came to believe it. The book is therefore arranged upon the positive principle of a riddle and its answer. It deals first with all the writer's own solitary and sincere speculations and then with all the startling style in which they were all suddenly satisfied by the Christian Theology."

Chesterton died on June 14, 1936, a stalwart defender of orthodoxy and a literate apologist for the Christian faith. His work (69 books were published while he was alive, with an additional 10 after his death) is worthy of our acquaintance.[2]

Below are some of the salient observations by G. K. Chesterton, predominantly from his 1908 *Orthodoxy*. The following citations portray the real sense of the strength of orthodoxy in its beauty and order.[3]

---

[1] G. K. Chesterton, *Orthodoxy* (London: Lane, 1909), p. 153. The page numbers in parentheses are to this edition until otherwise noted.

[2] Mike Piff has summarized a few other important glimpses into Chesterton's life. See his brief biography on the WWW at: http://ws-mj3.dur.ac.uk/gkc/index.html. Piff notes that, "Chesterton had no difficulty standing up for what he believed. He was one of the few journalists to oppose the Boer War. His 1922 *Eugenics and Other Evils* attacked what was at that time the most progressive of all ideas, the idea that the human race could and should breed a superior version of itself. . . . His politics fitted with his deep distrust of concentrated wealth and power of any sort. Along with his friend Hilaire Belloc and in books like the 1910 *What's Wrong with the World*, he advocated a view called 'Distributionism' that is best summed up by his expression that every man ought to be allowed to own 'three acres and a cow.' Though not known as a political thinker, his political influence has circled the world. Some see in him the father of the 'small is beautiful' movement and a newspaper article by him is credited with provoking Gandhi to seek a 'genuine' nationalism for India."

[3] Several ideas prompted me to cite Chesterton so extensively. *First*, I find that few evangelicals have had direct access to Chesterton's own words; thus, this is my attempt to acquaint them with as much original material as possible. *Second*, in order to appreciate the great authors of the past—one of the aims of this present volume—earlier thinkers need to be allowed equal time at the microphone. One may well criticize them later, but this is at least an attempt to allow Chesterton to speak for himself. I, for one, am not uncritical of his thought, but at the same time, I wanted him to be heard in full. *Third*, I prefer his own style over summaries that may inadvertently distort. In short, I am pleased to confess that Chesterton says these things far better than I can summarize. I hope the reader will come to a greater appreciation of his thought after hearing these lengthy quotes; but don't stop there. Read him yourself.

Unimpressed with the expertise of modern prophets, Chesterton tweaked them: "The sages, it is often said, can see no answer to the riddle of religion. But the trouble with our sages is not that they cannot see the answer; it is that they cannot even see the riddle. They are like children so stupid as to notice nothing paradoxical in the playful assertion that a door is not a door." (55) He continueth: "The modern latitudinarians speak, for instance, about authority in religion not only as if there were no reason in it, but as if there had never been any reason for it. Apart from seeing its philosophical basis, they cannot even see its historical cause."

Chesterton sounded like a recovering modernist, skewering the previous generation's skeptics, when he wrote:

> When the business man rebukes the idealism of his office-boy, it is commonly in some such speech as this: 'Ah, yes, when one is young, one has these ideals in the abstract and these castles in the air, but in middle age they all break up like clouds, and one comes down to a belief in practical politics, to using the machinery one has and getting on with the world as it is.' Thus, at least, venerable and philanthropic old men now in their honoured graves used to talk to me when I was a boy. But since then I have grown up and have discovered that these philanthropic old men were telling lies. What has really happened is exactly the opposite of what they said would happen. They said that I should lose my ideals and begin to believe in the methods of practical politicians. Now, I have not lost my ideals in the least; my faith in fundamentals is exactly what it always was. What I have lost is my old child-like faith in practical politics. I am still as much concerned as ever about the Battle of Armageddon; but I am not so much concerned about the General Election. As a babe I leapt up on my mother's knee at the mere mention of it. . . . As much as I ever did, more than I ever did, I believe in Liberalism. But there was a rosy time of innocence when I believed in Liberals. (79)

But there is one thing that, from his youth up, Chesterton was never able to grasp: "I have never been able to understand where people got the idea that democracy was in some way opposed to tradition. It is obvious that tradition is only democracy extended through time. It is trusting to a consensus of common human voices rather than to some isolated or arbitrary record. The man who quotes some German historian against the tradition of the Catholic Church, for instance, is strictly appealing to aristocracy. He is appealing," explained Chesterton, "to the superiority of one expert against the awful authority of a mob."[4] He pointed out that, "Tradition may be defined as an extension of the franchise. Tradition means

---

[4] Chesterton also argued: "It is quite easy to see why a legend is treated, and ought to be treated, more respectfully than a book of history. The legend is generally made by the majority of people in the village, who are sane. The book is generally written by the one man in the village who is mad. Those who urge against tradition that men in the past were ignorant may go and urge it at the Carlton Club, along with the statement that voters in the slums are ignorant. It will not do for us. If we attach great importance to the opinion of ordinary men in great unanimity when we are dealing with daily matters, there is no reason why we should disregard it when we are dealing with history or fable." Op. cit., pp. 82-83.

giving votes to the most obscure of all classes, our ancestors. It is the democracy of the dead. Tradition refuses to submit to the small and arrogant oligarchy of those who merely happen to be walking about. All democrats object to men being disqualified by the accident of birth; tradition objects to their being disqualified by the accident of death. Democracy tells us not to neglect a good man's opinion, even if he is our groom; tradition asks us not to neglect a good man's opinion, even if he is our father. I, at any rate, cannot separate the two ideas of democracy and tradition; it seems evident to me that they are the same idea. We will have the dead at our councils. The ancient Greeks voted by stones; these shall vote by tombstones. It is all quite regular and official, for most tombstones, like most ballot papers, are marked with a cross." (83)

Chesterton observed "an imbecile habit . . . in modern controversy of saying that such and such a creed can be held in one age but cannot be held in another. Some dogma, we are told, was credible in the twelfth century, but is not credible in the twentieth. You might as well say that a certain philosophy can be believed on Mondays, but cannot be believed on Tuesdays." Chesterton argued:

> You might as well say of a view of the cosmos that it was suitable to half-past three, but not suitable to half-past four. What a man can believe depends upon his philosophy, not upon the clock or the century. If a man believes in unalterable natural law, he cannot believe in any miracle in any age. If a man believes in a will behind law, he can believe in any miracle in any age. Suppose, for the sake of argument, we are concerned with a case of thaumaturgic healing. A materialist of the twelfth century could not believe it any more than a materialist of the twentieth century. But a Christian Scientist of the twentieth century can believe it as much as a Christian of the twelfth century. It is simply a matter of a man's theory of things. Therefore in dealing with any historical answer, the point is not whether it was given in our time, but whether it was given in answer to our question. And the more I thought about when and how Christianity had come into the world, the more I felt that it had actually come to answer this question. (134)

Later Chesterton alluded to the fatuity of claiming than ancient creeds cannot be believed in modernity. He contended, "Of course, anything can be believed in any age. But, oddly enough, there really is a sense in which a creed, if it is believed at all, can be believed more fixedly in a complex society than in a simple one. . . . For the more complicated seems the coincidence, the less it can be a coincidence. If snowflakes fell in the shape, say, of the heart of Midlothian, it might be an accident. But if snowflakes fell in the exact shape of the maze at Hampton Court, I think one might call it a miracle. It is exactly as of such a miracle that I have since come to feel of the philosophy of Christianity. The complication of our modern world proves the truth of the creed more perfectly than any of the plain problems of the ages of faith. . . . This is why the faith has that elaboration of doctrines and details which so much distresses those who admire Christianity without believing in it. . . . If it is right at all, it is a compliment to say that it's elaborately right. A stick might fit a hole or a stone a hollow by accident. But a key and a lock are both complex. And if a key fits a lock, you know it is the right key." (149)

Chesterton is sagacious when warning against subjectivism:

> Of all conceivable forms of enlightenment the worst is what these people call the Inner Light. Of all horrible religions the most horrible is the worship of the god within. Any one who knows any body knows how it would work; any one who knows any one from the Higher Thought Center knows how it does work. That Jones shall worship the god within him turns out ultimately to mean that Jones shall worship Jones. Let Jones worship the sun or moon, anything rather than the Inner Light; let Jones worship cats or crocodiles, if he can find any in his street, but not the god within. Christianity came into the world firstly in order to assert with violence that a man had not only to look inwards, but to look outwards, to behold with astonishment and enthusiasm a divine company and a divine captain. The only fun of being a Christian was that a man was not left alone with the Inner Light, but definitely recognized an outer light, fair as the sun, clear as the moon, terrible as an army with banners. (136-137)

"Pantheism," Chesterton continued, "is all right as long as it is the worship of Pan. But Nature has another side which experience and sin are not slow in finding out, and it is no flippancy to say of the god Pan that he soon showed the cloven hoof. The only objection to Natural Religion is that somehow it always becomes unnatural. A man loves Nature in the morning for her innocence and amiability, and at nightfall, if he is loving her still, it is for her darkness and her cruelty. He washes at dawn in clear water as did the Wise Man of the Stoics, yet, somehow at the dark end of the day, he is bathing in hot bull's blood, as did Julian the Apostate. . . . Physical nature must not be made the direct object of obedience; it must be enjoyed, not worshipped. Stars and mountains must not be taken seriously. If they are, we end where the pagan nature worship ended." (137-138)[5] He concluded: "Mere optimism had reached its insane and appropriate termination. The theory that everything was good had become an orgy of everything that was bad." (138)

---

[5] If one wished to return back to a state of nature, Chesterton warned: "If you want to treat a tiger reasonably, you must go back to the garden of Eden. For the obstinate reminder continued to recur: only the supernatural has taken a sane view of Nature. The essence of all pantheism, evolutionism, and modern cosmic religion is really in this proposition: that Nature is our mother. Unfortunately, if you regard Nature as a mother, you discover that she is a step-mother. The main point of Christianity was this: that Nature is not our mother: Nature is our sister. We can be proud of her beauty, since we have the same father; but she has no authority over us; we have to admire, but not to imitate. This gives to the typically Christian pleasure in this earth a strange touch of lightness that is almost frivolity. Nature was a solemn mother to the worshippers of Isis and Cybele. Nature was a solemn mother to Wordsworth or to Emerson. But Nature is not solemn to Francis of Assisi or George Herbert. To St. Francis, Nature is a sister, and even a younger sister: a little, dancing sister, to be laughed at as well as loved." (205)

At several points in his writing, he provides a testimonial to his conversion away from modernity and its notions back to ancient orthodoxy. Listen in.

It was as if I had been blundering about since my birth with two huge and unmanageable machines, of different shapes and without apparent connection—the world and the Christian tradition. I had found this hole in the world: the fact that one must somehow find a way of loving the world without trusting it; somehow one must love the world without being worldly. I found this projecting feature of Christian theology, like a sort of hard spike, the dogmatic insistence that God was personal, and had made a world separate from himself. The spike of dogma fitted exactly into the hole in the world—it had evidently been meant to go there—and then the strange thing began to happen. When once these two parts of the two machines had come together, one after another, all the other parts fitted and fell in with an eerie exactitude. I could hear bolt after bolt over all the machinery falling into its place with a kind of click of relief. Having got one part right, all the other parts were repeating that rectitude, as clock after clock strikes noon. Instinct after instinct was answered by doctrine after doctrine. Or, to vary the metaphor, I was like one who had advanced into a hostile country to take one high fortress. And when that fort had fallen the whole country surrendered and turned solid behind me. The whole land was lit up, as it were, back to the first fields of my childhood. All those blind fancies of boyhood . . . became suddenly transparent and sane. (142-143)

His profession of coming to orthodoxy needs to be heard in full.

I was a pagan at the age of twelve, and a complete agnostic by the age of sixteen; and I cannot understand any one passing the age of seventeen without having asked himself so simple a question. I did, indeed, retain a cloudy reverence for a cosmic deity and a great historical interest in the Founder of Christianity. But I certainly regarded him as a man; though perhaps I thought that, even in that point, he had an advantage over some of his modern critics. I read the scientific and skeptical literature of my time . . . I never read a line of Christian apologetics. I read as little as I can of them now. It was Huxley and Herbert Spencer and Bradlaugh who brought me back to orthodox theology. They sowed in my mind my first wild doubts of doubt. Our grandmothers were quite right when they said that Tom Paine and the freethinkers unsettled the mind. They do. They unsettled mine horribly. The rationalist made me question whether reason was of any use whatever; and when I had finished Herbert Spencer I had got as far as doubting (for the first time) whether evolution had occurred at all. As I laid down the last of Colonel Ingersoll's atheistic lectures the dreadful thought broke across my mind, 'Almost thou persuadest me to be a Christian.' I was in a desperate way. (151-153)

Chesterton reported this "odd effect of the great agnostics in arousing doubts deeper than their own might be illustrated in many ways. . . . As I read and re-read all the non-Christian or anti-Christian accounts of the faith . . . a slow and awful impression grew gradually but graphically upon my mind—the impression that

Christianity must be a most extraordinary thing. For not only (as I understood) had Christianity the most flaming vices, but it had apparently a mystical talent for combining vices which seemed inconsistent with each other. It was attacked on all sides and for all contradictory reasons." (153) His egalitarian repudiation of inconsistencies is displayed below:

> I believed this doctrine of the brotherhood of all men in the possession of a moral sense, and . . . I was thoroughly annoyed with Christianity for suggesting (as I supposed) that whole ages and empires of men had utterly escaped this light of justice and reason. But then I found an astonishing thing. I found that the very people who said that mankind was one church from Plato to Emerson were the very people who said that morality had changed altogether, and that what was right in one age was wrong in another. If I asked, say, for an altar, I was told that we needed none, for our brothers gave us clear oracles and one creed in their universal customs and ideals. But if I mildly pointed out that one of men's universal customs was to have an altar, then my agnostic teachers turned clean round and told me that men had always been in darkness and the superstitions of savages. I found it was their daily taunt against Christianity that it was the light of one people and had left all others to die in the dark. But I also found that it was their special boast for themselves that science and progress were the discovery of one people, and that all other peoples had died in the dark. Their chief insult to Christianity was actually their chief compliment to themselves, and there seemed to be a strange unfairness about all their relative insistence on the two things. When considering some pagan or agnostic, we were to remember that all men had one religion; when considering some mystic or spiritualist, we were only to consider what absurd religions some men had. We could trust the ethics of Epictetus, because ethics had never changed. We must not trust the ethics of Bossuet, because ethics had changed. They changed in two hundred years, but not in two thousand. (159-160)

Chesterton expressed his alarm: "It looked not so much as if Christianity was bad enough to include any vices, but rather as if any stick was good enough to beat Christianity with. What again could this astonishing thing be like which people were so anxious to contradict, that in doing so they did not mind contradicting themselves? I saw the same thing on every side." (160) He discovered that his "rationalist teachers [had] no explanation of such exceptional corruption. Christianity (theoretically speaking) was in their eyes only one of the ordinary myths and errors of mortals. *They* gave me no key to this twisted and unnatural badness. Such a paradox of evil rose to the stature of the supernatural. It was, indeed, almost as super-natural as the infallibility of the Pope. An historic institution, which never went right, is really quite as much of a miracle as an institution that cannot go wrong. The only explanation which immediately occurred to my mind was that Christianity did not come from heaven, but from hell. Really, if Jesus of Nazareth was not Christ, he must have been Antichrist." (163) One can almost see the origin of C. S. Lewis' notorious trilemma in the quote above.

Chesterton's conversion continued along the lines below:

And then in a quiet hour a strange thought struck me like a still thunderbolt. There had suddenly come into my mind another explanation. Suppose we heard an unknown man spoken of by many men. Suppose we were puzzled to hear that some men said he was too tall and some too short; some objected to his fatness, some lamented his leanness; some thought him too dark, and some too fair. One explanation (as has been already admitted) would be that he might be an odd shape. But there is another explanation. He might be the right shape. Outrageously tall men might feel him to be short. Very short men might feel him to be tall. Old bucks who are growing stout might consider him insufficiently filled out; old beaux who were growing thin might feel that he expanded beyond the narrow lines of elegance. Perhaps Swedes (who have pale hair like tow) called him a dark man, while Negroes considered him distinctly blonde. Perhaps (in short) this extraordinary thing is really the ordinary thing; at least the normal thing, the centre. Perhaps, after all, it is Christianity that is sane and all its critics that are mad—in various ways. I tested this idea by asking myself whether there was about any of the accusers anything morbid that might explain the accusation. I was startled to find that this key fitted a lock. For instance, it was certainly odd that the modern world charged Christianity at once with bodily austerity and with artistic pomp. But then it was also odd, very odd, that the modern world itself combined extreme bodily luxury with an extreme absence of artistic pomp. The modern man thought Becket's robes too rich and his meals too poor. But then the modern man was really exceptional in history; no man before ever ate such elaborate dinners in such ugly clothes. The modern man found the church too simple exactly where modern life is too complex; he found the church too gorgeous exactly where modern life is too dingy. The man who disliked the plain fasts and feasts was mad on *entrées*. The man who disliked vestments wore a pair of preposterous trousers. And surely if there was any insanity involved in the matter at all it was in the trousers, not in the simply falling robe. If there was any insanity at all, it was in the extravagant *entrées,* not in the bread and wine.

I went over all the cases, and I found the key fitted so far. The fact that Swinburne was irritated at the unhappiness of Christians and yet more irritated at their happiness was easily explained. It was no longer a complication of diseases in Christianity, but a complication of diseases in Swinburne. The restraints of Christians saddened him simply because he was more hedonist than a healthy man should be. The faith of Christians angered him because he was more pessimist than a healthy man should be. In the same way the Malthusians by instinct attacked Christianity; not because there is anything especially anti-Malthusian about Christianity, but because there is something a little anti-human about Malthusianism. (163-165)

"Then," continued Chesterton, "the most difficult and interesting part of the mental process opened, and I began to trace this idea darkly through all the enormous thoughts of our theology. The idea was that which I had outlined touching the optimist and the pessimist; that we want not an amalgam or compromise, but both things at the top of their energy; love and wrath both burning. Here I shall only trace it in relation to ethics. But I need not remind the reader that the idea of this combination is indeed central in orthodox theology. For orthodox theology has specially insisted that Christ was not a being apart from God and man, like an elf, nor yet a being half human and half not, like a centaur, but both things at once and both things thoroughly, very man and very God." (167)

Following his conversion away from the sloppiness of non-Christian thought, Chesterton became an advocate of doctrinal precision. What seemed inconsequential to some was of profound importance. Chesterton explained: "It was only a matter of an inch; but an inch is everything when you are balancing. The Church could not afford to swerve a hair's breadth on some things if she was to continue her great and daring experiment of the irregular equilibrium. Once let one idea become less powerful and some other idea would become too powerful." (182)

So enamored was Chesterton with this ideological exactness that he referred to it as a "thrilling romance of Orthodoxy." He reproved progressivism:

> People have fallen into a foolish habit of speaking of orthodoxy as something heavy, humdrum, and safe. There never was anything so perilous or so exciting as orthodoxy. It was sanity: and to be sane is more dramatic than to be mad. . . . The Church in its early days went fierce and fast with any warhorse; yet it is utterly unhistoric to say that she merely went mad along one idea, like a vulgar fanaticism. She swerved to left and right, so exactly as to avoid enormous obstacles. She left on one hand the huge bulk of Arianism, buttressed by all the worldly powers to make Christianity too worldly. The next instant she was swerving to avoid an orientalism, which would have made it too unworldly. The orthodox Church never took the tame course or accepted the conventions; the orthodox Church was never respectable. It would have been easier to have accepted the earthly power of the Arians. . . . It is easy to be a madman: it is easy to be a heretic. It is always easy to let the age have its head; the difficult thing is to keep one's own. It is always easy to be a modernist; as it is easy to be a snob. To have fallen into any of those open traps of error and exaggeration which fashion after fashion and sect after sect set along the historic path of Christendom—that would indeed have been simple. It is always simple to fall; there are an infinity of angles at which one falls, only one at which one stands. To have fallen into any one of the fads from Gnosticism to Christian Science would indeed have been obvious and tame. But to have avoided them all has been one whirling adventure; and in my vision the heavenly chariot flies thundering through the ages, the dull heresies sprawling and prostrate, the wild truth reeling but erect. (183-185)

Chesterton summarized the "whole collapse and huge blunder of our age" as a confusion about the goal of progress. He explained the contrast: "We have mixed up two different things, two opposite things. Progress should mean that we are always changing the world to suit the vision. Progress does mean (just now) that we are always changing the vision. It should mean that we are slow but sure in bringing justice and mercy among men: it does mean that we are very swift in doubting the desirability of justice and mercy: . . . Progress should mean that we are always walking towards the New Jerusalem. It does mean that the New Jerusalem is always walking away from us. We are not altering the real to suit the ideal. We are altering the ideal: it is easier." (193)

If a person "altered his favorite color every day, he would not get on at all. If, after reading a fresh philosopher, he started to paint everything red or yellow, his work would be thrown away: there would be nothing to show except a few blue tigers walking about, specimens of his early bad manner." "This is exactly," noted Chesterton,

> the position of the average modern thinker. It will be said that this is avowedly a preposterous example. But it is literally the fact of recent history. The great and grave changes in our political civilization all belonged to the early nineteenth century, not to the later. They belonged to the black and white epoch when men believed fixedly in Toryism, in Protestantism, in Calvinism, in Reform, and not infrequently in Revolution. And whatever each man believed in he hammered at steadily, without skepticism: and there was a time when the Established Church might have fallen, and the House of Lords nearly fell. It was because Radicals were wise enough to be constant and consistent; it was because Radicals were wise enough to be Conservative. But in the existing atmosphere there is not enough time and tradition in Radicalism to pull anything down. There is a great deal of truth in Lord Hugh Cecil's suggestion (made in a fine speech) that the era of change is over, and that ours is an era of conservation and repose. But probably it would pain Lord Hugh Cecil if he realized (what is certainly the case) that ours is only an age of conservation because it is an age of complete unbelief. Let beliefs fade fast and frequently, if you wish institutions to remain the same. The more the life of the mind is unhinged, the more the machinery of matter will be left to itself. The net result of all our political suggestions, Collectivism, Tolstoyanism, Neo-Feudalism, Communism, Anarchy, Scientific Bureaucracy—the plain fruit of all of them is that the Monarchy and the House of Lords will remain. The net result of all the new religions will be that the Church of England will not (for heaven knows how long) be disestablished. It was Karl Marx, Nietzsche, Tolstoy, Cunningham Graham, Bernard Shaw and Auberon Herbert, who between them, with bowed gigantic backs, bore up the throne of the Archbishop of Canterbury. (194-195)

Chesterton offers this common sense advice to the ideological tourist: "You may alter the place to which you are going; but you cannot alter the place from which you have come. To the orthodox there must always be a case for revolution; for in the hearts of men God has been put under the feet of Satan. In the upper world hell once rebelled against heaven. But in this world heaven is rebelling against hell. For the orthodox there can always be a revolution; for a revolution is a restoration. At any instant you may strike a blow for the perfection which no man has seen since Adam. No unchanging custom, no changing evolution can make the original good any thing but good. Man may have had concubines as long as cows have had horns: still they are not a part of him if they are sinful. Men may have been under oppression ever since fish were under water; still they ought not to be, if oppression is sinful." (201)

Chesterton saw the infatuation with novelty of thought and progressivism as unfounded for several reasons:

> We have remarked that one reason offered for being a progressive is that things naturally tend to grow better. But the only real reason for being a progressive is that things naturally tend to grow worse. The corruption in things is not only the best argument for being progressive; it is also the only argument against being conservative. The conservative theory would really be quite sweeping and unanswerable if it were not for this one fact. But all conservatism is based upon the idea that if you leave things alone you leave them as they are. But you do not. If you leave a thing alone you leave it to a torrent of change. If you leave a white post alone it will soon be a black post. If you particularly want it to be white you must be always painting it again; that is, you must be always having a revolution. Briefly, if you want the old white post you must have a new white post. But this which is true even of inanimate things is in a quite special and terrible sense true of all human things. An almost unnatural vigilance is really required of the citizen because of the horrible rapidity with which human institutions grow old. It is the custom in passing romance and journalism to talk of men suffering under old tyrannies. But, as a fact, men have almost always suffered under new tyrannies; under tyrannies that had been public liberties hardly twenty years before. (210-211)

On the contrary, Christianity cannot ignore men as "backsliders." Chesterton affirmed: "that human virtue tended of its own nature to rust or to rot; I have always said that human beings as such go wrong, especially happy human beings, especially proud and prosperous human beings. This eternal revolution, this suspicion sustained through centuries, you (being a vague modern) call the doctrine of progress. If you were a philosopher you would call it, as I do, the doctrine of original sin. You may call it the cosmic advance as much as you like; I call it what it is—the Fall." (213)

Moreover, he noted: "I have spoken of orthodoxy coming in like a sword; here I confess it came in like a battle-axe. For really . . . Christianity is the only thing left that has any real right to question the power of the well-nurtured or the well-bred. I have listened often enough to Socialists, or even to democrats, saying that the physical conditions of the poor must of necessity make them mentally and morally degraded. I have listened to scientific men (and there are still scientific men not opposed to democracy) saying that if we give the poor healthier conditions vice and wrong will disappear. I have listened to them with a horrible attention, with a hideous fascination. For it was like watching a man energetically sawing from the tree the branch he is sitting on. If these happy democrats could prove their case, they would strike democracy dead." (214)

On the contrary, "there is only one answer, and that answer is Christianity. Only the Christian Church can offer any rational objection to a complete confidence in the rich. For she has maintained from the beginning that the danger was not in man's environment, but in man. Further, she has maintained that if we come to talk of a dangerous environment, the most dangerous environment of all is the commodious environment." (216)

Of the embarrassment of thinking that he had discovered something brand new, Chesterton confessed: "As usual, I found that Christianity had been there before me. The whole history of my Utopia has the same amusing sadness. I was always rushing out of my architectural study with plans for a new turret only to find it sitting up there in the sunlight, shining, and a thousand years old. . . . Without vanity, I really think there was a moment when I could have invented the marriage vow (as an institution) out of my own head; but I discovered, with a sigh, that it had been invented already." (224)

Particularly disdainful toward the modernization of theology, Chesterton suggested: "Now let us take in order the innovations that are the notes of the new theology or the modernist church. . . . The very doctrine which is called the most old-fashioned was found to be the only safeguard of the new democracies of the earth. The doctrine seemingly most unpopular was found to be the only strength of the people. In short, we found that the only logical negation of oligarchy was in the affirmation of original sin. So it is, I maintain, in all the other cases." (231-232)

As an exemplar *contra modernus*, Chesterton realized that a broader reference point than that of a single generation was required. He commented: "Here again, therefore, we find that in so far as we value democracy and the self-renewing energies of the West, we are much more likely to find them in the old theology than the new. If we want reform, we must adhere to orthodoxy." (247)

Chesterton believed that the main advantage of orthodoxy was that it was "the most adventurous and manly of all theologies." (255) Of the *kamikaze* nature of opposing God, Chesterton asserted: "This is the last and most astounding fact about this faith: that its enemies will use any weapon against it, the swords that cut their own fingers, and the firebrands that burn their own homes. Men who begin to fight the Church for the sake of freedom and humanity end by flinging away freedom and humanity if only they may fight the Church. This is no exaggeration; I could fill a book with the instances of it. Mr. Blatchford set out, as an ordinary Bible-smasher, to prove that Adam was guiltless of sin against God; in maneuvering so as to maintain this he admitted, as a mere side issue, that all the tyrants, from Nero to King Leopold, were guiltless of any sin against humanity. I know a man who has such a passion for proving that he will have no personal existence after death that he falls back on the position that he has no personal existence now." (256)

Chesterton contended that "orthodoxy is not only (as is often urged) the only safe guardian of morality or order, but is also the only logical guardian of liberty, innovation and advance. If we wish to pull down the prosperous oppressor we cannot do it with the new doctrine of human perfectibility; we can do it with the old doctrine of Original Sin. If we want to uproot inherent cruelties or lift up lost populations we cannot do it with the scientific theory that matter precedes mind; we can do it with the supernatural theory that mind precedes matter." (259)

Christianity, according to Chesterton, "preaches an obviously unattractive idea, such as original sin; but when we wait for its results, they are pathos and brotherhood, and a thunder of laughter and pity; for only with original sin we can at once pity the beggar and distrust the king." He understood the necessity of confessing depravity: "The ancient masters of religion were quite equally impressed with that necessity. They began with the fact of sin—a fact as practical as potatoes. . . . Certain new theologians dispute original sin, which is the only part of Christian theology which can really be proved. . . . The new theologians seem to think it a highly rationalistic solution to deny the cat." (22-23)

To wound the pride of the modern rationalist, Chesterton observed a perennial circularity to their foundational argument: "It is we Christians who accept all actual evidence—it is you rationalists who refuse actual evidence being constrained to do so by your creed. But I am not constrained by any creed in the matter, and looking impartially into certain miracles of medieval and modern times, I have come to the conclusion that they occurred. All argument against these plain facts is always argument in a circle. If I say, 'Medieval documents attest certain miracles as much as they attest certain battles,' they answer, 'But medievals were superstitious'; if I want to know in what they were superstitious, the only ultimate answer is that they believed in the miracles. If I say 'a peasant saw a ghost,' I am told, 'But peasants are so credulous.' If I ask, 'Why credulous?' the only answer is—that they see ghosts. Iceland is impossible because only stupid sailors have seen it; and the sailors are only stupid because they say they have seen Iceland. It is only fair to add that there is another argument that the unbeliever may rationally use against miracles, though he himself generally forgets to use it." (277-278)

Chesterton was not as infatuated with novelty as are many moderns. He said, "As long as the vision of heaven is always changing, the vision of earth will be exactly the same. No ideal will remain long enough to be realized, or even partly realized. The modern young man will never change his environment; for he will always change his mind. This, therefore, is our first requirement about the ideal towards which progress is directed; it must be fixed. But it does frightfully matter how often humanity changes its ideal; for then all its old failures are fruitless." (197) He argued, "If we are bound to improve, we need not trouble to improve. The pure doctrine of progress is the best of all reasons for not being a progressive." (202)

To round out the thought of Chesterton, consider a few of his sayings on the family. Many other structures, methods, and beliefs will come and go, Chesterton asserted, but God will continue to use the family. G. K. Chesterton asserted: "The family is radically subversive of the state-control." What he meant was that the family was the one institution that the state could not possess, enslave, intimidate, nor control. He said, "If we wish to preserve the family we must revolutionize the nation."[6]

---

[6] G. K. Chesterton, *Brave New Family* (San Francisco: Ignatius, 1990), p. 24.

The earliest sphere of government was the family; it was a small state. "The family is the model state," said Benjamin M. Palmer.[7] Long before mammoth governmental bureaucracies, and long before the growth of democracies, society was ordered in simple fashion—by families. These family-states performed basic tasks in lieu of civil government performing them. Families cared for one another, they protected from enemies, and they passed on values and wealth. The family is an adequate governmental sphere as well. In fact, if government crumbled or if a cataclysmic holocaust occurred, the survivors would probably begin with the new state based on the family. The family is "the ultimate human institution . . . Christianity, even enormous as was its revolution, did not alter this ancient and savage sanctity; it merely reversed it."[8]

Chesterton was again perceptive when he wrote: "This is the social structure of mankind, far older than all its records and more universal than any of its religions; and all attempts to alter it are mere talk and tomfoolery."[9] He asserted, "When we defend the family we do not mean it is always a peaceful family; when we maintain the thesis of marriage we do not mean that it is always a happy marriage. We mean that it is the theater of the spiritual drama, the place where things happen, especially the things that matter."[10]

Chesterton, of course, was not perfect in all ways. He maintained an inordinate antipathy toward orthodox Calvinism and espoused more ideas associated with Roman Catholicism than many will embrace. His idiosyncracies were numerous, and some of his poetry is ribald. However, an acquaintance with his work would steel many a mind against the onslaught of overbearing progressivism.

Dorothy Sayers

Lincoln once asked, "What is conservativism? Is it not adherence to the old and tried, against the new and untried?"[11] Another British thinker who championed the virtues of the tried and true was Dorothy Sayers, an admirer of Chesterton. She noted:

> It is worse than useless for Christians to talk about the importance of Christian morality unless they are prepared to take their stand upon the fundamentals of Christian theology. It is a lie to say that dogma does not matter; it matters enormously. It is fatal to let people suppose that Christianity is only a mode of feeling; it is vitally necessary to insist that it is first and foremost a rational explanation of the universe. It is hopeless to offer Christianity as a vaguely

---

[7] Benjamin Palmer, *The Family in its Civil and Churchly Aspects* (1876, rpr. Greenville, SC: Greenville Presbyterian Theological Seminary Press, 1992), p. 174.

[8] Chesterton, *Brave New Family*, p. 37.

[9] Ibid., p. 57.

[10] Ibid., p. 24.

[11] Cited in William J. Bennett in *The De-Valuing of America* (New York: Summit Books, 1992), p. 35.

idealistic aspiration of a simple and consoling kind; it is, on the contrary, a hard, tough, exacting, and complex doctrine, steeped in a drastic and uncompromising realism. And it is fatal to imagine that everybody knows quite well what Christianity is and needs only a little encouragement to practice it.[12]

"The task is not made easier," observed Sayers, "by the obstinate refusal of a great body of nominal Christians, both lay and clerical, to face the theological question. 'Take away theology and give us some nice religion' has been a popular slogan for so long that we are likely to accept it, without inquiring whether religion without theology has any meaning. And however unpopular I may make myself, I shall and will affirm that the reason why the churches are discredited today is not that they are too bigoted about theology, but that they have run away from theology." (36)

In "Creed or Chaos," Sayers aimed at two targets: "First, to point out that if we really want a Christian society, we must teach Christianity, and that it is absolutely impossible to teach Christianity without teaching Christian dogma. Secondly, to put before you a list of half a dozen or so main doctrinal points that the world most especially needs to have drummed into its ears at this moment—doctrines forgotten or misinterpreted but which (if they are true as the Church maintains them to be) are cornerstones in that rational structure of human society that is the alternative to world chaos." (36)

She observed "the inevitability of dogma," if Christianity was to be "more than a little, mild, wishful thinking about ethical behavior." When a contemporary of Sayers argued against ecclesiastical disputes and "the rise of the new dogmatism, whether in its Calvinist or Thomist form, constitut[ing] a fresh and serious threat to Christian unity," she responded: "Now I am perfectly ready to agree that disputes between the churches constitute a menace to Christendom. And I will admit that I am not quite sure what is meant by the new dogmatism; it might, I suppose, mean the appearance of new dogmas among the followers of St. Thomas and Calvin, respectively. But I rather fancy it means a fresh attention to, and reassertion of, old dogma, and that when Dr. Selbie says that all this is irrelevant to the life and thought of the average man, he is deliberately saying that Christian dogma, as such, is irrelevant." (37)

"But," she continued, "if Christian dogma is irrelevant to life, to what, in Heaven's name, is it relevant?—since religious dogma is in fact nothing but a statement of doctrines concerning the nature of life and the universe. If Christian ministers really believe it is only an intellectual game for theologians and has no bearing upon human life, it is no wonder that their congregations are ignorant, bored, and bewildered." (37) Even critics like Selbie admitted there was "something more" to Christianity than a reaction against paganism.

---

[12] Dorothy L. Sayers, "Creed or Chaos?" *The Whimsical Christian* (New York: Macmillan, 1978). pp. 34-35. Page numbers in parentheses are taken from this edition.

Sayers' rejoinder to him on this point is instructive. "The 'something more,'" asserted Sayers, "is dogma, and cannot be anything else, or between humanism and Christianity and between paganism and theism there is no distinction whatever except a distinction of dogma. That you cannot have Christian principles without Christ is becoming increasingly clear because their validity as principles depends on Christ's authority." (38) She continued her argument by referring to the totalitarian states, which once "having ceased to believe in Christ's authority, are logically quite justified in repudiating Christian principles." She argued for the inescapability of dogma: "If the average man is required to believe in Christ and accept his authority for Christian principles, it is surely relevant to inquire who or what Christ is, and why his authority should be accepted. But the question, 'What think ye of Christ?' lands the average man at once in the very knottiest kind of dogmatic riddle. It is quite useless to say that it doesn't matter particularly who or what Christ was or by what authority he did those things, and that even if he was only a man, he was a very nice man and we ought to live by his principles; for that is merely humanism, and if the average man in Germany chooses to think that Hitler is a nicer sort of man with still more attractive principles, the Christian humanist has no answer to make." (38) She further averred:

> It is not true at all that dogma is hopelessly irrelevant to the life and thought of the average man. What is true is that ministers of the Christian religion often assert that it is, present it for consideration as though it were, and, in fact, by their faulty exposition of it made it so. The central dogma of the Incarnation is that by which relevance stands or falls. If Christ were only man, then he is entirely irrelevant to any thought about God; if he is only God, then he is entirely irrelevant to any experience of human life. It is, in the strictest sense, necessary to the salvation of relevance that a man should believe rightly the Incarnation of Our Lord, Jesus Christ. Unless he believes rightly, there is not the faintest reason why he should believe at all. And in that case, it is wholly irrelevant to chatter about Christian principles. (38)

Sayers found the clergy infatuated with modernistic reformulation and faulted them for unnecessary epistemological obfuscation: "If the average man is going to be interested in Christ at all, it is the dogma that will provide the interest. The trouble is that, in nine cases out of ten, he has never been offered the dogma. What he has been offered is a set of technical theological terms that nobody has taken the trouble to translate into language relevant to ordinary life." (39) She blamed:

> Teachers and preachers never, I think, make it sufficiently clear that dogmas are not a set of arbitrary regulations invented *a priori* by a committee of theologians enjoying a bout of all-in dialectical wrestling. Most of them were hammered out under pressure of urgent practical necessity to provide an answer to heresy. And heresy is, as I have tried to show, largely the expression of opinion of the untutored average man, trying to grapple with the problems of the universe at the point where they begin to interfere with daily life and thought. To me, engaged in

my diabolical occupation of going to and fro in the world and walking up and down in it, conversations and correspondence bring daily a magnificent crop of all the standard heresies. I am extremely well familiar with them as practical examples of the life and thought of the average man, though I had to hunt through the encyclopedia to fit them with their proper theological titles for the purposes of this address. For the answers I need not go so far, they are compendiously set forth in the creeds. (41)

Sayers discovered "an interesting fact: that nine out of ten of my heretics are exceedingly surprised to discover that the creeds contain any statements that bear a practical and comprehensible meaning." She repeated her experience: "If I tell them it is an article of faith that the same God who made the world endured the suffering of the world, they ask in perfect good faith what connection there is between that statement and the story of Jesus. If I draw their attention to the dogma that the same Jesus who was the divine love was also the light of light, the divine wisdom, they are surprised. Some of them thank me very heartily for this entirely novel and original interpretation of Scripture, which they never heard of before and suppose me to have invented. Others say irritably that they don't like to think that wisdom and religion have anything to do with each other, and that I should do much better to cut out the wisdom and reason and intelligence and stick to a simple gospel of love. But whether they are pleased or annoyed, they are interested; and the thing that interests them, whether or not they suppose it to be my invention, is the resolute assertion of the dogma." (41)

In opposition to the approach of Selbie and others (i. e., to avoid dogmatic assertion lest affront be given), she contended:

> First, I believe it to be a grave mistake to present Christianity as something charming and popular with no offense in it. Seeing that Christ went about the world giving the most violent offense to all kinds of people, it would seem absurd to expect that the doctrine of his person can be so presented as to offend nobody. We cannot blink at the fact that gentle Jesus, meek and mild, was so stiff in his opinions and so inflammatory in his language that he was thrown out of church, stoned, hunted from place to place, and finally gibbeted as a firebrand and a public danger. Whatever his peace was, it was not the peace of an amiable indifference; and he said in so many words that what he brought with him was fire and sword. That being so, nobody need to be too much surprised or disconcerted at finding that a determined preaching of Christian dogma may sometimes result in a few angry letters of protest or a difference of opinion on the parish council. The other thing is this: that I find by experience there is a very large measure of agreement among Christian denominations on all doctrine that is really ecumenical. (42)

Of the exaltation of rhetoric to replace rational evaluation—a tactic used in Sayers' time and greatly increasing into our own times—she noted: "'Any stigma,' said a witty tongue, 'will do to beat a dogma;' and the flails of ridicule have been brandished with such energy of late on the threshing floor of controversy that the true seed of the Word has become well-nigh lost amid the whirling of chaff. Christ, in his divine innocence, said to the woman of Samaria, 'Ye worship ye know not what'—being apparently under the impression that it might be desirable, on the whole, to know what one was worshiping. He thus showed himself sadly out of touch with the twentieth-century mind, for the cry today is: 'Away with the tedious complexities of dogma—let us have the simple spirit of worship; just worship, no matter of what!' The only drawback to this demand for a generalized and undirected worship is the practical difficulty of arousing any sort of enthusiasm for the worship of nothing in particular." (23)

Michael Oakeshott

Some Brits in modern times have exposed the penchant toward an unexamined bias for the progressive on secular grounds. Michael Oakeshott, Professor of Political Science at the London School of Economics from 1951-1967, provided a helpful definition of the "disposition" of a conservative. Amidst the confusion of many modern movements, one that is frequently misunderstood is the conservative movement. To clarify, Oakeshott said, "The general characteristics of this disposition are not difficult to discern, although they have often been mistaken. They centre upon a propensity to use and to enjoy what is available rather than to wish for or to look for something else; to delight in what is present rather than what was or what may be . . . an appropriate gratefulness for what is available, and consequently the acknowledgment of a gift or an inheritance from the past."[13] Thankfulness may indeed be a distinguishing feature of the conservative as opposed to various progressivist idolatries.

In "On Being Conservative," Oakeshott continues to define: "In short, it is a disposition appropriate to a man who is acutely aware of having something to lose which he has learned to care for; a man in some degree rich in opportunities for enjoyment, but not so rich that he can afford to be indifferent to loss. . . . To be conservative, then, is to prefer the familiar to the unknown, to prefer the tried to the untried, fact to mystery, the actual to the possible, the limited to the unbounded, the near to the distant, the sufficient to the superabundant, the convenient to the perfect, present laughter to utopian bliss. Familiar relationships and loyalties will be preferred to the allure of more profitable attachments: to acquire and to enlarge will be less important than to keep, to cultivate and to enjoy; the grief of loss will be more acute than the excitement of novelty or promise." (409)

Oakeshott warns that conservatives will have a decided bias against mindless alteration or inferior innovation: "Changes are without effect only upon those who notice nothing, who are ignorant of what they possess and apathetic to their circumstances; and they can be welcomed indiscriminately only by those who

---

[13] Michael Oakeshott, *Rationalism and Politics* (Indianapolis: Liberty Press, 1991), p. 408. Citations from Oakeshott are from this edition.

esteem nothing, whose attachments are fleeting, and who are strangers to love and affection." (409) He reminds us that innovation and change can also yield actual loss: "A storm which sweeps away a corpse and transforms a favorite view, the death of friends, the sleep of friendship, the desuetude of customs of behavior . . . involuntary exile, reversals of fortune, the loss of abilities enjoyed and their replacement by others—these are changes, none perhaps without its compensations, which the man of conservative temperament unavoidably regrets." (409) As a result, the conservative "will find small and slow changes more tolerable than large and sudden . . . he will value highly every appearance of continuity." Oakeshott is perceptive to note that "every change is an emblem of extinction." Innovation that is specific and salutary, on the other hand, is an improvement.

Oakeshott observes that "not all innovation is, in fact, improvement; . . . to innovate without improving is either designed or inadvertent folly. Moreover, even when an innovation commends itself as a convincing improvement, [the conservative] will look twice at its claims before accepting them. . . . the disruption entailed has always to be set against the benefit anticipated." (411) This British economist advised: "The total change is always more extensive than the change designed; and the whole of what is entailed can neither be foreseen nor circumscribed. . . . there is the chance that the benefits derived will be greater than those which were designed: that there is the risk that they will be off-set by changes for the worse." (411)

Most contemporaries are so enamored with change or innovation that they forget that,

> First, innovation entails certain loss and possible gain, therefore the onus of proof, to show that the proposed change may be expected to be on the whole beneficial, rests with the would-be innovator. Secondly, he believes that the more closely an innovation resembles growth . . . the less likely it is to result in a preponderance of loss. Thirdly, he thinks that an innovation which is a response to some specific defect, one designed to redress some specific disequilibrium, is more desirable than one which springs from a notion of a generally improved condition of human circumstances, and is far more desirable than one generated by a vision of perfection. Consequently, he prefers small and limited innovations to large and indefinite. Fourthly, he favors a slow rather than a rapid pace, and pauses to observe current consequences and make appropriate adjustments. And lastly, he believes the occasion to be important; and, other things being equal, he considers the most favorable occasion for innovation to be when the projected change is most likely to be limited to what is intended and least likely to be corrupted by undesired and unmanageable consequences. (412)

"The man of conservative temperament," continued Oakeshott, "believes that a known good is not lightly to be surrendered for an unknown better. He is not in love with what is dangerous and difficult; he is unadventurous; he has no impulse to sail uncharted seas; for him there is no magic in being lost, bewildered or shipwrecked. If he is forced to navigate the unknown, he sees virtue in heaving the lead every inch of the way. What others plausibly identify as timidity, he recognizes in himself as rational prudence; what others interpret as inactivity, he recognizes as a disposition to enjoy rather than to exploit. He is cautious, and he is disposed to indicate his assent or dissent, not in absolute, but in graduated terms. He eyes the situation in terms of its propensity to disrupt the familiarity of the features of his world." (412)

To Oakeshott "the disposition of adolescence is often predominantly adventurous and experimental; when we are young, nothing seems more desirable than to take a chance; *pas de risque, pas de plaisir*." (413) For the progressive and liberal, "the fascination of what is new is felt far more keenly than the comfort of what is familiar. We are disposed to think that nothing important is happening unless great innovations are afoot, and that what is not being improved must be deteriorating. There is a positive prejudice in favor of the yet untried. We readily presume that all change is, somehow, for the better, and we are easily persuaded that all the consequences of our innovating activity are either themselves improvements or at least a reasonable price to pay for getting what we want. . . . We are acquisitive to the point of greed; ready to drop the bone we have for its reflection magnified in the mirror of the future. . . . Pieties are fleeting, loyalties evanescent, and the pace of change warns us against too deep attachments. We are willing to try anything once, regardless of the consequences." (414) More than anything else, the modernists wants to be up-to-date—even if it means jettisoning the tried and true. *Neophilia* (the love of the new) seems to value fashion over fact, presentation over substantiation, and recency of reporting over certainty of content.

The habit of this analytic adolescence is further characterized by Oakeshott: "Everybody's young days are a dream, a delightful insanity, a sweet solipsism. . . . we live happily on credit. There are no obligations to be observed; there are no accounts to be kept. Nothing is specified in advance; everything is what can be made of it. . . . We are impatient of restraint . . . we readily believe . . . that to have contracted a habit is to have failed. These, in my opinion, are among our virtues when we are young; but how remote they are from the disposition appropriate for participating in the style of government I have been describing." (436)

The next time some bureaucrat from any realm announces that he has the secret and can remedy our problems (which we frequently do not even know we have until the elite explains) with his "novel" contraption, recall this or read the following to him:

> [M]odification of the rules should always reflect, and never impose, a change in the activities and beliefs of those who are subject to them, and should never on any occasion be so great as to destroy the ensemble. Consequently, the conservative will have nothing to do with innovations designed to meet merely hypothetical situations; he will prefer to enforce a rule he has got rather than invent a new one; he will think it appropriate to delay a modification of the rules

until it is clear that the change of circumstances it is designed to reflect has come to stay for a while; he will be suspicious of proposals for a change in excess of what the situation calls for, of rulers who demand extraordinary powers in order to make great changes and whose utterances are tied to generalities . . . and of Saviors of Society who buckle on armor and seek dragons to slay; he will think it proper to consider the occasion of the innovation with care; in short, he will be disposed to regard politics as an activity in which a valuable set of tools is renovated from time to time and kept in trim rather than as an opportunity for perpetual re-equipment. (431)

The ideas from these three thinkers were written over four decades ago—which further proves that truth is timeless. Chesterton and Sayers were even earlier than Oakeshott.

Charles Spurgeon could be added to the list as a precursor of this British analytic *contra modernus*. Spurgeon said, "Rest assured that there is nothing new in theology except that which is false; and the facts of theology are today what they were eighteen hundred years ago. . . . self-styled 'men of progress' . . . degenerate as they advance, and their divinity, like the snail, melts as it proceeds."[14]

These Brits were correct in their analysis. Perhaps Karl Barth's flirtation with orthodoxy (in 1924 when he discovered Heinrich Heppe's collation of *Reformed Dogmatics*) should have been detected as an indication that he was applying for British citizenship. Barth, perhaps in a fit of paleo-orthodoxy, testified:

> . . . out of date, dusty, unattractive, almost like a table of logarithms, dreary to read, stiff and eccentric on almost every page I opened; in form and content pretty adequately corresponding to what I, like so many others, had described to myself decades ago, as the 'old orthodoxy.' . . . I studied, I reflected; and found that I was rewarded with the discovery, that here at last I was in the atmosphere in which the road by way of the Reformers to H[oly] Scripture was a more sensible and natural one to tread, than the atmosphere, now only too familiar to me, of the theological literature determined by Schliermacher and Ritschl . . . I found . . . a dogmatics which by adopting and sticking to main lines of the Reformation attempted alike a worthy continuation of the doctrinal constructions of the older Church . . . I had cause for astonishment at its wealth of problems and the sheer beauty of its trains of thought. In these old fellows I saw that it can be worth while to reflect upon the tiniest point with the greatest force of Christian presupposition, and, for the sake of much appealed-to 'life,' to be quite serious about the question of truth all along the line. . . . Orthodoxy may be but one stop on the way to this goal. . . . Success can come only if we have previously learned to read the Reformers as the Church's teachers and, with them, Scripture as the document for the Church's existence and nature, and therefrom to ask what Church science might be. That precisely may be learned, nay must be, from the early Orthodox men.[15]

---

[14] Charles Spurgeon, *An All-Round Ministry* (Edinburgh: Banner of Truth, 1986), p. 10.

[15] Karl Barth's Preface to *Reformed Dogmatics*, Heinrich Heppe, ed. (rpr. Grand Rapids: Baker Bookhouse, 1956), pp. v-vii.

Heresies That Transform, Deform, and Re-Form

Heresy exhibits a decipherable continuity. Some heresies are more persistent than others, and these recurring heresies are as comprehensive as they are old. The Second Law of Solomon as applied to theological error (the first law being that "There is nothing new under the sun.") might well be formulated as: *There are no new heresies under the sun; only recycled ones.* Or perhaps old errors never pass away; they only reappear in new garb.

Of course, some heresies—wrong as they might be—are of lesser consequence and barely worth opposition. However, any heresy that denies a portion of God's Word is also likely derivative from some philosophical root. Insofar as any heresy is related to a comprehensive whole, it is dangerous and bears the potential for large-scale destruction.

Those comprehensive heresies with such a potential are the mirror-opposites of "Truths that Transform" (to borrow the name of a popular religious radio program). Indeed, the major heresies are transformational. They change a person's life to be sure; only for the worse. A better knowledge of those errors might prevent us from committing the self same mistakes because just as surely as they transform, they also re-form. Of course, if one is too proud to receive assistance from his earlier siblings, then this historic aid will be of no avail.

G. K. Chesterton observed that to the "modern critics of the history of Christianity," the "monstrous wars about small points of theology, the earthquakes of emotion about a gesture or a word" were inexplicable. Of the narrow margin between orthodoxy and heresy, Chesterton explained:

> It was only a matter of an inch; but an inch is everything when you are balancing. The Church could not afford to swerve a hair's breadth on some things if she was to continue her great and daring experiment of the irregular equilibrium. Once let one idea become less powerful and some other idea would become too powerful. It was no flock of sheep the Christian shepherd was leading, but a herd of bulls and tigers, of terrible ideals and devouring doctrines, each one of them strong enough to turn to a false religion and lay waste the world. Remember that the

Church went in specifically for dangerous ideas; she was a lion tamer. The idea of birth through a Holy Spirit, of the death of a divine being, of the forgiveness of sins, or the fulfillment of prophecies, are ideas which, any one can see, need but a touch to turn them into something blasphemous or ferocious. The smallest link was let drop by the artificers of the Mediterranean, and the lion of ancestral pessimism burst his chain in the forgotten forests of the north. Here it is enough to notice that if some small mistake were made in doctrine, huge blunders might be made in human happiness. . . . Doctrines had to be defined within strict limits, even in order that man might enjoy general human liberties.[1]

One of the reasons that heresies are so difficult to detect—and so fatal when undetected—is that they rarely are overt or explicit. Indeed, the heretic hides among the flock, disguising himself under the cloak of similarity until he can break away and create his own religion. In addition, heresies, as counterfeits of truth, by their very nature seek to be close to the truth. It is this proximity to the truth that makes them difficult to expose.

Francis Turretin said that "heretics are masters of equivocation."[2] He also stated: "So invariably heretics are accustomed to laud the Scriptures 'speaking the same things, but thinking differently.'"[3] Irenaeus, a millennium and a half earlier, likewise noted: "Error, indeed, is never set forth in its naked deformity, lest, being thus exposed, it should at once be detected. But it is craftily decked out in an attractive dress, so as, by its outward form, to make it appear to the inexperienced (ridiculous as the expression may seem) more true than truth itself."

In the seventeenth century, William Perkins commented that preachers should "get help from orthodox Christian writers, not only from modern times but also from the ancient church." He explained:

For Satan raises old heresies from the dead in order to retard the restoration of the church . . . The Antitrinitarians have simply painted a new coat of varnish on the views of Arius and Sabellius. The Radical Anabaptists repeat the doctrines of the Essenes, Catharists, Enthusiasts, and Donatists. The Swenkfeldians revive the views of the Eutychians, Enthusiasts, and others. Menno follows the Ebionites, and Roman Catholicism resembles the Pharisees, Encratites, Tatians and Pelagians. The Libertines repeat the views of the Gnostics and Carpocratians. Servetus has revived the heresies of Paul of Samosata, Arius, Eutyches, Marcion, and Apollinarius. Lastly, schismatics who separate themselves from evangelical churches revive the opinions, facts and fashions attributed by Cyprian to Pupianus and of the Audians and Donatists. We do not need to look for any novel way of rejecting and refuting these heresies; the ancient ones found in the Councils and the Fathers are well-tested and still reliable.[4]

---

[1] G. K. Chesterton, Orthodoxy (London: Lane, 1909), pp. 182-183.
[2] Francis Turretin, *Institutes of Elenctic Theology*, James T. Dennison, ed. (Phillipsburg, NJ: Presbyterian and Reformed Publishing Co., 1994), vol. 2, p. 70.
[3] Ibid., vol. 1, p. 259.
[4] William Perkins, *The Art of Prophesying* (rpr. Edinburgh: Banner of Truth, 1996), p. 24.

An acquaintance with these errors of the past, similar to the manner in which federal agents detect phony currency by studying counterfeits, will help Christians be on guard against future errors. Seven major "transforming" heresies are reviewed below with the intent of showing how they also spawn modern offspring.[5]

Gnosticism

Two modern examples of gnosticism may be mentioned among many. In fact, this heresy may win the award for the most frequently recurring. Many Christians have met another professing believer who says something like this: "I love Jesus and his Word, but organized religion squeezes the life out of faith. I will remain free and not settle down under the authority of any particular church. If one buries himself in a formal church, the spiritual life becomes bondage."

Such expressions of modern gnosticism demonstrate the hatred of formality, structure, organization, or regularity. In lieu of those, the Gnostic prefers absolute spontaneity, independence, liberty, and so-called spirit. It is hardly debatable that our age much prefers the second set of variables.

In another instance, a charismatic cheers on the suffering saint with something like the following: "C'mon, you've got to believe and have faith. You need to claim health, ignore the symptoms—they're from the devil—and walk in faith. Don't let the world get you down with this talk about sickness. It's only an invention of the mind. Let your spirit soar."

Gnosticism, named after the early *gnostikoi* ("knowing ones"), manifests itself in a variety of ways, but consistently attempts to elevate the higher realm of spirit while denigrating the worldly or physical. The Gnostic calls devotees to be more attentive to heavenly ideals than earthly or physical realities. Admittedly, most believers could benefit from a little more exhortation to be more spiritual; there is no objection to that. However, the Gnostic pushes that dynamic to an extreme, resulting in the distortion of nearly every other biblical virtue. Gnosticism, at its simplest, rejects the physical and extols the spiritual; it despises the external and lauds the invisible. It is a reality-denying faith that is totalitarian.

An early founder of this original heresy was Cerinthus (a contemporary of Polycarp in the mid-second century), who believed that the divine "Christ" temporarily came on Jesus from his baptism until his crucifixion. The Gnostic has an insurmountable theological quarrel with the notion of God suffering bodily. For the Gnostic this is blasphemy. The Gnostic view of God is that he is so far removed from physicality that he could not possibly suffer in the flesh. Thus, the Gnostic Jesus was someone other than the Bible describes. The Gnostic, like all heretics, must become excessively creative in exegesis in order to explain away autogenic

---

[5] Robert C. Walton's *Chronological and Background Charts of Church History* (Grand Rapids: Zondervan, 1986) is helpful; cf. also *Modern Reformation*, Jan./Feb. 1994, pp. 11, 15-18. Harold O. J. Brown's *Heresies* (New York: Doubleday, 1984) is also very helpful.

(self-generated) problems. The Gnostic denial of the possibility of physical suffering generates a problem with the reality of Jesus' own suffering. Thus, the Gnostic posits that Jesus was not fully God, at least not all the time. According to Cerinthus and mainline Gnostic thought, the Second Person of the Trinity was not really born to a virgin; for he could not develop in the birth canal. Neither could Jesus suffer hunger when he fasted for 40 days; nor could the Son of God suffer on the cross. Neither would such suffering be either very spiritual or victorious.

Due to his root theological error, the Gnostic must eisegete a host of biblical passages, resulting in a distorted Jesus. Whenever heresy distorts Jesus, rest assured that Christian living—which is organically connected to Christology, always and everywhere—will soon be corrupted as well.

It did not take long for this philosophical error to challenge orthodox Christianity. By the end of the first century AD, Gnostic elements were evident in the NT.

Colossians 2:21-23 refers to extra-biblical rules that forbade the handling, tasting of touching of physical things. Such prohibitions, the apostle Paul wrote, had an attractive visage of spirituality. However, even "with their self-imposed worship, their false humility and their harsh treatment of the body, they lack any value in restraining sensual indulgence." The various monastic movements in the succeeding centuries were but attempts to put out the fires of bodily urge with the tonic of hyper-spirituality. Yet, earlier Paul had also warned against any believer being taken captive by hollow, deceptive, or man-generated philosophy (Col. 2:8).

Later, in his correspondence to Timothy, Paul continues to castigate such reality-denying heresy and also speaks positively of physicality. In 1 Timothy 1:4, he warns against those who are fixated upon secret myths, Gnostic teachings, and endless genealogies. The NT *ethos* is that God's truths are public, visible, and revealed—precisely the opposite of the secret, invisible, and concealed.

The apostle alludes to such early Gnostic errors when he rebuked those who forbid marriage and command abstinence from food (1 Tim. 4:3). The NT, far from being Gnostic propaganda, is in favor of the right use of food and sexuality (cf. 1 Cor. 7:5); it is only heretics that re-create these good God-given things after the image of evil. The root problem is that they deify the spiritual rather than use the good creation provided by the Deity. Paul acknowledges, "God created [them] to be received with thanksgiving by those who believe and who know the truth. For everything God created is good, and nothing is to be rejected if it is received with thanksgiving because it is consecrated with the word of God." (1 Tim. 4:3-5) Paul also warns against those conceited hedonists who "have a form of godliness" but in reality repudiate his very power (2 Tim. 3:5).

The apostle John, toward the end of the first century, contended with incipient gnosticism. His first epistle begins with an affirmation that the incarnate Word was heard, seen, touched, and experienced physically (1 Jn. 1:1-3). Far from "the Christ" being a spirit only, he is One who walked among these eyewitnesses. John, for this reason, associated the Gnostic tendency with the anti-Christ. The liar, or the anti-Christ, denied that Jesus is the Christ (1 John 2:18, 22-23). The Apostle subsequently stated: "This is how you can recognize the Spirit of God: Every spirit that acknowledges that Jesus Christ has come in the flesh is from God, but every spirit that does not acknowledge Jesus is not from God. This is the spirit of the antichrist . . ." (1 Jn. 4:2-3; cf. also 2 John 7) Other passages (e.g., 2 Peter 2) apparently repudiate gnosticism in its early forms. The trouble with gnosticism, however, is that it is still with us.

The following are traits of this heresy:

- Denial of divine incarnation; God could not become man.
- Spirit is totally good; matter is totally evil.
- Physical is bad and must be escaped; redemption is liberation from flesh.
- Special knowledge (*gnosis*) is championed; immediate illumination or alleged vision is preferred over observation or reflection.
- Gnosticism "runs ahead" (2 John 9) in creating rules of abstinence.
- The body is treated as either (a) deprived or (b) unbridled (Libertine). Gnosticism, as an unbalanced totalitarian error, may swing both ways: it may be ascetic (denying urges by privation) or it may be libertine (urges are hopefully repressed if restraint is lifted).

Gnosticism took the revelation of Christianity, and added to it several layers of philosophy, reducing it in effect to solipsism. It clashed with orthodox Christianity at the following points according to Harold Brown's synopsis:

> Gnosticism totally denied the Creation. In the first place, the supreme Deity . . . was altogether too exalted to be capable of having anything to do with base matter; . . . For biblical thought, the world is radically distinct from God because he is the Creator, it is his creation. Gnosticism not only opposed the idea that God could have been involved in an act of creating a material world, but it also denied that the material world is meaningful in itself. . . . The material world, if not totally illusory, is meaningless, and no true wisdom can be gleaned by studying it. . . . While Gnosticism repudiated Creation, it accepted Christ, although it gave him a drastically different interpretation from that of developing orthodox theology. Christianity might conceivably have accepted a Gnostic Christology, for the Christ of orthodoxy also has a cosmic dimension. If it had done so, it would have lost its roots in history, for the Christ of Gnosticism was not the real, human Jesus of Nazareth and did not die under Pontius Pilate.[6]

Each generation may have to reject these heresies itself. However, if one wanted to save much heartache, he could refer to the earlier Councils of the Church which condemned such errors long ago. It might be easier if Christians did not assume that they are the only ones ever to face similar errors, or at least consult history to see if modern reiterations of earlier error can be classified under a previous precedent. If modern Christians could benefit from the past, they might find many resources that could spare them dalliances with danger.

---

[6] Harold Brown, op. cit., pp. 49-50.

The condemnation of gnosticism was issued as early as the pages of the NT. Romans 12:1-2 calls Christians to present their *bodies* to God as living sacrifices. Their bodies are not to be ignored but sanctified. The NT explicitly refutes a Gnostic Christology: "He appeared in a body, was vindicated by the Spirit, was seen by angels . . ." (1 Tim. 3:16) Christ was definitely not an invisible *logos*. Moreover, God himself dignified bodily imagery when the church is denominated the "Body" of Christ (1 Cor. 12). The church's various diaconal ministries (1 Tim. 5; Acts 6) further sanctify the propriety of ministering to bodily needs. Such physical needs are not to be ascetically ignored; rather they are to be kept in the right place.

Many ramifications of gnosticism occur. One is the despising of flesh or form. Gnostics believe that structure, form, order, law, or regulation inherently detract from the spiritual. Gnostics cannot comprehend how something can simultaneously be orderly and passionate. They view these categories as mutually exclusive.

Gnosticism also detracts from the sacrifice of Christ. Gnostics must explain away the atoning death of Christ on the cross. Disbelieving that God can suffer, they must remove Christ from the suffering on the cross—to the detriment of orthodox Christology.

Another effect is the Gnostic elevation of spiritual superiority. Francis Schaeffer had this in mind in his short 1976 pamphlet, *The New Super Spirituality*. That booklet was a gentle admonition to evangelicals with unintentional Gnostic elements in their doctrine. Schaeffer and others warned against the tendency for the super-spiritual to inadvertently view themselves as spiritual superiors. Whenever standards of asceticism are elevated, some believers will be seen as competent and others will not be up to the superior performance of the gnostics. Gnostics may also fall prey to legalism with more regularity than those who espouse grace.

Accordingly, gnosticism, if unbridled from immutable ethical standards, invariably leads to immorality. Over time gnosticism that has rejected structures—moral or otherwise—leads to libertinism.

Tertullian (c. 200) described early gnosticism. The following account almost sounds like Tertullian anticipated many modern expressions of the heresy.

> First, one does not know who is a catechumen or a believer. . . . they do not care if they profess different doctrines . . . All are proud, all promise knowledge. The catechumens are perfect before being instructed. . . . they appoint neophytes . . . so as to bind with vainglory those whom they cannot bind with the truth. Nowhere is it easier to obtain promotion than among the enemy, where simply being there is considered an achievement. And so, today one man is a bishop, tomorrow another. Today one is a deacon who tomorrow will be a lector. The presbyter of today is the layman of tomorrow.[7]

---

[7] Cited in Giovanni Filoramo, *A History of Gnosticism*, Anthony Alcock, trans. (London: Basil Blackwell, 1990), p. 173.

Eric Voegelin and others have noted the Gnostic disdain for order or role. He has also helpfully analyzed the evolution of original gnosticism from its medieval faces up to the present. Voegelin notes: "And the transformation is so gradual, indeed, that it would be difficult to decide whether contemporary phenomena should be classified as Christian because they are intelligibly an outgrowth of Christian of the Middle Ages or whether medieval phenomena should be classified as anti-Christian because they are intelligibly the origin of modern Anti-Christianism. The best course will be to drop such questions and to recognize the essence of modernity as the growth of gnosticism."[8]

Voegelin is particularly perceptive to note the tendency of historic speculation to result in gnosticism. He goes so far as to claim that "Scientism has remained to this day one of the strongest Gnostic movements in Western society," warning against its "immanentistic pride."[9] Voegelin describes modern gnosticism as generating a "dream world" of counter-existential principles that defy logical and ordinary explanation, thus, the necessity for Gnostic secrets.

Gnostics grow impervious to reason, argument, even scriptural interpretation—all which are too tedious and formal for such high-spirited arrogance. Knowing Voegelin's description of the sociology of gnosticism a generation ago could have spared many headaches and heartaches in our own generation.

> Once a social environment of this type is organized, it will be difficult, if not impossible, to break it up by persuasion. . . . They [gnostics] are impermeable to argument and have their answers well drilled. Suggest to them that they are unable to judge in such matters, and they will answer, 'God hath chosen the simple.' Show them convincingly that they are talking nonsense, and you will hear, 'Christ's own apostle was accounted mad.' . . . In brief: the attitude is psychologically iron-clad and beyond shaking by argument.[10]

The Gnostic, according to Voegelin, is led to a militaristic confrontation with existing powers, invariably applying passages from the Revelation to himself with his adversaries viewed as apocalyptic agents of the anti-Christ. The Gnostic secret about eschatological outcomes grants superiority to the *illuminati*, while those not in the clique are sub-spiritual.

Closer to our own time than the first century, Richard Hooker described puritans as gnostics because they appealed to "special illumination of the Holy Ghost, whereby they discern those things in the word, which others reading yet discern them not."[11] Hooker, perhaps because he was a pro-Anglican establishmentarian, thought all puritans were crazed revolutionaries. He viewed them as radicals who "prefer each other's company to that of the rest of the world; they will

---

[8] Eric Voegelin, *The New Science of Politics* (Chicago: The University of Chicago Press, 1952), p. 126.
[9] Ibid., p. 127.
[10] Ibid., p. 176.
[11] Idem.

voluntarily accept counsel and direction from the indoctrinators, they will neglect their own affairs and devote excessive time to service of the cause, and they will extend generous material aid to the leaders of the movement."[12]

When one looks for modern manifestations of gnosticism, abundant examples could be given. The Branch Davidians were a Gnostic cult. They believed that their leader had a secret interpretation of The Book of Revelation that justified their confrontation with authorities. Neverthemind that no one else believed their doctrine, they were so "Spirit-led" that they were not exposed to objectivity or criticism.

Some aspects of Pentecostalism operate by the same dynamic. When Pentecostals insist that "the Spirit's leading" is valid even though it may be contrary to the clear teaching of Scripture, or when charismatics believe that an inner voice is more normative than the objective teaching of the Bible, they are exhibiting gnosticism, no matter how sincere they may be. Pleas to "set my spirit free that I might worship Thee" are more often than not reiterations of gnosticism. A variety of common slogans—such as calls for simplicity of lifestyle, anti-intellectualism, emphasis on experientialism, yearning for special illumination, and even calls for intimate accountability groups—may in the end stem more from gnosticism than from biblical Christianity.

The Gnostic temptation does not appeal only to evangelicals. It is also seductive for the waning mainline American churches that seem to be mirroring much New Age thought.[13] At a recent discussion of homosexuality, leaders of one mainline denomination presented arguments reminiscent of ancient gnosticism, with one professor defending homosexuality under the rubric of "hospitality." Johanna Bos claimed, "The Presbyterian Church is not hospitable to strangers and is in violation of the biblical text—we are estranging them, not only lesbian and gays but other sexual orientations."[14] Appearing to believe that patriarchy was worse than gnosticism, a study committee for the liberal Presbyterian church recognized the following as valid—even though Scripture was objectively clear on this matter: "The guideline for the study includes these items: the witness of the biblical text alongside the insights of sociological, psychological, and medical disciplines; the insights of any who may find themselves aggrieved by current practices, policies, or law relating to homosexuality and membership, ministry and ordination."[15] This is an example of elevating subjective concerns over objectively revealed moral standards.

Gnosticism, an extremism of the spirit, will probably continue as long as people are interested in spirituality. It is the *abuse* (or extremism) of the realm of the spirit that is wrong, not its lawful *use*. It is important for Christians to realize,

---

[12] Idem. Of course, not all puritans were anti-authoritarian nor inherently revolutionary.

[13] Cf. Peter Jones, *The Gnostic Tendency: The New Age Movement* (Phillipsburg, NJ: Presbyterian and Reformed, 1993).

[14] *The Presbyterian Layman*, July/August 1993, p. 4.

[15] Idem.

however, that many errors in the twenty-first century will be reiterations of errors in the first century. Errors, particularly the totalitarian kind, recur. One step toward spiritual security might be to diagnose some of the errors of the past, mindful that errors recycle themselves if not resisted.

Pelagianism

Pelagianism is nearly as manifold as gnosticism. Named after Pelagius, the fourth century heretic, this heresy is most associated with its belief in the goodness or perfectibility of man. It recurs in many different fields as witnessed below:

> The risks of modernity . . . are real enough. Decoupled from tradition and history and from any genuine transcendental faith, with inherited religious traditions having succumbed to the Pelagian heresy of the indefinite *improvability of the human lot*, modern man is defenseless when faced by the myriad political religions, projects of social engineering, and psychotherapeutic technologies that promise an exorcism of tragedy from human life. It is this spiritual emptiness from which the Enlightenment project—that is to say, the liberal project—emerges and which it aspires to cure.[16]

Michael Horton analyzes the penchant for Pelagianism—partially typified by its belief in the inherent goodness of man—even among evangelicals as follows:

> The fact that recent polls indicate that 77% of the evangelicals today believe that human beings are basically good and 84% of these conservative Protestants believe that in salvation 'God helps those who help themselves' demonstrates incontrovertibly that contemporary Christianity is in a serious crisis. No longer can conservative, 'Bible-believing' evangelicals smugly hurl insults at mainline Protestants and Roman Catholics for doctrinal treason. It is evangelicals today, every bit as much as anyone else, who have embraced the assumptions of the Pelagian heresy. It is this heresy that lies at the bottom of much of popular psychology (human nature, basically good, is warped by its environment), political crusades (we are going to bring about salvation and revival through this campaign), and evangelism and church growth (seeing conversion as a natural process, just like changing from one brand of soap to another, and seeing the evangelist or entrepreneurial pastor as the one who actually adds to the church those to be saved).[17]

Above all tenets, Pelagians laud man's will, experience, or potential goodness. Pelagianism, in its various forms, places more emphasis on the creation than the Creator. It imbues man with power and prowess that the Bible does not.

Pelagius (ca. 350-419) was a knowledgeable Englishman who taught an early form of perfectionism. He jousted with Augustine on several occasions, particularly

---

[16] *National Review*, June, 1993. Emphasis mine.

[17] Michael Horton, "Pelagianism," *Modern Reformation*, January/February 1994, 31-32.

over the matter of free will. He thought the church belonged only to adult-baptized perfectionists and he emphasized human capacity for virtue. Pelagius, the spiritual father of Arminius (1560-1609), laid the groundwork for the following closely-related doctrines: free will prior to regeneration, perfectionism in sanctification, human ability, and various ideas that leave ultimate determination up to persons.

Pelagius' foundational aberration lay in his misunderstanding of the Fall. "Denying the doctrine of original sin," Pelagius viewed grace as "given to all to enable them to know and choose the good; in Augustine's view, no one can choose and love the good apart from the grace of God. . . . The dangerous aspect of the Pelagian position for Christology lies in the possible implication that without original sin and a naturally corrupt will, man does not need a Savior so much as a good example. . . . The danger to our doctrine of God in this controversy lies in the fact that the alternative to Pelagianism seems to be a kind of rigid determinism that would make the unique God the author of all things . . . the author of sin and evil as well as of good."[18]

Pelagianism has bequeathed several distinguishing tenets.

- The church consists of voluntarily committed adults (emphasis on "will").
- Perfectionism and freedom from sin is promised.
- Grace reversed the Fall, but people are not totally fallen.
- Men can come to truth on their own apart from grace.
- Christ died to provide an option; atonement was made potential at best.

Official condemnation of Pelagianism was issued as early as 431 at the Council of Ephesus. Although Pelagius himself was not mentioned, his thought (and his chief exponent, Celestius) was clearly condemned in 431. Later, the Council of Orange (529) even more explicitly decreed:

> If anyone denies that it is the whole man, that is both body and soul, that was 'changed for the worse' through the offense of Adam's sin, but believes that the freedom of the soul remains unimpaired and that only the body is subject to corruption, he is deceived by the error of Pelagius and contradicts the Scripture . . . (Canon 1) If anyone asserts that Adam's sin affected him alone and not his descendants also [he is condemned] . . . (Canon 2) If anyone says that the grace of God can be conferred as a result of human prayer, but that it is not grace itself which makes us pray to God, he contradicts the prophet . . . (Canon 3) If anyone says that not only the increase of faith but also its beginning and the very desire for faith by which we believe . . . if anyone says that this belongs to us by nature and not by a gift of grace . . . it is a proof that he is opposed to the teaching of the Apostles . . . For those who state that the faith by which we believe in God is natural make all who are separated from the Church of Christ by definition in some measure believers. (Canon 5) If anyone makes the assistance of grace depend on the humility or obedience of man and does not agree that it is a gift of grace itself that we are obedient and humble, he contradicts the Apostle . . .

---

[18] Harold Brown, op. cit., pp. 201-202.

(Canon 6) If anyone affirms that we can form any right opinion or make any right choice which relates to the salvation of eternal life . . . he is led astray by a heretical spirit and does not understand the voice of God . . . (Canon 7) If anyone maintains that some are able to come to the grace of baptism by mercy but others through free will, which has manifestly been corrupted in all those who have been born after the transgression of the first man, it is proof that he has no place in the true faith. (Canon 8)

If this statement were read in many evangelical churches today, many of their members would protest its truth—a lamentable indicator of how much we have allowed novelty to shape our thinking. If the Council of Orange was so clear on this, then we are either inferior to their level of insight or else the early church was not on target. The former may be true; the latter is certainly false in this instance. Moreover, much of modern evangelicalism has lost its nerve and hesitates to even denominate similar views as heretical.[19]

A beginning refutation of Pelagian ideas occurs in Genesis 6:5 where God pronounces that humans only do evil all the time, even in their inclinations and motivations. Sin, far from being external, is also present in the innermost springs of our person. In the NT, Romans 3:10-23 catalogues typical human sin. Romans 6 also depicts us as slaves to sin. We are not portrayed in that passage as free and willing, rather as slaves in bondage. In addition, that passage retains the slavery imagery and applies it to righteousness even subsequent to conversion.

Romans 9:16-18 portrays our wills as, to use Luther's word, "bound." They do not soar in freedom before conversion, nor totally so after rebirth. Even Philippians 2:13-14, the presumed *classicus locus* of Pelagianism, semi-Pelagianism, and Arminianism, does not (rightly interpreted) prove an unrestricted will.

What is at stake with Pelagianism in its full-blown form is the entire system of belief. These heretical seeds of thought can hardly be isolated parts of the faith. In Pelagianism, God the Father is transformed into a supporting actor in the cast, with human will inflating itself to the leading role; it becomes all-determinative. God the Son becomes an exemplar. He cannot, according to Pelagianism and its posterity, act for us—for that would presuppose either fallenness or inability. For the Pelagian, man must do all the important things, with Christ relegated to being an inspirational model at best or else a Great Encourager. Sound familiar? God the Spirit becomes the comforter and counselor but seldom the convictor or powerful worker. The Trinity itself is sacrificed to Pelagian ideas.

Humans become the really important players. They are the ones who decide for or against Christ; humans give God a break or do not. God is limited, according to these will-olatries; he may act only within the range we permit. He can never be seen as presiding over the all-important will of man; his sovereignty is not

---

[19] The shudder among most evangelicals at the very vocabulary of "heresy" reveals the weakness of epistemology among evangelicals.

countenanced by Pelagians. In the end, as in the beginning, it is up to the disciple of Pelagius to keep himself in the good graces of God.

The ministry of Pelagianism looks much like modern evangelicalism. Paige Patterson (cf. pp. 282-283 below) and others candidly, albeit painfully, admit that all too often we have resorted to gimmickry rather than the gospel. The gospel and its radical portrayal of fallen man and powerful grace keep the Christian from excessive gimmickry. However, without this correct doctrine the heresy of Pelagianism turns Christianity totally on its head.

Examples of modern Pelagians abound. Most do not like that appellation, but if the ideological shoe fits, they should wear it. Charles Finney was a Pelagian. His formulaic method for revival (roughly equated as means plus effort equals success) was an outgrowth of his underlying view of mankind. The sad thing in our day is to note how many disciples Finney has. The various church growth methods, many of the evangelistic gimmicks, and the reliance on the response of the will all flow from the line of Pelagius-Arminius-Finney rather than from Paul or John.

Arminius' thought was called the "cousin-German of Pelagianism" by Dabney. "Feeling-ism" (see below) and other new gospels may be methodologically utilitarian, but they are hardly orthodox. Pelagian views of man, God, the will and grace, destroy the very foundations of not only our churches, but our homes and societies as well. Indeed, if I were the devil, I could hardly concoct a more appealing and more terminal heresy to lull the world into unwarranted confidence about its own prowess than the various strains of Pelagianism, ancient or modern. Will-worship is most enticing in the ambiance of arrogance.

Arianism

Among the cults of modernity, Arianism abounds. Two notorious examples of Arianism are the search for the Liberal Jesus and the Jehovah's Witnesses. In the 1980s, a group of critical scholars began a democratic project that sought to decide which canonical sayings were authentically uttered by Jesus. The Sayings of Jesus Study Group polled the members of the American Academy of Religion, asking them to rate select sayings of Jesus as to whether they were certain, likely, the product of accrued tradition or propaganda, or dubious altogether. With four colors for beads to express the referenda, the scholars voted. Amazingly, the composite of Jesus that returned was a Jesus who was very scientific, psychologistic, and pacifistic, but not very religious.[20] In fact, this Jesus looked much like the mirror-image of a liberal theologian. The Jesus of modern theology is not the divine Son of God. He may have shared a few god-like tendencies, but he was certainly not, according to this modern Arian Academy of Religion, divine. The Liberal cult emphasized the manhood of Jesus.

---

[20] More amazing, few from this group ventured to suggest that such cumulative results stemmed from looking into a mirror.

Jehovah's Witnesses reached a similar conclusion. Though vastly different in origin than the proponents of the modern-liberal Jesus, the Witnesses could not countenance the doctrine of the Trinity as a native part of scriptural teaching. Like the earlier Arians, Jehovah's Witnesses could not comprehend both how God could be the only God and how Jesus could also be fully divine. Thus, they felt compelled to demote Jesus by a sophisticated but worn tactic.

The father of this heresy was Arius (d. 336), an Alexandrian presbyter who rejected the full deity and eternality of Christ. He argued that if Jesus was begotten then he had a point of origination; thus he could not be eternal. Athanasius stood against this heresy, sensing its strategic potential to cripple the Christian faith.[21]

In keeping with Irenaeus' observation that error is masked in an attractive garb lest it be detected, Arius cloaked his mistaken Christology under the Greek phrase *homoiousion*.[22] The orthodox believed that Jesus was the same (*homo*) substance (*ousion*) as God the Father. Arius, on the other hand added a heretical *iota*; he taught that Jesus was similar (*homo*i) in substance (*ousion*) to God the Father. Similarity (*homoi*), as opposed to sameness (*homo*) of substance, makes all the difference in the world. The addition of the heretical *iota*, which perverts the essence and foundation of the Christian faith, may serve as a beneficial reminder that even small alterations in the faith may lead to gross heresies. Those who detest precision may profit from a review of the Arian chapter of history.

The articles below reflect the peculiarities of Arianism, ancient or modern:

- Jesus is created, subordinate in being to God.
- The Father alone is truly God.
- Non-Trinitarianism is justified.
- Jesus may be "Son" of God, but not God.

The Council of Nicea (325 AD) pronounced this condemnation of Arianism:

We believe in one God, the Father All Governing [*pantokratora*, Acts 4:24], creator [*poieten*] of all things visible and invisible;

---

[21] While some castigate orthodoxy as little more than a reaction to the heretical, it should also be recalled that in each of the major heresies, a major defender of the faith contended against the strategic error. Tertullian, not to mention the NT epistle authors, vied against gnosticism; Athanasius battled Arianism; Augustine fought Pelagianism; Calvin and others wrestled against Socinianism and Anabaptism. After history is written, the defender of the faith becomes the definer of orthodoxy. Cheers to the polemicists.

[22] As an interesting reminder to modern common denominatorists, a review of Arius' private creed will illustrate that sometimes a heretic is not so much condemned by what he affirms as by what he omits. Arius affirmed his belief in the "one God, the Father Almighty; And in the Lord Jesus Christ his Son, who was begotten of him before all ages, the Divine Logos, through whom all things were made, both those in heaven and those in earth; who came down and was made flesh; and suffered; and rose again; and ascended to the heavens; and shall come again to judge the quick and the dead. And in the Holy Ghost; and in the resurrection of the flesh; and in the life of the world to come; and in a kingdom of heaven; and in one Catholic Church of God which extends to the ends of the earth." Philip Schaff, *The Creeds of Christendom* (rpr. Grand Rapids: Baker, 1993), pp. 28-29.

And in one Lord Jesus Christ, the Son of God, begotten of the Father as only begotten, that is, from the essence [reality] of the Father, [*ek tes ousias tou patros*] God from God, Light from Light, true God from true God, begotten not created [*poiethenta*], of the same essence [reality] as the Father [*homoousion to patri*], through whom all things came into being, both in heaven and in earth; Who for us men and for our salvation came down and was incarnate, becoming human [*enanthropesanta*]. He suffered and the third day he rose, and ascended into the heavens. And he will come to judge both the living and the dead.

And [we believe] in the Holy Spirit.

But, those who say, Once he was not, or he was not before his generation, or he came to be out of nothing, or who assert that he, the Son of God, is of a different *hypostasis* or *ousia*, or that he is a creature, or changeable, or mutable, the Catholic and Apostolic Church anathematizes them.

This old error does not need novel condemnations; it already stands condemned. Unless errors are new, they are already anathematized.

John 10:29-30 teaches the oneness of the Father and the Son. Not only are they one in nature, but they are also one in activity (e.g., keeping the saints). Jesus is depicted as fully God and the sole mediator between God and men in 1 Timothy 2:5. Acts 20:28 is more subtle, but stunningly convincing. The apostle Luke taught the whole counsel of God, reminding his readers of Paul's earlier admonition to "be shepherds of the church of God, which he bought with his own blood." The serendipitous dilemma presents itself as a deduction from this verse: Either God the Father shed blood for his church or the Person who shed his blood for his church [Jesus] is divine.[23]

At the time of the heresy, Athanasius sensed the damage of minimizing the dotting of the heretical 'i'. Later, Harnack recapped his doctrinal aberration:

Athanasius has exposed the internal difficulties and contradictions . . . A Son who is no Son, a Logos who is no Logos, a monotheism that does not exclude polytheism, two or three essences to be worshiped, although only one is really distinct from that of the creatures, an indefinable being that becomes God only in that it becomes man, and that is neither God nor man, etc. On each individual point, there is apparent clarity, but everything is hollow . . . a childish self-satisfaction in the activity of contentless syllogisms.[24]

Even though the Arians began their presentation of their Christology with affirmations like "the Word of God, God of God, Light of light, life of life, the only begotten Son, firstborn of all creation, begotten of the Father before all ages, by whom all things were made," such affirmations were inadequate in what they did not affirm: the simple, clear, and full deity of Jesus. Lest modern Christians fall prey to similar errors in the future, more attention to theological detail is warranted.

---

[23] Many other verses support this orthodox Christology: e. g., John 1:1, 14; John 5:23; and John 14:5-11, among others.

[24] Cited in Harold Brown, op. cit. p. 116. Brown has an excellent summary of Arianism in op. cit., pp. 112-127.

Passing acquaintance with Athanasius and other parents in the faith would help immensely to inoculate us from recurring doctrinal heresies.

Modern descendants such as Unitarians and the Socinians (below) followed Arian thought in the main. Faced with challenges such as these, surely if past weapons are proven and still available, it would be folly to avoid this helpful arsenal simply because they were forged in an earlier age.

Socinianism

A newspaper advertisement for a local church typifies the *ethos* that animates many a heresy: the urge to find cordial acceptance in the minds of contemporaries. A local Unitarian congregation recently ran this ad (emphasis added).

> Being a Unitarian Universalist means taking personal responsibility for your own religious life. No one will try to remake you religiously. We won't offer you 'final and absolute truths' or rigid dogma. Instead, we try to provide a stimulating and *congenial* atmosphere in which you may seek answers, in which you may ask new questions, in which you are free to *discover the best that is in you*. We *reject the idea that a book or institution is superior to the conscience and intellect* of a morally responsible human being. We affirm that your spiritual well-being is yours to determine. No one else can live your own life for you.

This, of course, could well appeal to a Pelagian . . . or many a modern evangelical attract-seekers-at-any-cost approach, if pressed. What is not always realized is that this approach is at least 500 years old.

Lelio (1525-1562) and Fausto Socinius (1539-1604) were the pioneers of a revolt from orthodox Trinitarianism toward modernistic Unitarianism. In search of what they thought to be a restoration of pristine Christianity, Socinianism "taught a rationalistic interpretation of Scripture . . . an acceptance of Jesus as the revelation of God but nevertheless solely a man; the separation of church and state; and the doctrine of the death of the soul with the body except for selective resurrection of those who persevered in obeying Jesus' commandments."[25] The teachings of the Socinians became calcified in the Racovian Catechism (1605). Later descendants would espouse a latitudinarian approach that consistently led to doctrinal laxity followed by spiritual aridity. In England, giants such as Isaac Newton and John Locke became involved in latter-day Socinianism or early day Unitarianism.

Socinianism did not, however, await centuries of reflection in order to be repudiated. During Calvin's own time, he opposed the early disciples of these ideas. The notorious Michael Servetus was one such person. Along with a disavowal of the sovereignty of God and the Trinity, Socinians subjected biblical teaching to the canon of the human intellect. Later the Unitarians would extend this

---

[25] J. D. Douglas, ed. *The New International Dictionary of The Christian Church* (Grand Rapids: Zondervan, 1979), p. 912.

humanism to such lengths that it became noticeably heretical. However, initially Socinianism was difficult to diagnose.

This heresy added rationalism to the earlier Arian views. Skepticism toward miracles positioned this heresy to conspire with modern skepticism and the growing awe of science. Furthermore, the Socinians and Unitarians were the first real critics of Scripture. A thoroughly modern cult, Socinians reveled in their anti-authoritarianism and extolled the virtue of individual conscience, elevating both to *summae*. This heresy trusted in the inherent goodness of man, and could not bring itself to believe in anything as harsh as the biblical teaching about punishment or Hell. Not wishing to offend any, Socinians and Unitarians still loathe formal doctrine and honor personal opinion above all things.

A scriptural refutation of Unitarianism can be found in any orthodox defense of either the Trinity or the deity of Christ (see above on Arianism).

Unitarianism *per se* is of more recent vintage, originating in modern England. Unitarians promoted creedlessness as a virtue and eventually championed universalism. What is helpful to note, however, is the organic connection between Arian, Socinian, and Unitarian views of man, God, revelation, ethics, and spirituality. Although successive generations of this particular heresy grow worse, it is not fundamentally different from its predecessors. Familiarity with these past movements can critically aid to modern believers, if they will but resort to a standard theological dictionary.

Interestingly, many other modern cults, e. g., "Unity" and the New Age Movement, are far closer to Unitarianism than to orthodox Christianity. These ecumenical movements are syncretistic and remain as dire threats to real Christianity. To most successfully defeat them, some knowledge of their origin and theological incubation may be helpful.

Anabaptist

Another heresy that has survived its own funeral many times over is the Anabaptist heresy. I cannot stress too strongly that Anabaptists are not the same as modern Baptists. Most modern Baptists are legitimate heirs of the Protestant Reformation. In fact, in colonial America only minor differences (church government and infant baptism) separated the earliest Baptists and Presbyterians. While it may not be altogether clear today, three centuries ago Baptists virtually adopted the *Westminster Confession of Faith* with minor changes as the London Confession in England and as the Philadelphia Confession in America. The *Ana*baptists, however, were a different matter. The name Anabaptist comes from *ana* ("again") and *baptizo* ("baptize"). An Anabaptist was originally a person who believed that Roman Catholic baptism was invalid, thus requiring a professing Christian to be baptized again. Along with this was also the strongest of reactions against Roman Catholicism in the early sixteenth century. Anabaptists today are much closer to the Branch Davidians than to a typical Baptist congregation.

Shortly after the time of Martin Luther, a segment of Protestantism reacted so vehemently against Rome and the organized church that they formed themselves into communes and fought any who remained loyal to the Roman Catholic church. These groups called for the destruction of Roman Catholic Churches and viewed other reformers as less committed if they did not join the sundry fanaticisms. The chevron of commitment was a person's re-baptism, signifying his repudiation of the Catholic church. Calvin described members of this movement (that also became known as the radical Reformation) as "libertines" or "Enthusiasts."

In 1524-1525, a series of armed conflicts ("The Peasants Revolt") besmirched the reputation of Luther[26] and other reformers. Up to a third of a million radical reformers took up arms and fought the German King in reaction against pre-Reformation abuses in the Catholic Church. These Anabaptists were roundly defeated and humiliated, leaving a stench on the reputation of others who were seeking to reform the church. The errors of these "enthusiasts" were largely symbolized by their various extremisms. The Anabaptists insisted on little or no authority within the church; they did not recognize ordination or regular church government; they elevated subjective religious experience over a history-tested set of norms; and they stressed individual commitment as a test of sincerity. In addition, they frequently had excessive millennial fervor and believed that they had God's blessing regardless of what any external signs showed. What began as an anything-but-Roman-Catholic revolt soon degenerated into a cultish religion. Later, Anabaptists would drastically modify their earlier practice by becoming pacifists, with descendants such as Quakers, Moravians, and Mennonites stemming from this root, albeit with marked improvement.

Much of the error of Anabaptism was in its fanaticism and excess. Some secularists (e.g., Fredrick Engels) even saw the precursor to Marxism in the communal expression among some Anabaptist groups. Christopher Hill provided a telling description of Anabaptists:

> The most obviously political religious group was that of the Fifth Monarchists, who believed that the reign of Christ upon earth was shortly to begin. This view was held by many respectable Independent divines, who drew no directly political conclusions. . . . Only Christ's second coming could achieve what political action had failed to win. The duty of the elect was to eliminate hindrances to Christ's rule on earth. This often, in political terms, became 'overturn, overturn, overturn,' a doctrine of political anarchism. . . . The sense of the imminence of a new spiritual epoch, in which God's people should be free in a new way, was one of the many Fifth Monarchist concepts which the Quakers took over.[27]

---

[26] One Radical Reformer, Thomas Munzer went so far as to call Luther, "Brother Fattened Swine," "Dr. Liar," "Brother Soft Life," and "Pope of the Lutheran Scripture Perverters." If one was not committed to all the same causes as the Anabaptists were (and with equal zeal), evidently his character was called into question.

[27] Christopher Hill, *The Century of Revolution* (Edinburgh: Thomas Nelson, 1961), 168.

The movement virtually died after the Munster disaster, only to be rehabilitated by later leaders. The magisterial reformers and Reformation creeds[28] consistently condemned the Anabaptists.

One hallmark of the Anabaptist movement was its repudiation of civil authority. John Calvin did not mince words in detailing the errors of the Anabaptists. Calvin's thought can also be gleaned from his 1544 tract, "Brief Instruction for Arming all the Good Faithful against the Errors of the Common Sect of the Anabaptist,"[29] where he argued (*contra* the Anabaptists) that if the civil office was so impious, how could so many believers and Judges occupy positions of temporal power in the OT. Further, he argued for the legitimacy of the power of the sword: "We worship the same God that the fathers of old did. We have the same law and rule that they had . . ." Calvin found it inconsistent that Anabaptists could not admit that service as a civil officer was ordained since "they do not deny that a Christian can be a tailor or a cobbler. And yet these vocations are not expressly mentioned in the Scriptures. Why then don't they permit a Christian to be a minister of justice, seeing that this calling is so amply approved with praise by the mouth of God?"[30]

Calvin strongly reproved the Anabaptists as "miserable fanatics [who] have no other goal than to put everything into disorder, to undo the commonwealth of property in such a way that whoever has the power to take anything is welcome to it."[31] His critique of the sixth article of *The Schleitheim Confession* concluded:

> As for the end to which they lay claim, I only have two words to say: that in it they reveal themselves to be the enemies of God and of the human race. For they make war against God in wanting to revile what he has exalted. And we could not imagine a better way of trying to ruin the world and ushering in brigandage everywhere than in seeking to abolish the civil government or the power of the sword, which indeed is thrown down if it is not lawful for a Christian man to exercise it.[32]

Theodore Beza spoke of them as "the fanatical Anabaptists who abolish completely the authority of magistrates . . . and declare that trial and wars are

---

[28] The Second Helvetic Confession, the Confession of Basle, along with the French, Scottish, Belgic, and Augsburg Confessions assert the propriety of a Christian holding civil office contrary to Anabaptist teaching. Communism (an assertion by some Anabaptists) was also condemned by the French, Belgic, Augsburg, and Saxony Confessions. Cf. my *Savior or Servant? Putting Government in Its Place* (Oak Ridge, TN: Kuyper Institute, 1996), p. 252.

[29] John Calvin, *Treatises Against the Anabaptists and Against the Libertines*, Benjamin W. Farley, ed. (Grand Rapids: Baker, 1982), pp. 72-73, 77-82, and 82-91 for his critiques of *The Schleitheim Confession*.

[30] Ibid., p. 81.

[31] Ibid., p. 85.

[32] Ibid., p. 91.

unlawful things."[33] His stinging rebuke concluded that to so allege is "notorious; contrary to the Word of God, they set themselves above kingdoms and kings, there is no kind of person more rebellious to magistrates than they are; yet, they dare to charge us with a crime which they do not draw back from saying is permitted to them." In a 1591 work, *The Grounds and Principles of Christian Religion*, Beza reviled the Anabaptists who were "to be detested [for] despising all government and speak evil of the superior powers."

The Anabaptists, "the left wing of the Reformation," had their own distinctive view of the relationship of Christians to the secular state. John Eidsmoe summarizes their beliefs as follows:

> Many . . . of the early Anabaptists believed that the state was part of the evil world-system from which believers were to separate themselves. If Satan were not actually the founder of the state, he had at least taken control of it. Consequently, believers were to separate themselves from the state as much as possible; they were not to vote, hold public office, serve in the armed forces, or involve themselves with government in any other way.[34]

The Anabaptist tradition, which is the theological root of groups such as the Mennonites and Quakers, first enunciated its views on the state in the 1527 *Schleitheim Confession*. This confession regarded the use of the sword as "outside the perfection of Christ" and considered the use of the "ban" (excommunication) as the only acceptable form of coercion. In addition, this confession denied the propriety of Christians serving as civil magistrates, so contrary was the secular order to the plan of God: "The government magistracy's is according to the flesh, but the Christians' is according to the Spirit; . . . the weapons of their conflict and war are carnal and against the flesh only, but the Christians' weapons are spiritual . . ."[35] Such extreme dualism requires a separation from the world and worldly participation in matters of government. Anabaptists also extended this to deny the propriety of taking civil oaths. Although some recent efforts have been made to mitigate the earlier total "withdrawal" view, still the theological root of the Anabaptists disqualifies a Christian from full participation in the public square.

John H. Yoder has proffered modified proposals,[36] but still limits Christ's redemption to matters of the soul, arguing that "Christ's redemption does not redeem the Powers; it results in his sovereign control of the Powers for his

---

[33] Theodore Beza, *The Christian Faith*, James Clark trans. (East Sussex: Christian Focus, 1992), p. 117.

[34] John Eidsmoe, *God and Caesar: Christian Faith and Political Action* (Westchester, IL: Crossway, 1984), pp. 13-14.

[35] John Leith, ed., *Creeds of the Churches* (Atlanta: John Knox Press, 1963), 287-289.

[36] See John H. Yoder, *The Christian Witness to the State* (Newton, KS: Faith and Life Press, 1964) and *The Politics of Jesus* (Grand Rapids: Eerdmans, 1994).

redemptive purposes."[37] Instead of intending to impact the secular public square, Yoder calls for a strategy which relies nearly exclusively on personal redemption.

The traditional Anabaptist complex erects a wall between church and society, and it limits Christ's redemption to saved individuals. There is little room in practice for Christ's sovereignty over the unredeemed. One result of this view is to imply that matters of state and culture are beyond the Christian's calling. This pietism, while commendable in some of its motive, falls short of the scriptural realization that Christ is King over the Powers; he does express his sovereignty over even those unredeemed and uncooperative agents. Similarly, this extreme separatist view minimizes the salutary impact of Christians serving in government.

Calvin was quite critical of the Anabaptist approach, at times referring to exponents of that view as "men furiously striv[ing] to overturn the divinely established order" (*The Institutes*, IV, xx, 1), as "certain fanatics who delight in unbridled license" (IV, xx, 2), and as "anarchists" (IV, xx, 5) who manifested "their ignorance but devilish arrogance when they claim perfection of which not even a hundredth part is seen in them" (IV, xx, 5). He analyzed a flaw of Anabaptist thinking in the presumption that after true conversion, somehow after Christians "are transported to God's kingdom, and sit among heavenly beings, it is a thing unworthy of us and set far beneath our excellence to be occupied with those vile and worldly cares which have to do with business foreign to a Christian man" (IV, xx, 2). According to Calvin, these Anabaptist libertines claimed that "there ought to be such great perfection in the church of God that its government should suffice for law. But they stupidly imagine such a perfection as can never be found in a community of men" (IV, xx, 2).

Calvin's critique in principle is stated early in his treatment of the state:

> For certain men, when they hear that the gospel promises a freedom that acknowledges no king and no magistrate among men, but looks to Christ alone, think that they cannot benefit by their freedom so long as they see any power set up over them. They therefore think that nothing will be safe unless the whole world is reshaped to a new form, where there are neither courts, nor laws, nor magistrates, nor anything which in their opinion restricts their freedom. But whoever knows how to distinguish between body and soul, between this present fleeting life and that future eternal life, will without difficulty know that Christ's spiritual Kingdom and civil jurisdiction are things completely distinct. Since then, it is a Jewish vanity to seek and enclose Christ's Kingdom within the elements of this world . . . (IV, xx, 1).

One early Anabaptist leader was Felix Manz (1498-1527), who thought that Ulrich Zwingli was too moderate. Manz insisted on believer's baptism. Another

---

[37] Guenther Haas, "The Effects of the Fall on Creational Social Structures: A Comparison of Anabaptist and Reformed Perspectives," *Calvin Theological Journal*, vol. 30, no. 1 (April, 1995), p. 113.

early leader was Menno Simons (1495-1561), from whom the Mennonites derived their name.

The heretical tenets of Anabaptism are still manifest today. Those who limit the church to none but pure, adult believers, while well-motivated, deviate from the covenantal structure of the Scriptures. Anabaptists insist on adult professions, but in so doing overemphasize human intentionality. These groups are also notorious for their "no creed but Christ" motto. Anabaptists are rabidly anti-creedal; indeed, they seem to loathe any form or structure.

Anabaptists have often retreated from society, seeking refuge in a tightly communal expression of Christianity. Frequently, they have been preoccupied with "end-time" concerns. Perhaps most disconcerting is their similarity to an earlier gnosticism that posits a spirit/flesh dichotomy. Anabaptists believe that "what is truly spiritual cannot be confined to the flesh." This includes the text of Scripture.

A proper interpretation of the Sermon on the Mount refutes this error. Moreover, a proper exegesis of 1 Corinthians 12 would eliminate many of the recurring errors promoted by Anabaptists, as would proper interpretations for key texts like 2 Corinthians 3:6 and Acts 2. The Bible does not teach that Spirit and Flesh are inherent contraries as imagined by the Anabaptists.

The effects of Anabaptism still persist. After learning a little about this cult, one should beware of an excessive focus on independence or extremism. Some social movements today are reminiscent of earlier Anabaptism in their extremism. Christians in Arkansas who in 1987 sold their property thinking the Rapture was about to happen were more Anabaptistic than biblical. Christians could be better protected against such abuses with a little knowledge of church history.

In view of the fact that extreme Anabaptists fueled the Unitarian (Socinius) movement, it is wise to question whether such independence and unbridled individuality is so desirable. Modern descendants such as the Quakers express this heresy more benignly. Still, we must heed Chesterton's warning about the danger of prioritizing the 'inner light.' (cf. p. 41 above)

Pietism, the step-child of Anabaptism, became a dangerous and isolated movement. Christians can be as pious as God wants them to be, but they must not retreat from the world nor despise the world as a Gnostic would. Furthermore, pietism would fuel the nigh-total secularization of education and science in our time. Anabaptist thinking has more often than not forgotten to be salt and light.

Feeling-ism (The Heresy of sentimentolatry)

Subjectivism has been called the "Heresy of the Enlightenment." Much of modern Christianity is driven excessively by considerations of individual, emotional, or subjective factors. Indeed, a heresy has arisen that treats feeling or sentiment as the final arbiter of valid Christian experience. This transformational heresy—which colors the totality of one's existence if maintained—is of fairly recent birth. Although ancient pagan religions often elevated passion, ecstasy, or irrationality above truth or morality, only recently did Christianity entertain sentiment as a possible *summa*.

As with most heresies, emotionalism was likely a reaction to what was perceived as a sterile spirituality. That true Christianity can ever be sterile is, of course, impossible. Nonetheless, sentimentolatry was jump-started in the modern era with the thought of Friedrich Schleiermacher (1768-1834). Living at the peak of the Enlightenment, Schleiermacher rejected (properly) the reductionism of German pietism. Following his studies at Halle, he was seduced by literary Romanticism. Romantic emphases on personal expression, artistic sentiment, and emotional vigor greatly influenced Schleiermacher and his disciples.

Schleiermacher's first major work (*On Religion: Speeches to Its Cultured Despisers*) was in some respects an attempt to make the Christian faith acceptable to Romanticism. In it, Schleiermacher treated religion in affective terms, hoping to show children of the Enlightenment that Christianity could compete with the ideals and sentiment of humanism. Schleiermacher defined religion as "sense and taste for the infinite," and sought to avoid classic expressions of biblical orthodoxy— thinking that they were too confining for the romantic spirit. For Schleiermacher the foundation of spirituality was religious experience, and traditional theological topics were overhauled and recast in affective terms. Sin was a mistaken emotional orientation, Christ was the ultimate example of emotional dependence on God, and morality was the chief goal of religion. The disciples of Schleiermacher took his thought even further, making individual perspective and experiential feeling the main criteria for legitimacy. As a result of this attempt to make Christianity acceptable to modern schemes, secularism rose to ascendancy both inside and outside of the church.

As one reviews modern Christianity—even evangelical Christianity—the fingerprints of Schleiermacher are all too clear. After Schleiermacher, heresy was rarely spoken of, Christians preferring to emphasize sincerity. Much of modern spirituality is obsessed with reaching the feelings of the audience. Indeed, many ministries have made emotional penetration their goal, elevating subjective considerations over objective ones. A tell-tale attribute of sentimentalism is its loathing of the objective, the external, fixed truth, or creed. Emotionalism frequently caricatures strong commitment to truth as negative, having greater trust in natural sense than for revealed truth. Experience, or the "feeling of absolute dependence," becomes the norm.

Contrary to this, Romans 12:1-2 that tells us to present our entire person as a sacrifice, which is our reasonable (not emotional) worship. Worship, according to the Old and New Testaments, is not primarily emotional, although when carried out properly it normally results in due affect. Jesus told his disciples to "search the scriptures," rather than to fall for every expression of sentiment. He also stressed discernment (Jn. 7:24), as had the OT—particularly the Book of Proverbs. In addition, toward the end of the NT, John told his spiritual children to test the spirits to see if they were legitimate (1 Jn. 4:1). Nowhere in scriptural teaching are feelings given epistemological primacy. Even feelings of dependence are not absolutized; it is more important to follow God, and at times even the finest of Christians will not have his feelings aligned with God's will. The harsh reality is that sometimes emotions are crosses to bear.

This "heresy of the Enlightenment" leaves Christians with no standards by which to judge. Worship becomes valued chiefly for its effect. The Great "I" determines most matters, and results often become more prominent than faithfulness. Moreover, this religion is inadequate when attacked by strong intellectual concerns.

Modernity reflects this heresy when it despises fixed truth and authority. Emotionalism and anti-authority nearly always walk hand in hand. Romanticism and the elevation of the naïve are also undesirable attributes of sentimentolatry. The overemphasis of the self, along with its esteem and desires, has become its own heretical cult particularly in our day. When worship becomes more preoccupied with accommodation, when evangelism abandons confrontation, when missions becomes an exercise in contextualization, and when preaching degenerates to a variety of first person experiences, one can be sure that emotionalism—whether of the Schleiermacherean kind or not—is the dominant religious principle.

Doug Marlette, a cartoonist for *The Atlanta Constitution*, penned this spoof of modern evangelicalism—which may be a satirical presentation of the heresy of emotionalism.

> Amazing grace, how sweet the sound
> That saved a stunted self-concept like me.
> I once was stressed out, but now am empowered,
> Was visually challenged, but now I see.

Many would prefer John Newton's version.

Modernism

The worship of the new—modernism by any other name—is another in the long line of transformational heresies. Some Christians appear to have but one dogmatic commitment: Anything new must be better. They seldom stop to consider if some novelties might not be inferior. Chesterton was helpful in cautioning against this. In his 1905 book, *Heresies*, the 'rollicking journalist' commented that progress was "simply a comparative of which we have not settled the superlative. . . Progress . . . as used in opposition to precise moral ideas is ludicrous. . . . Nobody has any business to use the word 'progress' unless he has a definite creed and a cast-iron code of morals."[38] Chesterton rebuked modernism in these words: "Never perhaps since the beginning of the world has there been an age that had less right to use the word 'progress' than we. . . . It is, moreover, true that the people who have settled least what is progress are the most 'progressive' in it." (2)

---

[38] G. K. Chesterton, *Heretics* (New York: John Lane Company, 1905), posted on the WWW at: http://ws-mj3.dur.ac.uk/gkc/books/heret11.txt. Citations in parentheses from this work are referenced to the original chapters of this 1905 edition.

Preferring to "revert to the doctrinal methods of the thirteenth century, inspired by the general hope of getting something done," Chesterton observed that heretics in the modern era were now proud of their heresies. The term itself "no longer means being wrong; it practically means being clear-headed and courageous." (1) Chesterton seemed to realize that modernism was but a Schleier-macherean fixation with novelty, experience, practicality, or progress. In any visage, modernism extols the virtue of being practical.

It is sad to watch evangelicals fall into the trap of worshiping innovation. When this heresy re-forms, it sweeps its disciples away from fad to fad, in the end leaving nothing but the sediment of experiences and experiments as its legacy.

Heresies that deform are by nature corruptions that re-form. It is as unfortunate as it is predictable that present and future errors will inevitably be reiterations of prior heresy.

How similar heresies remain over time. While preparing for a particular historic commemoration, I returned to some of the early historical treatises on the Westminster Assembly. In one of those early histories I found a summary list of errors that one of the Assembly members combated. It sounded so similar to many of the errors faced by the church in our own age that I reproduce some of the list for the reader below.

One of the perennial tendencies—to reject normal church authority—was widely prevalent and partially nourished by Anabaptists and Independents. Things have not changed much today. Many pamphlets of that day attacked the orthodox ministers, but as one historian noted, "Religion suffered more by the low Arminianism and lax principles of morals . . . than by all the ranting and extravagances of the sectaries during the time of the Commonwealth."[39] It was also recognized by these divines that theological beliefs were interrelated. Thus seldom (if ever) would an erring group be deviant in a single area of doctrine.

For the sake of their flocks, orthodox ministers of the earlier day fought these heresies head on. Thomas Edwards, a defender of the Assembly, depicted the errors of the Westminster opponents as a composite beast: "Strange monsters, having their heads of Enthusiasm, their bodies of Antinomianism, their legs and feet of Anabaptism, their thighs of Familialism, their hands of Arminianism, and Libertinism as the great vein running through the whole."[40] From Edwards' catalogue of errors listed in his *Gangrenae* (which lists some 186 separate errors of the day), one can see the keen eye for the purity of the faith maintained by the divines. A select list of the errors of the day will indicate the kind of critics the Assembly enjoyed as well as reinforce the teaching that "there is nothing new under the sun."

Three and a half centuries ago, some held the following errors:

1) That the Scriptures cannot be said to be the word of God.
2) That the Scriptures are a mere human composition, and cannot discover a divine God.

---

[39] Anon., *A History of the Westminster Assembly of Divines* (Philadelphia, 1841), p. 145.
[40] Ibid., p. 146.

5) That the men who wrote the Scriptures were moved by their own spirit, and they were no more inspired in this than in anything else; for it is in God that we live and move.

8) That no Scripture obliges any further than our spirit reveals to us that it is the word of God.

10) That no man is cast into hell, for any sin, but only because God would have it so.

11) That man's soul is a part of the divine essence; and when he dies, it will return to God again.

23) That we cannot look for much from a Christ crucified at Jerusalem, sixteen hundred years ago; but it must be a Christ formed in us.

34) Christ Jesus came into the world to declare the love of God to us; not to procure it for us, or to satisfy God.

36) That Christ was a legal preacher; for until after his ascension, the gospel was not preached.

43) Perfection is attainable in this life, not by the word, sacraments, prayer, and ordinances, but by the experience of the Spirit in a man's self.

51) There is no original sin in us; Adam's sin was the only original sin.

59) The moral law is of no use to believers; it is no rule for them to walk by, nor to examine themselves by; and Christians are freed from the precepts as well as the penalty of the law.

83) God has connected the preaching of the gospel indissolubly with signs and miracles.

84) Many now have greater knowledge than the apostles, because the church was then in its infancy.

87) That Paedobaptism is unlawful and anti-Christian.

97) That there should be no ministry; but every one should preach that is moved to it.

99) That they who preach should not study or premeditate what they are to say.

105) That Presbytery is the false prophet spoken of in the Revelation.

106) That there ought to be, among Christians, a community of goods.

107) That parents should not catechize their children, nor teach them to pray.

109) That all war, however necessary for defense, is unlawful.

112) That there will be a general restoration, when all men shall be reconciled and saved.[41]

Neither these errors nor their critics have changed. Indeed, all the major errors of our time, including annihilationism, the "signs and wonders" movement, enthusiasm, denial of Scripture, etc., were extant in the days of the Westminster Assembly—three and a half centuries ago. As one historian put it a century and a half ago, "Almost every form of error prevalent in our times, has existed centuries ago; in heresy, it would be hard to find anything entirely new."[42]

Over time, and in all ages, the errors are approximately the same. Today's envirofeminism may be quite organically related to ancient, Baal fertility rites. New Age religion is little more than a mixture of old age pantheism, Christian Science, and mysticism *cum* quartz and holographic technique. Egalitarianism is based on a Pelagian foundation. The old errors persistently recur. Hence, Christians had better

---

[41] Ibid., pp. 146-154.
[42] Ibid., p. 154.

be prepared for their re-formation. "Been there, rejected that" might be a more appropriate motto than "been there, done that."

The first heresiarch was Satan. All error commenced with him. In a real sense, each error is normally manifested in some attitude of Satan. Thus, there can be no new heresies, only recycled ones. If that is the case, then foolish indeed is the church or individual who refuses to learn the lessons of history.

While we are at it, let us also rid our heads of the juvenile notion that love never confronts. To fail to oppose these transforming errors—to fail to love enough to assist in repudiating such errors—is indifference not love. One hundred and fifty years ago, J. W. Alexander said, "A spurious charity forbids every word . . . towards even gross error. Indifferentism is the mother of heresy." Pseudo-love can excuse evil.

Francis Turretin was wise enough to escape infatuation with the novel. He wrote: "For since each of the oldest things is most true, no better stamp can be given especially in sacred argument than that something has less novelty. Old is best here and that which goes back to earliest antiquity. It was discovered through much sad experience that they always dangerously go astray who spurn the well-known and well-worn paths in order to cut new ones which lead off as much as possible into the pathless heights and precipices."[43] Turretin warned against "novel doctrines" which "are introduced into the church as if those who preceded us lived in a fog and in shadows until now, and they are unable to purge religion from their own errors. . . . Let other books, then, be commended for their novelty. I do not want this statement to justify mine. I avoided it most diligently lest it should contain anything new, a stranger from the word of God and from the public forms received in our churches."[44] Turretin is worthy of emulation as he repeatedly analyzed "the ancient and modern Pelagians" or "the many headed Pelagian hydra." Evidently, earlier theologians had the good sense to realize that errors of innovation are not necessarily new.

In a letter to Epictetus in the fourth century, Athanasius remarked, "I thought that all vain talk of all heretics, many as they may be, had been stopped by the Synod which was held at Nicea." Notwithstanding his sanguine outlook, heresies are seldom ended once and for all. The transformational heresies recur and deform like mutant strains of ebola. The antidote to such viral outbreaks is frequently an acquaintance with previous vaccines.

---

[43] Francis Turretin, *Institutes of Elenctic Theology*, James T. Dennison, ed. (Phillipsburg, NJ: Presbyterian and Reformed Publishing, 1992), vol. 1, p. xliii.
[44] Idem.

Hermeneutics: With History or
With Hubris

Historiam esse vitae magistram, vere dixerunt ethnicic &c.—Calvin on Romans
4:23-24.

History is philosophy teaching by example.—Lord Bolingbroke

*. . . one method seems to me worth mentioning. It is a variant of the (at present
unfashionable) historical method. It consists, simply, in trying to find out what
other people have thought and said about the problem in hand: why they have
to face it; how they formulated it; how they tried to solve it. This seems to me
important because it is part of the general method of rational discussion. If we
ignore what other people are thinking, or have thought in the past, then rational
discussion must come to an end, though each of us may go on happily talking to
themselves; . . . I fear that the practice of philosophizing on this somewhat
exalted plane may be a symptom of the decline of rational discussion. No doubt
God talks mainly to Himself because He has no one worth talking to. But a
philosopher should know that he is nor more godlike than any other man.*[1]—Sir
Karl Popper*

Widely esteemed as one of the premier commentators on Scripture in his day,
Theodore Beza confessed in the preface to his commentary on Job (1587): "I am
minded to expound the *histories* of Job, in which . . . there are many dark and hard
places, insomuch as I must here of necessity sail, as it were, among the rocks; and
yet I hope I shall not make any shipwreck."[2]

Beza's awareness of the past, along with its complexity, led him to a humble
assessment of his own ability as an exegete. The two chief interpretive options for
him were: (1) a historically informed hermeneutic ("the histories of Job"), or (2) a
shipwreck resulting from an unawareness of the previous interpretations of Job. In

---

[1] Karl Popper, *The Logic of Scientific Discovery* (New York: Harper and Row, 1959), 17.
[2] "Calvin's Exposition of the Book of Job" by Derek Thomas, *The Banner of Truth*, no.
366, March 1994, p. 13. Emphasis added.

this instance, Calvin's disciple saw the choice between a hermeneutic *cum* history, and a hermeneutic with pride of discovery (*hubris*) but capable of shipwreck. He chose the former and, with an appreciation for the history of interpretation, not only found a sounder platform but also evidenced much more humility than many moderns. Many today would also profit from a history-induced humility.

Indeed the enterprise of hermeneutics would be vastly strengthened by an improved working knowledge of the history of interpretation of any event, theory, or text. If such is confirmed, then it is also predicted that—in any endeavor at interpretation, whether in science or religious or philosophical hermeneutics—not only will sounder interpretation result, but also that humility will be a by-product as well. Or in terms of a recipe: History (*historia*) added to hermeneutic (*hermeneia*) will yield more humility or less *hubris*.

Any interpreter who approaches his text, theory, or subject devoid of famili-arity with what has gone before will invariably be less progressive (necessarily having to dedicate much time to basic rediscoveries that others have already documented). He will also be prouder of his eventual discoveries. Such pride of discovery, while exhilarating and fulfilling, is also a fine fit with a self-centeredness that so characterizes our age, sometimes chiefly in evangelical communities. If one adopts a humbler position—holding out the possibility that prior interpreters may have been equal to or greater than ourselves—then one can more readily benefit from their previous foundation. As a result one will also arrive at a more sober assessment of one's own originality. Progress and humility go hand in hand, but *hubris* and static conditions characterize the approach that arrogantly and automat-ically discounts those who have preceded us. A preferred model, therefore, will value history as an interpretive variable over the *hubris* associated with claims to original (or novel) discovery.

For those who seek to avoid replication, biblical interpretations need not be ignored by each successive generation, nor rediscovered by the alternating gener-ations. We could profit by studying past interpretive efforts, and attempt to mold our inchoate exegesis after the progress of our spiritual ancestors. The same may be true for scientific progress. Frequently, the greatest heuristic value is found in an approach that embraces the validity of history and does not limit scientific knowledge to an individual scientist or his experience. The better part of wisdom is to rule out inefficacious modes of interpreting, with the past showing which routes were dead-ends.

Likewise, we can benefit from those who have already pioneered some of these paths for us; or we can disregard their work, presuming that we are sufficient to discover all biblical truth by ourselves in our own generation. In what other academic discipline would such folly exist as in the field of hermeneutics to ignore so consistently the history of our development? A rediscovery of the interpretations from the orthodox of the past is sorely needed in our own day. Such theological giants, exegetical exemplars, and confessions could teach us much. The choice, in the end, may be between *hubris* or humility.

Dutch theologian Abraham Kuyper showed how errors of interpretation may be ruled out by process of elimination through the use of history and confession. Kuyper put great stock in the information provided through a historical study of the church's official views. According to him, "The church tells you at once what fallible interpretations you need no longer try, and what interpretation on the other hand offers you the best chance for success."[3] Kuyper admonished us to "[t]ake account of what history and the life of the church teach" about various theological topics. Thus history is useful to highlight "which paths [are] useless to further reconnoiter." History has heuristic value in eliminating erroneous dead-end paths in hermeneutics as well as in any other scientific discipline.

Thus Kuyper advised that we cannot deny history, and advocated that the history of interpretation was a partial guarantor "for freedom from error." It would be an act of extreme arrogance to elevate our own limited experience and perspective over the sum of those who have gone before us. Rather, it is "by the history of the churches" that one "shall take the dogmas of the church as his guide that he shall not diverge from them until he is compelled to do so by the Word of God."[4] For Kuyper the theological enterprise is a thoroughly historical one that greatly values church history. As Santayana might have said regarding hermeneutics: exegetes who fail to learn the errors of past hermeneutics are doomed to repeat them. The same is generally true in science and philosophy.

Earlier exegetes actually have much to teach us today. Perhaps we would make fewer mistakes if we would return free expression to those spiritual researchers and exegetes who have preceded us. Of course, to do so, compels us to adopt the posture of John the Baptizer, accepting that they must increase while we must decrease—at least in terms of self-importance.

A recent observer made the same point respecting a philosophical concept. Richard Pipes wrote:

> In his *Astonishing Hypothesis*, Sir Francis Crick informs the world of his discovery that we have no 'soul' and that our feelings and thoughts 'are in fact no more than the behavior of a vast assembly of nerve cells and their associated molecules.' That this idea should strike him as a revelation indicates only that for all his scientific brilliance, Sir Francis is poorly versed in intellectual history. For this notion is over three hundred years old, having been first intimated by John Locke in his *Essay on Human Understanding* (1690), which denied the existence of 'innate ideas' and therefore anything resembling a soul as an entity separate from the body. The notion was taken over and pushed to its logical extremes by French eighteenth century materialists. . . . In other words, far from being an 'astonishing hypothesis,' the idea is old hat. It has also proved extremely pernicious. Popularized in Russia . . . it exerted profound influence on the future Bolsheviks, who concluded that since man was nothing more than material

---

[3] Abraham Kuyper, *Principles of Sacred Theology* (rpr. Grand Rapids, MI: Baker Bookhouse, 1980), p. 576.
[4] Ibid., p. 577.

substance, he could be molded and remade in any desired shape. It provided the philosophical justification for the Stalinist and Maoist attempts to create 'new men.' Seventy years of Communist experience, ending in utter failure, proved beyond a doubt that human beings are much more than mere matter.[5]

Who (whether in the laboratory or study) has not had the experience of extensively researching some problem or text, reaching a wonderful solution or interpretation, thinking that he is the first pioneer of this interpretation or phenomena, setting forth his theory or interpretation with self-accolades for uniqueness, only to find that: (1) in science, another less known (or even heterodox) scientist has already made such a discovery, or (2) in theology, that wonderful interpretation—for which we flatter ourselves with pride of discovery—was published centuries ago by Augustine, Chrysostom, Aquinas, Calvin, Luther, Wesley, a Puritan, or a papal encyclical prior to modernism? The same thing frequently happens to new pastors, graduate assistants, first-year law clerks, and anyone involved in any hermeneutical process. In each case, a little more acquaintance with the history of one's discipline would lead to less hermeneutical *hubris* and greater appreciation for history. The history of exegesis of any passage or the previous debates on a scientific problem, therefore, are essential prior to valid discovery. Those who prove to make the most enduring contributions will also be those who are more concerned with historical continuity than with headlines for purported discovery.

The central question is: Are we better off using a historically-sensitive hermeneutic or one that is naively buttressed only by the experience of one particular age? By the very framing of the question, the reader can guess my answer. I will seek to support it below.

For those involved in regular interpretation of texts or data, a humility tempered by broader historical horizons is needed. One severely restricts success in hermeneutical fields by philosophically constraining the universe to one's own experience. All along, God has given us a far more comprehensive community that is not nearly so limited to the experience or insight of a single generation or a single interpreter. Those who have gone before us—particularly those who were best at interpreting data or texts—should be considered first in the hermeneutical enterprise, not last.

Since the earlier exegetes' insights were more reliable than the average paperback Christian book or pop-exegesis, then by all means we ought to refuse to be so arrogant as to cling to an indefensible bias for the modern. A humbler approach will avoid an arrogance that despises the past. This humbleness in hermeneutic puts us in our place, so to speak, not as the first to discover something "new under the sun"—which if such discovery did occur might justify one's boast of originality—but rather locates us as one among many other interpreters in a

---

[5] *National Review*, Aug. 15, 1994, p. 2.

stream of continuity. To those who wish to stand out and attract fame to themselves, such humility will offend. However, to those who value faithfulness and truth, a knowledge of the history of some interpretive issue is more important than the gratification of making (or claiming) novel discoveries.

This is affirmed by Alister McGrath when he tells about his grandparents in Belfast who kept all kinds of memorabilia from their childhood. When asked why, they replied that one never knows when those things might be helpful. That led McGrath to comment about one particular era.

> That is what the Reformation is like in many ways. It is about realizing that we can turn to our Christian past and rediscover things that we have neglected, that we have forgotten; things that really can be useful today. Studying history is not simply nostalgia, a sentiment that says, 'Oh, they always did things better in the past.' Rather, it is saying . . . reach into the past to enrich the present by discovering things that we need to hear today. . . . The reformers [said]: There is no point in going forward, forward, forward. We're not saying that the Reformation is basically something we have to repeat like parrots. We *are* not saying that, as we seek to move the church into the future. It helps to look back at those great moments in Christian history and ask, 'Can we learn from that time? Is there anything that the Lord wants to say to us through those people of long ago as we face their task in today's age?'[6]

McGrath reflects the perspective that will assist any hermeneutical endeavor with its humble appreciation of the past:

> The Reformation is about that process of rediscovering, and bringing to life. That is still very much our agenda. . . . we are looking at a church today that very often has many of the same problems we find in the late Middle Ages. There is a need for us to think through what we can do about those problems. The Reformation gives us some bearings, some landmarks, some ideas about how to address today's issues, using the resources, the methods, and above all, the inspiration that comes from the past.[7]

Let me seek to illustrate the benefit of historical perspective by a few concrete examples of ahistorical *hubris* from the recent past.

One of the most fanciful instances of a historically deficient hermeneutic was the popular attempt to buttress self-esteem by a dubious interpretation of Jesus' words, "Love the Lord you God with all your heart, soul, and mind. This is the first and greatest commandment. And the second is like it: Love your neighbor as yourself." In the past generation—amidst a culture that has been infatuated with psychological counseling and its novel dogmas—Robert Schuller and others sought a biblical platform for the gospel of self-esteem. Not easily finding texts that

---

[6] Alister McGrath, "The State of the Church Before the Reformation," *Modern Reformation*, March/April 1994, pp. 4, 11.

[7] Ibid., p. 11.

supported that doctrine—indeed many teachings, such as the command to crucify self and take up one's cross, are profoundly stultifying to self-esteem but nevertheless commanded by our Lord—the apostles of self-esteem were pressed to create novel interpretations from texts that did not truly support their dogma.

In one glaring instance of this mistaken (and historically-deficient) approach, some even ventured to deny the history of hermeneutics on this verse, and emphasize the final phrase, "Love your neighbor *as yourself*" as mandating a type of self-love as a prerequisite for neighbor love. Nothing could be farther from the history of orthodox interpretation on this text. One would be hard-pressed to find any prior hermeneutic that translated the final phrase of this verse ("Love your neighbor as yourself") to a level of *summa*, as if one could not function as a Christian or fulfill the law until one first had fragile self-love in place, and intractably so! A simple knowledge of the history of interpretation of this classic text could have delivered the apostles of self-esteem from such exegetical error; although such history would fail to deliver the more self-inflating results. However, it seems that self-aggrandizing interpreters value originality of interpretation—which led to actual error—over a more humble interpretation that would have fit in with the continuity of Christian interpretation of this verse. The pursuit of the new, the effort to arrive at new truth, in this case led to a departure from orthodoxy. Had history been an advisor, such would not have happened so easily.

Another example is the creation *ex nihilo* of the "preferential option for the poor." The question may be legitimately asked: Does the Bible teach that the poor should be treated differently and with preference, or is it a prior philosophical commitment to the proletariat that teaches such? Certainly the Scriptures mandate showing compassion and giving the best help we can to the deserving poor. However, Leviticus 19:15 says, "Do not pervert justice; do not show partiality to the poor or favoritism to the great, but judge your neighbor fairly." The context of this is justice in inter-personal relationships, and for at least a second time in Scripture (see also Ex. 23:2), the poor are not to be shown any partiality in respect to justice. This must surely, if Scripture is our guide, call into question any concept of a preferential option to the poor. While we may be moved to help the poor and disadvantaged in light of their need, a lowering of ethical or judicial norms is not only disallowed but explicitly condemned by these texts.

It is time to reevaluate such statements, especially in light of the collapse of most of the twentieth century experiments in serving the poor, both in the East and in the West. The following question may be asked and answered: Does the Old Testament reveal a preferential option for the poor in terms of God's intrinsic attitude toward them or the church's attitude toward them?

An answer may be given: Preference in terms of compassion perhaps, but only relatively so at this. The Scriptures indicate the need for Christian compassion extended to all who repent and believe regardless of their plight. To elevate one environmental manifestation over others (e.g., ignorance, starvation, disease) is to elevate a value that Scripture does not so elevate—even if we do so stemming from soft-hearted motives. Genuine compassion for the poor does not necessitate a preference that expects less responsibility from the poor. Justice should not be sacrificed in our attempts to give compassion to the poor.

The values of responsibility, equity, and charity are finely balanced in the Old and New Testaments. Moreover, the Bible also recognizes several distinct groups who are to be treated mercifully (including those who may not be poor). Widows, orphans and other disadvantaged groups are called to the attention of the people of God in the Old Testament lest their normal routines obscure the needs of those who are genuinely downtrodden. Thus, the much-vaunted preference for the poor may be based only on an incomplete interpretation of Scripture—one that has not consulted the past exegetes on this subject.

Furthermore, there are indeed several OT texts that specifically militate against this favoritism. One such is in Exodus 23:2 which says, "Do not follow the crowd in doing wrong. When you give testimony in a lawsuit do not pervert justice by siding with the crowd, and *do not show favoritism to a poor man* in his lawsuit." This is at least one instance where the poor are explicitly prohibited from receiving a preferential treatment. To the contrary we are told not to show favoritism to them. It is understood that the psychology of those who would be making just decisions in this scenario is one that is apt to be sympathetic and somewhat soft on the poor. The command of God is that jurors are to resist this normal human tendency and not to show favoritism or injustice to a poor man in his lawsuit simply because of his poverty. Thus in this case and others, poverty alone is not sufficient to change the norms of Scripture.

One final clue that this preferential option for the poor is more of a modern cultural innovation than a valid biblical interpretation is discoverable when we consult church history. Whenever we are faced with a purported new discovery of biblical teaching, it is normally illuminating to test its longevity from the history of exegesis. Specifically, it is informative to ask of a new teaching, "Has this view been held before? When and under what conditions? Did this view have an approximate moment of arrival, such that prior to it virtually no one held that position?" The answer will reveal something about the genesis of the idea.

In regard to this preferential option for the poor, as best as I can tell, such position was not the orthodox one in any period of church history. It is basically undetected prior to the 1960s. That fact, unless disproved, is as damaging to this view as any other single piece of information. The preferential option is almost like the Rogerian 'unconditional positive regard,' a phrase that appears to have no antecedent prior to about 1950. Could it be that the 'preferential option for the poor' is to biblical social teaching, what 'unconditional affirmation' is to modern psychology? Both can be dangerous and both are devoid of historical foundation. Is it possible that the supposed 'preferential option for the poor' is as innovatively fabricated as 'unconditional positive regard' or other psychological chimera?

If all of a sudden, the 'discovery' of a new hermeneutical tidbit is proffered, upon what 'new evidence' is this founded? If the history of orthodox interpretation does not corroborate this specific teaching, is it one we wish to advocate? I can find nowhere that great biblical scholars, like Augustine, Calvin, or Luther maintained that God had preference for the poor. Neither do I find any teaching that God has a preferential option for the foolish, nor for the terminally ill, nor for inanimate forests. Apart from socio-political preconceptions, I do not see that Scripture singles out such preferences. Neither do the great creeds or confessional statements affirm such. To claim such, it would be helpful to have historical analog in support. We must at least question the veracity of a claim, when the *analogia fides* is absent.

Neither the reformers nor the puritans singled out the poor as preferential in deserving special treatment. The poor, have always been with us, too (In Matthew 26:11, Jesus predicted that they would always be with us.). Thus, we cannot explain the sudden epiphany of this 'preferential option' in terms of a new social phenomena. Even in the throes of the Industrial Revolution, with large-scale abuse and ill-treatment of the poor, the nineteenth century evangelicals do not speak of a preferential option of the poor as founded in Scripture. A dire call for ministry, yes, and in need of the church's constant attention are the poor; but not as a categorical difference among other needs. In the history of biblical exegesis and evangelical social interest prior to the twentieth century, there is scant evidence for any preferential treatment of the poor. They are to be cared for to be sure, and biblically so; but not by throwing all other biblical principles to the wind.

One can certainly find substantial and recurring documentation that the church has not always been a good steward of God's resources. That is clear in church history. One can also confirm the church's own confession of her inadequacy at this point in numerous previous writings. Moreover, one can detect from the study of church history that the church has repeatedly re-affirmed her duty, calling, and need to minister to the poor, and to provide 'charity.' What one cannot find is the church singling out the poor with preference as objects of ministry based on the record. Comparison to church history makes this modern claim of "preference to the poor" highly suspect to say the least.

In fact, not only does this idea not appear to be supported prior to the twentieth century, it is not even apparent in the theological literature in the first half of this century, making it even more suspect. Is this just an innovation invented after 1917 or 1950? Is it too much to ask that legitimate biblical claims be advocated *not solely* by our present generation with all its respectable myopiae? Or is it too much to raise the question that if there is a legitimate biblical teaching that it be historically maintained by others than ourselves? We might not be too far off to revisit the Latin *desideratum: quod semper, quod ubique, quod ad omnibus* ("held at all times, everywhere, and by everyone").

If, indeed, this idea of the poor as a *summa* arose shortly after 1960, it is likely another case of culture determining Scripture and not vice-versa. If no history is behind this idea, it tends to look suspiciously like a post-1960s invention. If so, we might want to recognize it as such. Most likely, that is the most reputable hermeneutical course.

Another example is the recent interpretation of the reference in 1 Corinthians 5 to the "handing over to Satan" of the immoral church member. Some fantastic interpretations of this verse have been suggested. Most popular is the historically-uninformed interpretation that interprets the reference above as a prayer for the unrepentant person to face some grave physical consequence—perhaps even death —at the hands of the unleashed evil one, if he does not repent. Some have even been encouraged to pray for their non-repentant loved ones or colleagues to be buffeted by Satan and their flesh destroyed if necessary, should they not repent. Such interpretation—although sensational and ingenius—reflects scant acquaintance with the previous exegesis and the received interpretation of this text.

A simple scan of several leading works on the history of church discipline (or most church order manuals) would quickly show that among the orthodox this phrase has been interpreted as synonymous with disciplinary excommunication. Johannes Wollebius interpreted 1 Corinthians 5:5 as "the greater excommunication by which a sinner is cast out of the church, yet not without hope of pardon and return."[8] Likewise, the Westminster Assembly's *Directory for Church Government* (1645) alluded to 1 Corinthians 5:5 in its prayer attending the service of excommunication: ". . . that this retaining of the offender's sin and shutting him out of the church, may fill him with fear and shame, break his obstinate heart, and be a means to destroy the flesh, and to recover him from the power of the devil, that his spirit may yet be saved."[9] The footnotes for the Westminster Confession of Faith's chapter on "Church Censures" (XXX:4) list 1 Corinthians 5:5 as a scriptural proof for excommunication. George Gillespie interpreted this verse as follows: "Sure I am an excommunicate person may truly be said to be delivered to Satan, who is god and prince of this world."[10] Further, in his *The Due Right of Presbyteries*, Samuel Rutherford also associates "acts of government, in rebuking, assuring, and joint consenting to deliver to Satan an incestuous man"[11] with excommunication.

Likewise, a familiarity with previous systematicians of note might steer interpreters away from some fanciful interpretations. Francis Turretin is another example of how earlier exegetes can be helpful for interpreting the early chapters of Genesis. On the early population of the world—to solve a perennial dilemma, if Cain and Abel were the only sons of Adam and Eve—Turretin interprets, "The expression of Eve at the birth of Seth [Gen. 4:25] does not signify that there were absolutely no other sons of Eve, but only that none existed similar in piety and virtue to Abel recently killed, whom the pious mother hoped and desired to be in

---

[8] Cited in David W. Hall and Joseph H. Hall, *Paradigms in Polity* (Grand Rapids: Eerdmans, 1994), p. 164.

[9] Ibid., p. 270.

[10] George Gillespie, *Aaron's Rod Blossoming* (1646, rpr. Harrisonburg, VA: Sprinkle Publications, 1985), p. 198.

[11] David W. Hall and Joseph H. Hall, *Paradigms in Polity*, p. 315.

some measure restored to life in Seth."[12] Later, in Turretin's discussion of angels, he shines the light of common sense on the fantasy interpretations often given to Gen. 6:2 ('the sons of God took wives from the daughters of men'): "'The sons of God' referred to are no other than the posterity of Seth, who on account of still retaining the purer worship of God, are distinguished from the profane posterity of Cain or 'the sons of men.'"[13] The significant point is that even at Turretin's time the exegetical option of rendering these as 'giants' was present. Yet, we have in Turretin a refutation of the inferior and an instance of superior interpretation. Is there any valid reason that such historical superiority should be ignored? Humility might thrust us back.

Let me draw one final set of illustrations of the thesis to show the utility of history in hermeneutics. In a recent issue of the *Journal of the Evangelical Theological Society* (I am sanguine that most issues would yield the same benefit.), I found several exegetical conclusions interesting, particularly those that were buttressed by earlier interpretations. In one article, Gerry Breshears sought to define the role of the church in modern political matters by borrowing from an ancient taxonomy of the church regarding the offices of Christ: Prophet, Priest, and King. Breshears acknowledges that he is following the thought of Calvin (not to mention Turretin[14]). To the degree that he follows such, he has a solid tradition behind him, as well as heuristic value in that such schema has received so little attention lately. Thus, we see a helpful categorization, but one that is not truly a unique discovery.

Like Chesterton, we might confess that such taxonomy could have been learned long ago had we known our catechism. Yet many (certainly not Breshears) are too vain to imagine that any generation prior to their enlightened one could have possibly known anything of value.

In the same issue, Joe Morgado, Jr. concludes with his own affirmation, one that also mimes a late NT scholar par excellence, Colin Hemer:

> Although I can say that this paper might contain a few shreds of new evidence that I have not observed in other literature dealing with the subject of Paul's Jerusalem visits in Acts and Galatians, my concluding position on the issue is not new or creative in any way. Perhaps I can relate to Colin Hemer when he says of his own conclusion that 'there is nothing novel in this position, but the correct solution to a puzzle of this kind is not likely to be novel: the ground has been too often explored.' It is more likely to be a matter of judgment between acknowledged alternatives than any radically new combination of the data.[15]

---

[12] Francis Turretin, *Institutes of Elenctic Theology*, James T. Dennison, ed. (Phillipsburg, NJ: Presbyterian and Reformed Publishing, 1992), vol. 1, p. 461.

[13] Turretin, *Institutes of Elenctic Theology*, vol. 1, p. 538.

[14] Cf. Turretin, *Institutes of Elenctic Theology*, vol. 1, p. 393.

[15] "Paul in Jerusalem: A Comparison" by Joe Morgado, Jr., *Journal of the Evangelical Theological Society*, vol. 37, no. 1 (March 1994), p. 68.

In the next article, T. David Gordon exposes, as unsubstantiated and biased by modernity's egalitarianism, the recent translation of Eph. 4:12 as "equipping the saints for the work of ministry." Rather, he advocates as superior—of all things scandalous to neophiles—the KJV and Vulgate translations as supported by commentators on the original text, ranging from Calvin to Owen to Hodge to the present (A. T. Lincoln): "The very fact that some ancient translations do not translate the text in such a way as to permit such conclusion should produce caution and should motivate those who are otherwise convinced to frame an exegetical argument. . . . I am satisfied that the candid and unprejudiced reader will agree that the more likely translation of Eph. 4:12 is that adopted by older translations."[16]

After helping to clarify this, he accounts for the popularity of the bastardized translation: ". . . we cannot account for its popularity on the basis of careful Biblical study. Rather, we must attribute it to the egalitarian, anti-authoritarian, populist *zeitgeist* so well documented by Nathan Hatch. This spirit is so pervasive and so impervious to self-criticism that it even projects itself onto others."[17]

Thus, Gordon opts for the more historic hermeneutic, and most likely he is correct. Nathan Hatch has provided a critique of earlier evangelical preaching *sans* classical frame stemming from the "hermeneutics of populism" that demanded a simultaneous rejection of hierarchicalism and the elevation of the individual's conscience.[18] He observes that "American churches' profound commitment to audience in the early decades of the nineteenth century shaped the way religious thinking was organized and carried out . . . Insurgent religious leaders . . . considered people's common sense more reliable, even in theology, than the judgment of an educated few . . . This shift involved a new faith in public opinion as an arbiter of truth."[19] Hatch illuminates the dominant ideology of American evangelicalism under the paradigm of populism, concluding that the driving force of this Christianity is not to be found so much in its organizational styles, nor even in sociological terms, nor in the quality of its leaders, nor ideas. Instead the "central force has been its democratic or populist orientation."[20] Many evangelicals in our day would be better off to begin to recognize this extreme in their own mirror of experience.

A correlate of this humble approach to history is that historical judgments must of necessity be made with some modicum of tentativeness and be open to revision by later events. Particularly definitive of all previous history will be the *eschaton*. Anthony Hoekema has also served notice that a biblical view of history will manifest a certain tentativeness respecting aspects of internal ambiguity and the

---

[16] T. David Gordon, "'Equipping' Ministry in Ephesians 4?," *Journal of the Evangelical Theological Society,* vol. 37, no. 1, p. 70.

[17] Ibid., p. 77.

[18] Nathan Hatch, *The Democratization of American Christianity* (New Haven: Yale University Press, 1989).

[19] Ibid., p. 162.

[20] Ibid., p. 213.

bias of the interpreter: "Until the final Day of Judgment, history will continue to be marked by a certain ambiguity. . . . Cross and resurrection are both together the secret of history. Lack of appreciation for either of the two factors or the isolation of one from the other . . . must be rejected. . . . We know that in the last judgment good and evil will be finally separated, and a final evaluation of all historical movements will be given. Until that time, as Jesus said, the wheat and the tares grow together. This implies that all of our historical judgments on this side of the final judgment must be relative, tentative, and provisional."[21]

If our task is to receive updated interpretations, modify to fit the latest social change, then analyze them, and then re-enter them as new data for a new program, then we will by the very nature of the case always be lagging behind our cultural change. The World will be setting the agenda for the Church—even in hermeneutics. We must be careful not to become dominated by the latest discoveries or the latest trends. For if we have our ear to the drum of those outside of the church too often, we may find that in the end we are following in their band.

We may even find ourselves more appreciative of recycling past exegeses than hurdling forward surrounded by so great a cloud of neo-pagan witnesses. We might even find, as some disciplines have, that the past affords more heuristic value than many contemporaneous studies.

As Michael Oakeshott has asserted in the political realm, it might be more profitable for us to "prefer the familiar to the unknown, to prefer the tried to the untried, fact to mystery, the actual to the possible, the limited to the unbounded, the near to the distant, the sufficient to the superabundant, the convenient to the perfect, present laughter to utopian bliss."[22] This is the humble option for hermeneutics: a hermeneutics *cum* history, rather than the *hubris* of the Enlightenment.

In closing, I argue that there are at least three additional reasons to be more humble and historical in one's hermeneutic. If for no other reasons, should we employ a more historically-sensitive hermeneutic, the following result.

1) A more historically sensitive hermeneutic tames some of the arrogance of imagined uniqueness. All too often we think of ourselves in a self-centered fashion. We tend to believe that the world revolves around our own lives and that the discoveries we make in our labs are the first and the finest. Some of this stems from an acceptable joy of discovery. However, even in this a little more humility would make us more cautious in our pronouncements and more circumspect in allowing for other possibilities in our interpretation.

The best scientists and exegetes will avoid the "You're so special" syndrome that appeals to me-centeredness. In light of biblical wisdom (1 Cor. 10:13), claims

---

[21] Anthony Hoekema, *The Bible and the Future* (Grand Rapids: Eerdmans, 1979), pp. 34-35, 37.

[22] Cited in R. Emmett Tyrell, Jr.'s *The Conservative Crack-Up* (New York: Simon and Schuster, 1992), p. 280 as one definition of a conservative, in tandem with Abraham Lincoln's famous definition of conservatism as "adherence to the old and tried, against the new and untried."

to utter uniqueness must be refracted through other truths. History added to any hermeneutic will strip it of some of the aggrandizement attendant with the pride of discovery.

2) A more historically informed hermeneutic recognizes that our predecessors may possibly have been as wise as we are. An acquaintance with history forces us to admit that other scholars have preceded us. Church historians are fond of saying, "We stand upon the shoulders of others." Might not scientists with a greater appreciation of the history of science begin to echo some such similar saying? If we can learn to agree with Solomon (that there is nothing new under the sun), then prior to trumpeting our discoveries we may wish to seek out other earlier pioneers to see if they have beat us to the punch. Moreover, a preference is given to that which is the received judgment as opposed to new discovery. The burden of proof rests on the shoulders of the novel, not the already-proven.

3) Historical hermeneutics leads to a healthy tentativeness in pronouncing novel judgment. Accordingly, we will have to learn to make friends with provisionality in some areas. Often, we will have to wait patiently as well as humbly on further confirmation. And indeed, some of our theorizing will have to be jettisoned and revised. Tentativeness in pronouncing judgment may be a sign of a mature scholar or scientist. Wolfhart Pannenberg has urged that scientific conclusions be subjected to ongoing revision, and also is helpful in reminding of the need to submit one's pre-understanding to the ontological flow of history.[23]

On the utility of history in general, Hilaire Belloc noted: "[H]istory adds to a man, giving him, as it were, a great memory of things—like a human memory, but stretched over a longer space than one human life." Would such not help in hermeneutics—legal, biblical, scientific, or otherwise? All in all, history appears to be the friend of humility; not to mention, the friend of hermeneutics.[24]

---

[23] See, e. g., W. Pannenberg, *Theology and the Philosophy of Science* (Philadelphia: Fortress, 1976). Pannenberg, as part of the hermeneutic movement in late twentieth century philosophy, sees any process of understanding—whether it is science or theology—as involving hermeneutic. He as much as says, "Where there is science there is hermeneutic and where there is hermeneutic there is science." Cf. my earlier "The Relation of Philosophy of Science to Theology: An Integrated Coexistence" (1978, unpublished).

[24] This is adapted from an earlier version of an essay that appeared in *Premise*, vol. 2, no. 9, Oct. 1995, p. 9 (http://capo.org/premise/95/oct/toc.html). Used with permission.

The Old Way: Confessional Adherence

To commit oneself to the particulars of a stated confession or creed is an ancient practice, but it is neither the exclusive property of Roman Catholics nor a token of dead legalism. It may even hold merit for consideration in an age where relativism runs rampant and truth is tortured. To adhere to a confessional document is a practice that was evident in some of the strongest Protestant churches. For example, Charles Briggs (who shunned the very idea of a confession as limiting) had to admit to several instances of this practice at the time of the Westminster Assembly.[1] Also during several Reformation era colloquies, various proponents would frequently sign their name to their theses as a sign of authenticity.[2]

A definite pre-history exists for the practice of confessional subscription, stemming at least as far back as the Reformation period. For example, Calvin himself advocated the formal adoption of a Catechism (1536) by all citizens of Geneva. The Ministers of the Presbytery (The Company of Pastors) frequently signed documents indicating both their authenticity as well as their affirmation. Numerous other Reformation confessions and creeds were signed. Later, the First Scots Confession—and subsequently even polity documents—were subscribed. Beza and others subscribed the French Confession of Faith at the Synod of Emden in 1571.[3] Moreover, the Lutheran tradition of subscription during the Reformation is eye-popping when it is remembered that certain prominent Lutheran leaders were not allowed to subscribe the Augsburg Confession (1530) because they demurred at one particular article concerning the uniquely Lutheran view of the sacrament. James R. Payton, Jr. observes, "Their request to subscribe with a proviso was denied: subscription had to be to the confession *in toto* or not at all. The rigor with which this defense of an unqualified confessional subscription was

---

[1] Charles Briggs, *American Presbyterianism* (New York: Charles Scribners & Sons, 1885), p. 63 refers to certain divines whose names were signed to a tract in 1643. Cf. also, p. 342.

[2] Jill Raitt, *The Colloquy of Montbeliard* (New York: Oxford, 1993), pp. 30-31, 74-76.

[3] Robert Kingdon, *Geneva and The Consolidation of the French Protestant Movement, 1564-1572* (Madison, WI: University of Wisconsin Press, 1967), p. 125.

maintained in the midst of exceptionally dangerous circumstances speaks volumes regarding the attitude of the early Protestants toward a confession."[4]

The Lutherans subscribed the 1537 Smalcald Articles.[5] The First Helvetic Confession had formally been read before each congregation annually, and ministers in that communion are still required to promise "to teach according to the direction of God's Word and the Basle Confession derived therefrom."[6] Subscription became so popular that by 1573 graduates of Oxford were required to subscribe prior to receiving degrees, and by 1576 subscription was applied even to entrants over the age of sixteen.[7] It is well-known that Scottish Christians subscribed national covenants in 1581, in 1638, and took part in subscribing the Solemn League and Covenant with the Westminster Divines ("Wherein we all subscribe, and each one of us for himself with our hands lifted up to the most high God, do swear"[8]) in 1643.

Thus, even from these few references, it is clear that the first generation of the Reformation churches—committed to biblical truth—had no qualms about composing, embracing, requiring, and subscribing to biblical re-statements of the faith. So accepted was this that there was very little debate among Protestants over the propriety of creedal subscription, except among the Anabaptists and other fringe groups of the Reformation. Debates would arise later, however.

Since there is so much disinformation on this subject, and since we have at hand several good examples of the utility of adhering to objective statements of faith, I would like to trace one tradition's attempt to hold to truth below. Since they were not ultimately successful, studying these parents is not to boast of their efficacy so much as it is an attempt to learn from their mistakes.

Confessions Among British Presbyterians

A moderately successful experiment in "presbyterianizing" was carried out in Northampton in 1571, with "prophesyings" (exposition of Scripture apart from liturgy) following the precedent of 1 Corinthians 14.[9] In Northampton, seven regulations were adopted, the first of which was: "That every minister, at his first allowance . . . of this Exercise, shall by subscription declare his consent in Christ's true religion, with his Brethren, and submit to the discipline and order of the same."[10] Further, a May 29, 1571 law allowed Presbyterian ordination as long as

---

[4] James R. Payton, Jr., "The Background and Significance of the Adopting Act of 1729," *Pressing Toward the Mark* (Philadelphia: Orthodox Presbyterian Church, 1986), p. 134.

[5] Philip Schaff, ed., *The Creeds of Christendom* (Grand Rapids: Baker, 1983), 1:254.

[6] Ibid., p. 388.

[7] Ibid., pp. 618-619.

[8] John L. Carson and David W. Hall, eds. *To Glorify and Enjoy God: A Commemoration of the Westminster Assembly* (Edinburgh: Banner of Truth, 1994), p. 295.

[9] A. H. Drysdale, *History of the Presbyterians in England: Their Rise, Decline, and Revival* (London: Publication Committee of the Presbyterian Church of England, 1889), p. 121. Hereafter cited as Drysdale.

[10] Drysdale, p. 124.

the Ordinand was supportive of the Thirty-Nine Articles.[11] Hence, it seems that the earliest practice of subscription in England was to the Thirty-Nine Articles. Furthermore, M'Crie asserts that, at the organization of the Presbytery of Wandsworth (1572), "it is certain that some general outline of discipline was drawn up, and privately subscribed by the members, in pledge of mutual agreement."[12] What exactly was subscribed to, M'Crie is not sure since the original minutes are not available. However, he speculates: "The Discipline had been subscribed to in various parts of England."[13] Daniel Neal also supports this,[14] and even Charles Briggs includes the subscription formula in his reprinting of Cartwright's *Book of Discipline*, to wit: "The Brethren of the conference of N. whose names are here under written have subscribed this discipline after this manner . . ."[15]

The next instance of subscription among our British parents was one that was used against the incipient Puritan movement. Its negative impact continued to shape the views of British Presbyterians for some time, frequently inciting violent reactions to subscriptions of any sort due to this tyranny. In 1583, as Archbishop Whitgift began to retaliate against the proto-Presbyterians, his first step was to issue "a paper of fifteen requisitions which all the clergy were at once to subscribe, on pain of deprivation. . . . The Sixth of these provisions was the hardest and most notorious, containing as it did the new subscription test, and requiring that none be permitted to preach, read, catechize, minister the Sacraments, or execute any ecclesiastical function, by what authority soever he be admitted thereunto, unless he first consent and subscribe to these Articles following . . ."[16] Whitgift required subscription to the Prayer Book, and "those subscribing bound themselves to use these forms and none other."[17] That these were indeed enforced can be seen in that shortly thereafter, Humphrey Fenn and others were suspended from ministry for refusing to subscribe.[18] John Udall, the first Presbyterian martyr of the Star Commission, had "subscribed *The Book of Discipline*" in 1592, thereafter becoming a marked man.[19] Following the first blush of subscription by British Presbyterians in Northampton, immediately thereafter subscription became associated with ecclesiological tyranny. So bitter was this experience with subscription,

---

[11] Drysdale, p. 131.

[12] Thomas M'Crie, *Annals of English Presbytery* (London: James Nisbet, 1872), p. 104. M'Crie also speaks of Presbyterian ministers "as having 'subscribed the discipline,'. . . in some form or other, it must have been this book that was subscribed . . ." (p. 108), referring to the 1587 *Book of Discipline*.

[13] Ibid.

[14] Daniel Neal, *The History of the Puritans* (New York: Harper, 1855), p. 445.

[15] Charles Briggs, *American Presbyterianism* (New York: Charles Scribners & Sons, 1885), p. xvii.

[16] Drysdale, pp. 186-187.

[17] George Rule, *Puritanism in Politics, 1640-1647* (Oxford: The Sutton Courtenay Press, 1981), p. 57.

[18] Drysdale, p. 188.

[19] Drysdale, p. 208.

as it was abused at the hands of Whitgift and the persecuting Anglicans, that it would be a wonder if such practice was ever revived by English Presbyterians.[20] Yet, later it was.

Early in the eighteenth century, the matter of subscription would resurface—nearly a decade prior to the Adopting Act in America. By the year 1717, at least five Presbyterian congregations were meeting together at Exeter. A controversy arose over the orthodoxy of James Peirce who had been accused of Arianism. When the committee from this Presbytery met (also to consider the orthodoxy of Joseph Hallett and others),[21] Peirce strenuously denied any deviation, and responded in 1719 with a vigorous pamphlet, "The Western Inquisition."

In May of 1719, this matter was then brought before the Exeter Assembly, a synod founded by Flavel and others (commencing as early as 1655—even in the face of the Act of Uniformity).[22] One attempt to resolve the conflict was by subscribing the First Article of the incontrovertibly trinitarian Thirty Nine Articles. Fifty-nine of the ministers agreed to so subscribe, while nineteen (including Peirce and Hallett) did not. The trial *per se* ended, with this Assembly resolving, "that no minister henceforth be ordained or recommended to congregations by the Assembly, unless he subscribed that First Article, or the 5th and 6th answers of the Assembly's Catechism, or assented to the Assembly's own declaration of faith, or sufficiently expressed the same sense in words of his own."[23] An attempt to prevent the triumph of Unitarianism, this method employed a formal principle of specific doctrinal subscription. In this early phase, subscription obviously meant submission to the stated doctrine and a whole-hearted embracing of the *credenda* without equivocation or mental reservation—the exact short-coming of Peirce *et al* that the Synod was trying to preclude.

Earlier the same year, the Salters' Hall Synod (Feb. 19, 1719) met, hoping to communicate some healing measure to the upcoming Exeter Assembly. According to Drysdale, all at that Synod were willing to affirm the First Article and Catechism answers #5 and #6. However, they faced a tactical decision—not altogether dissimilar from the American Adopting Act a decade later: What was the most irenic way to contend for orthodoxy, while simultaneously pleading for mutual understanding? By a narrow vote of 73-69 that Synod decided against the call for subscription.[24]

This led to a division among the London Presbyterians into Non-Subscribers, Subscribers, and Neutrals, a crucial division of which American Presbyterians

---

[20] Thomas M'Crie in *Annals of English Presbytery* (London: James Nisbet, 1872) notes the overreaction toward the practice of subscription stemming from this period: "And indeed, as we may see afterwards, if the English presbyterians went too far in any point, it was in their uniform dislike to the subscription of religious creeds." (p. 102)

[21] Drysdale, p. 500.

[22] Drysdale, p. 501.

[23] Drysdale, pp. 501-502.

[24] Drysdale, p. 502.

were certainly not unaware. [25] The Neutrals were led by Edmund Calamy, Jr. (also Isaac Watts and Daniel Neal). The Subscriptionists divided off and were led by Thomas Bradbury. The slim majority of Non-subscribers, led by Joshua Oldfield, sent a letter on March 10th to Exeter. It stated that the Salters' Hall Synod opted not to subscribe, merely out of respect for Scripture and the desire to impose only scriptural wording on the conscience: "We take it to be an inverting the great rule of deciding controversies among Protestants, making the explications and words of men determine the sense of Scripture, instead of making the Scriptures to determine how far the words of men are to be regarded."[26] Still, they desired to repudiate Arianism.

Notwithstanding, the next month the subscribing Assembly communicated their "Advices for Peace" on April 7th, prefaced with 77 signatures (including 48 from London) which subscribed to the First Article and the 5th and 6th Answers of the Westminster Catechism.

With such divided attempt at intervention, the Exeter Assembly, nevertheless, acted on its own, and in May of 1719 adopted the subscriptionist position by a vote of 3-1 (actually 59-19 as above). However, Presbyterianism was badly divided.[27] Both factions, of course, laid claim to the true chevron of the Protestant Principle. Drysdale caricatures the Non-subscribers as biblicistic, of greater learning and social status, and less ecumenical, while portraying the Subscribers as more devotional, saintly, ecumenical (with the Independent Dissenters), and older.[28] Of the Non-subscriber tendency toward accommodation he stated:

> The Non-subscribing Presbyterian ministers showed a tendency toward the reception of new ideas, whatever these ideas might be; and, to adapt themselves to altering tastes, committing themselves to the current speculations and spirit of the times. This was the section that slowly found themselves drifting away from former moorings, though they neither intended nor admitted to themselves that they were doing anything else than protesting against narrow, illiberal, and bigoted notions.[29]

Drysdale warns of an incipient rationalism[30] that can accompany some anti-subscriptionism, noting Chillingworth's observation that, "it [the practice of non-subscription] had become the grand bulwark of latitudinarianism; . . . subsequently it got to be freely used in defense of all sorts of laxity by many among this non-

---

[25] Richard Webster refers to five factions in the American synod: "the Protesters, the excluded, the silent, those who were dissatisfied with both parties, and the absent." Richard Webster, *A History of the Presbyterian Church in America from its Origin until the year 1760* (Philadelphia: The Presbyterian Historical Society, 1857), p. 174.

[26] Drysdale, p. 504.

[27] Drysdale notes that the tendency toward subscription was actually stronger among Independent Dissenters, than Presbyterian Dissenters, p. 505.

[28] Drysdale, p. 506.

[29] Drysdale, p. 506.

[30] In a footnote (p. 507), he even sees the "influence of Locke" on these non-subscribers.

subscribing class of Presbyterian ministers."[31] Sadly, by 1735 the Westminster Shorter Catechism was revised toward Arminianism and Arianism and, thereafter, British Presbyterianism careened toward Unitarianism or rationalism. In 1736, one attack on the Westminster Catechism went so far as to query whether Presbyterians held to it due to "Bigotry or from Reason."[32]

Drysdale offers several explanations for the decline of Presbyterianism in England, among which are the failure to enforce doctrinal conformity, the lack of control over schools and Academies, "the practical disuse of and departure from the more fully developed Presbyterial government and discipline as an operative and influential reality,"[33] and the temper of the times—which was loath to adopt strong convictions.

Notwithstanding, Drysdale notes the consequences of not holding to a creed:

> Given then all this: given this spirit of opposition to restraint and of resistance to any trammels of human authority, with dislike to all subscriptions of Articles and compulsory authority; then, with the other conditions of the age, and the state of the young, half-trained Presbyterian ministers, Arianism, with its vagueness and flexibility, just met their case, and was a convenient disguise, to any that sought it, to conceal a denial of all supernatural elements in revelation . . .[34]

Agreeing with John Black, author of *Presbyterianism in England in the Eighteenth and Nineteenth Centuries*, Drysdale affirms: "Perhaps nothing in ecclesiastical history is more remarkable than the change which came over the Presbyterianism of England between the Westminster Assembly and the Revolution, in the transition from a jealous guarding of the *complete truth*, even to *intolerance*, in the former period, to the broad and even *latitudinarian charity* which prevailed in the latter."[35]

Later, he averred that the 1719 Salters' Hall Synod was the "only instance perhaps that can be produced out of church history for many centuries, of an Synod of ministers declaring in favor of religious liberty."[36] Presbyterianism in England did decline thereafter, with Presbyterian ministers soon acquiring a reputation as

---

[31] Drysdale, p. 507.

[32] Part of the subtitle of Samuel Bourn's *An Address to Protestant Dissenters.* Drysdale, p. 508.

[33] Drysdale, pp. 509-513. On p. 511, he notes: "Organization, indeed, is not life; but as the highest life seeks the best organization, the want of it is apt to be death, and the disuse of it deprives Churches of that staying and self-recuperative power which is most needed at critical junctures; and so they are left a prey to the downward and deadening tendencies that may be at work. For want of Presbyterian supervision, the leaven of heresy had free course to work its way secretly." He goes on to note the invariable tendency to begin with a civil desire not to question personal honor that may degenerate into dishonesty.

[34] Drysdale, pp. 512-513.

[35] Drysdale, p. 513.

[36] Drysdale, p. 521.

those who "preferred speculative liberty to Evangelical orthodoxy."[37] The meeting at Salters' Hall appears to be a turning point, with the "Disuse of distinctively Presbyterian methods of procedure, depriv[ing] the Churches of their chief staying power, and [leaving] them a prey to the downward tendencies of the time."[38] Peirce of Exeter, and other Presbyterian ministers, "became semi-Arian... and rapidly did the infection spread, becoming more virulent and deep-seated as the years increased. Uncontrolled liberty... insisted on this as their right. The Salters' Hall controversy, in 1719, familiarized the people with the new destructive force that was to wreck the old Presbyterian interest, already sufficiently prostrate, under efforts to galvanize its departing and well-nigh exhausted energy."[39]

Drysdale saw a relationship—if not causal, certainly circumstantial—between the demise of English Presbyterianism and the slide toward Unitarianism. He does not overlook the "influence of the Non-subscribing or rather Anti-subscriptionist ministers."[40] Meanwhile the northern parts of England sought pulpit supply from Scotland.

Only the Scots helped preserve a small remnant, although "the Scottish ministers feeling repelled like their English subscriptionist brethren kept themselves more and more aloof from the heterodox party; and in self-defense created... 'the Scots Presbytery'"[41] in London in 1772. In 1755, when the Presbytery of Newcastle was revived, it saw wisdom in beginning its "Rules of Orderly Procedure" with the following emphases on subscription—likely having been learned from an earlier era:

> We, subscribers, Ministers of the Gospel, for the honor of our profession, the maintaining and promoting peace among us, do declare: (1) That we will study to cultivate a good understanding amongst ourselves... (2) As Infidelity, Error, and Profaneness... seem to be on the growing hand, we disclaim Deism, the Arian, Socinian, Antinomian, Pelagian, and Sabellian errors and heresies as such, and resolve on all occasions to give our testimony against them; (3) And whereas Confessions of faith and Creeds are unreasonably run down, we are determined by the grace of God to make His Holy Word and Confessions, thereunto agreeable, the standard of our faith or religious principles, and the Rule of our Practice...[42]

Shortly thereafter, in the 1784 "Formula and Rules," the British Presbyterians set forth:

> 1. Formula.—We, the Dissenting Ministers of the Newcastle Class, do own and believe the Scriptures of the Old and New Testaments to be the Word of God, the

---

[37] Drysdale, p. 533.

[38] Drysdale, p. 549.

[39] Drysdale, p. 550.

[40] Drysdale, p. 550.

[41] Drysdale, p. 556.

[42] Drysdale, p. 576. It is to be noted how similar this language is to various denials of heresy (and affirmation of orthodoxy) in early American Presbyterianism.

only infallible rule of faith and practice; we believe . . . [a list of theological affirmations]; and as these and all the other doctrines which we believe and profess are clearly comprehended and shortly and distinctly summed up in the Westminster Confession of Faith, we heartily acknowledge it to be the Confession of our Faith, and this we the rather do, as Arians, Socinians, Arminians, etc., have always recourse to Scripture, and wrest it to support their own erroneous tenets, whereas we are convinced, that the Westminster Confession gives us a view of the doctrines most agreeable to the mind of the Spirit of God in his holy word. And therefore we promise (through grace) to maintain them both in our profession and preaching, . . .
2. Rules.—As every Society has a right to make Rules and Regulations for the direction of their own conduct, so this Class think it highly necessary that the following be consented to and acquiesced in by all its members that either are or shall be admitted members of it:—(1) That no person, ordained or unordained, should be admitted a member of this Class until he subscribe the above Formula.[43]

In retrospect, it appears that Custer's Last Stand may have been at the Exeter Assembly in 1719, with both Subscriptionism and Presbyterianism quickly deteriorating thereafter. Drysdale perceptively summarized the fallout:

They had seen the evils of an imposed set of Articles, enforced by the State and statute law; and as conscious freedmen they learned to resent it, when practiced upon themselves. Their prejudice against tests and impositions, so natural and easy to be understood, led them to confound this with the very different thing of what is apostolically required—'a pattern or form of sound words,' as an exposition of a teacher's faith, *for mutual confidence and co-operation.* Doubtless they had seen some men keep the faith, without such bonds, through times of trial and persecution . . . But this guarantee is not available in quiet and peaceful times. Besides, while they persuaded themselves that they were wiser and more liberal than their fathers and founders in showing antipathy to all tests or standards or orthodoxy, they confounded *terms of Church communion* . . . with *terms of ministerial office and honor,* which has to do with the different question altogether of public and authorized teaching.[44]

Thus, Drysdale, the leading historian of British Presbyterianism, identified the "question of ministerial subscription [as that over which] the English Presbyterians began to fragment."[45] He asserted that although Arianism became the resting home for such Non-subscriptionists, "Any other form of doctrinal speculation that happened to emerge might have been as readily adopted."[46] He analyzes below:

---

[43] Drysdale, p. 577.
[44] Drysdale, p. 509.
[45] Drysdale, p. 519.
[46] Drysdale, p. 519.

For the great question among these anti-subscription Presbyterian divines of the [18th] century was not so much about any one specific doctrine or other, but it was the principle of *entire ministerial freedom of religious inquiry and profession*. This was an early and potent watchword with these non-subscribing Presbyterians, and under the spell of it there resulted many varying changes of doctrinal theory. . . . The absence of any provision for enforcing doctrinal unity beyond what was legally required by the Toleration Act, was a form of unrestrained liberty greatly relished by men embarking on a new departure in ecclesiastical life. Intoxicated with its exhilaration, there were those among them who began to praise and ultimately even to worship this newly-found principle of an untrammeled ministry. . . . Changes at length inevitably began to appear, according as the practical habit of acting on the easy and non-restrictive method led to a speculative recognition of its pleasantness. . . . Christian doctrine . . . degenerated into a mere set of scheme of 'opinions' . . . [47]

Drysdale—even though not contending for subscription as a principle—does lament the consequences of anti-subscriptionism. With a sadness of pen, he observed of the modernizing trends:

These views, which became so current, and which confound license with liberty and the lack of restraint with freedom, which mistake indifferentism and latitudinarianism for Christian charity, and which make ministerial laxness synonymous with Catholicity, soon began, like all empiricism to work its mischievous effects, to the detriment and ruin of the very interests which were meant to be safeguarded. [48]

Thus, in British Presbyterianism, it is clear that the concept of subscription had a definite meaning, one that was understood by friends and enemies alike as requiring adherence. Furthermore, the doctrinal specifics adhered to were expressed nearly identically to some of the wording invoked by American Presbyterians in the same era. Evidently, a tradition of subscription which was not unique to Americans was extant.

Is it conceivable that the American cousins knew nothing about this British experience a little later as they took their Adopting Act?[49] If, as Drysdale and

---

[47] Drysdale, pp. 519-520.

[48] Drysdale, p. 521.

[49] Acknowledging the communication between the Old World and the New, Webster observed both the inadvisability of duplicating the European experience in the colonies, and also the strength of colonial Presbyterian adherence:

The jealousy of the people for the integrity of the standards, and for exact and hearty adherence to them, was most reasonable, from their knowledge of the spread of the New Light "at home," and from the probability that errorists would cross the ocean to "corrupt our church." Great alarm prevailed on account of the progress of error in the British Isles. . . . And some American Presbyterian ministers, following the Hemphill trial wrote to the Synod pleading for a method of identifying and excluding possible

others concluded, much of American Presbyterianism was rooted in the British experience,[50] then it is the more imperative that we take seriously this English context, perhaps as definitive for interpreting our own tradition. At the very least, this British pre-history illuminates the nuances that were likely in the minds of American Presbyterians when they first practiced subscription. Add to this the knowledge of the Scottish and Irish controversies, and it seems that a tradition of confessional adherence can be ascertained—even though some hesitate to admit these historical realities.

Scotland and Ireland Prior to the Adopting Act

In the beginning of his treatment of the background of the Adopting Act, Charles Briggs noted that in 1693 the General Assembly of Scotland allowed for a rather clear-cut subscription statement. That 1693 vow was: "I do sincerely own and declare the above Confession of Faith, approved by former General Assemblies of this Church, and ratified by law in the year 1690, to be the Confession of my faith, and that I own the doctrine therein contained to be the true doctrine, which I will constantly adhere to."[51] Later in 1698, the Synod of Ulster resolved: "That young men licensed to preach be obliged to subscribe to our Confession of Faith and all the articles thereof, as the confession of their faith."[52] Further, Briggs noted that this 1698 Act was renewed in 1705. He contends that, "the year 1705 was the first formal subscription among Protestant churches"—surely a dubious claim in light of the Elizabethan churches a century earlier, not to mention the reformed churches in Europe in the sixteenth century (see pp 99-100 above). Still later Briggs reported that the Synod of Belfast, "[i]n 1716 debated the matter, and expressed themselves as in favor of including subscription to the Westminster Confession of Faith and the Toleration Act." Hence, there was some precedent for the American style of subscription, and many of these earlier acts could provide a hermeneutic for the Adopting Act.

'wolves in sheep's clothing,' suggesting "our earnest desires, that ministers, besides credentials, should bring letters from brethren who are well known to us to be firmly attached to our good old principles and schemes."(Webster, op. cit., pp. 114-115)

[50] James R. Payton notes: "Contact [by early American Puritans] with their confreres in the British Isles, however, kept them abreast of developments there and the question soon received a considerable amount of attention. In the decade of the 1690s, the Presbyterian churches in Scotland, England, and Ireland had each adopted the Westminster Confession and come to require subscription to it. . . . These churches in the British Isles were still embroiled in their controversies when in 1721 an overture moving in the general direction of requiring subscription to the Westminster standards came on the floor of the Synod of Philadelphia." "The Background and Significance of the Adopting Act of 1729," *Pressing Toward the Mark* (Philadelphia: Committee for the Historian of the OPC, 1986), p. 135.

[51] Briggs, p. 201.

[52] Idem. The next references are to pp. 201-203.

Leonard Trinterud, an antagonist of subscription, does an able job of recounting some of the controversies in Scottish Presbyterianism over subscription. He admits that in 1690 and in 1696 the General Assembly of Scotland both allowed subscription to the Confession of Faith as a test of ministerial communion and further forbade anyone to "speak, write, preach, teach, or print anything whatsoever that would be contrary to or even inconsistent with, any view contained in the Confession."[53]

A sense of the earliest colonial practice is found in the adoption of the Heads of Agreement (associated with Cotton Mather). One could re-read such standards and find the earliest colonists adopting an Americanized version of the Westminster Confession of Faith (hereafter WCF) without equivocation.[54] The record itself is unambiguous. "Own" was the common usage of that day as in the 1711 Scottish terminology that probably inspired the 1784 British "Formula and Rules" above.

For students of confessional history, Ian Hamilton has provided a fine study[55] chronicling the decline of confessional orthodoxy among Scottish Presbyterians from 1730-1879. Since American Presbyterianism followed a similar course, any who wish to see an antecedent to our own symbological history would do well to absorb this chapter from Scottish history.

Hamilton notes that the Westminster Confession of Faith held a position of prominence among confessional documents within the reformed Presbyterianism of an earlier day. Proceeding chronologically, Hamilton begins by detailing the Scottish subscription formulae of the early eighteenth century. Documenting that from 1711 on, the General Assembly of Scotland required a strict subscription, Hamilton discusses the early evolution of the pertinent ordination vow, illuminating how it eroded from unequivocal adoption of the WCF as "ones own" and as "believing the whole doctrine contained" to an ambiguous and less specific adoption of the confession as containing a "general sense." Hamilton shows how this erosion considerably weakened the doctrinal orthodoxy of the Scottish church by 1840. Hamilton's discussion refutes the claim that prior to the 1840s Scottish Presbyterianism accepted a latitudinarian approach to subscription.

In a subsequent chapter chronicling the atonement controversy in the 1840s, Hamilton opines that this was the beginning of evident deterioration in confessional orthodoxy. Hamilton continues his anatomy of erosion, focusing on the Union discussion between Scottish Presbyterians from 1863-1873 which reveals more cleavage. Growing theological laxity is noticed when during the Union discussions the participants maintain that they still believe and have an unwavering commitment to the WCF, despite clear denials of particulars. If this sounds similar to what

---

[53] Leonard Trinterud, *The Forming of an American Tradition,* (Philadelphia: Westminster, 1949), p. 39.

[54] Cf. Cotton Mather, *The Great Works of Christ in America* (Edinburgh: Banner of Truth, 1979), p. 275.

[55] Ian Hamilton, *The Erosion of Calvinist Orthodoxy: Seceders and Subscription in Scottish Presbyterianism* (Edinburgh: Rutherford House, 1990).

American Presbyterians would hear a few decades later, that is likely due to the organic strain of the common theological virus. In fact, it may be that precedent-setting American Presbyterian cases, such as those surrounding Charles A. Briggs, were indeed guided by these controversies. Briggs himself (although Hamilton does not extend these lessons to the American venue) no doubt was aware of this very strategy, noting its success. This chapter in Scottish history should at least be seen as a probable precursor to Briggs and other American trends in terms of confessional orthopraxy.

The main point could be summed up briefly in Hamilton's own words as follows: "The effect . . . was to undermine the belief that truth was absolute and unchanging, and to initiate the conviction that it was rather relative, genetic, and evolutionary."[56] Hamilton identifies the pathology of confessional relaxation in a sequence which moved first from a general ambiguity over the "sense" of the confession to particular denials (principally over the atonement and other particularities of Calvinism), then on to the failure to discipline in practice, onward to a zeal for union valued over purity, and finally to actual revision of the confession and dilution of the subscription vow itself. For those who have seen this repeated in American Presbyterianism, this could be a helpful caution for the future.[57]

Moreover, it should be noted that this era of Scottish history was important for American Presbyterians in two regards. First, it was substantially the same drama

---

[56] Hamilton, *op. cit.*, p. 123.

[57] Other venues are also instructive. In a study of late seventeenth century Genevan Formularies, Martin Klauber has pointed out how even the progeny of the orthodox, in this case Jean-Alphonse Turrettini, "contributed to the demise of . . . Reformed scholasticism through the abrogation of the Formula of Consensus," so reducing subscription to the bare essentials by 1725 that the Genevan Company of Pastors, a century and a half after the death of Calvin, voted to alter their ordination Formula, thus creating a lesser form of subscription henceforth. Consequently, the earlier standard of subscription (prior to 1725) is seen to be a clear one, in need of change only if the requirements for ordination were lessened. See, "Jean-Alphonse Turretinni and the Abrogation of the Formula of Consensus in Geneva," Martin I. Klauber, *Westminster Theological Journal*, Fall 1991, vol. 53, no. 2, pp. 326, 336. In another study, "Reformed Orthodoxy in Transition: Benedict Pictet (1655-1724) and Enlightened Orthodoxy in Post-Reformation Geneva," Martin Klauber mentions that the 1675 Formula Consensus "had to be signed by all graduates of Reformed academies as a prerequisite for ordination." Further, he cites Benedict Pictet (1655-1724) as a moderate representative who "defended the requirement that candidates for ordination at the Academy sign the Formula. He did so for several reasons, including the preservation of the unity of the faith, at least within the Swiss confederation. In addition, Pictet feared that the orthodoxy of Dort could potentially be lost. He exclaimed: 'Take care, should you remove the Formula. . . . I fear for the future; I see that the exhortations will be useless; one will attack the Synod of Dort . . . the confessions of the faith. I fear for the establishment of Arminianism and I dread even worse things; the minds of the century are extremely disposed to innovation. . . .' Pictet countered the charges that the requirement for subscription was divisive by saying that such a formulary had never caused disunion among the Genevan Church and those of Holland, Switzerland, the University of Marburg, and many others." Cf. W. Fred Graham, ed., *Later Calvinism: International Perspectives* (Kirksville, MO: Sixteenth Century Essays and Studies, vol. xxii, 1994), p. 98.

that would be re-enacted on American soil a few years later. Second and more importantly, the Scottish views in the early 1700s, since the tie between Scottish and American Presbyterianism was still very close—almost umbilically connected—form some of the best interpretive backdrop from which to understand the intent of the American Presbyterian Adopting Act and the subsequent affirmations of the WCF in American Presbyterianism. Our understanding of the need and tenor of confessional subscription should be aided by this, even if it has the potential of overturning some of the work by latter-day American Presbyterian historians who favored confessional relaxation.

These vignettes from Great Britain are essential pre-history for the American events. Notwithstanding, if an *ethos* of the intent prior to the Adopting Act is found, then there is still a need to ascertain what the adopters themselves intended.

Is and Ought

One of my concerns is to be fair to history and not to confuse prematurely our own blaring concerns with those of an earlier age. It is a question well worth considering: Even if an earlier age held to a stricter or looser view, ought we in our day hold to the same view? Of course, good reasons might be (and have been) proffered for either answer.

All too often, even the finest of historians and churchmen are guilty of proof-texting church history, similar to a fundamentalistic approach to biblical exegesis. Frequently, while trying to buttress our present position, we eisegete the past, and attempt to make our forefathers speak the same word as we do. As Luther phrased it, we take this web of issues and twist it into a "nose of wax" to reflect our own biases.

Most of us would benefit by correctly dividing the very important question about confessional adherence. In the process we will learn some valuable things both about ourselves and our parents in the faith. What I suggest is that we first interpret what our forefathers intended with as little eisegeting as possible. Our predecessors should certainly be permitted the right to define for themselves what they intended and how they subscribed.

Then a second and separate question (Should we follow their train?) can be examined, but only after we have a clear understanding with which to begin. Efforts that compare the 1990s to the 1690s or 1720s with either too much similarity or too little continuity may stand in need of correction; they may be but impositions of our own ideas jammed back into history. The history and the normative ecclesiology ought to be kept separate, unless there is a presupposition that the one will automatically follow the other. If that second area (normative ecclesiology) is kept separate, it liberates us to hear from earlier siblings in our spiritual family.

Two questions—which are applicable in nearly every age—persist: (1) What *did* the best tradition of our Presbyterian forefathers hold as the wisest manner for confessing orthodoxy? and (2) *Ought* we hold to the same manner of confessional practice today, or have the dynamics changed so as to justify a departure from the earlier practice? The second question is the "payoff" question, but we will not approach this with a bald pragmatism characteristic of William James. All too often, the impatient and ahistorical among us insist on attempting to answer the second query before the first, which is as naive as it is imprudent.

I realize, of course, that if Query Number One is answered in one way, it might disappoint many a modern. Yet surely the pursuit of truth must be held in higher esteem than the psychological affect or comfort zones of *homo modernus*. Conversely, even if Query Number One is answered in favor of the Old School, that does not automatically compel ecclesiological bodies to perpetuate such tradition. There are times to change the tradition—if it is inferior or not biblically rooted—and correspondingly there should be bold justifications from a superior paradigm to do so. Hence another underlying question is: "If the early tradition of Presbyterianism was (or was not) in favor of confessional subscription, upon what basis (or change of bases) do we continue or discontinue that tradition?" After answering the first Query, what is the justification to change? Have times, people, ecclesiological issues, or ministry changed so as to justify the jettisoning of the earlier tradition? And upon what sufficient grounds? Or, was that tradition mistaken from the beginning?

A word of caution, however, is in order lest we transform subscription into a golden calf. By itself, it will neither heal nor preserve. That is rather easily demonstrated; further, it is such an instance of stating the more than obvious, i.e., that confessional subscription alone will not preserve the purity of the church, that it should by now produce yawns when uttered as a defense for non-subscription. Its very utterance still misses the real issue, and once again blurs the is/ought distinction. Even under the best case scenario, confessional subscription must also be supported by the entire community, and, if lacking, be reinforced or disciplined.

Perhaps Drysdale is correct both in his analysis of earlier subscription as well as in his estimate of its maximum utility:

> For subscription, to be free and unoppressive yet *secure*, must be *preceded* by thoroughly good and efficient training in the theology to be taught, and *followed up* by a process of *constantly operative discipline* by mutual consent. They forgot, too, that the easy-going state of goodwill toward all speculative tendencies was only a latitudinarian or intellectual charity—the charity of an easy-going and secularly-minded indifferentism, and very far removed indeed from the *Christian charity* which, in a very different sense, *believeth all things*. They forgot that the charity of speculative intellectualism is painfully deficient in enthusiasm, self-sacrifice, and *life*.[58]

Toward the end of our third century of American Presbyterianism, debate and discussion still linger over the meaning of a formative act defining the nature of

---

[58] Drysdale, p. 510.

American Presbyterianism i.e., the Adopting Act of 1729. Part of the confusion is that many hesitate to face the historical past fearing that the present might not measure up or else that present practice might stand in need of alteration. Inadvertently, therefore, it is customary to yoke these two aspects—the "is" and the "ought" of the Adopting Act.

To rescue the present, theories based more on non-Synodical sources have skewed the debate over an event which appears to be capable of simple interpretation. What is likely at the heart of the confusion is a blurring of the (1) historical significance (the "is"), and (2) an unconscious awareness of normative significance (the "ought"). As a result, sometimes secondary factors surrounding this act and its history take precedence for some interpretations. A differentiation between the historical and the normative is needed. In short, it is desirable to view this historic event without necessarily shaping it to fit any particular set of preconceived ecclesiological ramifications.

Until relatively recent times, the tradition of interpreting the meaning of the Adopting Act was fairly uniform. This Act was, in fact, further interpreted and reiterated on numerous occasions. After 1729, the intent was reaffirmed in every decade for over a century. Indeed, this is *the* single most reiterated and reaffirmed act of early American Presbyterianism, establishing a tradition of interpretation through the repetitions of intent. Often the post-1729 declarations of Synod seem to be minimized or disregarded altogether. Regardless of interpretations of the Adopting Act in the abstract, one should at least consider the rather consistent and frequent commentaries on it put forth subsequently by those who could clarify or correct its nuance.[59] Such consideration discloses a strong American tradition of upholding—possibly strengthening—but not retreating from the original.

Before the New School attempted to defend their case, there were few, if any, reinterpretations of the Adopting Act supporting a lax subscription. Following the Civil War and in connection with the reunion of Old School and New School branches in the North (1869), some attempts were made to provide justification for relaxed practices of confessional adherence—but not so much on historical grounds. Thus, the history of Presbyterian confessional subscription seemed rather uniform until the late nineteenth century. Prior to the later 1800s, agreement over the meaning of this important act met with hearty agreement among nearly all Presbyterians. However, as the winds of modernity began to blow through the churches, the normal and, heretofore uncontested, historical understanding of this Act was clouded.

The contention that a uniform interpretation of the Adopting Act existed is not the same as the claim that there were no detractors or critics. Detractors of the Adopting Act are not difficult to unearth. Of course, there were some critics from

---

[59] From a scan of the minutes from 1729-1829, on at least fourteen different occasions the intent of the Adopting Act is iterated. For a more chronological display, see *Paradigms in Polity*, David W. Hall and Joseph H. Hall, eds. (Grand Rapids: Eerdmans, 1994), pp. 348-365.

the beginning, such as Jonathan Dickinson, who perhaps acquiesced later, or who properly should be seen not so much as an opponent of creedal subscription as a proponent of religious toleration. Throughout most of the eighteenth century, the Presbyterian church did indeed attract critics, critics specifically irritated at her strong practice of subscription—not to mention the ire vented at this particular confession's tenets.

It is equally certain that later critics—both of the method of subscription as well as of the content of the WCF—were numerous. Statements such as "The Adopting Act never intended to bind the conscience" abound. By 1956, James H. Nichols would assert: "None of the major Reformed churches are any longer willing to be bound rigidly to the peculiarities of the federal theology of the Westminster standards."[60] Others who opposed the Calvinism contained in the heart of the Confession were critical of the *enforcement* of such doctrine. And of course, many a well-meaning evangelical opposed the adoption of any confession with the naive slogan, "No creed but Christ," which sentiment was extant among some evangelicals several centuries ago.

However, with the sea-change of modernity beginning after the Civil War, critics gradually arose from within the ranks. To further shed light, we would do well to consider one of the most potent critics of subscriptionism to the West-minster Confession. Re-examining critics will also unveil the Synodical traditions of comment on the intent of subscriptionism within American Presbyterianism. These can serve as models to avoid, regardless of views of subscription or confessional practice. They can also remind us not to confuse the historical with the normative. They remain as lasting examples of distorting the "is" of history in deference to the "ought" preferred by modernity.

Charles Briggs (1841-1913) refracted the Adopting Act's significance—not in terms of the official acts of the Synod—but in light of the Irish Pacific Act of 1720.[61] He opined that the American adopters likely had that context in mind when they approved the Adopting Act; thus conforming his understanding of the Adopting Act to an Irish precedent. For Briggs, the earlier act determines the meaning of the Adopting Act, even if explicit interpretation of that controverted American act by the adopters themselves is provided.

A recent study goes so far as to recognize that underlying much of Briggs's "painstaking scholarship and often brilliant interpretive analysis was a quite specific *political* agenda . . . Basic to Briggs's historiographic purposes [for *American Presbyterianism*] was an almost transparent political move to win American Presbyterians to the cause of creedal revision. Such a victory would be brought about by using the historico-critical methodology to elucidate the Adopting

---

[60] James H. Nichols, "Colonial Presbyterianism Adopts its Standards," *The Journal of the Presbyterian Historical Society*, vol. xxxiv, no. 1 (March 1956), p. 63.

[61] Another classic linkage of the Irish and Scottish influence on the Adopting Act, although more traditional than Briggs, was Frederick W. Loetscher's "The Adopting Act," *The Journal of the Presbyterian Historical Society*, vol. xiii, no. 8 (Dec. 1929), pp. 337-354.

Act of 1729 . . ."[62] Briggs also feared that confessionalism was a limiting factor for liberal biblical scholarship: "Subscription to the Westminster standards imposed very clear limitations on the hermeneutical explorations of Reformed scholars, limitations that were violated by 'any opinion inconsistent with the inerrancy of Scripture, or belief in the non-Mosaic authorship of the Pentateuch.'"[63] Thus, one may be wise to discern the politically-driven penchant in Briggs's historical reconstructions. His history was not value-free; certainly it was not immune from bias. Of course, it presumes from the outset that modernity is superior to the past.

Briggs' adamant opposition to subscription to creeds in general should be recalled. For example, in 1887 he cited several great barriers to his desired catholic ecumenism: "The first great barrier to Christian Unity is the theory of *submission to a central ecclesiastical authority claiming divine right of government . . .* Another great barrier to the reunion of Christendom *is subscription to elaborate creeds.* This is the great sin of the Lutheran and Reformed churches . . ."[64] Holding the view that subscription to an elaborate creed was a "great sin" could certainly taint the author's reconstruction of the Adopting Act.

A partial glimpse into Charles Briggs's earlier "Documentary History of the Westminster Assembly,"[65]—the fruit of his research into the origins of Elizabethan Puritanism—uncovers Briggs's attitude in general toward the substance of the Westminster Confession. Drawing widely on original writings from many of the divines at Westminster, Briggs contended that the Westminster Confession was a consensus-building instrument reflecting many of the strong compromises necessarily arising from the Westminster Assembly.[66] With such opinions, obviously his desire to see the Adopting Act carry any continuing significance would be lessened.

By the late 1880s, Briggs' debates with A. A. Hodge (whose mantle was later assumed by the likes of Patton, Shedd, and Warfield) led to a firestorm of calls for confessional revision. Briggs' sentiments, e.g., "The Westminster Standards are the banners of Protestantism, but they did not claim infallibility, inerrancy, or completion. They did not propose to speak the final word in theology. . . .

---

[62] Mark J. Massa, *Charles Augustus Briggs and the Crisis of Historical Criticism* (Minneapolis: Fortress, 1990), p. 75. Perhaps it takes a non-Presbyterian Jesuit to get to the truth of this.

[63] Massa, op. cit., p. 67.

[64] Charles A. Briggs, "The Barriers to Christian Union," in *Presbyterian Review*, VIII, 1887, pp. 445 ff.

[65] *Presbyterian Review*, vol. 1, 1880, pp. 127-163.

[66] I have argued elsewhere that the mere presence of diverse elements at the Westminster Assembly (particularly, the Independents) in no way demands that we reconstruct each controverted issue as a compromise. For example, just because Independents were present does not prove that they *won* the debates. In many cases compromises were reached. In church government, however, a *jure divino* government was embraced as the majority view, despite the Independents' presence and obstruction. See *Jus Divinum*, revised and edited by David W. Hall (Dallas: Naphtali Press, 1995), pp. i-xx.

Theological progress is not in the direction of simplicity, but of variety and complexity,"[67] proved provocative, as Benjamin Warfield (and others) of the Old School tradition spewed responses. By 1890, the subject of creedal revision was so discussed that 134 presbyteries had called for revision, with some even proffering shrunken forms of consensus models.[68]

Briggs saw the 1720 Pacific Act of the Irish courts as determinative for the backdrop of the 1729 American Adopting Act. He identified: "This Pacific Act is of great importance to the American Presbyterian Church, for it was the *basis* of the Adopting Act."[69] Hence Briggs defended the Adopting Act as a compromise vehicle in light of the 1720 Pacific Act. The next faulty pillar of Briggs's defense is his dependence on correspondence from Jonathan Dickinson. In a personal letter dated April 10, 1729, Dickinson denied that subscription was proper and contended that it violated conscience.[70] Later, Trinterud and others based their claim of the Adopting Act as a compromise vehicle on similar extra-synodical sources. Still later, Briggs concluded at the end of his discussion of the Adopting Act that there is no evidence of "*jure divino* presbyterianism"[71]—a claim which could be true only upon the proof of a total divorce from the presbyterian ecclesiology less than a century earlier.[72]

Later Briggs builds much of his case on the earliest heresy trial involving Samuel Hemphill[73] and on a second idiosyncrasy, i.e., an assertion that between the years 1729 and 1736 the composition of the Synod that decided these matters was radically changed. Briggs is responsible for originally introducing this theory (upon which Trinterud later builds) as he seeks to document an imaginary radical discontinuity between the constituency of the 1729, 1730, and 1736 Synods. In a

---

[67] Charles Briggs, *Whither? A Theological Question for the Times* (New York: Charles Scribners & Sons, 1889), p. 160.

[68] For an excellent summary of this whole period that is sympathetic to Briggs, see *Charles Augustus Briggs and the Crisis of Historical Criticism* by Mark S. Massa (Minneapolis: Fortress Press, 1990), pp. 59-84. Warfield responded with numerous ripostes, such as "The Presbyterians and Revision," and "The Presbyterian Churches and the Westminster Confession of Faith." *Presbyterian Review*, Vol. 10, 1889, pp. 646-657. Also in this issue were articles by Philip Schaff on "The Revision of the Westminster Confession of Faith," John de Witt on "Revision of the Confession of Faith," and later Shedd offered a contribution, all of which were printed under the title *Ought the Confession of Faith to be Revised* (New York, 1890). W. G. T. Shedd's 1893 *Calvinism: Pure and Mixed* contained several essays defending the lasting usefulness of the Westminster Confession of Faith.

[69] Charles A. Briggs, *American Presbyterianism* (New York: Scribner's, 1885), p. 205.

[70] Briggs, *American Presbyterianism,* pp. 212-213.

[71] Briggs, *American Presbyterianism,* pp. 221.

[72] Briggs denied this, despite his clear recognition of *jure divino* presbyterianism in his earlier "The Provincial Assembly of London, 1647-1660," *The Presbyterian Review*, No. 5 (Jan. 1881), e.g., pp. 57, 71, *passim,* where he noted that the London Ministers did not hesitate to *subscribe* other public expressions of their faith (pp. 62-64).

[73] Briggs, *American Presbyterianism,* pp. 232-233.

lengthy footnote,[74] Briggs contends that nearly half of the original signers of the Adopting Act were no longer present and that an in-house insurrection against the New Side approach had been devised by Old Siders. Thus Briggs' argument is that a revolution of personnel in this seven year period led to a 180 degree reversal of the earlier intent. The question begs to be raised: "Will such hypothesis be sustained when compared to the actual action and decisions of the subsequent Synodical courts of the church?" [75]

In contrast to a re-examination hermeneutic, George Knight responds to Briggs' thesis on subscription and does a commendable job in rebutting the idea of an in-house revolution between 1729 and 1736. Knight points out that there was at most a 50% change between the personnel, and moreover that there was an even greater continuity between the 1730 and 1736 Synods. Moreover, Knight points out that both the 1730 and the 1736 Acts were approved *without objection* (unanimously) and, furthermore, that no subsequent objections from later Synods were brought to seek to correct the interpretations of 1730 and 1736. Knight, along with Hodge earlier, notes that these were indeed men of high character. As formidable witnesses, if their 1730 and 1736 after-the-fact interpretations were in fact contrary to the 1729 declaration, they certainly would have had the courage to correct a *coup d'etat* against original intent—had there been such.

It must be noted that it would have been difficult for the original intent to have changed so much in a mere seven years. Knight concludes his argument in another section, while at the same time pointing out the hermeneutical choices. He says: "The decision of 1730 is unanimous and the decision of 1736 is without dissent! . . . the Synods of 1730 and 1736 can speak for themselves. One must urge that the Synods did speak for themselves . . ."[76] Thus Knight is helpful in correcting the charge that there was a revolution between 1729 and 1736.

Certainly courts may err; and as the Confession itself suggests, many have. Individual synods do not always perfectly represent the views of all the church, although over time the synodical actions of duly constituted church courts are a fair representation of history. Moreover, when individual court actions do not represent the true sentiment of an ecclesiological body, such misrepresentations may be corrected and normally are. It is interesting to note of the Adopting Act, Briggs' hypothesis notwithstanding, that at no later date was the Adopting Act revoked, diluted, contradicted, nor modified. To the contrary, if there are any epexegetical commentaries on the Adopting Act by the subsequent Synods, they are glosses that routinely strengthen the original. Perhaps, if there was any change after 1729, it was consistently to strengthen—not to relax—the adherence to the WCF. Not only would Briggs have to account for the change of personnel, he would also have to

---

[74] Briggs, *American Presbyterianism*, p. 237.

[75] Cf. David W. Hall, ed., *The Practice of Confessional Subscription* (Lanham, MD: University Press of America, 1995), pp. 268-274.

[76] George Knight, "A Response to Dr. William Barker's Article 'Subscription to the Westminster Confession of Faith and Catechisms,'" *Presbuterion*, Spring/Fall, 1984, p. 58.

positively demonstrate that "new" personnel held views that were radically unacceptable to the 1729 adopters. Yet, this is not to be found in the record itself; however, the record does contain numerous reiterations of the 1729 Act.

Briggs' argument rests upon the slim hope of a statistical deviation between the 1729 and 1736 Synods. His argument can be paraphrased as: The 1736 Synodical declaration did not represent the true intents of the American Presbyterian Church. Many who were present in 1729—to keep things from the extremism of 1736—were absent by 1736. Hence, the 1736 pronouncement should be nullified as not truly reflective of the broader tradition championed mainly by Dickinson.

In answer to this, several things must be noted. First, it is undeniable that ecclesiastical bodies do, at times, make mistakes and then reverse their field. It is possible for political manipulation or demagoguery to occur, so that one Assembly or Presbytery does not truly represent the views of the church. However, in order to prove this, it must be very clear that such manipulation has occurred. Where is such contemporaneous accusation or evidence that the 1729 and 1736 Synods were not the true sentiment of American Presbyterianism? Strangely, Briggs' line of argument arises only after the fact and is ensconced amidst his politically motivated historical revision. No contemporaneous claims to chicanery were presented; only the notation that the claim by the stronger adherents won the day after 1729. If anything, such an admission may be an incipient acknowledgment that since this strong view prevailed after 1729, then far from being a unique American deviation, the strong view indeed prevailed with 1729 representing the most compromised (perhaps atypical) and not the strictest sentiment as purported by revisionists. That being the case, the question as to whether or not things changed between 1729 and 1736 can be answered in terms of subsequent clarifications by those present.

The question then may be: If 1736 was such a deviation from the broader 1729 norm (as Briggs alleges) where is that stated *after 1736*, and where is the 1736 standard repudiated or lessened over the next hundred years? Again, Briggs is lacking in proof for such. To the contrary, had 1736 been an accident or the fluke of political manipulation ("packing the court"), it would be expected that a subsequent Synod would have overturned the prior act or would have clarified that the Adopting Act did not really intend to set strict terms for ministerial communion. Yet, no such later nullification occurs—until the age when arrogant liberalism threw out the baby with the bathwater. The record is clear: Briggs' contention about a radical dissimilarity of constituency between 1729 and 1736 was not maintained by any contemporaries. Trinterud, too, follows this chimera that could be dismissed by a simple reading of the records themselves. His, and like arguments based on extra-synodical factors, are stretched to the breaking point. They are shown to be weak attempts to read back into history a rather liberal and open approach—likely animated by ecclesiastical politics and a bias for progressive modernism—which was not present in the first place, nor advisable in the second place.

To agree with Trinterud's reconstruction, one would also need to see an accounting for the dissimilarity as well as at least some testimony that later courts disavowed the 1736 pronouncement. Apart from liberalizing trends, where is the record of such official disavowals by the ecclesiastical bodies? The matter seemed to have been settled for nearly two centuries, at least until modern interpreters sought to re-interpret the original intent.

Whatever one may learn from these details of history, it seems clear that the Presbyterian church showed no lack of fortitude in seeking out and prosecuting heresy. This was not a church that had an undefined tradition, nor an unacknowledged confession, nor an absence of clarification on the subject. She was consistent with her earlier positions and not about to alter them at this later date. Whatever interpretations any subsequent historians place on these acts, it is difficult to disprove that this church adhered to the confessional standards as adopted. Even though they wished to adhere to those standards in a non-offensive manner, they nonetheless rigorously adhered—in principle and in practice—to the adopted Confession. Moderns may not agree that this ought to be so, but the history of the American communion is strong and clear.

Beginning with the Briggs case in the late nineteenth century, a serious undermining of this central defining act of American Presbyterianism was underway. One of the results of this was to call into question the binding nature of adherence to the Confession of Faith. Another unfortunate by-product of this new tradition was the countenancing of ministers' holding their credentials in a confessional church without *necessarily* adhering to all that the church maintained. Even critics could see this dilution as a typical case of the camel with his proverbial nose under the tent. Once the undermining of confessionalism began, the Presbyterian church would find itself unable to resist the enlargement of the camel's position, ultimately leading to the pluralistic logic of the multi-confessionalism of today that is so encompassing as to be virtually non-definite.

With the rise of modernity, the Presbyterian church gradually increased its disinheritance of its own noble past adherence to a confession. To persist in this would necessitate a reinterpretation of history either ignoring the past or else discounting it as wayward and irrelevant to modern times. [77]

For most of the second half of the twentieth century, this "new" interpretation had gained the ascendancy and was subsequently taught to future generations of students as the "reexamination" of previously held theories. Hence the majority of Presbyterians came to value later reconstructions over the original documents and the original understanding of the makers of colonial Presbyterian tradition.

As the Presbyterian tradition moves into the twenty-first century there is a large and predominant understanding of confessional subscription exemplified in the Presbyterian Church (USA). However, despite this tradition's present norms or

---

[77] Most clearly presented in Trinterud's classic, *The Forming of an American Tradition: A Re-examination of Colonial Presbyterianism* (Philadelphia: Westminster Press, 1949).

practice, it seems at least on the surface to be at variance with the earliest history. On the other hand, there is a smaller, more conservative, tradition of stricter confessional subscription which, as exemplified by sectors of the Associate Reformed Presbyterian Church, the Reformed Presbyterian Church North America, the Presbyterian Church in America, and the Orthodox Presbyterian Church (and others), professes to be in strict continuity with earlier history

Do some re-examiners unconsciously revise history in order to adjust the past to their present (abnormally low) norms of subscription? Perhaps it is appropriate to revisit this formative question: Were modern re-examinations after-the-fact justifications for the emerging view of loose subscription? Or more objectively put: Were they accurate and compatible with the documentary history? Or were revisions demanded by the evolution of a new paradigm reflecting contemporaneous norms and ecclesiastical politics?[78] If these ideological biases can be acknowledged, then perhaps we can return to some of the other corroboratory history and establish a case other than the modernist's rendition.

The canon of interpretation for constitutional law (and most church history) gives preferential weighting to the official acts unless there is explicit indication to the contrary. The Preliminary Act is certainly preliminary—and certainly important. But it is not more important than the final act. To reverse such weighting—as Briggs does—is to impose our will on our forefathers 250 years after the fact; it also disallows them a rebuttal. Such an interpretation of the Preliminary Act as final fails to take into account the changes of mind, the refining of opinions, and the role of deliberative reflection in that Synod. Instead, it would be the better course to admit priority of interpretation for the actual Adopting Act. It was, after all, the Act adopted by the 1729 Synod. Short of explicit (not inferential as with Briggs and Trinterud) proof that these churchmen did not mean what they said, we must be satisfied with their act. Hence the meaning of the morning act should be conformed to the final afternoon act—not vice-versa.[79]

The Act's own wording does indeed provide sufficient explication of the original intent. A little later, these Adopting Act authors affirm the WCF as the confession of *their* faith and affirm the right of Presbyteries to reject any candidate for the ministry who does not declare his agreement "with all the essential and necessary articles of said Confession" either in written or oral form. The phrase "essential and necessary articles" is referred to in this Adopting Act six times.

In light of this, it is possible to understand the minds of the framers of this document. There are few cases in all of history that provide so clear a contem-

---

[78] Interestingly, in an early review of Trinterud's "Re-Examination," Paul Wooley spoke of it as "propaganda . . . Trinterud has not only not hit the bull's eye; he is not even on the target. . . The book then is, in fact, a piece of propaganda . . . this book is a tract for the times . . . it will serve for one in the current campaign . . . to depreciate the importance of creedal standards and doctrinal emphases . . ." Wooley also called for a reduction of "the propaganda bias." *Westminster Theological Journal*, vol. xii, no. 2 (May 1950), pp. 167-171.

[79] Cf. Hall, *The Practice of Confessional Subscription*, pp. 279-286.

poraneous account of original intent. It is almost as if anticipating later questions, these presbyters provided a proleptic answer. Fewer cases of original intent could be imagined. Equally, it would require an agenda of denial to distort this.

In fact, to see a great divorce between the actions of 1729 and 1736 may require one to posit an uncommon degree of memory loss or deliberate falsification. That is the exact refuge of James H. Nichols: "Here is the historical puzzle with regard to the Adopting Act. How could the Synod unanimously adopt, only seven years after passing the Act, a declaration so manifestly out of accord with their own minutes of what they had done? . . . Were memories so short, or can we believe that this unanimous action was deliberate falsification?"[80] All the while, one obvious answer—which Nichols finds incredible—is that indeed the "true intent of the New Castle men at the Synod of 1729" was to adopt the Confession. A historical answer —which is simple and consistent—may be given, provided that political considerations do not seduce us into revising the clear history.

It is readily admitted that this does indeed present a number of normative questions for a modern church. The plea at this point, however, is not to allow normative questions to becloud the historical facts. It might even help to decide the normative question—if first the historical question could be reviewed without the bias of the tradition of Trinterud. All the while, a contrasting hermeneutical consensus—one that is not countenanced by Briggs and Trinterud—can be gleaned from European predecessors immediately prior to 1729.

Following Trinterud's revisions, the floodgates for further relaxation of confessional adherence were opened. Quick on the heels of Trinterud's study was the 1956 article by James H. Nichols mentioned above. A short time later, a death knell for confessionalism clanged as the northern Presbyterians adopted a new consensus, the *Confession of 1967*, which simultaneously struck a blow at both the substance of the confession and the method of adhering to it. The 1967 *Confession* had numerous relaxations of the original Westminster system of doctrine. Furthermore, this new consensus attained the status of Confession with the ordination vows being altered entirely shortly thereafter so as to allow for adherence to a multitude of confessional options.

The mainline Presbyterian church, once the tradition of the Adopting Act was dispatched, in less than a generation after Trinterud's "re-examination," became a multi-confessional church. By adopting this pluralistic approach to theological orthodoxy, they left behind their exclusive commitment to the system of doctrine derived from Westminster. After 1967, the mainline Presbyterians put their faith more in confessional relativism and modernizations of ancient traditions, than in those time-tested truths. The fall was swift and decisive as the epistemology of modernism took root, but it was hardly an improvement.

Shortly thereafter, another philosophical movement would further bury adherence to a seventeenth-century confession. Latter twentieth-century deconstruc-

---

[80] Nichols, op. cit., p. 62.

tionism would assert that the ideologies of our older siblings—particularly those who lived in capitalist Britain and who were white (privileged) European males—were necessarily and altogether suspect. For the truly modern person, meaning or truth (if there were such things) rests in the personal apprehensions of the world; the testimonies of others (particularly the group above) were deemed beneath the enlightened understanding of even the poorest of moderns. This elevation of the modern over the ancient, the denigration of the historic, and ascribing preferential treatment to the progressive over the traditional meant that each individual was epistemologically free to deconstruct any test; and then reconstruct its meaning after his own image. In some ways, the *Confession of 1967* was an ecclesiastical harbinger of this epistemology. Yet, pluralism and deconstructionism are certainly inadequate substitutes for the practice of confessional adherence.

Indeed, as modernity's flaws are now abundantly obvious, and even as postmodernity is collapsing, it may be an opportune time to re-examine these modern re-examinations and, after having made such re-examinations with less philosophical bias, to return to a stronger hermeneutic—not dissimilar to the one expressed by A. A. Hodge a century ago:

> If [students attempting to find a harmonious system of truth from Scripture] refuse the assistance afforded by the statements of doctrine slowly elaborated and defined by the Church, they must make out their own creed by their own unaided wisdom. The real question is not, as often pretended, between the Word of God and the creed of man, but between the tried and proven faith of the collective body of God's people, and the private judgment and the unassisted wisdom of the repudiator of creeds.[81]

---

[81] A. A. Hodge, *The Confession of Faith* (Edinburgh: Banner of Truth, 1983), p. 2.

Dabney and the
Utility of History

It was neither accidental nor inconsequential that when Robert Dabney assumed the Professorship of Ecclesiastical History and Polity at Union Theological Seminary in 1854 he chose for his topic: "Uses and Results of Church History."[1] Dabney himself had a great appreciation for the Vincentian emphasis on those things held at all times, everywhere, and by all.[2] History, obviously not a revelatory muse, nevertheless had great use in the theological curriculum. Dabney's estimate of its preeminent value hinted at the theological slant he would maintain over the next decades. All the while, history—supporting and interpreted by Scripture—was at his side.

Dabney's inaugural address committed him to be guided by the following historically-induced truths:

> That the first great requisite for the Christian minister is fervent piety; and that to cultivate this should be the chief aim of his training; that there is no royal road to mental improvement, but the faculties are only improved by honest and diligent labor; that the doctrines, government and mode of worship of the Presbyterian Church in the United States compose the wisest and most scriptural set of religious institutions known to us; that the sacred Scriptures possess plenary inspiration, and are infallible truth in every word; that to the dictates of these Scriptures, interpreted according to the fair and customary sense of human language, all philosophy, all speculations, and all inferences must implicitly bend; and that the Holy Spirit, to be obtained by constant prayer and holy living, is the only sufficient interpreter of God's word. (5)

---

[1] Reprinted in Robert L. Dabney, *Lectures and Discussions*, vol. III (Edinburgh: Banner of Truth Trust, 1982), pp. 5-26. References in parentheses are to page numbers in this edition.

[2] In *Christ our Penal Substitute* (rpr. Harrisonburg, VA: Sprinkle, 1985), Dabney explicitly refers to the canon suggested by Vincent of Laurins: "The valid tests of such an intuition are these: *Quod semper, quod ubique, quod ad omnibus, creditur.*" (36)

Hence, at the outset, his sympathies were clear. One of the reasons for his emphasis on history was that "[t]here is no department of human study requiring wider or more profound knowledge, and a rarer union of varied talents, than are requisite for him who would be master of the science of history. The study of this science is no dull treadmill of names, dates, and events, as some seem still to imagine." (6) For Dabney, a mastery of the historical was indicative of comprehensiveness: "All the faculties which are requisite for eminence in judicial transactions are here called into play; for the historian must sit in judgment on a multitude of competing witnesses, and hold the balance of truth with an acute eye and steady hand." (6) When a student mastered history, he necessarily also knew the literature of the matter, the spirit of the age, the nature of events, and "the contemporary sources of information." (6) In addition, Dabney thought that such would also insure that the teacher of church history (not to mention the students) would have "ample knowledge of all the theories of philosophy" (7) as well.

Moreover, the goal of this spiritual view of history was a divinely-centered interpretation of human events. Dabney taught that "[t]he secret operations of men's hearts are among the most important elements of human events, and our synthesis of those events cannot be complete, because our analysis cannot be complete, unless the annalist of the events could exercise the attribute of the Searcher of hearts." (9) Dabney's candid confession of incompleteness is a sign of his true humility, a virtue that should also adhere to the best of historians and historically-informed Christians.

Robert Louis Dabney (1820-1898) was one of the most influential thinkers among southern Presbyterians following the Civil War until the twentieth century. Having received his college and theological training among Virginia Presbyterians and having graduated from Union Theological Seminary, he was ordained to the Presbyterian ministry in 1847. He served as a pastor in Virginia and was called to the chair of Ecclesiastical History and Polity at Union Seminary in 1853. His inaugural address was given on May 8, 1854.

By the late 1850s, he moved to the department of Systematic Theology. Princeton Seminary esteemed Dabney so highly that at the height of Charles Hodge's ministry in 1860, they extended a call to Dabney to join the faculty. However, due to his allegiance to the Confederacy, Dabney declined.

During the Civil War, in addition to serving as chaplain to Stonewall Jackson, he also served as his Chief of Staff and was influential in assisting a genuine revival among the Confederate troops. After the war in 1866, Dabney compiled *The Life and Campaigns of Lt. General Thomas J. Jackson,* which was a lasting testimony to Stonewall Jackson. Following the war, Dabney returned to teach at Union Theological Seminary, remaining there until 1883. At age 63, he moved to the frontier and joined the faculty of the infant University of Texas where he taught until 1894. Along with others, he also helped establish the Austin Theological Seminary.

Dabney was a prolific writer. Among his writings were: *A Defense of Virginia* (1867); *A Defense of Slavery, Sacred Rhetoric* (1870), a treatise on homiletics;

and *Lectures in Systematic Theology* (1871), which was reissued in 1878. He also wrote two separate volumes on philosophy.

Dabney's method of theological instruction is reflected in his *Lectures*. Each week he devoted the class lecture to a major topic and then scheduled an intervening two days for readings. The topic was discussed in the first lecture; subsequently, students were to research and discuss the topic when they returned for the second class meeting. The textbook used by Dabney, reflecting his Old School heritage, was Turretin in Latin. At this second class meeting on the topic for the week, Dabney would require a recitation based on Turretin. The students were required during the intervening days to write an essay on the text—this time without the aid of Latin interpreters.

The use of Turretin's *Elenctic* as a text reveals the historiaphilia of Dabney. This text, nearly two-centuries old, was itself one of the more historically based. Dabney sounds similar to others who have recently rediscovered the value of history as he said: "No branch of history has been a fruitless study . . . if I shall succeed in imparting to my pupils only those old and known lessons which church history has taught all along, I shall consider the course by no means useless." (11)

Dabney had a distinct aversion to "neo"-hyphenates. Instead, his epistemological view acknowledged: "To the lessons of history we owe all our experimental knowledge of human affairs." (12) Further, "[i]t is the knowledge of the past which gives to the young man the experience of age. While yet he retains the energy and enterprise of youth, and it is not too late for action, history guides his activity with the prudence and wisdom of venerable infirmity." (12) History could function like an ancient Greek pedagogue, enlightening youth, if they were not so oriented to the shrill muse of modernity as to ignore it.

Dabney believed that church history could actually be prophylactic:

Here the narrow but increasing experience of the young man, united with caution, may protect him from all ruinous errors. But public institutions or influences, whose operations are far-reaching, whose right conduct involves the welfare of many passive persons subject to them, should never be committed to any man who has not gained a wide experimental knowledge of similar institutions in all former times. The man who undertakes to teach, to legislate, or to govern, either in church or state, without historical wisdom is a reckless tyro . . . The incidents of one human lifetime, or one era, constitute but a single 'case,' a single turn of the diseases of society. And no man has experience of those diseases who has not studied the symptoms and results through many generations. (13)

Another significant asset of history was its efficacy in rebutting heresies and other errors: "The readiest way to explode unreasonable pretensions [of faulty ideals] is to display their origin." (13) Dabney states what many evangelicals have only recently learned: "Often there is no way so practical and so efficacious to disarm a modern heretic as to prove that his pretended improvements are substantially the same with the errors of some schismatic who has been stamped with the reprobation of Christendom in ages long past. To affix just reprobation to a wicked thing is often its most effectual punishment." (13-14)

Not merely as a rhetorical blast but as a faithful diagnosis, Dabney saw, for example, Pelagianism as an ever-recurring heresy that can take some by surprise. In this context, history is frequently one of our best friends. Of Arminianism as the lineal descendant of earlier Pelagianism, Dabney noted: "Affix to it, as it may be justly done, this name, which has met the execrations of Christendom for thirteen hundred years, and it dies in merited shame and contempt." (14) He advocated that "[t]he most instructive and profitable way to study theology is to study the history of theological opinions. It has been often remarked that he who thoroughly knows past errors is best prepared to refute the errors of his own day." (14) "Indeed," of this rampant Arminianism that is of the same root as the Pelagianism of Molina, Dabney attests, "I have always found a knowledge of the origin of a dogma, and of the creed and tendencies of the man who originated it, invaluable as a guide to its logical affinities and consequences." (15) Familiarity with the past clues us into the future of errors, even while they are enjoying present favor. Dabney recognized that some "crooked policy crowned with apparent success" may be merely "specious but vicious principles of action applauded" (16), which later will ripen into putrid fruit. Sounding nearly like Abraham Kuyper who stressed the organic connection of ideas, Dabney also believed that errors were connected to and should be as exposed as flowing from a "parent system." (15)

Dabney consistently reserved great condemnation for continuing Pelagianism in its various forms, and he was quick to point out that a knowledge of history made one see such Pelagian errors as non-novel. Accordingly, he wrote that the, "Arminians disclosed themselves as being, under a pretended new name, nothing in the world, but the old semi-Pelagianism which had been plaguing the churches for a thousand years, the cousin-German of the Socinian or Unitarian creed."[3]

Of the short half-life of heresies, Dabney realized that a thorough knowledge of church history can save much time. He analyzed the process:

> But here, to the mind of the instructed man, history intervenes and forbids the heart to be depraved by the example of prosperous vice, or misled by the seeming success of dangerous measures. She lifts the veil of the past and unrolls similar scenes, showing not only the gaudy beginnings, but the gloomy end, to which these principles have conducted. (16)

A historical perspective "protects us from confounding the errors and vices which are the true poison of society with its pleasant food, and the wholesome and necessary medicine with its poison. It teaches us to distrust the temporary and specious prosperity or gain which attends immorality and error, and tells us, with solemn and monitory voice, to remember, amidst all the clash of unthinking

---

[3] Robert L. Dabney, *The Five Points of Calvinism* (rpr. Harrisonburg, VA: Sprinkle Publications, 1992), p. 5.

applause, that "the lip of truth shall be established forever, but a lying tongue is but for a moment." (17)

Dabney understood the continuity both of human thought and thinkers as a commendation of the utility of history.

> God has impressed a general sameness upon the hearts and understandings of all the generations which produce these recurring opinions. The history of theology, therefore, is a complete arsenal, which furnishes us with all the weapons of discussion. There we shall find in regular array the arguments which were found most efficient to slay the heresiarchs of their day; and when the old enemies revive, it is our wisdom to grasp those same weapons and burnish them again; their temper has been tried. (14)

He made this recommendation to his students and to public servants: "Whether in church or state, man's true political wisdom is only learned from experience; in other words, from history. This is the only source from which any safe light can be obtained as to the future workings of proposed opinions and institutions." (19) When faced with new policy options, only omniscience could search out all possible ramifications. Thus, history is the chronicle of many of the tried-and-failed options.

He challenged those who expect novel brilliance from modernity-revised programs:

> The only political wisdom which is worth having, is that of historical experience. And we repeat the reason, that the conditions under which any proposed new institution will have to act in the future will be endlessly diversified . . . Man has no pole star and no compass, by which he may boldly break away from the track of experience and navigate the ocean of the future. The province of his wisdom is to follow the ways explored by previous voyagers, and only to venture into the uncertain storms of the untried so far as the light of the past is reflected forward upon it. (20)

Dabney was even so astute as to warn that new institutions and ideas will not be created "which shall run of themselves, like some improved carriage of locomotive, forgetting that their machine must meet diversities of positions and relations in its course of which they can foresee nothing." (19) The assumption of ever-upward progress is the drive-shaft of an optimism which thinks we are constantly on the verge of some organizational *coup d'etat*. Seldom are our discoveries so revolutionary, although frequently we are so proud to believe they are. A more prominent place for history in the curriculum forces one toward less hubristic claims.

In his inaugural address, Dabney elaborated on one of his favorite historical examples—the French Revolution. Dabney saw this revolution as the quintessential expression of *hubris*, its leaders exhibiting an inflated arrogance toward their own contributions to world history. Dabney estimated:

The [French] Revolution announced its mission as one of destruction to the past, to its abuses, its principles, and even its recollections, and of new and independent creation for the future. They disdained the safe and gradual reform of institutions tried, and known because tried, but partially perverted. They swept all away; and proceeded to reconstruct on the basis of their own airy speculations. (21)

In another article, on the subject of rights, Dabney identified the French Revolution as the cradle of modern selfishness. Following Jeremy Bentham, who was astute enough to diagnose the social compact view of rights as nothing more than the "anarchical fallacy,"[4] Dabney made some salient observations in his 1888 "Anti-Biblical Theories of Rights."[5] Of the French Revolution, he was prescient to identify "another hostile banner" that was already unfurled and ready to attack millions. This assault, which proceeded from "professed social science," was derived from the "atheistic French radicals" (22) and was in process of being unwittingly adopted by thousands of American Protestants. At its heart, this new anti-biblical theory of rights posited an absolute mechanical equality (23) in contrast to the earlier-held and historically orthodox moral equality.

This new radical theory asserted that "all men are born free and equal" in the beginning and logically led to the following:

Consequently the theory teaches that exactly the same surrender must be exacted of each one under this social contract, whence each individual is inalienably entitled to all the same franchises and functions in society as well as to his moral equality; so it is a natural iniquity to withhold from any adult person by law any prerogative which is legally conferred on any other member in society. The equality must be mechanical as well as moral or else the society is charged with natural injustice. (24)

This contends that, if we do not treat people absolutely the same (mechanical equality), then we have somehow violated their rights. Tragically, the mechanical has now superseded the moral with the spectacle of countless demands for rights, subsidies, and corrective *panaceae*. Dabney lamented both the confusion created by this new nomenclature and the lack of discernment by Christians:

So widespread and profound is this confusion of thought, that the majority of the American people and of their teachers practically know and hold no other theory than the Jacobin one. . . . history and science show that it is a fatal heresy of thought, which uproots every possible foundation of just freedom, and grounds only the most ruthless of despotism. But none the less is this the passionate belief of millions, for the sake of which they are willing to assail the Bible itself. (24)

---

[4] *Encyclopedia of Religion and Ethics*, vol. x, p. 773.
[5] Robert L. Dabney, *Lectures and Discussions* (Edinburgh: Banner of Truth, 1982), pp. 21-46. The page references in parentheses are from that article.

Sadly, many Christians did not heed these early words of warning that so clearly foresaw the inherent contradiction between the social compact view of rights and the biblical view. As Dabney stated his goal, his sole object was "to examine the scriptural question, whether or not the integrity of the Bible can be made to consist with the Jacobin theory and its necessary corollaries" (26). Thus Dabney's warning of the "coming contest" (27) went largely unheeded as few entertained the question raised by Dabney: "Will you surrender the inspiration of Scriptures to these assaults of a social science—so-called?" (27) Had Dabney's audience learned their history, they might have benefited from this accurate assessment of the French Revolution and its offspring.

To Dabney, this view of rights was one reason for the decline of erstwhile stalwart evangelical bodies (39) who "piously borrowed even from French atheism" (39). To him, it was clear that a student of Scripture should detect that "this radical theory of human rights and equality, born of atheism, but masquerading in the garb of true Biblical republicanism" (38) had numerous and definite corollaries. Despite being "passionately held by millions of nominal Christians" (38), the theory of rights meant, according to Dabney, the collision between a biblical ethic and "the popular political theory, so flattering to the self-will and pride of the human heart, and so clad in the raiment of pretended philanthropy." (38) He went on to assert that this anti-biblical theory of rights had "become the occasion of tens of thousands making themselves blatant infidels, and of millions becoming virtual unbelievers" (38). Dabney analyzed the rightist advance in these terms: "Those who wish to hold both the contradictories have indeed been busy for two generations weaving veils of special pleadings and deceitful expositions of Scripture wherewith to conceal the inevitable contradiction. But these veils are continually wearing too thin to hide it, and the bolder minds rend them one after another and cast them away." (38)

Predicting that "the struggle cannot but be long and arduous" (43), Dabney gave some advice for those who contend against rightsism. His caveat was:

> Since the opinions and practices hostile to the Scriptures are so protean, so subtle, and so widely diffused, there is no chance for a successful defense of the truth except in uncompromising resistance to the beginnings of error; to parley is to be defeated. The steps in the 'down-grade' progress are gentle, and slide easily one into the other, but the sure end of the descent is none the less fatal. He who yields the first step so complicates his subsequent resistance as to insure his defeat. There is but one safe position for the sacramental host: to stand on the whole Scripture, and refuse to concede a single point. (44)

Thus, the French Revolution offered a potent illustration of the utility of history.

Another reason for would-be pastors to be knowledgeable about history is their influence on other public leaders. To this end, Dabney explained:

> This reason is to be found in the neglect of such reading, and the ignorance of the potency of the religious element in public affairs, which prevail among our

legislators. The time was when enlightened statesmen were aware of the fact that they, their measures and their institutions, were but the driftwood upon the great current of moral influences which pervade the nations, indicating its direction and power. They were aware that *religion* is the great mistress of these influences, for good or for evil. (21)

When these citizen-legislators do not benefit from regular historical instruction, inevitably "[t]hey put forth a rash hand to the springs of a nation's energies in ignorant unconsciousness of the tremendous powers with which they tamper. (22) Without religion as the "great mistress" (21), public leaders become "the driftwood upon the great current of moral influences which pervade the nations." (21) A sad result is that "[t]hey do not know the history of the church. And hence the necessity that these great lessons of the past shall be everywhere studied, everywhere discussed." (23)

As a final commendation for the study and use of history, Dabney relates history to the decree of God. Believing that since "that decree is one, so is history a unit" (23), Dabney affirms the proposition that: "The history of the church and of the world, regarded as a whole, is but the evolution of the eternal purpose of that God who 'worketh all things after the counsel of his own will.'" (23) The fruit of historical study is a "unified plan, from which the pattern is gradually unfolded on the tangled web of human affairs." (23)

However, such history is not to be construed apart from a thorough-going Christian epistemology. The noetic effects of the Fall limit what can be known by those who reject revelation. Hear Dabney:

No man but the believer is capable of understanding the philosophy of history. He who learns from the Scriptures, and he alone, can possibly understand the meaning of events or interpret them aright. Your infidel historian must needs blunder on in Egyptian midnight. . . . The science of history will only attain that philosophic completeness which some have desired and prophesied for it, after the course of human events is ended. (23)

Along with this, however, is also a caveat about the possible misinterpretation of or ambiguity within history. Dabney wisely counseled, "But it is only after the field is fought, as we review it in the leisure of our triumph, that we will understand the complicated whole and appreciate the perfection of the plan." (23) Modern restatements about the ambiguity of history have been given by those ranging from Reinhold Niebuhr to Anthony Hoekema.[6]

A correlate of this humble approach to history is that historical judgments must, of necessity, be made with some modicum of tentativeness and be open to revision by later events. Particularly definitive of all previous history will be the *eschaton.* Dabney advised:

---

[6] See Anthony Hoekema *The Bible and the Future* (Grand Rapids: Eerdmans, 1979).

When we look back thence upon the field fought and won, when we have before us the finished whole, and above all, when we have the tuition of him into whose hand 'all power in heaven and on earth is given,' to explain to us the eternal plan, then we shall know fully what is the teaching of history. (25)

Correspondingly, the biblical historian will humbly agree that "[s]uch an undertaking cannot fail to result in a life-long sense of deficiency. Let it be mine to feel this sense as a stimulus to the greater diligence." (25) And if understood properly, Dabney was not hesitant to posit that when viewed from this final and ultimate hermeneutical vantage, "the history of the church is one of the studies and enjoyments of heaven." (25)

Thus, history is given a status than which few could be higher. In other works, too, Dabney's emphasis on history's utility is apparent. Referring to certain views of the atonement, if students and pastors had a better grasp on history they might even avoid some previous errors. Dabney put it this way:

These facts show that an exhaustive and triumphant refutation of the objections and a final establishment of this vital doctrine are among the urgent needs of the day. If the innovators would but study the masterly demonstrations of the church theologians, of an Anselm, a Calvin, a Turretin, a Witsius, a Hill, a Hodge, a Shedd, they would not need further discussion.[7]

Thus, a historical acquaintance with earlier formulations would spare new theologians from error.

In one of Dabney's final pieces, "The Doctrinal Contents of the Confession," an address prepared for the 250th anniversary of the completion of the work of the Westminster Assembly, he praised the Westminster divines as "those profound and illustrious scholars [who] were enriched with all the stores of sacred learning gathered from previous ages, and culminating in their glorious epoch."[8] Moreover, "they knew the past history of the church, and of doctrine, and of philosophy, and had before them all the great symbols of the previous ages . . . It is impossible to question the full acquaintance of the Westminster divines with the history of doctrine and philosophy."[9] Dabney recognized them for their historical knowledge of the Middle Ages, of the pre-Socratic philosophers, even of the most modern scientists—Bacon, Descartes, Copernicus, and Galileo. This full-orbed knowledge, with history as the capstone is the Dabneyian ideal.

It may be time for seminaries to recapture this dynamic today. Perhaps it would aid them in producing graduates who produce fruit that would last. Dabney's grasp of the utility of history was certainly one example of that.

---

[7] Robert L. Dabney, *Christ our Penal Substitute*, supra., p. 19.

[8] Robert L. Dabney, "The Doctrinal Contents of the Confession," in *Memorial Volume*, ed. by Francis Beattie, et al (Richmond: The Presbyterian Committee of Publication, 1897), p. 92.

[9] Ibid., p. 93.

PROCEEDING WITHOUT CONTEMPT

Revolutionary Pulpits

Suffice it to say that the majority of modern communicators, political analysts, and even Christians do not believe an activity as traditional and as seemingly impotent as preaching could be the engine that drives a nation's politics. But that has not always been the case. One of the grandfathers of western democracies, Thomas Hobbes, castigated the preaching by Puritans and Presbyterians in mid-seventeenth century England for the large social and political change it brought. In his analysis of the causes of the British Civil War, Hobbes attributed part of the blame for the anti-monarchical movement to the Presbyterian preachers. Hobbes, the royalist, accused the Puritans of "horrible designs . . . covered with the cloak of godliness" and of being used by aspiring parliamentarians to limit the power of the crown. Ascribing much of the effectiveness to the rhetorical style and affect of Puritan preachers, not to mention the envy of the nobility, Hobbes acknowledged: "It was not their own art alone that did it, but they had the concurrence of a great many gentlemen, that did no less desire a popular government in the civil state than these ministers did in the Church."[1]

Not only did this affect church politics, but more importantly Hobbes thought it made them "in love with democracy by their harangues in the Parliament, and by their discourses . . . continually extolling liberty and inveighing against tyranny, leaving the people to collect of themselves that this tyranny was the present government of the state. And as the Presbyterians brought with them into their churches their divinity from the universities, so did many of the gentlemen bring their politics from thence into the Parliament."[2] Hobbes believed that the Puritans worked by artifice to "change government from monarchical to democratical." Their method, according to him, was to decry oppression by hierarchies either in church or state. Moreover, Hobbes commented that the challenge to the monarchy was not directly against sovereignty *per se*, but against the various and essential acts of sovereignty. From this one can see that the pulpit bears revolutionary promise.

---

[1] Thomas Hobbes, *Behemoth or The Long Parliament* (London: Frank Cass and Co., Ltd, 1969), p. 23.
[2] Idem.

More recently, Cornell University Professor Barry Alan Shain has determined that rather than a generic republicanism or seventeenth century libertarianism nourishing the root of American democracy, a much older religion did: the biblical faith. The preaching of this biblical faith was a staple in the intellectual life of colonial America. For a century before the earliest settlers arrived in America and for the 150 years of colonial experience prior to the US Revolution, regular preaching was formative for the ideas of the American revolutionaries. Shain notes: "Americans in the late eighteenth century were not a people who had founded colonies and then a nation around a pervasive, indeed, almost monolithic commitment to classic ideas such as individualism, freedom, and equality. . . . Americans did not hold to a republican outlook that was anthropocentric and independent of a Christian or a rationalist faith in an omniscient God. . . . [E]ighteenth century Americans were a parochial reformed Protestant people whose thought was (to the contemporary republican apologist, inconveniently) strikingly dependent on a Christian origin or natural ordering in the Cosmos."[3] Shain continues to note that the founders of the American republic were more interested in biblical dynamics than "in personal development through direct participatory political activity."[4]

Shain takes issue with the currently regnant secular paradigm that seeks to explain America's origin in predominantly secular terms. His research leads him to believe that neither the 'classical republican' explanation nor the 'libertarian individualistic' model sufficiently explains America's unique cradle. Although those features certainly "have their place in the totality of the Revolutionary drama," Shain admits, nevertheless, "the defenders of each model have been guilty of greatly exaggerating the coherence, hegemony, and institutional strength in Revolutionary America of their preferred body of thought. They do so while virtually ignoring more powerful, though today less useful, influences on the speech and practices of the majority of European Americans; such as the reformed Protestant foundations of almost all the Colonies and their citizens; . . . The confusion is understandable because it is so easy today to forget that in the years 1765-1785 . . . America was a nation of Protestant and communal backwater polities . . . only in 1776 did republic, republican, and republicanism change from defamatory clichés to being taken generally as terms with affirmative connotations."[5] Shain explains that rather than being based in "the revolutionary and atheistic liberalism of Hobbes and Mandeville," American foundations were based on other ideological platforms. Indeed, historian Henry May has argued that such humanist authors were generally reviled by pre-revolutionary Americans, today's vast secular *mythos* notwithstanding. "In short," Shain concludes, "the exaggerated attention shown to liberal individualism and classical republicanism probably speaks more to the needs and sensibilities of contemporary urban and secular commentators in search of a useful past than to the historic reality of a rural and Protestant people nestled in a caring and purposeful universe of divinely

---

[3] Barry Alan Shain, "The Protestant Communitarian Basis for American Political Thought," *Religion and Liberty*, vol. 6, no. 2 (March-April 1996), p. 6.

[4] Idem. Cf. also Shain's *The Myth of American Individualism* (Princeton University Press, 1994).

[5] Idem.

inspired meaning."[6] If that is our true history, then the preaching in early America was more powerful and enduring than most revisionists care to admit.

Earlier commentators were quicker to admit more of the religious infrastructure than our contemporaries who are more concerned with other factors. For example, John Wingate Thornton believed: "One nationality, and that of a Protestant people, was essential to constitutional liberty in America."[7] Begrudgingly, even Perry Miller acknowledged concerning the preaching at the American revolution: "[A]mong the masses the Hebraic analogy was at least as powerful an incentive as the declaration of inalienable right."[8] David R. Williams surmises: "Old Testament imagery thus inspired Revolutionary zeal by tying personal identity to communal identity and tying them both into the larger cosmic identity of scripture."[9] Believing that "the rhetoric of the [Revolutionary] war was often political, but its passions were religious," Williams reports: "Between 1740 and 1800, over 1800 sermons were published in Massachusetts and Connecticut alone . . . the weekly sermon was an important and often the only source of information as well as inspiration."[10] He interprets that preaching helped portray the British as primary threats to religious freedom, while also reflecting the religious form of colonial piety. More recently, Donald Weber sought to disprove the strong Protestant underpinning among the colonial American clergy who supported the Revolutionary War. However, as the documentary evidence hijacked his preconceptions, he discovered that Jonathan Edwards, Jr. and others "preached throughout that critical interval on virtually every important event of battle of the war in a homely language that would have been grasped by most of his audience. In fact, Edward's sermons incorporated every trope characteristic of whig political discourse."[11]

While the secular cant[12] seeks to ward off much, if any, impact of real piety on politics, a longer stretch of history shows that religion and preaching have frequently

---

[6] Ibid., p. 7.

[7] John Wingate Thornton, *The Pulpit of the American Revolution* (Boston: Gould and Lincoln, 1860), p. iii. Cf. also, Frank Moore, *The Patriotic Preachers of the American Revolution* (1860).

[8] Cited by David R. Williams, *Revolutionary War Sermons* (Delmar, NY: Scholars' Facsimiles and Reprints, 1984), p. xxxiii.

[9] Williams, op. cit., p. xxxiv.

[10] David R. Williams, Ibid., p. x.

[11] Donald Weber, *Rhetoric and History in Revolutionary New England* (New York: Oxford University Press, 1988), p. viii. Besides the studies referenced above, others are important for a full grasp of this topic. Cf. Bernard Bailyn's *The Ideological Origins of the American Revolution* (1967), Nathan Hatch's *The Sacred Cause of Liberty* (1977), Peter Carroll's *Religion and the Coming of the Revolution*, Alice Baldwin's *The New England Clergy and the American Revolution* (1928), Alan Heimert's *Religion and the American Mind* (1965), Mason Lowance's *The Language of Canaan*, Ursula Brumm's *American Thought and Religious Typology*, and Carl Bridenbaugh's *Mitre and Sceptre*. For a recent study, cf. Keith L. Griffin's *Revolution and Religion: American Revolutionary War and the Reformed Clergy* (New York: Paragon House, 1994).

[12] Of course, the opponents of the Revolution saw these insurrectionist sermons as "windows onto this world of weeds, luxuriant evidence of a wild and unkempt growth different from the cultivated garden." Cited in David R. Williams, *Revolutionary War Sermons* (Delmar, NY: Scholars'

shaped the basic moral issues facing various nations. Indeed, a vital enunciation of the faith may be the most common accent of political discourse—a statement that only comes as a surprise to an extremely secular audience.[13]

What we wish to lend a hand to in this discussion is a renewal of the proper place of Christian thinking and preaching to inform political notions.

Pulpits and Politics: 1620-1776

Puritan theologies and sermons led to the colonization of the New World. The charter documents of nearly all colonial American settlements contain some overt reference to religious purpose. The Mayflower Compact opened on an unadulterated religious note: "In the name of God. Amen. . . . Having undertaken for the Glory of God and Advancement of the Christian Faith, and the honor of our King and Country, a voyage to plant the first colony in the northern parts of Virginia . . ." Such civic purpose was rooted in Reformation beliefs. Similarly, the 1639 *Fundamental Orders of Connecticut*, sometimes referred to as the first written constitution in the New World, began: "For as much as it has pleased Almighty God by the wise disposition of his divine providence so to order and dispose of things . . . and well knowing where a people are gathered together the word of God requires that to maintain the peace and union of such a people there should be an orderly and decent Government established according to God . . . [we] enter into such Combination and Confederation together, to maintain and preserve the liberty and purity of the Gospel of our Lord Jesus which we now profess, as also the discipline of the Churches . . ."[14] Following this preamble, the colonists covenanted to hold two General Assemblies per year to elect a Governor and (at least six) magistrates for no more than a year who were to "administer justice according to the Laws here established, and for want thereof, according to the Rule of the Word of God." Magistrates were elected by ballot, with a Secretary who presided only "for the time being" (and who could not himself nominate candidates). The governor could serve no more than two consecutive years and was to "always be a member of some appointed Congregation." Due public notice was to be given for the convening of these legislative assemblies, with a proviso that if the sitting politicians refused to do so, the Freemen could petition the lower magistrates to convene the assembly which could lawfully "proceed to do any act of power which any other General Court" could. Most of these tenets are best understood as Reformation theological notions.

Facsimiles and Reprints, 1984), p. xxiv. Indeed, Tories thought the revolutionaries to be so religious as to speak of them as "descendants of Cromwell's elect."

[13] Donald Weber concludes: "It is not surprising that many secular academics, themselves partisans of the Enlightenment, have with considerable success portrayed the Revolution as a secular, rational, political movement." Weber, op. cit., p. 1.

[14] This term, discipline, was shorthand for presbyterian polity from the time of Thomas Cartwright in England.

The pastors of the early American colonies exposed their parishioners to the ideas of Knox, Calvin, Beza, Althusius, and Rutherford more than acquainting them with secular thinkers like Locke, Hobbes, or Rousseau. Despite the fact that the First Amendment was passed in 1791, to support this reading of original intent, one should note that Connecticut did not dis-establish the state-sponsored congregational church until 1818; nor did Massachusetts until 1833.[15] Further, the 1783 Treaty with Paris began "in the name of the most Holy and undivided Trinity."[16] Religious establishments and regular pulpit exposition of political themes were regular features of the colonial experience.

It is against this backdrop that election sermons are best understood. One of the most influential ideological sources for American politics in the seventeenth and eighteenth centuries was preaching. Harry Stout has proffered the following summary:

> Over the span of the colonial era, American ministers delivered approximately 8 million sermons, each lasting one to one-and-a-half hours. The average 70-year old colonial churchgoer would have listened to some 7,000 sermons in his or her lifetime, totaling nearly 10,000 hours of concentrated listening. This is the number of classroom hours it would take to receive ten separate undergraduate degrees in a modern university, without ever repeating the same course! . . . Events were perceived not from the mundane, human vantage point but from God's . . . Thus colonial audiences learned to perceive themselves not as a ragtag settlement of religious exiles and eccentrics but as God's special people . . . [17]

Such preaching saw tyranny as idolatry and America as a destined colony. The oratory of Patrick Henry, the writing of James Madison, and the leadership of George Washington cannot be grasped apart from the preaching of pre-Revolutionary pulpits.

A survey of popular discourse in the period preceding the American Revolution illustrates how the American colonialists viewed civil government as resting on biblical foundation.[18] Many of the sermons in the eighteenth century discussed and applied biblical themes. Charles Chauncy, in "Civil Magistrates Must Be Just, Ruling in the Fear of God," (1746) reasoned that in view of sin, those who desire a stable society and mutual defense must, "combine together in distinct societies, lodging as much power in the hands of a few, as may be sufficient to restrain the irregularities of the rest, and keep them within the bounds of a just decorum." Moreover, in his sermon (from 2 Sam. 23:3), he based the rise of civil government on the reality of human depravity: "And from

---

[15] *Christian History*, Issue 50, p. 3. Harry S. Stout notes that "Baptists, Quakers and Anglicans were free to worship as they pleased, but until 1727 they were still required to pay religious tithes to support the majority church and minister" in New England. Cf. Harry S. Stout, *The New England Soul: Preaching and Religious Culture in Colonial New England* (New York: Oxford University Press, 1986), p. 149.

[16] Idem. Cf. Also Harry S. Stout, *The New England Soul: Preaching and Religious Culture in Colonial New England* (New York: Oxford University Press, 1986), pp. 3-4, 70-75.

[17] Harry S. Stout, "Preaching the Insurrection," *Christian History*, Issue 50 (Vol. XV, no. 2), 12.

[18] Among others, Rousas J. Rushdoony, *This Independent Republic* (Fairfax, VA: Thoburn Press, 1978), pp. 94-96 *passim* supports the claim that "civil government was inescapably religious."

hence, strictly and properly speaking, does that civil order there is among men take rise. Nor will it from hence follow, that government is a mere humane constitution. For as it originates in the reason of things, 'tis, at the same time, essentially founded on the will of God. . . . The suitableness of order and superiority, both to the nature of man, and his circumstances in the world, together with its necessary connection, in the nature of things, with his safety and happiness, is such an indication of the divine pleasure, that there should be government, as cannot be gainsaid nor resisted."[19]

A generation later, as the New Hampshire Legislature was gathered (1784) to enact the New Hampshire Constitution, Samuel McClintock addressed the body, arguing from Scripture: "1st. That God exercises a sovereign dominion over the nations and kingdoms of this world, and determines their rise, growth, declension and duration, and; 2nd. That his sovereign power is invariably directed by perfect and infinite rectitude; in plucking up and destroying, and in building and planting them, he treats them according to their moral character." McClintock stated, "God is an absolute sovereign. He presides with an uncontrolled sway over all the nations of this earth, and orders all the events, changes and revolutions by which they are either exalted to power and dignity, or brought to dishonor and ruin. By a turn of the wheel of providence, he can form a people into a respectable and happy, or a mean and contemptible nation; more easily than the potter, of the same lump, [he] can make one vessel to honor and another to dishonor."[20]

Later in this same sermon, McClintock noted that, "the history of all nations and ages, shews that public virtue makes a people great and happy, vice [makes them] contemptible and miserable . . . unless God should change, that is, cease to be God, we cannot be a happy, unless we are a virtuous people . . . but as virtue is the basis of republics, their existence depends upon it, and the moment that the people in general lose their virtue, and become venal and corrupt, they cease to be free."[21] Such sentiment was a far cry from the contemporaneous French Revolution.

Sounding very similar to Calvin, McClintock even asserted that the duty of rulers was "to give all that countenance and support to religion that is consistent with liberty of conscience. . . . to punish profane swearing, blasphemy, and open contempt of the institutions of religion." He also believed: "The religion of Christ, where it has its proper influence on the hearts and lives of men, will not fail to make the best rulers and the best subjects." That the biblical doctrine of human depravity was affirmed, in diametric opposition to the French Revolution, may be seen from this sermon:

> If mankind were in a state of rectitude there would be no need of the sanctions of human laws to restrain them from vice or to oblige them to so what is right. . . .
> But in the present disordered state of our nature there would be no safety of life or property without the protection of law. A state of nature would be a state of continual war and carnage. The weak would be devoured by the strong, and every affront avenged with the death of the offender. Even under the best governments,

[19] Ellis Sandoz, ed., *Political Sermons of the American Founding Era, 1730-1805* (Indianapolis: Liberty Press, 1991), p. 143.

[20] Ibid., p. 796.

[21] Ibid., p. 805.

we see the human passions often break through all the restraints of law in acts of violence and outrage! which shews what reason we have to be thankful to God for that excellent Constitution we live under, and how incumbent it is on every one who is a friend to the order, peace and happiness of society, or who even regards the safety of his own life and property, to support and maintain it.[22]

Of the intersection of depravity and religious virtue as the foundation of the state, Elizur Goodrich argued ("The Principles of Civil Union and Happiness"):

Hence religion and virtue are the great principles on which the happiness of human societies must be built; and from these principles must be derived the knowledge of all laws, which determine the order of that benevolence, we owe to one another, and point out the means of attaining the greatest good. . . . There can be no beneficial union among the members of a community, where these great principles of righteousness and truth integrity and the fear of God, are not maintained, both among themselves, and towards all mankind.[23]

Prior to the American Revolution, sermons directed to the common person frequently drew on biblical instances of government to support the republic. Samuel Langdon, for example, stated of the Mosaic period: "Thus a senate was evidently constituted, as necessary for the future government of the nation, under a chief commander. And as to the choice of this senate, doubtless the people were consulted, who appear to have had a voice in all public affairs from time to time, the whole congregation being called together on all important occasions: the government therefore was a proper republic."[24] He proceeded to state the value of the judicial laws of Moses:

A government, thus settled on republican principles, required laws; without which it must have degenerated immediately into aristocracy, or absolute monarchy. But God did not leave a people, wholly unskilled in legislation, to make laws for themselves: he took this important matter wholly into his own hands, and beside the moral laws of the two tables, which directed their conduct as individuals, gave them by Moses a complete code of judicial laws. They were not numerous indeed, but concise and plain, and easily applicable to almost every controversy which might arise between man and man, and every criminal case which might require the judgment of the court. Of these some were peculiarly adapted to their national form, as divided into tribes and families always to be kept distinct; others were especially suited to the peculiar nature of the government as a theocracy, God himself being eminently their king, and manifesting himself among them in a visible manner, by the cloud of glory in the tabernacle and temple. This was the reason why blasphemy, and all obstinate disobedience to his laws, were considered as high treason, and punished with death; especially idolatry, as being a crime against the fundamental principles of the constitution. But far the greater part of

---

[22] Ibid., p. 812.

[23] Ibid., pp. 915-916.

[24] Ibid., p. 947.

the judicial laws were founded on the plain immutable principles of reason, justice, and social virtue; such as are always necessary for civil society.[25]

In 1793, Samuel Miller argued that civic liberties did not depend on the form of government in a nation, but upon something of greater importance:

> Human laws are too imperfect, in themselves, to secure completely this inestimable blessing. It must have its seat in the hearts and dispositions of those individuals which compose the body politic; and it is with the hearts and dispositions of men that Christianity is conversant. When, therefore, that perfect law of liberty, which this holy religion includes, prevails and governs in the minds of all, their freedom rests upon a basis more solid and immoveable, than human wisdom can devise. . . . The prevalence of real Christianity, tends to promote the principles and the love of political freedom, by the doctrines which it teaches, concerning the human character, and the unalienable rights of mankind; and by the virtues which it inculcates, and leads its votaries to practice.[26]

Miller also believed that rulers were "not intrinsically greater than those whom they govern; and that all the rational and justifiable power with which they are invested, flows from the people, and is dependent on their sovereign pleasure. There is a love of dominion natural to every human creature; and in those who are destitute of religion, this temper is apt to reign uncontrolled. Hence experience has always testified, that rulers, left to themselves, are prone to imagine, that they are a superior order of beings, . . . But the religion of the gospel, rightly understood, and cordially embraced, utterly disclaims such unworthy sentiments, and banishes them with abhorrence from the mind."[27] In contrast to unbelieving theological systems, Miller affirmed that wherever Christianity had exerted its "native influence," citizens had been bold, energetic, considerate of others, not to mention contemptuous of "that abject submission to the encroachments of despotism, to which the ignorant and the unprincipled readily yield." "Christianity forbids us to call, or to acknowledge, any one master upon earth," said Miller, "knowing that we have a Master in heaven, to whom both rulers, and those whom they govern, are equally accountable." He said:

> In a word, Christianity, by illuminating the minds of men, leads them to consider themselves, as they really are, all coordinate terrestrial princes, stripped, indeed, of the empty pageantry and title, but retaining the substance of dignity and power. Under the influence of this illumination, how natural to disdain the shackles of oppression, to take the alarm at every attempt to trample on their just rights; and to pull down, with indignation, from the seat of authority, every bold invader![28]

Rather than humanism or Deism holding ideological preference among the political heirs of the Reformation, in reality, the Christian doctrines flowing from the Reformation were at the forefront during the formation of America. Furthermore, they positively

---

[25] Idem.
[26] Ibid., pp. 1155-1156.
[27] Ibid., p. 1157.
[28] Idem.

impacted social and political affairs. These were the essential beliefs at about 1750 that have been lost to many segments of the church, and which will take some time to re-inculcate. Theology was influencing politics. It always will. Likewise, eternal political principles were proclaimed from pulpits with regularity and vigor.

The Constitution of the United States was conceived in this *ethos* of skepticism about human ability. One result was that no human being would be given unlimited power. Another safeguard was that states were governed best with the input of the people and under fixed constitutional principles. At first, the American Constitution stood alone, rather unique. In time, many other nations came to follow aspects of this pattern that was so rooted in Scripture. Some would even imitate American democracy driven by human-centered populism; nevertheless, it is most difficult to ignore the God-centered principles at the base of American government. These were hardly evil intrusions of religion into politics.

Evangelicals in America: Populist Realignments

If anything, the religious *ethos* of the founding era expanded over the next century. Richard Carwardine's study, *Evangelicals and Politics in Antebellum America*, makes several points that reflect this surge. Among his points, three bear special highlighting: (1) evangelicals in the mid-nineteenth century were not hamstrung from political involvement; (2) evangelicals focused on moral issues; and (3) evangelicals led to a crucial re-alignment of the traditional two-party system.

His thesis is: "Evangelical Protestants were amongst the principal shapers of American political culture in the middle years of the nineteenth century. . . . deeply engaged in the processes which tore political consensus apart and which opened the door to armed conflict."[29] Speaking of the large public role manned by evangelicals, Carwardine reminds that elections seemed to converge with revivals. Evangelicals were quite committed to electing other righteous believers to office, and encouraged politicians to focus on issues of moral character.

He is dubious that "the extraordinary popular interest in politics, the huge electoral turnouts, and the impressive mobilization of the electorate in that era could have occurred without the engagement of evangelicals, and their organizational structures, in the new order."[30] Similar to late twentieth century evangelical resurgences, Carwardine and others note the evangelical impact in increasing voter turn-out: "At the same time the level of voter turnout at elections was one of the most impressive in the whole of American history. In presidential elections between 1840 and 1860 average turnout in the North as a whole never dropped below 72 percent, and even the less passionately fought non-presidential contests regularly achieved participation levels of over 60 percent; figures in the South were lower, but still impressive."[31] He even suggests that

---

[29] Richard Carwardine, *Evangelicals and Politics in Antebellum America* (New Haven: Yale University Press, 1993), p. ix.

[30] Ibid., pp. 50-51.

[31] Ibid., p. 54.

elections appeared to "supersede religion as the principal source of popular excitement." The effectiveness of evangelical involvement is noted: "Examination of campaigns for the presidency, where excitement and turnouts tended to be highest of all, confirms that evangelicals possessed a realistic sense of their political authority as voters and as molders of political agendas."[32]

Carwardine reminds a secular age that, "ministers customarily offered prayer at the opening of . . . conventions, which were often accommodated in churches. Some regarded their party as a political church and its activists as a hierarchy of quasi-evangelists. . . . Political sermons, triumphalist and doom laden, redolent with biblical imagery and theological terminology, were a feature of the age."[33]

Some evangelicals were so identified with a particular party as to speak of Martin Van Buren (1848)

> as a sort of political divinity, whose political resurrection has been vouchsafed as a providential boon to rescue the country from peril. They faced, on the other hand, the forces of darkness, 'false Christs,' 'political sinners' groaning in the 'anxious seat,' those 'second only, in the violations of trust, to him who sold his Lord and Master for thirty pieces of silver.' A Free Soiler in 1848 bluntly asserted 'that God Almighty was the leader of the free soil party, and that the Devil was the leader of the two opposing parties,' while the Democratic candidate for the governorship of New Jersey in 1850, George F. Fort, believed the 'powers of hell' had been let loose against him and that 'the devil himself' had an interest in his defeat.[34]

To remind both exponents and opponents of evangelical political involvement of earlier efforts, Carwardine avers that "much of the passion of the campaign was religious in origin, as an analysis of campaign propaganda, especially of the Whigs, and of the state of mind of the evangelical community will make clear. For pious evangelicals the election of 1840 was not a campaign devoid of issues, nor was the economic collapse their main preoccupation; the contest between Whig and Democrat had a profound religious significance, Whig propagandists encouraged evangelicals to turn Harrison into a spiritual and religious symbol, and the campaign was thereby invested with a strong moral dimension."[35]

Not only were evangelicals politically charged in the antebellum period and not only did they focus on moral issues, but they became a third force.[36] Carwardine sees this evangelical participation as a major factor that generated a new political re-alignment, compelling political leaders to address their concerns.[37] For some time, segments of Protestantism had been cheering for a re-alignment of a theological nature.

---

[32] Idem.

[33] Ibid., pp. 51-52.

[34] Ibid., p. 53.

[35] Ibid., p. 55.

[36] Ibid., p. 132.

[37] "Evangelical Protestants actively participated in this process of political realignment, taking initiatives that forced politicians to address both sets of issues." Carwardine, op. cit., p. 133.

Things which began small soon led to laudatory optimism: "Evangelicals watched with wide-eyed wonderment what Daniel Eddy called a 'political earthquake' and James W. Alexander [called] a 'political rage.'. . . A northern correspondent of the Southern Christian Advocate marveled at this 'strange and wonderful' chapter of the country's history. William Brownlow declared 'the hand of God . . . is visible in this thing. Divine Providence has raised up this new Order to purify the land.'"[38] Many ministers were introduced to political involvement. Indeed, these mid-nineteenth century crusades attracted ministers, editors of church periodicals, and leading laymen.[39]

Evangelicals did take a leading role in shaping popular attitudes in the mid-nineteenth century.[40] Ministers "addressed political meetings, peppered their representatives with private and public protests, and filled the columns of church newspapers with diatribes against an abomination."[41]

The opponents of this evangelical uprising confirm its potency. Democrats wailed that the 33rd Congress took on "the semblance of an ecclesiastical council more than that of a legislative assembly." They were concerned over the engagement of ministers as "viceregents of the Almighty . . . as a left-handed attempt to put the state in subordination to the dictates of the church."[42] These Democrats complained against "the fanatical Methodist and Baptist preachers . . . hurling their anathemas at us from their pulpits on Sundays and from the stump on week days."[43] Henry Ward Beecher was notorious for taking leave of his congregation to be employed by a political party's national committee to speak up to three times a week, reaching tens of thousands.[44] Carwardine found that, "Through the weeks immediately before polling day, numerous denominational gatherings at state and regional level resolved to resist by all means, including political, the slave power's threat to free territory, free speech, and the Union."[45]

The election of 1856 presaged late twentieth century "culture wars" with one minister expressing: "Truth and falsehood, liberty and tyranny, light and darkness, holiness and sin . . . the two great armies on the battlefield of the universe, each contending for victory. There could be no cessation of hostilities . . . till righteousness triumphs."[46] On election day, a marriage between Republican politics and religion was

---

[38] Ibid., pp. 218-219.

[39] Ibid., p. 223.

[40] This evangelical surge led to re-alignment. In the decade prior to the Civil War: James Rollock, an ardent Presbyterian was a gubernatorial candidate in Pennsylvania in 1854; "In the Virginia contest of 1855 prominent Presbyterians were known supporters of Flournoy, whom Wise sneeringly dismissed as 'the Presbyterian Elder.' Robert J. Breckinridge and Andrew B. Cross represented the most influential of a substantial Presbyterian contribution to the American party in Maryland." Carwardine, op. cit., p. 236.

[41] Ibid., p. 236.

[42] Idem.

[43] Idem.

[44] Idem.

[45] Ibid., p. 268.

[46] Ibid., p. 269.

witnessed in this song: "Think that God's eye is on you;/ Let not your faith grow dim;/ For each vote cast for Fremont/ is a vote cast for Him!"[47]

Although it would be difficult to sustain a proof that the Republican party was "the political expression of pietistic Protestantism,"[48] evangelicals were a force with their postmillennial impetus. Both friends and critics recognized the role that the church played in the "unholy and fratricidal war . . . [which] began with hard-shell Reformed Presbyterians, and soft-shell new-school Presbyterians, and with Baptists, Methodists, and such like."[49] Carwardine concludes:

> Like these earlier parties, the Republicans acquired their essential moral energy from evangelical Protestantism, and their unique fusion of religion and politics drew on established modes of mobilizing revivalist enthusiasm. . . . Most strikingly, the movement's pious Protestant supporters went further than evangelicals had ever done before in identifying the arrival of the kingdom of God with the success of a particular political party. When during the climax of the campaigns of 1856 and 1860 ministers officiated with equal enthusiasm at revival meetings and at Republican rallies, it was clear that religion and politics had fused more completely than ever before in the American republic.[50]

Such studies confirm that religion was expressed publicly and persistently for over a century after the American Revolution. Religion and evangelical preaching buttressed—rather than repressed—the founding of the nation. If it was beneficial once, what compelling argument has been made to demonstrate that it is less necessary or less salutary today?

John Wingate Thornton assembled a number of political sermons from an earlier period in American history in 1860.[51] He found the pulpit of the American Revolution to be a genre of its own with distinctive rhetorical and philosophical commitments. Interpreters of these founding era sermons acknowledge how the preachers interpreted current events in light of revelation: "Their sermons also demonstrate the existence and effectiveness of a popular political culture that constantly assimilated the currently urgent political and constitutional issues to the profound insights of the Western spiritual and philosophical traditions. That culture's political theorizing within the compass of ultimate historical and metaphysical concerns gave clear contours to secular events in the minds of Americans of this vital era."[52]

Tocqueville and others confess that religion, specifically Protestant Christianity, lie at the foundation of America. The court prophets of that religion were the clergy of the day. Most preachers believed that creatures were distinct from their Creator, and that due

---

[47] Idem.

[48] Ibid., p. 277.

[49] Ibid., p. 319.

[50] Ibid., p. 322.

[51] John Wingate Thornton, *The Pulpit of the American Revolution* (Boston: Gould and Lincoln, 1860, rpr. New York: Da Capo, 1970).

[52] Ellis Sandoz, *Political Sermons of the American Founding Era, 1730-1805* (Indianapolis: Liberty Press, 1991), p. xiii-xiv.

to the Fall, citizens had to turn to the Sovereign Creator for guidance and sustenance. Their beliefs were "not merely parochially Puritan or Calvinistic but Augustinian and biblical."[53] Of course, the British background of the past century—complete with the views of English Libertarianism—and the various tyrannies of the eighteenth century form an interpretive relief for most of these sermons. Still, among the most important factors, if not the most important, was the role of biblical religion as prime interpreter for the political matters of the day.

Following the Great Awakening, the pulpit in America had an even more pronounced position. The liberty so discussed in the founding period of America was not a secular liberty, but rooted in God's created order. Earlier political sermons spoke of liberty as "most truly exercised by living in accordance with truth; . . . the obligation to obey the laws of the Creator only checks his licentiousness and abuse."[54] Thus, it is a mistake to strip these early orations from the framework of a biblical view of liberty.

Election sermons were preached to the Governor and legislature in Massachusetts for 256 years, in Connecticut for 156 years, and in Vermont (beginning in 1778) and New Hampshire (beginning in 1784; cf. Samuel McClintock's sermon below). John Wingate Thornton asserted that the annual Election sermons actually began as early as 1633 and served as a "perpetual memorial, continued down through the generations from century to century, still bearing witness that our fathers ever began their civil year and its responsibilities with an appeal to Heaven, and recognized Christian morality as the only basis of good laws."[55] The first of the election sermons occurred in 1633, but it was in 1641 that the homiletical style became mature.[56] By 1691, the election days and their accompanying sermons were fixed by colonial law, with Gordon Roxbury observing: "Two sermons have been preached annually for a length of time, the one on general election day, the last Wednesday in May, when the new general court have been used to meet . . . the other, some little while after, on the artillery-election day, when the officers are re-elected, or new officers chosen. On these occasions political subjects are

---

[53] Ibid., p. xvi.

[54] Ibid., p. xx.

[55] John Wingate Thornton, *The Pulpit of the American Revolution* (Boston: Gould and Lincoln, 1860), p. xxii.

[56] Harry Stout's description of Election Days is worth reviewing: "The setting of the election sermon, initially Boston's First Church and after 1658 the Boston Town House, reinforced the solemnity of the occasion. There, seated before the speaker in the principal building of the province, were the three orders of authority: the magistrates who represented the oligarchy, the deputies who represented the democracy, and the ministers who represented the theocracy. Each would be addressed in turn so that all aspects of government and authority would be illuminated by the Word of God. Unlike fasts and thanksgivings that were delivered irregularly in every town by a multitude of ministers, the election sermon was limited to a single day in the year and was spoken by only one minister. The communities would come together through their representatives and meet as one national assembly. . . . As the speaker entered the pulpit, the mood was expectant. What followed marked the moment of superb oratory in a culture that valued the spoken word above all other art forms. The speaker's goal was not to be innovative or entertaining, but to recall for his audience the vision that first impelled New England's mission." Stout, *The New England Soul*, p. 29.

deemed very proper; but it is expected that they be treated in a decent, serious, and instructive manner."[57] These sermons were distributed to colonial representatives who were also to convey copies to the chief ministers in their communities. Roxbury continued: "As the patriots have prevailed, the preachers of each sermon have been the zealous friends of liberty; and the passages most adopted to promote the spread and love of it have been selected and circulated far and wide by means of newspapers, and read with avidity and a degree of veneration on account of the preacher and his election to the service of the day.... Thus, by their labors in the pulpit, and by furnishing the prints with occasional essays, the ministers have forwarded and strengthened, and that not a little, the opposition to the exercise of that parliamentary claim of right to bind the colonies in all cases whatever." [58]

A few samples will confirm Thornton's conclusion, i.e., "Thus it is manifest, in the spirit of our history, in our annals, and by the general voice of the fathers of the republic, that, in a very great degree, To the pulpit, the PURITAN Pulpit, we owe the moral force which won our independence."[59] In 1663, John Higginson of Salem stated: "It concerneth New England always to remember that they are originally a plantation religious, not a plantation of trade. The profession of the purity of doctrine, worship, and discipline is written upon her forehead. Let merchants, and such as are increasing ... remember this: that worldly gain was not the end and design of the people of New England, but religion."[60]

In 1677, Increase Mather proclaimed: "It was love to God and to Jesus Christ which brought our fathers into this wilderness.... They did not, in their coming hither, propound any great matters to themselves respecting this world; only that they should have liberty to serve God, and to walk with him in all the ways of his worship.... There never was a generation that did so perfectly shake off the dust of Babylon, both as to ecclesiastical and civil constitution, as the first generation of Christians that came into this land for the gospel's sake."

In an 1682 Fast-day sermon, William Hubbard declared that the founding fathers "came not hither for the world, or for land, or for traffic; but for religion, and for liberty of conscience in the worship of God, which was their only design." This was later confirmed by then-President of Yale, Ezra Stiles: "It is certain that civil dominion was but the second motive, religion the primary one, with our ancestors, in coming hither and settling this land. It was not so much their design to establish religion for the benefit of the state, as civil government for the benefit of religion, and as subservient, and even necessary, towards the peaceable enjoyment and unmolested exercise of religion—of that religion for which they fled to these ends of the earth."

Thus Thornton concluded: "The true alliance between Politics and Religion is the lesson inculcated in this volume of Sermons, and apparent in its title ... It is the voice of

---

[57] Ellis Sandoz, op. cit., p. xxvi.
[58] Idem.
[59] Ibid., p. xxxviii.
[60] Thornton, op. cit., p. xviii. The following examples are taken from Thornton, pp. xvii-xxi.

the Fathers of the Republic, enforced by their example. They invoked God in their civil assemblies, called upon their chosen teachers of religion for counsel from the Bible, and recognized its precepts as the law of their public conduct. The Fathers did not divorce politics and religion, but they denounced the separation as ungodly. They prepared for the struggle, and went into battle, not as soldiers of fortune, but, like Cromwell and the soldiers of the Commonwealth, with the Word of God in their hearts, and trusting him. This was the secret of that moral energy which sustained the Republic in its material weakness against superior numbers, and discipline, and all the power of England. To these sermons—the responses from the Pulpit—the state affixed its *imprimatur*, and thus they were handed down to future generations with a two-fold claim to respect."[61]

These sermons were usually published as pamphlets and distributed to civil magistrates and ministers. Other occasions, e.g., the gathering of the army ("the artillery sermons"), "Market Day" sermons, anniversaries of important days, Thanksgiving Day sermons, Independence Day sermons, and those in conjunction with Election Day ceremonies provide a rich resource of political hortatory of the day. Most latter-day Christians will hardly hear better sermons than these, although the ones in this volume are intended to supplement the earlier vital tradition.

Several collections of political sermons exist. A variety of libraries contain some of the great manuscripts. If one can locate a copy of John Wingate Thornton's *The Pulpit of the American Revolution* (Boston, 1860), more of these early sermons can be reviewed. Others are contained in Frank Moore's *The Patriot Preachers of the American Revolution* (1860), Bernard Bailyn's *Pamphlets of the American Revolution* (Cambridge, MA, 1965), or two recent releases by Liberty Press in Indianapolis: *American Political Writing during the Founding Era, 1760-1805*, Charles S. Hyneman and Donald S. Lutz, editors (1983) or *Political Sermons of the American Founding Era, 1730-1805*, Ellis Sandoz, editor (1991). One would also do well to consult Harry S. Stout's *The New England Soul: Preaching and Religious Culture in Colonial New England* (New York: Oxford, 1986) or Donald Weber's *Rhetoric and History in Revolutionary New England* (New York, 1988). Many of these earlier classics provide instructive models for the present and the future.

Interestingly, with the revival of these fine anthologies above, most of them contain sermons that are at least 200 years old. Several of the collections were made in the mid-nineteenth century, and most of these laid dormant until very recent reprintings, leading one to query: What happened to political preaching? Did it stop after 1860? Or was it of diminished proportions? Why? Whatever answers are ultimately given to these queries, we believe that a revival of political preaching—as long as it is truly biblical—can only help a country such as ours. We do not believe that the proclamation of the whole counsel of God has ceased; only that it is not appreciated in some quarters and perhaps not anthologized in others.

According to a recent survey, political topics remain frequent staple of many preachers. A six-year survey of approximately 8,000 American pastors found that

---

[61] Thornton, op. cit., p. i.

evangelicals were adopting a new civic gospel that viewed the government as "playing a critical role in setting moral parameters and, therefore, government policies do make a difference." [62] In an attempt both to give guidance to their own and also to influence those outside the church, the percentages below reflect the frequency that certain topics have been recently addressed:

Abortion	89%
Pornography	89%
Homosexuality	67%
School Prayer	60%
Civil Rights	33%
Environment	25%[63]

Pulpits and politics evidently do mix—and have. Amidst the Civil War, James A. Lyon attempted to harmonize religion and politics: "That religion and politics should be separated, the one wholly divorced from the other, is a popular fallacy so assiduously cultivated by a certain interested party, and so widely disseminated, that it may be justly termed one of Lord Bacon's 'idols'. . . . Of the many popular fallacies that are generally afloat in society, there is perhaps none that is deeper rooted or more damaging in its effects than the one just stated. How it originated, and became so deeply implanted in the popular mind, it may be rather difficult to explain. It is, however, a modern notion."[64]

James H. Thornwell also believed that virtue would not ensue unless connected to religion. He affirmed, "The moral nature of man is inseparably linked with immortality, and immortality as inseparably linked with religion."[65] Moreover, Thornwell trumpeted the inescapably religious foundation of politics: "Subjects that have no religion are incapable of law. . . . Every State, therefore, must have a religion, or it must cease to be a government of men. Hence no Commonwealth has ever existed without religious sanctions. . . . man must have a religion."[66]

Citing the Princeton President, James McCosh, Thornwell approved:

When a religion waxes old in a country; when the circumstances which at first favored its formation or introduction have changed; when in an age of reason it is

---

[62] *Christianity Today*, April 29, 1996, p. 58.

[63] As to party affiliation, 89% of the clergy from the Assemblies of God were Republicans (with only 5% claiming to be Democratic), 68% of the SBC were Republican (22% were Democratic), 59% of the Reformed were Republicans (with 30% identifying themselves as Democratic), 44% of the UMC were Republicans (with 46% identifying themselves as Democratic), 33% of the PCUSA were Republicans (with 59% identifying themselves as Democratic), and 31% of the Disciples of Christ were Republicans (with 60% identifying themselves as Democratic. Ibid.

[64] James A. Lyon, "Religion and Politics," *The Southern Presbyterian Review*, vol. 15 (April, 1863), p. 569. He also noted that, "the separation of religion and politics, as a cardinal maxim in the foundation and superstructure of civil society, is of recent growth, the birth of modern infidelity." Ibid., p. 570.

[65] James Henley Thornwell, "Sermon on National Sins," *The Collected Works of James H. Thornwell* (Edinburgh: Banner of Truth, 1986), Vol. IV, p. 515.

[66] Ibid., pp. 515-516.

tried and found unreasonable; when in an age of learning it is discovered to be the product of the grossest ignorance; when in an age of levity it is felt to be too stern; then the infidel spirit takes courage, and with a seal in which there is a strange mixture of scowling revenge and light-hearted wantonness, of deep-set hatred and laughing levity, it proceeds to level all existing temples and altars, and erects not others in their room.

Thornwell believed that if such abandonment occurred, "The void which is created is soon filled with wantonness and violence. The State cannot be restored to order until it settles down upon some form of religion again. . . . a Commonwealth can no more be organized which shall recognize all religions, than one which shall recognize none. . . . A Godless State is, in fact, a contradiction in terms."[67] Notwithstanding, he maintained that this religious infrastructure of the state was not the same as "favoring a Church Establishment. To have a religion is one thing, to have a Church Establishment is another; . . . The Church and the State, as visible institutions, are entirely distinct, and neither can usurp the province of the other without injury to both. But religion, as a life, as an inward principle . . . extends its domain"[68] to the state. Yet, this extension is carried out *qua* citizen, not *qua officium*: "The State realizes its religious character through the religious character of its subjects; and a State is and ought to be Christian, because all its subjects are and ought to be determined by the principles of the Gospel." Thornwell agreed that religion "cannot be enacted as a law, or enforced by authority."

In light of the above, still a caveat needs to be proffered. James H. Thornwell also provided a fine definition of the proper place for preaching. One of the hallmarks of this earlier evangelical approach was the great reticence of theologians to address matters of secular politics. On one occasion, Thornwell averred that in a quarter-century of preaching he had never introduced politics into the pulpit: "Questions of law and public administration I have left to the tribunals appointed to settle them, and have confined my exhortations to those great matters that pertain immediately to the kingdom of God. I have left it to Caesar to take care of his own rights, and have insisted only upon the supreme rights of the Almighty." Thornwell and others believed that the commission of preachers only extended to expound on Scripture; not expounding "to senators the Constitution of the State, nor to interpret for judges the law of the land. In the civil and political sphere the dead must bury their dead."

The dividing line of propriety was whether the topic addressed was a moral issue or merely political. Thornwell said: "There are cases in which the question relates to a change in the government, in which the question of duty is simply a question of revolution. In such cases the Minister has no commission from God to recommend or resist a change, unless some moral principle is immediately involved. He can explain and enforce the spirit and temper in which revolution should be contemplated and carried forward or abandoned. He can expound the doctrine of the Scriptures in relation to the nature, the grounds, the extent and limitations of civil obedience; but it is not for him, as

---

[67] Ibid., pp. 517, 519.
[68] Ibid., p. 517.

a preacher, to say when evils are intolerable, nor to prescribe the mode and measures of redress. These points he must leave to the State itself."[69]

As an individual citizen, the minister was certainly free to engage in political discourse and measures. However, as to his office, he was to restrict his expositions to the revealed mind of God. Thornwell delicately found the balance: "I can truly say that my great aim is not to expound our complex institutions, but to awaken the national conscience to a sense of its responsibility before God. It is not to enlighten your minds, but to touch your hearts; not to plead the cause of States' rights or Federal authority, but to bring you as penitents before the Supreme Judge."[70]

Ellis Sandoz concluded his anthology of political sermons: "This rhetorical form expressed the philosophical mean that free government is based on liberty, and liberty is founded in truth and justice as framed by eternal laws. Republicanism and virtue were far from split apart by James Madison and his colleagues at the Federal Convention, as the clergy understood our constitutional system. For these preachers and their flocks, the two remained essentially bound together. The political culture of this country was not only all the things it is most frequently said to be . . . but was deeply rooted in the core religious consciousness articulated above all by the preachers; theirs were the pulpits of a new nation with a privileged, providential role in world history. What America's religious consciousness consisted of in the tumultuous and triumphant years of founding is what this book will disclose."[71]

We invite churches to rediscover this sturdy tradition. If pastors and other teachers in the church take their calling seriously and resume leadership in this area, such preaching promises great reformation; indeed, perhaps faithful preaching for a consistent period will result in more positive change in our land than any other single form of activism. And it will be difficult to fault preaching within the church for breaching the imaginary iron curtain between church and state. We call on Christians merely to apply the Scriptures to the issues to the day. See if that can be kept exclusively under a bushel so as not to revolutionize the political theater. This old method can breathe life into the dry bones and re-awaken the church from her undogmatic slumber.

---

[69] Ibid., p. 513.
[70] Ibid., pp. 513-514.
[71] Sandoz, op. cit., p. xxiv.

Ten Commandments Of Nineteenth Century Church Planting

When I am asked to do a new task or something with which I am not familiar, I often find it helpful to look backward before looking forward. That may sound contrary to some approaches that are inordinately focused on future prediction. We often imagine that the future is the best determinant for successful action in the present. However, I have found that looking backwards at history can also offer guidance about methods for the future. Even in something as practical as church planting, history can be our friend and a helpful guide.

Having been faced recently with a new regional assignment for church planting in Southeast, and not being an expert on a particular methodology, I found it helpful to glance backwards first to see where the Presbyterian Church in North America had some of its successful beginnings in church planting methodology.[1] From my review, I would like to extract ten principles for church planting adopted by the Presbyterian Church at an early period of her life. While these "Ten Commandments of Church Planting" are assuredly not revealed from Sinai, I believe that they are exemplary and could be helpful in all situations.

The *First Commandment* is: "In our motive we shall have no other motive other than to honor the Lord our God." In 1791, as the American Presbyterian Church in her infancy began to consider domestic missions (or home missions), she considered sending missionaries to the "frontiers of our Country." The motive for such was stated in these words: "To carry into effect so noble a design we cannot doubt that all who have a *supreme regard* to the glory of God and the salvation of their fellow man will cheerfully contribute." Further, in that same historic statement of motive the 1791 General Assembly of the PCUSA said:

---

[1] No doubt other denominations have similar stories to unearth. I have focused on the tradition with which I am most familiar; others will have opportunity to concentrate on other communions.

The honor of God, the eternal salvation of precious souls, the increase of the society to which you belong, and may we not add, your own peace and comfort, all conspire to prompt you to ardor in this generous undertaking. We are ready to anticipate the times, when by similar exertions to these, our holy religion will extend its influence over the vast regions of this western continent, and songs of salvation be heard from its remotest corners; and is it possible that pious Christians, that friends to the best interest to the world, that men of public spirit, should withhold their aid in bringing forth so glorious an event?

They added:

Christians can you look around you and behold such multitudes of souls ignorant of that Savior whom you love and through whom only they can be saved; ignorant of those truths so important to the happiness which you have received and even perishing for the lack of knowledge and not be willing to do everything in your power to rescue them from such a condition?

Thus at its outset the Presbyterian Church stated that its conjunct motives for church planting were the *supreme glory of God* and love of fellow man. The first and inviolable commandment of older church planting was: Thou shalt have no other gods before the sovereign God in any efforts and motivations for church planting. That commandment rules out church planting motivated by guilt; in pursuit of success; church planting for the glory of man, men, or a particular organization; and any other kind of church planting that is not radically oriented toward the exclusive glory of God. Church planting must be directed to please God—not ourselves—and be for his glory alone. That is to be our *supreme* regard. In practice, that means that we shall often return to re-examine our motivation to certify that we are not seeking some other kind of glory. It is hard to pass over the opportunity to ask if modern church planting efforts might be more enduring if founded on this first, greatest, and doxological mandate.

Commandment #2: "Home missionaries shall be assigned by the higher governing body." In 1795, the Presbyterian Church in the United States of America appointed several missionaries. It is important to understand that these earliest home missionaries were assigned or appointed; they were not free-lancers. They were far from lone rangers who worked apart from the lawful jurisdiction of the proper church court. These were men under authority. That is distinctive for Presbyterians as compared to congregational attempts at church planting. The higher courts retained that authority and that is where the practice of itineration saw its first gleams of light in American Presbyterianism. Further, in 1795 they appointed one John Porter for three months to set out from particular areas and visit a route.[2] The next year, to show that the church was serious about this effort,[3] it

---

[2] Guy Klett, ed., *Minutes of the Presbyterian Church in the USA* (Philadelphia: Presbyterian Historical Society, 1976), p. 98.

[3] Ibid., p. 113. Hereafter, page numbers in parenthesis are taken from the *Minutes of the Presbyterian Church in the USA* unless otherwise noted.

was resolved that a Mr. Sample be recorded as having not fulfilled his mission according to the directions of the General Assembly, apparently based on his own admission that his route had not been covered. This shows that the earliest Presbyterian church planting efforts in America operated under the accountability of the college of presbyters. This second commandment of church planting requires home missionaries and church planters to be under the oversight of the higher governing authorities, to be assigned certain areas, and to be responsible for those itinerations. They shall not act as independent contractors.

The second commandment of church planting involves accountability to the church courts. In the year 1800, the minutes (p. 208) state that missionaries were to be employed for certain time periods and were to cover certain routes about which they should "[r]eport annually to the Assembly of the manner in which [they] hath fulfilled the objects of [their] appointment; also the whole state of the frontier country in with regard of the number of organized churches, distinguishing between such as are able and willing to support a minister in a single united capacity." The early Presbyterian missions did not see themselves as independent; rather they were accountable and organically related to the higher court.

Commandment #2 is evident in that these early Presbyterians desired to maintain a board or committee overseeing the whole of this work. In 1816, the Presbyterian Church raised the committee of home missions to the status of a commission, gave it a title 'The Board of Missions,' and in so doing they conferred on that missionary board significant authority. At this early stage it was realized that this important work must be, of necessity, overseen by a competent board that would also be accountable to the General Assembly. These church planters were connectional through and through—not independent—else they would not have bothered with the accountability of such board.

Commandment #3: "Church planters shall possess distinctive qualifications." As the maturation of the church planting movement in the Presbyterian Church was beginning, the 1799 Assembly (p. 183) stated these qualifications for church planters:

> That those who carry out these missions ought to be conducted by men of ability, piety, zeal, prudence and popular talents; that missionaries should be employed in preaching the most important doctrines, the Gospel, commonly called the doctrines of grace, . . . that they organize churches when opportunity offers and administer ordinances; and they catechize and instruct from house to house as far as practicable . . . that they refrain from all political or party discussions of mind.

The early church planting movement understood that certain qualifications were required for those who plied the trade of church planting full-time. Every minister of the gospel was not gifted to be a church planter. The Presbytery, as the visible steward of those gifts, was to employ those best qualified for these unique works.

Commandment #4: "Certain target areas were chosen." At that same General Assembly in 1799, two sites were targeted. From that we can learn that these earlier efforts saw the value of setting target sites, instead of randomly roaming the countryside hoping that a church will just erupt on its own. We infer from this also that there must have been some strategy involved along with designated targets of concentration. The first two sites chosen to be operating centers or target sites were Ft. Schuyler on the Mohawk River and Geneva on the Seneca Lake. It was also advised at this time that these home missionaries should go out "two by two." The early American Presbyterian church planting was intentional, strategic, and well-thought out (as opposed to haphazard and unresearched)—complete with demographically ripe targets.

The *fifth commandment* of nineteenth century church planting was that the reformed faith—the doctrines of grace—were to be unashamedly taught and proclaimed as central to the foundation of newly developed churches. These Presbyterians did not sublimate the reformed faith in these attempts, nor did they relegate their distinctively Presbyterian approach to the hinterlands. In fact, one of the signs of genius of this church planting explosion was that this missionary church was also a doctrinal church that maintained great substance. A strong case can be made that one of the main *causes* of this unprecedented growth was because of—not in spite of—the prominent emphasis on this distinctive "whole counsel of God." Our Presbyterian forefathers would not dream of planting churches that were less than Presbyterian. The 1799 General Assembly had already expressed its priority on the reformed faith, urging "that the missionaries should be employed in preaching the most *important doctrines*, the Gospel, commonly called the doctrines of grace." Hence, the early church planters did not view the specific doctrines of grace (the reformed faith) as embarrassing step-children to be shunned. As will be seen from the tenth commandment (below) the church planting effort grew most quickly during the Old School dominance—i.e., during the most doctrinaire time. Hearty doctrinal churches were planted by these domestic missionaries. It is a needed corrective to re-emphasize that the best and most lasting fruit of church planting grows from churches with a strong doctrinal root that transcends the storms and fads *du jour*.

The *sixth commandment* is: "Thou shalt employ all other gifted Christians in this work." Also in the year 1800 (p. 197), the General Assembly approved using an order of men called catechists. These early Presbyterians knew that many Christians other than ordained church planters should be included in these frontier works. These "catechists" were not to be clothed with "clerical functions, but [were to] confine themselves to the private instruction of those to whom they are sent." These catechists were teachers who went from house to house ministering to the families. They were involved in a follow-up capacity and were also solid in the faith. Today, good ruling elders, Sunday School teachers, and other gifted Christians are still needed to assist in church planting.

The *seventh commandment* is: "Church planting efforts shall be sensitive to cross-cultural opportunities." At the heart of these earliest plantings was the desire to reach out to the American Indians (and later blacks in the South). The very first domestic missionaries for the nineteenth century Presbyterian church were commissioned to go to the Indians. The church seized upon this cross-cultural opportunity and made the most of it. Today we would be wise to do the same. Often, re-settled peoples and ethnic minorities are more open to new churches than many anglos. Today's strategists might do well to recall the faithful missions such as those by the Rev. Gideon Blackburn who labored for years in Kentucky and Tennessee, planting many churches, braving many dangers, and reaching out to hundreds of native Americans.

Commandment #8 is: "Thou shalt draft settled pastors as well." By the year 1839, there was both a growth in home missions but also an increasing need. In the General Assembly of 1839, only two years after one of the most serious splits in history of the young Presbyterian denomination, the church adopted a measure to use settled pastors to serve as helpers in these itinerant tours. The Assembly passed this resolution (p. 167):

> That in furtherance of this great work which is of equal importance to this *Country*, in its civil and religious aspects this assembly recognizes the great importance of itinerant missionary labors among the more destitute districts in the newly settled portions of our country, and would urge its necessity, not only upon the employed missionaries of the board, but also upon all pastors, who by an annual missionary tour of this character might render equal benefit to themselves, their churches, and to the church at large, and thus greatly extend the boundaries to the Kingdom of Christ.

Two years later (p. 444) the General Assembly said,

> That until a sufficient number of suitable men can be found to occupy this field of labor [home missions], it is the duty of the churches enjoying regular pastoral labor, and of settled pastors, to take part in the work by devoting a portion of their time to missionary labor; and it is recommended that every Presbytery take order on the subject, and see that the burden of this work is equally distributed among its churches.

This was one of the strongest contributions of the nineteenth century model to church planting. It reflected great ingenuity and the true zeal to reach the nation, whatever it took. It may be that one of the things we can best learn from the nineteenth century church planting model is that we should employ even church pastors who are settled in this great work. It could be a marvelous challenge to denominations or to whole Presbyteries to ask each pastor to give one or two weeks (annually) of time released from his regular pulpit ministry for the spade work in the initial stages of church planting. Presbyteries could coordinate this effort, in effect creating an additional full-time church planter, if all pastors took their turn. This might be a quick solution to some pressing needs that stem from lack of manpower. Here again, we can learn much about method from these spiritual ancestors.

Commandment #9 is: "The General Assembly *must* visibly keep church planting before the churches as a chief concern." The early nineteenth century Assemblies did an excellent job at stoking the fires of interest for church planting. This can be seen dramatically in two ways. One of those is to note that from 1802-1826 nearly every Assembly set aside a unique time for "special prayer for the revival of religion."[4] The General Assembly considered it its duty to keep this matter before the court as a matter of special prayer.

The second clue to the high importance of church planting to the Assemblies themselves can be seen from the types of moderatorial sermons preached at the commencement of the General Assemblies during this era. During the period of 1798-1806 the Assembly seemed especially interested in spurring on interest in evangelism and extension. The moderators of the Assemblies in those years, chosen as representatives of sentiment as well as respect, seemed concerned to publicly state the mandates for such extension, as for example:

Wm. Tennent (1798) preached on	Matthew 28:20.
Jn. McKnight (1799) preached on	2 Corinthians 2:16.
S. S. Smith (1800) preached on	Jude 3.
Jos. Clark (1801) preached on	Matthew 28:18-20.
Nathaniel Irwin (1802) preached on	Luke 14:23.
Jas. Hall (1804) preached on	Romans 10:1.
Jas. Armstrong (1806) preached on	John 3:16-17.

This is quite a collection of evangelistic passages. The Assembly did its best to keep the extension of the kingdom through church planting and evangelism regularly and visibly before the Presbyters in Assembly.

Also in 1839 (p. 167), the Assembly's mission statement was given in these words: "That it is not only the duty of this board to supply vacant churches with an intelligent, orthodox, and devoted ministry—not only to render assistance to feeble churches in supporting such ministry when enjoyed, but also to extend the boundaries of the church to organize new congregations and to establish churches in the hitherto neglected and waste places of the land." Home missions was seen as a great task and the extent of this field was not small. It was up to the General Assembly as the expression of the entire church to keep this concern visibly before its churches.

Commandment #10 is: "Thou shalt grow." The Presbyterian Church in the early nineteenth century had its most dramatic spurt of growth in home missions in

---

[4] Cf. *Minutes 1789-1820*, pp. 248, 269, 286, 322, 350, 375, 396, 412, 435, 519, 576, 605, 670, 698, and *Minutes 1821-1838*, pp. 68, 135, and 163.

its history using these methods. In more modern communions, ministers are often pleased with their our own church growth or proud of their successes. However, compared to early nineteenth century growth, our late twentieth century successes are small. The Presbyterian Church went from *zero* home missionaries in the year 1800 to over 100 by the year 1830. The first home missionaries were appointed to reach the Indians. Soon other missionaries were added, and by the year 1810 there were 30 full-time ministers involved in domestic missions. By the next year, 1811, this number had risen to 40 (an increase of 33% in one year!), and by 1814 the corps of home missionaries numbered *51*. Home missionaries went from:

- 0 to 30   from 1800-1810.
- 30 to 40   by   1811.
- 40 to 51   by   1814.
- 51 to 100   by   1830.

They went from zero to 100 in one generation!

However, in 1851, looking back on the previous 21-year period (from 1830 to 1850 inclusive), the 1851 General Assembly (p. 27) noted several increases: home missionaries rose from 101 to 570; the church planting fund increased from $12,000 to $79,000 (a large amount in that day!); *943 new churches* were organized; *1,484 houses of worship* were erected; and over 40,000 souls were added to the missionary churches on profession of their faith. Such were the great results of an unprecedented twenty-year spurt of home missions that saw a nearly six-fold increase. Surely something is to be learned from these earlier models and their methods.

It should be also noted that this great increase happened during one of the most tumultuous periods of the life of the Presbyterian Church. A great division had been brewing and was consummated in 1837 between the Old School and the New School. Also the labor pains of the Civil War were commencing. Notwithstanding these oppositions from inside and from outside of the church, the church planting movement in early nineteenth century Presbyterianism exploded across the country, and despite all obstacles, she experienced unprecedented growth.

What can we learn from this? For one thing, we can see a strong and vibrant church that was doctrinally centered and doctrinally sound. It was an era that was predominately Old School, and in that climate the church was growing. It was a church that did not hesitate to practice its faith. It was a church that, dare say, outgrew most modern church growth rates. We would be a step ahead of the latest technique if we first learn from these forefathers and employ these methods. These "Ten Commandments of Church Planting in the Nineteenth Century" should also become the "Ten Commandments of Church Planting in the late Twentieth and Twenty-first centuries."

For those who consider numerical success and result-orientation as all-determinative, until we surpass the era described above we should respect these earlier methods. A healthy dose of paleo-correctness might be just what the doctor ordered for this or the next church expansion wave. How can we possibly ignore these great forward movements of real evangelism—not merely transfer growth —of our forefathers?

The only justification for such ignorance is an arrogance that presumes our generation to somehow be inherently superior than others. A more humble approach might be to inquire of our parents and their methods before we claim superiority.

Holding Fast the Great Concession of Faith: Science, Apologetics, and Orthodoxy

One of the most contentious arenas for apologetics in this century has been the creation-evolution debate. Of late, some of the hostility seems to be diminishing as it has become fashionable to argue that there should be little debate because the ancients were amazingly anticipatory of modern notions. This harmonic convergence, however, appears to be simple revisionism. A central argument of this essay[1] is that neither science nor apologetics is strengthened by ill-founded revisions of earlier Christian thought.

Rather than deal exclusively with the historical dimensions, I also intend to use this as a case study of the interaction of science and apologetic method. One might even view this study as an application of the scientific method (hypothesis, experimentation, conclusion) to these theories: "Pre-Darwinian theologians admitted the possibility of a long period for creation. The best apologetic method conforms itself to the science of the day." What follows is a testing of these hypotheses to see if they are capable of falsification.

It is frequently claimed, for example, that evangelicals need not hold out for a short sequence of creation insofar as earlier fathers and earlier biblical interpreters did not. Professor John A. McIntyre has warned against a "Christian amnesia," which allegedly forgets the earlier commentators on creation: "[Some] Christians have introduced a modern, naive 24-hour interpretation for days in Genesis, disagreeing with the classical, sophisticated analysis of these days by Augustine, Aquinas, and Calvin. . . . How can Christian scholars today ignore so completely the great Christian scholars of the past?"[2] Is it correct that Augustine, Aquinas, Calvin, and the current of orthodox expounders of creation held to a view that has

---

[1] This essay is adapted with permission from *Premise*, vol. 4, no. 1 (Feb. 1997; http://capo.org/premise/97/feb).

[2] John A. McIntyre, *The Misuse of Science*, unpublished manuscript, 1993, p. 24.

immense "semantic elasticity"[3]? To isolate the matter, if those who lived before Darwin—thus uninfluenced by that type of evolutionary thought—believed in long periods of continuous creation or progressive creation, or if they believed in a developmental gradualism that did not demand a special creation, then indeed, perhaps later Christians, too, are justified in jettisoning *creatio simul et ex nihilo*.

As one examines these questions, openness and humility are fitting. In our search of ancient interpretations of the creation narratives, we desire to avoid haughty or provincial approaches which insist that one's own tradition or generation is superior to all past generations and interpretations. We do not wish to arrogantly disqualify earlier Christians from the discussion simply because of their moment in history. We seek to follow their path as a historical question arises that must be answered humbly even if it calls into question now-dominant theories: Did earlier Christians hold to instantaneous creation *ex nihilo*, or did they allow for lengthy evolutionary gradualism?

The modern hypotheses for creation by developmental and gradual means over long periods of time seem foreign to earlier evangelicals. Even if an idiosyncratic or ambiguous reference may be unearthed (often capable of alternative explanation) in some writers, an altogether compelling case to view ancient evangelicals as compatible with a framework hypothesis still remains to be made.[4] If one wishes to make the case against short periods of creation, he will likely have to move closer to the present than the Reformation. Yet, this mistake is becoming fairly common.

Older antagonists such as Andrew Dickson White claimed that Augustine (a major focus of this essay), "revolted against the conception of an actual creation of the universe by the hands and fingers of a Supreme Being."[5] White also put into Augustine's mouth a "belief in the pre-existence of matter," and asserted that "Calvin opposed the idea of an instantaneous creation," accusing those who hold such view of "basely insult[ing] the Creator, [and] expect a judge who will

---

[3] This phrase is taken from an excellent summary, "How Old is the Earth: Anthropomorphic Days in Genesis 1:1-2:3" by C. John Collins, *Presbuterion* (Fall 1994), vol. xx, no. 2, p. 110. In that essay, Collins also suggests that to label as the "path to compromise" the thought of the likes of Charles Hodge, William Shedd, E. J. Young, and Francis Schaeffer is to cast reproach on them. However, it is also possible to retain high regard for men like these in general, while disagreeing with some particulars in their thinking. Our respect for fathers in the faith does not mandate that they be held as infallible (as Collins notes), nor that their conclusions be granted immunity from revision. Rather, as this essay intends, high respect for their work can best be maintained by honest criticisms of their weak points.

[4] C. John Collins (op. cit., p. 110), agrees that the framework hypothesis as set forth by M. G. Kline is ruled out on exegetical grounds (op. cit., p. 116, n. 29). Moreover, he confirms that much of the argumentation for long days based on idiomatic considerations in Gen. 2:4 "give[s] us no information on the range of meanings of *yom* outside this bound form" and that "the day-age theorists have not been able to say by what criteria we may discern an extended sense of *yom* as 'age,' or what contextual clues seem to tip us off. This seems to be a fatal weakness."

[5] Andrew Dickson White, *A History of the Warfare of Science with Theology* (New York: D. Appleton and Co., 1896), p. 49.

annihilate them."[6] He even attributed to Augustine the lead in the purported medieval revolt away from literalism—and this due to Augustine's reliance on Scripture as more authoritative than human ingenuity.[7]

More recently, Hugh Ross has conceded: "Many of the early church fathers and other biblical scholars interpreted the creation days of Genesis 1 as long periods of time. The list includes . . . Irenaeus . . . Origen . . . Basil . . . Augustine, and later Aquinas to name a few."[8] Ross includes an argument for long days of creation[9] and blames fundamentalism for the genesis of creationism. However, the best that Ross, White, and others can do in their presentation of Augustine's and Calvin's views is to demonstrate that symbolic language is appreciated in earlier commentaries.[10] It is a reach, nevertheless, to infer a repudiation of traditional (pre-Darwinian) creationism from these authors' use of a symbolic hermeneutic.[11]

Furthermore, despite Henry Morris's interpretation that Augustine's doctrine of "seed principles" sounds like a "modern theistic evolutionist,"[12] it would take far more to transform Augustine into a theistic evolutionist than these claims—if the rest of his writing is taken into account. Morris even concedes that Augustine grants continuous creation in De Trinitate.[13] Did Augustine stand out from his day and hold to views of creation that are more akin to twentieth century views? Can one really agree with Henry Morris that, "The end result of the teachings of Augustine, Aquinas, and other well-intentioned theologians was an undermining of biblical authority"?[14] It seems that Augustine can speak for himself and should be consulted prior to accepting revisionary studies. Is either science or apologetics enhanced by re-imagining earlier theologians to be so tony as to conform to late twentieth century views of continuous creation which putatively developed over billions of years?

---

[6] Ibid., p. 73.

[7] Ibid., p. 72.

[8] Hugh Ross, The Fingerprint of God, 2nd edition (Orange, CA: Promise Publishers, 1991), p. 141. For support, particularly of Augustine's view, Ross cites the following: The Literal Meaning of Genesis, Books four and five; The Confessions, Book XIII, chaps. 48-52 (a mistake); The City of God, Book XI, chaps. 7-8, 30-31.

[9] Ibid., pp. 146-158. Cf. also Hugh Ross, Creation and Time (Colorado Springs: NavPress, 1994), pp. 45-71.

[10] It is not necessary to assert that biblical narratives on creation are intended to be literal in every aspect. Non-literal or symbolic hermeneutical conclusions are different from the positive assertion that earlier exegetes maintained notions compatible with quite modern theories.

[11] Collins is helpful to note the distinction between allegory and anthropomorphism (op. cit., p. 120, note 48). While it might be sustained that ancient evangelicals used an anthropomorphic interpretation in numerous places, that is not necessarily the same as pleading that they lobbied for long days in this instance.

[12] Henry Morris, The Long War Against God (Grand Rapids: Baker, 1989), p. 203.

[13] A search of De Trinitate (especially III, 9, 16) did not turn up any such notions. In The Literal Meaning of Genesis, however, Augustine makes it clear that the 'rest' of God demonstrates that God completed the work of creation after the sixth day. Cf. 4:11-12 and 5:3.

[14] Morris, op. cit., p. 205.

In what follows, I dispute the claim that Augustine, Aquinas, Calvin, and others erected theories compatible with a 16-18 billion year old cosmos—an apologetic revision of epic proportions. The strategic revision is clarified by contrasting the exegesis of two eras: (1) pre-Darwinian theology, and (2) post-Darwinian theology.[15] The bulk of this essay examines the frequent assertion that the orthodox strain of beliefs on creation has always allowed wide latitude in this *loci*, rendering the ancients virtually indistinguishable from moderns.

It was, after all, the same Andrew White above who—despite his wish to the contrary—admitted that Calvin had a "strict" interpretation of Genesis, and that "down to a period almost within living memory [1896], it was held, virtually 'always, everywhere, and by all,' that the universe, as we now see it, was created literally and directly by the voice or hands of the Almighty, or by both—out of nothing—in an instant or in six days . . ."[16] Even opponents find it difficult to mangle this testimony, although with the effect of cumulative misrepresentations that is becoming more frequent.

Pre-Darwin

A representative survey of pre-Darwinian theologians will not prove that the ancients uniformly endorsed long periods of creation, non-momentary creation, or original cosmological development—purported citations notwithstanding. Many of the claims alleged to support a dubious point—when set in their proper context—allow an alternative interpretation and do not necessarily buttress the more modern schemes. Such citations are often based on inaccurate quotations, or are contradictory to the larger context, or are idiosyncratic (not necessarily typical of mainstream orthodoxy).

Ambrose of Milan (339-397) was one of the first theologians to explicate a mature view of creation. In his *Hexameron,* he admitted that even in his day some believed that matter "is considered to have given the power of creation to all things."[17] His view, however, was: "The language is simple: 'God created heaven and earth.' He created what was not, not what was."[18] Regarding the creation of the cosmos by divine Word, he added later: "When the word 'light' is used, it is not intended to mean merely the preparation for performance; rather, it is the splendor

---

[15] In another essay, I have examined leaders from reformed evangelicalism in the nineteenth century, Cf. my "Angels Unaware: The Ascendancy of Science over Orthodoxy in Nineteenth Century Reformed Orthodoxy," *Proceedings of the Wheaton Theology Conference*, Timothy Phillips, ed. (forthcoming, Wheaton: National Association of Evangelicals, 1994).

[16] Andrew White, op. cit., p. 60.

[17] *The Fathers of the Church: St. Ambrose, Hexameron, Paradise, Cain and Abel*, John J. Savage, trans. (New York: Fathers of the Church, Inc., 1961), vol. 42, p. 3. Ambrose also believed in the Mosaic authorship of Genesis (p. 5 *et passim*) and that the work of creation should not be confused with the eternality of God (p. 4).

[18] *Hexameron*, p. 34.

of the operation itself in action. . . . He did not speak in order that action should follow; rather, that action was completed with the Word [followed by a reference to Ps. 148:5]."[19] While there is no suggestion that the days were long, Ambrose affirmed that by God's command on the fifth day, "the waters immediately poured forth their offspring. The rivers were in labor. The lakes produced their quota of life. The sea itself began to bear all manner of reptiles and to send forth according to its kind whatever was there created. . . . Dolphins frolicked in the waves. Shell-fish clung to the rocks. Oysters adhered to the depths and the sea-urchins waxed strong."[20] He apparently believed that multiple species were created instantaneously rather than by gradual development: "The whale, as well as the frog, came into existence at the same time by the same creative power. Without effort does God produce the greatest things. He is not averse to creating the least."[21]

Elsewhere, Ambrose affirmed, "God created day and night at the same time. Since that time, day and night continue their daily succession and renewal."[22] In his fullest discussion of the lengths of the creation days, Ambrose commented:

> The beginning of the day rests on God's word: 'Be light made, and light was made.' The end of day is the evening. Now, the succeeding day follows after the termination of night. The thought of God is clear. First He called light 'day' and next He called darkness 'night.' In notable fashion has Scripture spoken of a 'day,' not the 'first day.' Because a second, then a third day, and finally the remaining days were to follow, a 'first day' could have been mentioned, following in this way the natural order. But Scripture established a law that twenty-four hours, including both day and night, should be given the name of day only, as if one were to say the length of one day is twenty-four hours in extent.[23]

The earliest full treatise on creation ends with these sentiments: "But now we seem to have reached the end of our discourse, since the sixth day is completed and the sum total of the work of the world has been concluded. . . . we should now make our contribution of silence, since God has rested from the work of the world. . . . He the Creator rested."[24]

With such clarity, a fair question is: Will Augustine (354-430) later differentiate his position from Ambrose's? Does Augustine distance himself from the *Hexameron* to advocate an immense period of creation? At least on the surface, Augustine did not seem aware of being contrary to Ambrose.

Augustine's view of creation is not always opaque. In his *Enchiridion*, he stated that the Christian believes "that the cause of all created things, whether in heaven or on earth, whether visible or invisible, is nothing other than the goodness

---

[19] *Hexameron*, pp. 38-39.

[20] *Hexameron*, p. 160.

[21] *Hexameron*, p. 163.

[22] *Hexameron*, p. 72.

[23] *Hexameron*, pp. 42-43.

[24] *Hexameron*, pp. 282-283.

of the Creator, who is the one true God. . . . By this Trinity, supremely and equally and immutably good, were all things created." (chap. III). A similar affirmation is given in *The City of God*, while arguing for the consubstantiality of the Son: ". . . the only-begotten Son who is the wisdom by which all things were created." (Bk. 11, ch. 24) In *The City of God*, Augustine affirms: "There is no creator higher than God" (Bk. 11, ch. 21); "nothing can exist apart from creation by God" (Bk. 11, ch. 23); "[man's] natural being is created from nothing" (Bk. 12, ch. 6); "But only a nature created out of nothing could have been distorted by a fault." (Bk. 14, ch. 13; cf. also Bk. 14, ch. 11). Augustine had no hesitancy employing the *ex nihilo* terminology, and even accepts a chronology that seldom accompanies an evolutionary view: "From Adam to the flood there were 2,262 years according to the calculation data in our versions of the Scripture." (Bk. 15, ch. 20) He concluded with a summary: "But to return to the three answers which, as I suggested above, should be given when we asked concerning any creature—Who made it? How? and Why?—the answers are: 'God'; 'by the word'; and 'because it is good.'" (Bk. 11, ch. 23)

In *Faith and the Creed*, Augustine stated: "If they admit that the world was made by an omnipotent God they must admit that he made what he has made out of nothing. If he were omnipotent there could be nothing of which he was not the Creator. Even if he did make something out of something else, as he made man out of clay, he did not make it out of something which he had not himself made. For he made the earth out of nothing, and clay comes from the earth. . . . we must by no means believe that the matter out of which the world was made, however formless or invisible, could have existed as it was by itself, as if it were co-eternal and coeval with God."[25]

Contrary to the claims by moderns searching for support, Augustine's statements in *The Confessions* do not lend support to viewing him as a precursor of evolutionary theory. At various places he affirmed: "this earth was invisible and without order . . . before you formed this unformed matter and fashioned it into kinds, there was no separate being, no color, no shape, no body, no spirit." (XII, 3);[26] "Lord, you made the world out of formless matter . . . 'Let it be made,' and so it was made." (XII, 8); "all these visible things were made and set in order during those various days . . ." (XII, 17). At a trenchant summation in *The Confessions*, Augustine said, "True it is that you, from whom are all things, have made not only created and formed being, but also whatsoever is capable of being created and formed." (XII, 19) Later he argued: "Why should we not understand, with Truth teaching us, that also formless matter, which Scripture calls earth invisible and unformed . . . was made by God out of nothing, and therefore is not co-eternal with

---

[25] *Augustine: Earlier Writings*, John H. S. Burleight, ed. (Philadelphia: Westminster Press 1953), p. 354.
[26] Citations taken from John K. Ryan, ed. *The Confessions of St. Augustine* (New York: Doubleday, 1959).

him . . . ?" (XII, 22) A long age of development or progressive creation does not seem compatible with these sentiments. He went so far as to pray for "patience" when dealing with those who oppose Moses' intent "because they are proud and have not known Moses's meaning, but love their own, not because it is true, but because it is their own." (XII, 25) He accused those of "rash judgment; not insight but pride" who would distort the meaning of Moses.

Augustine repeatedly affirmed that God made heaven and earth in the beginning (XIII, 2): "Out of nothing have they been made by you, not out of yourself, not out of anything not your own, or which previously existed, but out of concreated matter, that is, out of matter simultaneously created by you, since without any intervening time you gave form to its formlessness . . . you made the matter entirely out of nothing." (XIII, 33)

Despite the claim that Augustine manifested a "striking anticipation of some modern evolutionary doctrines,"[27] such claim is at best a classic case of conforming the ancient to the modern—whether the revisionary shoe fits or not. Augustine should also be remembered for asserting that God "would not be omnipotent, if he were unable to create anything good, unless he were assisted by that matter which he had not created." (VII, 5) The following should be factored into revisionary claims about Augustine's view of creation: "What was your engine for doing this mighty work? You did not work as does the human artist, who transforms one body into another . . . You made the artist's body; you, the soul that gives orders to his members; you, the matter out of which he fashions things . . . All these praise you, the creator of all things . . . You did not hold in your hand anything out of which to make heaven and earth . . . You spoke, therefore, and these things were made, and in your Word you made them." (XI, 5). This robust view of creation embraces special creation *ex nihilo simul et verbe*. Gradualism—absent some super-imposed presupposition—is not obvious in these early writings which are, of late, so misrepresented.

In *The Literal Meaning of Genesis*, Augustine—the alleged adherent to the framework hypothesis—commented: "Hence it seems that this work of God was done in the space of a day, at the end of which evening came on, which is the beginning of night. Moreover, when the night was spent, a full day was completed, and the morning belonged to a second day, in which God then performed another work."[28] In light of this and many other comments, Augustine's sensitivity to symbolism ought not be transformed into a cosmology which fits with a 16 billion year old cosmos apart from numerous, explicit, and consistent iterations.

---

[27] *The Confessions of St. Augustine*, op. cit., p. 415.

[28] "The Literal Meaning of Genesis" in *Ancient Christian Writers: The Works of the Fathers in Translation*, Johannes Quasten, Walter J. Burghardt, and Thomas Comerford Lawler, eds. (Ramsey, NJ: Paulist Press, 1982), vol. 1, p. 29.

It is true that Augustine's discussion of certain topics is somewhat bizarre and difficult to interpret.[29] For example, he averred that the Sabbath had been annulled,[30] that the seventh day "kept recurring to make up months and years and ages,"[31] (4:14), and that the sixth day symbolized completeness because it is the first number which is the sum of its parts. Despite these eccentricities, he theorized: "The more likely explanation, therefore, is this: these seven days of our time, although like the seven days of creation in name and in numbering, follow one another in succession and mark off the division of time, but those first six days occurred in a form unfamiliar to us . . ."[32] (4:14)

However, lest one think that Augustine was arguing for an expanded period of creation so as to permit lengthy development, he also argued that the entire creation happened in only one day: "Perhaps we should say that God created only one day, so that by its recurrence many periods called days would pass by. . . . All creation, then, was finished by the sixfold recurrence of this day, whose evening and morning we may interpret as explained above."[33] (4:20, 26) Augustine believed: "Thus, in all the days of creation there is one day, and it is not to be taken in the sense of our day, which we reckon by the course of the sun; but it must have another meaning, applicable to the three days mentioned before the creation of the heavenly bodies. This special meaning of 'day' must not be maintained just for the first three days . . . But we must keep the same meaning even to the sixth and seventh days."[34] (4:26) He continued to explain: "That day in the account of creation, or those days that are numbered according to its recurrence, are beyond the experience and knowledge of us mortal earthbound men."[35] (4:27) Still, he did not want to be confused with figurative or allegorical interpretations,[36] (4:28) and he believed that, "the whole of creation was finished in six days."[37] (4:14) He suggested that as angels beheld the creation, there were no intervals of time, i. e., that time stood still[38] (4:29-30; cf. also 2:8); however, there was order of sequence.

Augustine argued that the firmament, the waters, plants, trees, heavenly bodies, and all living creatures were "made simultaneously."[39] (4:33) So far was he from advocating a gradual evolution that he said: "Perhaps we ought not to think of

---

[29] Even Aquinas admitted that "Augustine differs from other expositors" and in Augustine's interpretation: "angelic knowledge is appropriately called day." St. Thomas Aquinas, *Summa Theologica* (London: Burns Oates & Washbourne, 1921), Q. 74, art. 2, p. 268.

[30] St. Augustine, *The Literal Meaning of Genesis*, John Hammond Taylor, trans. (New York: Newman Press, 1962), vol. 1, p. 119.

[31] Ibid., p. 125.

[32] Ibid., p. 125.

[33] Ibid., p. 128, p. 133.

[34] Ibid., p. 134.

[35] Ibid., p. 135.

[36] Ibid., p. 135.

[37] Ibid., p. 125.

[38] Ibid., pp. 136-137.

[39] Ibid., p. 141.

the creatures at the moment they were produced as subject to the processes of nature which we now observe in them, but rather as under the wonderful and unutterable power of the Wisdom of God . . . For this power of Divine Wisdom does not reach by stages or arrive by steps. It was just as easy, then, for God to create everything as it is for Wisdom to exercise this mighty power. . . . Creation, therefore, *did not take place slowly in order that a slow development might be implanted in those things that are slow by nature; nor were the ages established at the plodding pace at which they now pass.*"[40] (4:33) That Augustine is incompatible with modern notions is seen from his comment: "[B]ut there was no passage of time when they [creatures] received these laws at creation. Otherwise, if we think that, when they were first created by the Word of God, there were the processes of nature with the normal duration of days that we know, those creatures that shoot forth roots and clothe the earth would need not one day but many to germinate beneath the ground, and then a certain number of days, according to their natures, to come forth from the ground; and the creation of vegetation, which Scripture places on one day, namely the third, would have been a gradual process."[41] (4:33) Augustine believed that there was no "before" or "after" in the moment of creation: "It follows, therefore, that he, who created all things together, simultaneously created these six days, or seven, or rather the one day six or seven times repeated."[42] (4:33)

One can conclude the following about Augustine's views:

(1) they were directed toward a certain set of ideas of his day;
(2) his argumentation should be set in that context and not snatched from that context to argue for later ideas that are incompatible;
(3) his views of creation seem rather unique and idiosyncratic in the history of theology; i. e., few, if any, theologians approached the Genesis narratives as creatively as did Augustine (For example, his concern for the angelic observation of creation is rather unparalleled.);
(4) he did not wish to be interpreted as using the allegorical method; his intent was to be as literal as possible;
(5) he recognized that the day of creation was a non-normal day;
(6) he maintained that it was not a solar day, insofar as at least three "days" occurred prior to the creation of the sun;
(7) he did not believe that creation took a long period of development, but to the contrary;
(8) Augustine believed that all of creation occurred simultaneously, at one instant.

---

[40] Ibid., p. 141. Italics added.
[41] Ibid., p. 142.
[42] Ibid., p. 142.

(9) He also believed that Jesus' saying in John 5 ("My Father is still working") applied only to governance, not "of creating any new nature."[43] Thus, it is difficult to sustain the argument that Augustine believed in continuous creation.

(10) Augustine believed that Adam was "made from the slime of the earth and the woman from the side of her husband."[44] (6:5)

Ernan McMullin confirms that Augustine concurred with the Alexandrine fathers who believed that creation was in a single moment; he clearly did not believe that creation "days" were indefinitely long periods of time: "In fact, he insisted that the creative action whereby all things came to be was instantaneous; the six 'days' refer (he suggests) to stages in the angelic knowledge of creation. In properly temporal terms the 'days' reduce to an indivisible instant, so that all the kinds of things mentioned in Genesis were really made simultaneously."[45] Nor did Augustine "hold that one species could arise out of another."[46]

At best, when debaters try to convert Augustine into a theistic evolutionist who held to long unspecified days and continuous creation, they can be understood as presuppositionally selective in their choice of quotations; for even their choicest of citations do not prove their point, nor do other statements within the corpus prove compatible with such anachronisms. Even if the benefit of the doubt is given to interpretations which conform Augustine to the modern, other pre-Darwinian supporters of such interpretations are few and far between—certainly not the analogy of faith.

Augustine, Anselm, Lombard, and Aquinas are frequently alleged to have supported long days. John Collins confirms that: "Augustine and Anselm do not actually discuss the length of the creation days. . . . Certainly Augustine and Anselm cannot be called as witnesses in favor of a day-age theory."[47] Augustine having been discussed above, Anselm rarely drawn upon for this issue, and Lombard noted below,[48] suffice it to say that neither did Aquinas consistently nor explicitly hold to "long days."[49] Aquinas (1224-1274) believed: "The words *one day* are used when day is first instituted, to denote that one day is made up of twenty-four hours."[50] Moreover, he commented elsewhere: "But it [cosmos] was not made from

---

[43] Ibid., p. 117.

[44] Ibid., p. 183.

[45] Ernan McMullin, *Evolution and Creation* (Notre Dame: University of Notre Dame Press, 1985), pp. 11-12.

[46] Ibid., p. 15.

[47] Collins, op. cit., pp. 113-114.

[48] Shedd's citation of Lombard (*Dogmatic Theology*, p. 475) likely should be surrendered in light of the recent study and conclusions of Marcia Colish (*infra*).

[49] Collins admits that Hugh Ross's claim that Aquinas held to long days is mistaken, even though in other ways Aquinas did follow Augustine (op. cit., 125-126).

[50] St. Thomas Aquinas, *Summa Theologica* (London: Burns Oates & Washbourne, 1921), Q. 74, art. 3, p. 274.

something; otherwise the matter of the world would have preceded the world . . . Therefore, it must be said that the world was made from nothing."[51]

Later, one of the greatest medieval theologians, Peter Lombard, continued the analogy of faith on the subject of creation. Lombard, along with other contemporaries, recognized creation *ex nihilo*, Adam and Eve's special creation, and affirmed that "the Catholic faith believes that there was one principle, one cause of all things, namely God."[52] Moreover, Lombard affirmed the "essentially hexameral plan" of creation, taking a clear position that God: "creates the angels and the unformed matter *simul* and *ex nihilo*. Then, in the work of six days, he produces individual creatures out of the unformed matter . . . The days referred to in Genesis are to be understood literally as lasting twenty-four hours."[53] If one retains a proper understanding of the philosophical audiences and contexts of the great theologians prior to the Reformation, one discovers that a majority of orthodox commentators did not explicitly hold to long days, gradual development, or an old earth as is frequently claimed.[54]

John Calvin (1509-1564) had a quite consistent view of creation, speaking of it as a "mirror" through which the invisible God makes himself visible. He was quick to affirm: "God, by speaking, was Creator of the universe."[55] Moreover, Calvin agreed: "Indeed, the testimony of Moses in the history of creation is very clear" that God created out of "formless matter."[56]

Rather than speaking of continuous creation, Calvin noted that, "we are drawn away from all fictions to the one God who distributed his work into six days that we might not find it irksome to occupy our whole life in contemplating it."[57] He

---

[51] St. Thomas Aquinas, *Summa Theologica* (London: Burns Oates & Washbourne, 1921), Q. 46, art. 2, pp. 248-249.

[52] Marcia Colish, *Peter Lombard* (Leyden: E. J. Brill, 1994), vol. 1, pp. 330-331.

[53] Ibid., pp. 337, 340-341. Marcia Colish, a leading historian of medieval theology summarizes Lombard's ideas as follows: "According to Peter, God and God alone is the cause of creation *ex nihilo*. He rejects the idea of exemplary causes, however understood, along with preexistent matter. Further, he sees God as such as doing the whole work of creation . . . God cannot be equated with the forces of nature he creates . . . In all these respects, God transcends the world he creates." (Ibid.)

[54] In an appendix, David Kelsey collects a number of earlier opinions on the subject. Cf. his "The Doctrine of Creation from Nothing," Ernan McMullin ed., *Evolution and Creation* (Notre Dame: University of Notre Dame Press, 1985), pp. 192-195. He cites, among others, Anselm as affirming creation *ex nihilo*; the Fourth Lateran Council (1215): "Firmly we . . . confess . . . the true God . . . who by his own omnipotent power at once from the beginning of time created each creature from nothing . . ."; and The Council of Florence (1441): "God . . . is the creator of all things visible and invisible, who, when he wished, out of his goodness created all creatures, spiritual as well as corporal; good, indeed . . . since they were from nothing . . ."

[55] John Calvin, *The Institutes of the Christian Religion*, J. T. McNeill, ed. (Philadelphia: Westminster Press, 1960), 1.13.7. Citations to *The Institutes* are from this McNeill edition and are referenced by book, chapter, and section, e. g., 1.5.5 refers to Book 1, chapter 5, section 5.

[56] *The Institutes*, 1.13.14.

[57] *The Institutes*, 1.14.2.

repeatedly and consistently referred to Moses as "a sure witness and herald of the one God, the Creator."[58] Calvin also wrote: "[C]reation is not inpouring, but the beginning of essence out of nothing."[59]

In his major discussion of creation, Calvin began by stating agreement with earlier orthodox treatments of this subject by Basil and Ambrose (see above). Summarizing the "first history of the creation of the universe, as it has been set forth briefly by Moses," Calvin noted:

> From this history we shall learn that God by the power of his Word and Spirit created heaven and earth out of nothing; that thereupon he brought forth living beings and inanimate things of every kind, that in a wonderful series he distinguished an innumerable variety of things, that he endowed each kind with its own nature, assigned functions, appointed places and stations.[60]

The aim of his discussion was practical knowledge, i. e., to have the believer not merely know the truths about creation, but also to be led to praise of the Creator. God is so powerful that, far from six days being too short a span of time to create all the beauty around us, Calvin averred: "For it is not without significance that he divided the making of the universe into six days, even though it would have been no more difficult for him to have completed in one moment the whole work together in all its details than to arrive at its completion gradually by a progression of this sort."[61] In fine, *The Institutes* do not proffer a doctrine of progressive or theistic evolution nor creation from already existing matter.

Calvin's view may be confirmed from a perusal of his *Commentaries* on key verses. Commenting on Genesis 1:1, the Genevan reformer stated:

> When God in the beginning created the heaven and the earth, the earth was empty and waste. He moreover teaches by the word 'created,' that what before did not exist was not made . . . Therefore his meaning is, that the world was made out of nothing. Hence the folly of those is refuted who imagine that unformed matter existed from eternity; and who gather nothing else from the narration of Moses than that the world was furnished with new ornaments, and received a form of which it was before destitute.[62]

Commenting on the fifth day of creation, Calvin observed that even God's shaping of new life from that which does exist is praiseworthy: "Therefore, there is in this respect a miracle as great as if God had begun to create out of nothing those things which he commanded to proceed from the earth. And he does not take his material from the earth, because he needed it, but that he might the better combine

---

[58] Ibid.

[59] *The Institutes*, 1.15.5.

[60] *The Institutes*, 1.14.20.

[61] *The Institutes*, 1.14.22.

[62] John Calvin, *Commentary on Genesis* (Grand Rapids: Baker, 1979), 1:70.

the separate parts of the world with the universe itself."[63] Calvin did not preclude that God created out of existing elements; rather he was constrained to praise God for any and every mode of creation. However, praise for creation out of something in no way was intended to denigrate creation *ex nihilo*.

Calvin commented on Hebrews 11:3: "For they who have faith do not entertain a slight opinion as to God being the Creator of the world, but they have a deep conviction fixed in their minds and behold the true God. And further, they understand the power of his word, not only as manifested instantaneously in creating the world, but also as put forth continually in its preservation."[64] On this passage, he had noted earlier that "even infidels acknowledge" creation.[65] On Isaiah 40:22, Calvin observed: "Formerly he spoke of the creation of the world, but now he comes to the continual government of it; for God did not only for a single moment exert his power for creating the world, but he manifests his power not less efficaciously in preserving it. And this is worthy of observation; for our minds would be little impressed by knowing that God is the creator of the world, if his hand were not continually stretched out for upholding it in existence." Once again, in context, it is seen that Calvin—far from minimizing momentary creation—extolled it; but also urged upon the sanctified mind the importance of continually knowing God and his governance.

Interestingly, had Calvin wanted to lobby for "long days," two ideal verses presented themselves: Psalm 90:4 and 2 Peter 3:8. Oddly, while commenting on both of them, Calvin refrained from injecting the idea that the first days of creation could be as long as millennia. The exegesis which is becoming so common was avoided by earlier exegetes. These verses were not interpreted to satisfy certain scientific theories; rather they were interpreted simply to mean that God is above time. All in all, Calvin presents a rather consistent view on this subject, and it is antithetical to the modern attempts to recraft it after their own image.[66]

Martin Luther's view is largely uncontested, so explicit is it.[67] Numerous other citations could be assembled, but interestingly Luther is rarely misappropriated. It

---

[63] Ibid., p. 90.

[64] John Calvin, *Commentary on the Epistle to the Hebrews* (Grand Rapids: Baker, 1979), pp. 264-265.

[65] Ibid.

[66] His disciple, Theodore Beza, also affirmed that Hebrews 11:3 taught creation *ex nihilo*. Moreover, Beza explained: Mundum conditum ex nihilo: nemo potest compraehendere, quod ex eo quod non est fiat id quod est. ("The world is formed *ex nihilo*. We are not able to comprehend how from this which is not made, is that which is [made].") Cf. Theodore de Beze, *Cours Sur les Epitres aux Romains et aux Hebreaux (1564-1566)* in *Travaux d'Humanism et Renaissance* (Geneva: Library Droz, 1988), vol. 226, p. 311. Further, in his *Confession de Foi du Chretien* (1558), Beza affirmed that God the Father "has created all out of nothing" (2.2), and "We believe that he has not only created the visible world, the heaven and the earth and all that they contain, but also invisible spirits." (2.3; Cf. the English translation, *The Christian Faith* by James Clark (East Sussex: Christian Focus Ministries Trust, 1992), p. 3.

[67] Cf. e.g., Martin Luther, *Luther's Works*, vol. 17 (Concordia: St. Louis, 1972), 29, 118.

deserves to be stated, however, that the frequent omission of reference to Luther (and others) illustrates the selectivity of sources drawn upon. A search for the mainstream of orthodox interpretation on this subject should not omit Luther, even if he mitigated the propositions ardently maintained by modern revisionists.

These claims that ancient Christians believed in anything less than a strong view of special creation are akin to other revisionist efforts. Upon scrutiny, the claim is found to be indefensible, relatively recent, and more a function of accommodating ideology than historical accuracy. If the scientific method (hypothesis, experimentation, conclusion) is applied to the hypothesis: "Pre-Darwinian theologians admitted the possibility of a long period for creation," then such hypothesis is falsified by these experiments. Prior to Darwin, evangelicals did not recognize creation as occurring apart from the direct involvement of God intervening in space and time to initiate the cosmos. Robert Bishop concurs: "Neither the original audience of that book [Genesis] nor anyone else until about two hundred years ago would have understood a 'geological era' to be a meaningful concept."[68] There is scant evidence, if any, that prior to the nineteenth century any view of creation that accorded with macro-evolution was anything but aberrant.[69]

The point deserves stating: Apologists ought be leery of surrendering aspects of historic orthodoxy if for no other reason than yielding obeisance to current scientific theories. A vigilant apologetic, one based on sound principles, will not be so culture-accommodating. It will be less trusting of the human mind unaided by revelation and more suspect of the noetic effects of sin. It will also be an apologetic that guards against strategic concessions, especially those which claim to reinterpret history. This earlier apologetic was less accommodationistic than the post-Darwinian one.[70] Perhaps we should let the scientist, Isaac Newton, have the

---

[68] Robert C. Bishop, "Science and Theology: A Methodological Comparison" in *Journal of Interdisciplinary Studies*, vol. v, no. 1/2 (1993), p. 155.

[69] Similarly, C. S. Lewis noted that many ancient scientists knew many of the concepts that are considered quite modern. However, a historical discrimination often occurs, as Lewis noted: "Here is a simple historical falsehood. Ptolemy (*Almagest*, bk. I, ch. v) knew just as well as Eddington that the earth was infinitesimal in comparison with the whole content of space. There is not question here of knowledge having grown until the frame of archaic thought is no longer able to contain it. The real question is why the spatial insignificance of the earth, after being known for centuries, should suddenly in the last century have become an argument against Christianity. I do not know why this has happened; but I am sure it does not mark an increased clarity of thought, for the argument from size is, in my opinion, very feeble." C. S. Lewis, "Dogma and the Universe," *God in the Dock* (Grand Rapids: Eerdmans, 1970), p. 39. Cf. also, pp. 74, 99.

[70] John Collins, who has presented one of the more-researched and balanced studies of these issues, argues that William Shedd was more tolerant in this area. However, in keeping with my thesis, it must be noted that Shedd's claims were made nearly 30 years after Darwin and modern geological dating; thus indirectly supporting my central claim. While still holding high regard for Shedd in many *loci*, it appears that he fell in with Hodge, Warfield, and Dabney in committing this apologetic mistake. Collins's reference to John Macpherson's 1882 work is answered similarly.

final word on whether or not the days in Genesis 1 were fictitious. His view in 1681 may be gleaned from his comment: "methinks one of the Ten Commandments given by God in Mount Sinai, pressed by divers of the prophets, observed by our Savior, his Apostles, and first Christians for 300 years . . . should not be grounded on a fiction."[71]

Post-Darwin

Most modern American evangelicals have tremendous respect and admiration for nineteenth century stalwarts such as Charles Hodge and Benjamin B. Warfield. Yet, indebted as one may be, it is nonetheless curious to review one glaring weak link: they seemed oblivious to the danger of apologetic revision in the area of evolution. As intentionally orthodox as these were, still, they seem to have adopted aspects of secular scientific methodology rather uncritically. It appears that these angels were unaware of the inherent dangers of accommodation at this juncture. As Theodore Bozeman perceptively wrote at the conclusion of his book:

Collins raises challenging testimony to my thesis by his reference to William Ames (op. cit., p. 114). Collins suggests that Ames was certainly "not under pressure from modernism to allow for" six days, with "intervening spaces" between the days. However, an amplified translation of Ames' *Medulla Theologica* I, 8. 28 from the Latin edition (1634) is: "Creation [*creatio*] of these parts [*harum partium*, various parts of the creation; cf. I, 8, 27] of the world, however [*autem* signifies the connection to the previous paragraph], was not done simultaneously and in one moment [*contra* Augustine], but was accomplished through parts, each in its turn, succeeding in six days, with [normal] intervention [between each day]." Robert Bailey, a Latin instructor from Yazoo City, MS has kindly provided an accurate translation from Ames' original: "However, the creation of these parts of the world did not occur at the same time and in one moment, but it was accomplished through parts, succeeding themselves in the space of six intervening days." Macpherson's commentary on *The Westminster Confession of Faith* (1882) refracts Ames to support "that the active creative periods were six natural days, with indefinite intervals between them." However, it seems that this addition of "indefinite" is Macpherson's redaction, not so much a direct citation from Ames. Moreover, when section 28 is compared with the previous paragraph, it seems clear that the reference is not to creation *en toto*, but to the creation of various parts (*partes, partium*) of the cosmos. Thus, what Ames asserted was that—contrary to Augustine—the entire cosmos was not created *simul & uno momento* (simultaneously and in one moment); rather, the various *parts* were created "each in turn, succeeding in six days, with [normal] intervention [between each day]." If Ames is understood as opposing the Augustine/Alexandrine view that all six days of creation occurred in a singular instant, then Ames' claim is little more than a reaffirmation of Ambrose's (traditional) view. Further, insofar as Ames was not commonly understood as holding to long periods of creation (nor was that the majority view of the other testimony above), more than Macpherson's redaction is needed to prove that Ames had such a modern view.

Collins' appendix is honest, but not exhaustive. The references to Josephus and Irenaeus (as claimed by Hugh Ross) only show that they believed in a young earth. Collins' appendix contains no reference to Basil (also claimed by Hugh Ross), Ambrose, or Luther. Anselm, Aquinas, and Calvin are represented fairly.

[71] H. S. Thayer, ed. *Newton's Philosophy of Nature: Selections from his Writings* (New York: Hafner Publishing Company, 1953), pp. 64-65.

It may be questioned whether religious leaders at any previous point in the nation's past had achieved a more unabashed union of gospel and culture than this. Doubtless if the Old School could have foreseen Darwin or the triumph of a physics of forces undermining the older empiricism they would not have been so eager either to canonize Bacon or to embrace scientific endeavor as a natural patron of belief.[72]

Indeed, for Bozeman: "It is revealing that [other] prominent Old Schoolers . . . were now willing to suggest that if an 'indisputable' result of thorough induction manifestly contradicted an existing doctrine of the church, the theologian *must reconsider* his interpretation of God's word, and see if he has not misunderstood it. In view of the firm biblical literalism and the unbending confessionalism to which the Old School was committed, this was a substantial concession."[73] Science could at least *theoretically* have preeminence over Scripture—at least as an intermediate hermeneutic.

Hodge and other evangelicals had a categorically different attitude toward science than did another evangelical apologist, Abraham Kuyper.[74] In fact, Kuyper rebuked Hodge for conceding on this apologetic point.

Abraham Kuyper: An Apologetic Contrast and Earlier Critic

Jonathan Wells observes that as early as 1863 Hodge was indeed accused of "Remaining open to the possibility that Scripture would have to be re-interpreted in light of scientific evidence."[75] Further, the *New York Observer* accused Hodge of being guilty of letting "Science lead the way and the Bible followed."[76] On several occasions Hodge had to defend himself from his contemporaries that he was "not guilty of subordinating Scripture to science." Thus, in at least this one instance, other contemporaries suspected that Hodge could be "persuaded by scientific evidence to modify his interpretation of Scripture," and that he served to "reconcile Scripture with established scientific facts."[77] That Hodge was contouring the Bible to the findings of science is seen from his comment in an 1856 review: "If science should succeed in demonstrating that the earth is millions of years old, then we will with the utmost alacrity believe that the days of creation were periods of indefinite duration."[78]

---

[72] Theodore Bozeman, *Protestants in an Age of Science* (Chapel Hill, NC: University of North Carolina Press, 1977), p. 174.

[73] Ibid., p. 118.

[74] Cf. my "Angels Unaware: The Ascendancy of Science over Orthodoxy in Nineteenth Century Reformed Orthodoxy" in Timothy Phillips, *supra*.

[75] Jonathan Wells, "Charles Hodge on the Bible and Science," *Journal of Presbyterian History*, Fall 1988, vol. 66, no. 3, p. 161.

[76] Ibid., p. 160.

[77] Ibid., p. 161.

[78] Ibid., p. 160.

Although Hodge was at times able to resist the strong pull of certain scientific theories, still he exhibited a lofty "Confidence in the harmony of religion and science . . . [which led] to some extent, [to] the independence of science and religion."[79] Wells perceptively remarks: "Although Hodge died without conceding that evolution could be reconciled with the Bible, his theology contained the seeds for such a reconciliation."[80]

Another more potent criticism is contained in the criticism by Abraham Kuyper, a later contemporary of Hodge, who was greatly respected by the Princeton theologians. Abraham Kuyper implicitly and explicitly accused Hodge of conceding too much to the realm of autonomous fact. Kuyper at one point said, "There is, to be sure, a theological illusion abroad . . . which conveys the impression that, with the Holy Scripture in hand, one can independently construct his theology from this principium."[81] In this criticism, Kuyper was likely thinking of Hodge and others who championed scientific orthodoxy based on their presupposition of the finality of facticity.

Kuyper criticized Hodge by name in another section. He faulted Hodge for his "combination of facts and truths" which overthrows his own system. Kuyper said that Hodge demanded that the "theologian be the one to authenticate these truths."[82] Further, Kuyper accused Hodge of succumbing "to the temptation of placing Theology formally in line with the other sciences."[83] Continuing his critique, the Dutch theologian said: "The authentication of his facts brought him logically back again under the power of naturalistic science. And though as a man of faith he bravely resisted this, his demonstration lacked logical necessity . . . the entire subsequent development of theological study has actually substituted an utterly different object, has cut the historic tie that binds it to original theology, and has accomplished little else than the union of the sub-divisions of psychology and of historic ethnology into a new department of science, which does not lead to the knowledge of God, but aims at the knowledge of *religion* as a phenomenon in the life of humanity."[84]

Kuyper protested "every appearance of neutrality, which is after all bound to be dishonest at heart." In contrast to Hodge, Kuyper maintained that there could be no neutrality toward the scientific datum—an early form of a presuppositional apologetic. Ahead of his time, Kuyper was keen to note that even the knowing observer was not isolated from "the stream of history in which he moves," nor is this observer "able to make an all-sided and complete exhibition of the object of his investigation."[85]

---

[79] Ibid., p. 158.
[80] Ibid., p. 163.
[81] Abraham Kuyper, *Principles of Sacred Theology* (Grand Rapids: Baker, 1980), p. 574.
[82] Ibid., p. 318.
[83] Ibid.
[84] Ibid., p. 319.
[85] Ibid., pp. 49-50.

Whatever the root cause, Kuyper's apologetic approach to science was starkly different from that of Hodge. Kuyper consistently stressed the inescapability of the religious presupposition: "There is, therefore, no perception or observation possible, unless there is a receptivity for the object in our human consciousness, which enables our consciousness to grasp it after its nature and form."[86] Thus he would not allow evidence alone to speak by itself.

Kuyper spelled out the inherently presuppositional nature of science: "All prosecution of science which starts out from naturalistic premises denies the subjective fact of *palingenesis*, as well as the objective fact of a special revelation, which immediately corresponds to this."[87] Kuyper warned that not only is science affected by sin, but further science will be reduced if it does not acknowledge the effect of sin on its own varied behavior. He warned that sin "exercises a mighty dominion upon the whole content of our consciousness . . .—what used to be called one's life-and-world-view, by which the fundamental lines lie marked out in our consciousness."[88] Affirming the noetic effects of sin, he cautioned: "If, then, we make a mistake, or a single inaccurate move, how can it fail but communicate itself disastrously to our entire scientific study?"[89] He further warned, "that every scientific reproduction of the knowledge of God must fail, as long as this sense remains weakened and this impulse falsified in its direction . . . it will not do to omit the fact of sin from your theory of knowledge. . ."[90] Kuyper said, "sin modifies so largely all those data with which you have to deal in the intellectual domain and in the building-up of your science. Ignorance wrought by sin is the most difficult obstacle in the way of all true science."[91] So persuasive was the spread of sin that Kuyper must maintain, "it cannot be denied that a false representation of the real has made its way into almost every department of life . . ."[92] His was a superior apologetic in this instance; it estimated the observer's role as well as sheer evidence.

B. B. Warfield shortly thereafter plowed the same furrow. In a 1915 work entitled "Calvin's Doctrine of Creation," even Warfield is found defending one of the claims of modern science. One must marvel at Warfield's hermeneutical gymnastics as he tried to make Calvin into a proto-evolutionist. Warfield was to the point of saying: "Calvin doubtless had no theory of evolution; but he teaches a doctrine of evolution. He had no objection and so teaching it, cut to preserve the creative act . . ."[93] Warfield even speculated that had certain preconditions come

---

[86] Ibid., p. 71.
[87] Ibid., p. 224.
[88] Ibid., p. 109.
[89] Ibid., p. 110.
[90] Ibid., p. 113.
[91] Ibid., p. 114.
[92] Ibid.
[93] Mark Noll, ed., *The Princeton Theology, 1812-1921* (Phillipsburg, NJ: Presbyterian and Reformed Publishing Co., 1983), p. 298.

about "Calvin would have been a precursor of the modern evolutionary theorist."[94] In a footnote rebutting Herman Bavinck, Warfield concluded: "Calvin accordingly very naturally thought along the lines of a theistic evolutionism."[95] If one consults Calvin's *Institutes* or other Calvinalia, the possibility that Calvin might have been an evolutionist is quite remote.

It is a distinct irony that such stalwarts and defenders of orthodoxy as Hodge and Warfield were unwittingly part of the problem instead of part of the solution. That myopia reveals a structural deficiency in their apologetic. Perhaps this study will illuminate some of the warning signs of revisionism. We might do well to be a little more leery of an epistemology that seeks conformity to modernity. A naivete regarding scientific totalitarianism is beneficial neither for the progress of science or apologetics.

The point is that often as believers grapple with the epistemology of modernism they veer more toward true accommodation than true apologetics. In order to avoid this apologetic mis-step in the future, one must have a better apologetic methodology—one that is more resistant to the winds of modernity and its stepchild, revisionism.

Perhaps it has been underestimated: hand-to-hand combat apologetics is insufficient. Indeed, a purely evidentialistic approach will never bring about conclusive proof. One weakness of this method is the virtually naive acceptance of current cosmological theories. The preference for the inflationary version of the big bang theory may still concede too much priority to current-but-ever-changing theory. Would that the apologists' rigorous evidentialism not be forgotten when they examine these latest cosmologies, lest they fall into an uneasy alliance with contemporaneity. Evidentialists would do well to recall that these latest cosmologies may one day be disproven as well. The adopted evidentialistic posture guarantees that outmoded theories be discarded upon discovery of evidential novelty. Yet, along with that is also the canonization of the latest in empirical findings. Sadly, the evidentialist approach proves to be a two-edged sword. While it cuts the prior errors of cosmology, the blade swings back and eviscerates other accounts as Scripture is regrettably submitted to the newer evidences of the latest fads in cosmology, which themselves may be based on high proportions of theory and little observation.

A Plea for a More Cautious Reconstruction and a Humbler Apologetic

The recent dating of the universe at 7.3 billion years[96] means that some foundational premise of the cosmology that Hugh Ross, e. g., follows is faulty. With recent estimates trending toward a younger cosmos, theories are not given up

---

[94] Idem.
[95] Idem.
[96] *Newsweek*, Nov. 7, 1994, p. 55.

easily. At the latest date-setting, one commentator noted that astronomers could be fooled, "into believing that the universe got to its present size in less time than it really took. The effect is akin to measuring the average speed of a race-walker without realizing that she sprinted when no one was looking."[97] Would the evidentialist at some point serve the cause better by admitting that the evidence does not exist apart from a theory? Apparently, the theory itself is foundational.

In light of this evidentialistic flaw, two erroneous claims should be recognized as specious: (1) Ancient evangelicals did *not* propagate views compatible with theistic evolution or modern mutants of it; and (2) Some post-Darwinian evangelicals—even though stalwarts in many other areas—conceded at some points; but they should not necessarily be imitated. Thus, no norm from either period compels concession to modern claims, if respect for our earlier siblings is a criteria.

The proposed presuppositional apologetic also yields two other areas of benefit: (1) In evidentialism, the noetic effects of sin are understated, but should not be minimized. Remembering the biblical teaching on the fallenness of the will and the darkness of the heart (Eph. 4:17-19; 5:8), one should suspect that the majority of non-Christians will not easily affirm revealed truths based on mere evidences. Theoretically (and in practice) the set of excuses to deny biblically interpreted truths can be infinite, thus sheltering the unbeliever from ever conclusively and logically being convinced. One should not underestimate the fallen creativity that is capable of spawning a seemingly infinite number of substitutions for God (Rom. 1:21-25) rather than simply accepting and submitting to the only living God.

(2) It is unwise to concede to unbelieving notions—which is not the role of apologetics. This study has sought to show how it is also unfruitful. The earlier apologists did not concede at these points. We have no obligation from a fair reading of history to concede to revisionist views of creation.

Good science and good theology should be compatible. However, inaccurate history, theological revisionism, and inferior apologetics seldom advance the discussions. Both science and apologetics will be strengthened by more cautious and respectful treatments of the history of ideas and evidence. Neither science nor apologetics will proceed as well if they are more infatuated with the idea-fads of modernity than with the well-worn paths of truth. When certain scientific theories which were once treated with immunity from criticism *do finally tumble* from the weight of their own errors, one wonders if certain thinkers who are blindfolded to the past (not to mention the present) will still defend erroneous philosophical platforms. A small modicum of historical research can at least diminish the band wagon's peer pressure that expects everyone who is modern to affirm the dogmatic errors of inaccurate theories. Evidentialism hardly assists that cause, while the Kuyperian model above does. Of course, simply holding to the earlier orthodox interpretations could have spared much travail, too.

---

[97] Ibid.

Early Prototypes of Welfare Reform: The Reformation

In a thorny topic such as the church's role in social welfare, one is fearful to brave theories or make suggestions for reform without sensing he is out on a limb even if the limb is connected to the immovable root of Scripture. That very phobia, of course, is more related to the suffocating dogmatism of modernity which maintains that certain social programs should be afforded unamendable status than it is to a lack of confidence in Scripture. One of the stalwart aids in mature reflection on a subject like this is the employment of church history as a corroborating guide to the subject. In this brief study, I would like to present some of the principles and practices of welfare from a period nearly five centuries ago. One assumption is that over even long periods of time the human condition and social solutions are basically constant. Therefore, one is unwise to fail to benefit from what has successfully worked in other eras. This study highlights some of the best practice from three different traditions—the Calvinist, the Lutheran, and the Romanist. In our survey of the *first* tradition we concentrate on the contribution to the diaconate by John Calvin and others from the reformed tradition. The *second* part of this study switches to a northern European model derived from Luther and the early adherents to Lutheranism. And the *third* examination is a summary of the work of Juan Luis Vives, a leader of the Roman Catholic amelioration of poverty. Of these three, the Calvinistic tradition from this era provided the most substantial break and likely provided more influence in our own society; thus that tradition will be highlighted in more detail.

Jeannine Olson's fine historical work, *Calvin and Social Welfare: Deacons and the Bourse Francaise,*[1] provided a study of Calvin's impact on Reformation culture, particularly highlighting the enduring effect of Calvin's thought on the institution of the diaconate. In her treatise, she noted that, contrary to some modern caricatures, the reformers were not only sensitive to the need to protect institutions

---

[1] Published by Susquehanna University Press, 1989.

that fostered care for the poor, but also that the reformers worked diligently to shelter refugees and minister to the poor. The Bourse Francaise became a pillar of societal welfare;[2] indeed, this was one of Calvin's contributions to Western civilization. This diaconal ministry may have had nearly as much influence in Calvin's Europe as his theology did in other areas.

Calvin's welfare program in Geneva was contoured to the theological emphases of the reformers, providing an earlier illustration that welfare practice was and is (and still should be) erected upon definite principles that were religious or ideological in nature. Moreover, the theology of the Reformation was the guiding force for this welfare, just as the theology of medieval Roman Catholicism was the guiding principle for almsgiving. Ultimate principles contoured the practice of welfare 450 years ago as they do today, which is to say, that at no time is welfare truly divorced from underlying ideological values.

Of course, the Genevan model for welfare did not claim uniqueness; rather, it viewed itself as the culmination of a number of factors. Among other precedents, it saw itself built upon the earlier texts of the OT, the *Acts* narratives, and earlier canonical precedents (e. g., the Synod of Tours in 567 which assigned the responsibility of caring for the poor to each parish priest) describing the work of the diaconate. Thus the Bourse saw itself as standing on the shoulders of the work of Christians who had preceded.

The activities of the Bourse were numerous. Its diaconal agents were involved in housing orphans, the elderly, or those who were in any way incapacitated. They sheltered the sick, and dealt with orphans and those involved in immoralities. This ecclesiastical institution was a precursor to voluntary societies in the nineteenth and twentieth centuries.

The Bourse Francaise was founded under the leadership of John Calvin sometime between 1536 and 1541 (exclusive of the time of his Strassbourg exile). Its initial design was to appease the suffering brought onto French residents who, while fleeing sectarian persecution in France, came to Geneva. It has been estimated that in that single decade alone (1550-1560) some 60,000 refugees came through Geneva, a number significantly large to produce significant social stress.

Early on in the *Ecclesiastical Ordinances* first proposed in 1541, John Calvin had written a charter for the deacons, distinguishing them as one of the four basic offices. This Reformation church order stipulated that among the fourth biblical office, that of deacon, "There were always two kinds in the ancient Church, the one deputed to receive, dispense, and hold goods for the poor, not only daily alms, but also possessions, rents and pensions; the other to tend and care for the sick and administer allowances to the poor."[3] In addition, the 1542 charter prescribed, "It will be their duty to watch diligently that the public hospital is well maintained, and

---

[2] Jeannine Olson, *Calvin and Social Welfare: Deacons and the Bourse Francaise* (Cranbury, NJ: Susquehanna University Press), pp. 11-12.

[3] *Calvin Theological Treatises*, J. K. S. Reid, ed. (Philadelphia: Westminster, 1954), 64.

that this be so both for the sick and the old people unable to work, widowed women, orphaned children and other poor creatures. The sick are always to be lodged in a set of separate rooms from the other people who are unable to work . . . Moreover, besides the hospital for those passing through which must be maintained, there should be some attention given to any recognized as worthy of special charity."[4] In the conclusion of this section, Calvin advocated "to discourage mendicancy which is contrary to good order, it would be well, and we have so ordered it, that there be one of our officials at the entrance of the churches to remove from the place those who loiter; and if there be any who give offence or offer insolence to bring them to one of the Lords Syndic."[5] Begging without honest work was an affront to the biblical Protestant work. With sophistication of adminis-tration and discrimination of root causes among physical needs, this model can still inform our practice today.

Calvin was so interested in seeing the diaconate flourish that Calvin not only left an inheritance for his family in his will but also provided for the Boys School and poor strangers.[6] Yet, this Bourse was not an entirely new institution, although its roots were decidedly connected to the theology and the experience of Geneva. The deacons cared for a large range of needs, not wholly dissimilar to the strata of welfare needs in our own society.

In the 1541 *Ecclesiastical Ordinances* of Geneva, Calvin recommended a strong role for the diaconate, especially in almsgiving. After two decades, those *Ecclesiastical Ordinances* were revised in 1561. A recent translation of the 1561 *Ecclesiastical Ordinances* shows the sophistication and refinement of the diaconate even prior to the death of Calvin.[7] The following sections taken from the 1561 revision make clear that ministry to the poor was significant and well-ordered in Calvin's time. It was neither a low priority nor slip-shod in organization. The Swiss and French Reformed churches were agreed on "The Fourth Order of the Ecclesiastical Government, the Deacons," which was chartered as follows in the 1561 revision:

56. There were always two kinds in the ancient church: some delegated to receive, dispense and conserve the goods of the poor, daily alms as well as possessions, allowances, and pensions; others to attend to and care for the sick and administer the daily pittance. (It is indeed right for all Christians cities to conform to this, as we have tried to do and intend to continue [doing] in the future.) For we have trustees and hospital administrators; and to avoid confusion, let one of the four trustees of the hospital be the receiver of all the

---

[4] Ibid., p. 65.

[5] Ibid., p. 66.

[6] Cited by Geoffrey Bromiley, "The English Reformers and Diaconate," *Service in Christ* (London: Epworth Press, 1966), p. 113.

[7] Cf. Mary Crumpacker, "Ecclesiastical Ordinances, 1561," David W. Hall and Joseph H. Hall, eds., *Paradigms in Polity* (Grand Rapids: Eerdmans, 1994), pp. 148-149.

possessions of the above, and let him have funds sufficient to perform his task better.

57. Let the number of four stewards remain as it has been: one of whom will have charge of receipts, as stated, both that provisions may be laid in more promptly and also that those who wish to give alms to the poor may be more certain that the goods will not be used otherwise than they intended. And if the revenue were not sufficient, or even if it exceeded extraordinary necessity, let the Synod advise adjustment in accordance with the poverty they observe . . .

60. It will be necessary to watch carefully that the common hospital is well maintained and that it is as much for the sick as for the elderly who are unable to work, such as widows, young orphans, and other poor. However, the sick shall be kept together in a lodging apart and separated from the others.

61. Item, let the care of the poor who are scattered throughout the city return there as the trustees direct.

62. Item, besides the hospital for transients, which needs to be retained, there shall be some ward apart from those perceived to be especially deserving of charity; and to accomplish this, there shall be a room reserved for their use . . .

64. Let the ministers, commissioners or elders with one of the Syndics take the responsibility for inquiring whether in the above-mentioned administration of the poor there be any fault or indigence, in order to beseech and warn the Synod to settle the matter. And to do this, some of their company with the stewards shall visit the hospital quarterly to ascertain whether all is in good order.

65. It will also be necessary for the poor of the hospital as well as those of the city who have no way of helping themselves to have a doctor and a qualified surgeon on the city's payroll who, even if they practice in the city, were nevertheless engaged to care for the hospital and visit the other poor.

66. And because not only the old and sick are taken to our hospital but also young children because of their poverty, we have ordered that there always be a teacher to instruct them in morality, and in the rudiments of the letters and Christian doctrine. For the most part, he shall catechize, teaching the servants of the aforesaid hospital and conduct the children to the college.

67. As to the hospital for infectious diseases, it shall be entirely separate, especially if the city happens to have been visited by some scourge from God.

68. Moreover, to prevent begging, which is contrary to good order, it will be necessary (and so we have ordered) that the Synod station some of its officers at the exits of the churches to remove those who would like to beg, and if they resist or are recalcitrant to take them to one of the Syndics. Similarly for the rest of the time let the leaders of the groups of ten see to it that the prohibition on begging is well observed.

The deacons actively encouraged a productive work ethic. They provided interim subsidy and job-training as necessary; on occasion, they even provided the necessary tools or supplies so that an able-bodied person could engage in an honest vocation. They were discriminating as they ascertained the difference between the truly needy and the indigent. If necessary, they would also suspend subsidy. Over time, they developed procedures that would protect the church's resources from being pilfered, even requiring new visitors to declare their craft and list character witnesses to vouch for their honesty.[8] Within a generation of this welfare work, the diaconate of Geneva discovered the need to communicate to recipients the goal that they were to return to work as soon as possible.

In sixteenth century Geneva, there were cases of abandonment; the Bourse was frequently called upon to raise children. They supported the terminally ill who also left their children to be supported. Special gifts were given to truly needy children. The Bourse also included a ministry to widows who often had dependent children and a variety of needs.

Still, it must be noted that although the Bourse resembled many other contemporary welfare funds, it had its own peculiarities. Naturally there were theological peculiarities, and these theological distinctives led to certain practical commitments. For example, there were no guaranteed food hand-outs. Furthermore (as I note later), there were certain pre-requisites for receiving care, including the possibility that certain moral deficiencies would nullify the opportunity to be assisted by the Bourse.

The Bourse was not concerned only with spiritual or internal needs. On many occasions they hired medical doctors to take care of the ill. Their records indicate that the deacons oversaw medical care for the needy, reflecting that the full scope of diaconal ministry was not limited only to evangelism. Those who led the Bourse were also prudent. By January of 1581, the Bourse adopted a set of constitutional rules underscoring the need to have a vital and well thought out disciplined approach to poverty amelioration.[9]

For our own times it is perhaps instructive to note that in Calvin's era social welfare was not totally egalitarian. Olson notes:

> There was an effort in Geneva to maintain the image of the Bourse Francaise as a fund to help people who were considered worthy, rather than as an institution that indiscriminately aided everyone. The funds were intended for those who were in genuine need, particularly those who were ill or handicapped. The deserving poor were numerous in this age before modern medicine or surgery, when a simple hernia or poorly aligned broken bone could render one unable to work. The limited funds of the Bourse were not intended for derelict poor, those who are considered unwilling to work, lazy and slothful vagrants and vagabonds, to use the popular English terminology of the era. The assumption that welfare recipients should be worthy of aid had long been common in Europe, but the definition of worthiness varied from one milieu to another.[10]

---

[8] Olson, op. cit., pp. 39-40.

[9] Ibid., pp. 104-106.

[10] Ibid., p. 139.

Despite the rigor with which the deacons distinguished between the deserving and undeserving poor, charity motivated these to err on the side of generosity. Still, however, there were times and instances in the records of the Bourse when the deacons would not give assistance to those because of attitudinal or moral blights. Charity did not imply a style of giving that mitigated against personal industry and responsibility. There were a number of instances in which if one were to behave immodestly or unchastely then he/she would not receive certain aid. Recipients of subsidy were expected to uphold Christian standards of morality; if not, the Bourse might well withhold support until immoral behavior was jettisoned. The deacons attempted to use the Bourse as a means of discipline and encouragement.

In his *Commentaries,* Calvin also consistently set forth similar principles. On 2 Thessalonians 3:10, Calvin commented, "When, however, the Apostle commanded that such persons should not eat, he does not mean that he gave commandment to those persons, but forbade that the Thessalonians should encourage their indolence by supplying them with food . . . Paul censures those lazy drones who lived by the sweat of others, while they contribute no service in common for aiding the human race."[11] In commenting on Psalm 112:9, the Genevan reformer elaborated,

> . . . by dispersing [to the poor], the prophet intimates, that they did not give sparingly and grudgingly, as some do who imagine that they discharge their duty to the poor when they dole out a small pittance to them, but that they give liberally as necessity requires and their means allow; for it may happen that a liberal heart does not possess a large portion of the wealth of this world . . . Next he adds, they give to the poor, meaning that they do not bestow their charity at random, but with prudence and discretion meet the wants of the necessitous. We are aware that unnecessary and superfluous expenditure for the sake of ostentation is frequently lauded by the world; and consequently, a larger quantity of the good things of this life is squandered away in luxury and ambition than is dispensed in charity prudently bestowed. The prophet instructs us that the praise which belongs to liberality does not consist in distributing our goods without any regard to the objects upon whom they are conferred, and the purposes to which they are applied, but in relieving the wants of the really necessitous, and in the money being expended on things proper and lawful.[12]

Thus the experiment in welfare in Geneva offers a clinic in what may happen when welfare is conformed to biblical impulses.

It is helpful to remember also that the Bourse Francaise was a transitional institution. Occurring at the consummation of centuries of medieval welfare, yet renewed by the Protestant Reformation, the founders of the Bourse did not hold to the utopian notion that poverty would be entirely eliminated. In reference to Jesus' statement in Mark 14:7 ("you will always have the poor with you"), these founders

---

[11] *Calvin's Commentaries (*rpr. Grand Rapids: Baker, 1979), vol. xxi, p. 355.
[12] *Calvin's Commentaries* (rpr. Grand Rapids: Baker, 1979), vol. vi. pp. 328-329.

of the Genevan Diaconate were realists who consulted the past as they formed new manifestations of earlier models. As reformers they were most attracted to the institution of the early church, finding that model most fruitful for their reforms. These reformers lived on a cusp of a reform movement, learning from what had gone before them.

As those who look to the past and to the inadequacies of the present, perhaps we should replicate some of that posture, too. We might be better off from this and other studies to see what we can learn from the past, rather than looking exclusively to the future. In fact, if we find ourselves advocating practices markedly different from what the Bourse in Geneva did nearly five centuries ago, then it may be that our novel methods should be suspect to the extent that we deviate from earlier sound practice in the area of public welfare.

In summary thus far, we have seen the following as principles of Reformation welfare reform:

1) It was only for the truly disadvantaged.
2) Moral prerequisites accompanied assistance.
3) Private or religious charity, not state largesse, was the vehicle for aid.
4) Ordained officers managed and brought accountability.
5) Theological underpinnings were normal.
6) Productive work ethic was sought.
7) Assistance was temporary.
8) History is valuable.

Another study confirms many of these points. Emphasizing the value of historical studies, Elsie McKee comments:

> Before one can reform or even evaluate some part of life, whether individual or corporate, it is important to understand how present practices developed. What other ages have taught and done is not necessarily normative for the twentieth century, but failure to understand what we have inherited can make us puppets of the unknown past. It can also deny us the gifts of the faith and the wisdom of the communion of the saints.[13]

Moreover, McKee's own study independently corroborates the previously noted "work ethic," as she explains one difference between the Reformed and Romanist approaches to welfare:

> From this Protestant viewpoint, Roman Catholic almsgiving to healthy beggars who could work seemed indiscriminate; it was not charity but irresponsible stewardship. The new valuation of work—not as a means of earning or even proving salvation but as an expression of gratitude and responsible use of God-

---

[13] Elsie McKee, *Diakonia in the Classical Reformed Tradition and Today* (Grand Rapids: Eerdmans, 1989), p. xi.

given talents—was clearly a critical factor in the prohibition of begging among Protestants.[14]

In her more thorough scholarly treatment, *John Calvin on the Diaconate and Liturgical Almsgiving*,[15] McKee notes the emphasis on the role of the diaconate in ministering to the poor in Calvin's thought as follows:

> The portion of John Calvin's ecclesiology known as the office of the diaconate is, paradoxically, a doctrine as important as it is neglected. The modern Reformed tradition suffers ecclesiologically for this amnesia, but the importance of this doctrine is glimpsed also in scholarly controversies agitating other disciplines of modern research . . . Not infrequently, Calvin—or rather, fragments of Calvin—figure in one or another of these scholarly debates. However accurately quoted the fragments may be, they sometimes make limited theological sense because their full context is not seen or at least not made clear . . . despite the relative lack of emphasis on it, Calvin's teaching on the diaconate is a coherent and not insignif-icant theological development. Studied alongside his equally neglected views on liturgical almsgiving, this doctrine answers apparently diverse questions by showing their mutual relationships within the single doctrine of the Church; its development also contributes to a richer understanding of Reformed ecclesiology.[16]

Much of McKee's treatise includes numerous references to other contemp-orary reformers whose writings reveal a consensual teaching on the need and scripturalness of the office of deacon ministering to the poor. McKee notes, for example, that John á Lasco's *Forma ac ratio* (1555, London 1550) actually associated the final benediction with the collection of alms by deacons stationed at the doors of the church, viz.:

> Then, a psalm having been sung, the whole church is dismissed in peace by the preacher, with the commendation of the poor and the blessing, in these words: 'Remember your poor and let each in turn pray for the others. And may God have mercy on you and bless you. May the divine countenance shed his light upon you for the glory of his holy name, and keep you in his holy and saving peace. Amen.'
> When, however, these things are said by the preacher, the deacons according to their turns place themselves in order at the doors of the church, and after the church is dismissed, they diligently collect alms at the very doors of the church, and immediately they write down whatever they have collected, in the church itself. Moreover, this is also customarily always observed in all other gatherings of the church.[17]

---

[14] McKee, *Diakonia*, p. 54.

[15] Elsie Anne McKee, *John Calvin on the Diaconate and Liturgical Almsgiving* (Geneva: Librarie Droz, 1984). The references in parentheses for the next three pages are to this work.

[16] Ibid., p. 13.

[17] Ibid., p. 40.

Moreover, she notes that the same was "also the practice in the order of service used by Martin Micronius in London (1554) and Eastfriesland (1565). In a brief pamphlet (1551), Peter Paul Vergerio described the worship of the London Strangers' Church . . . [á Lasco's liturgy], which associates the final blessing with a collection at the door." [18]

Even Phillippe Mornay at the end of the century described the practice of the reformed community in France as set out in the church order proposed at Poitiers in 1557: "The collection for the poor shall be made at each preaching, at the end, and the said collection shall be written down by the hand of the minister on the paper of the deacons and kept by the said deacons to be placed in the hands of the treasurer on the day of the consistory meeting." [19]

In a sermon on 1 Timothy 3:8-10, Calvin associated the early church's compassion as the canon to measure our Christianity: "When there were neither lands nor possessions nor what is called property of the church, it was necessary that each give his offering and from that the poor be supplied. If we want to be considered Christians and want it to be believed that there is some church among us, this organization must be demonstrated and maintained." Later in that same sermon he enjoined, "Now when that property has been distributed as it ought, if that still does not meet all needs, let each give alms privately and publicly, so that the poor may be aided as is fitting.

The testimony of Calvin is quite full. In one of his sermons on 1 Timothy 3:8-13, he remarked:

> We saw this morning what position St. Paul discusses here, that is, that of those who in the ancient church were ordained to distribute the alms. It is certain that God wants such a rule observed in His church: that is, that there be care for the poor—and not only that each one privately support those who are poor, but that there be a public office, people ordained to have the care of those who are in need so that things may be conducted as they ought. And if that is not done, it is certain that we cannot boast that we have a church well-ordered and according to the gospel, but there is just so much confusion. [20]

Later in the same source, Calvin commented, "And yet the deacons are those ordained to have the care of the poor and to distribute alms, the care not only of distributing what is entrusted to them, but of inquiring where there is need and where the property ought to be used . . . We must find people who may govern the property of the poor. These are the sacrifices offered to God today, that is, alms. Therefore it is necessary that they be distributed by those whom God considers suitable for such a position, and that the deacons who are chosen should be as the

---

[18] Ibid., pp. 40-41.
[19] Ibid., p. 40.
[20] Ibid., p. 183.

hands of God, and be there in a holy office."[21] So strong was Calvin's view that he preached,

> Inasmuch as it is a question of the spiritual government which God has put among His own, St. Paul wants those who are ordained, whether to proclaim the gospel or to have the care of the poor, to be of irreproachable life . . . We must carefully note these passages where it is proclaimed to us what order God has established in His Church, so that we may take care to conform ourselves to it the best we can . . . Because if we want to have the Church among us, we must have this government which God has established as inviolable, or at least we must strive to conform ourselves to it.[22]

Calvin, whose name is not always and immediately identified with compassionate advocacy for welfare to the poor, even on one occasion rhetorically asserted, "Do we want to show that there is reformation among us? We must begin at this point, that is, there must be pastors who bear purely the doctrine of salvation, and then deacons who have the care of the poor."

Commenting on Romans 12:8, John Oecolampadius made this point about deacons and ministry to the poor:

> Sixth, those who show mercy, who differ in this way. For those who give mutually, and form their own means supply the hungry and the naked, are said to impart. And these ought to give simply and freely, without respect for temporal concerns, or friendship, or convenience. Those indeed who visit the sick and captives and are present with the afflicted are called those who show mercy, and their office ought to be done with a cheerful spirit and with promptness. Seventh are those who preside in any congregation; these ought to be courteous and diligent . . .[23]

McKee summarizes the Genevan practice as follows:

> Two or three things about most Protestants' almsgiving are notably different from the late medieval equivalent. One is the new organization, the coordination and centralization. This, however, was common to Roman Catholic as well as Protestant charity, and became universal. Another point is the matter of the poor begging for alms, whether in church or in the streets. . . . Protestants permitted only designated people to collect alms for the poor . . . A third point, however, the fact that Protestant almsgiving was repeatedly, explicitly or implicitly associated with the central official act of worship, distinguishes it from sixteenth century Roman Catholicism as well as from the late medieval church. Among the great majority of the Reformed churches, an alms collection became part of the regular worship order. . . . The common custom was a collection at the door, and it is probable that at least in a significant number of cases this was associated with a

---

[21] Ibid., p. 184.
[22] Idem.
[23] Ibid., p. 191.

concluding exhortation to remember the poor. It seems probable that Calvin himself collected alms during his Strasbourg Communion service, and it is certain that he believed no person should come before God empty-handed. . . . At least for the Reformed tradition, an adequate understanding of the relationship of worship and benevolence can be more fully, perhaps, better, achieved by an investigation of the diaconate. It is the doctrine of the diaconate which determines the ecclesiastical or civil nature of charity in the sixteenth century.[24]

The emphases of Calvin lived on after his death. Even one of the adversaries of Theodore Beza (Calvin's disciple), Jean Morely, affirmed a strong role for the church to care for those in poverty. In his 1562 *Treatise on Christian Discipline*, Morely asserted that in some organized manner, the church should "relieve the poor, and property should be set aside for its support. For poverty creates temptations to vice and corruption which few can resist. . . . In fact many of the arrangements are designed primarily to keep the able-bodied but indolent poor from receiving aid on a regular basis, so that all the church's resources for poor relief can go to those victims of circumstance who are deserving and helpless"[25]

Of all the reformers, Martin Bucer was considered the "theologian of the diaconate" since he wrote most directly about the function of the church in caring for the poor. Bucer argued in his 1560 *De Regno Christi* that, "there must be in the 'Christian Republic' a thorough organization of poor relief and assistance to the sick . . . for the fulfillment of these ends discipline is essential, and so there must be a thorough organization of labour and leisure."[26]

For a slightly fuller description of Bucer's view of the diaconate, Basil Hall records:

'Deacons are joined to the ministry of bishops and presbyters to minister to them and especially to care for the poor,' he wrote in his commentary on Ephesians 4. In *De Vera Animarum Cura* he wrote that 'the *officium et munus* of Deacons . . . is for the sustaining of the poor . . . Private men, great or small in condition, must contribute to the work of God in the Churches, both from their immovable and movable goods . . . [the Deacons are] diligently to distribute from this to all the poor in the Church, whether local people or strangers.' Butzer, thereafter, having referred with approval to *pulchra iudicia* in the Epistles of St. Gregory—*qui pius fuit Romanus pontifex*—on the subject of the work of deacons, added indignantly, 'this office and function are now in the Church, alas, wholly fallen in ruins through pontifical tyranny . . . so that few if any who are Deacons . . . know what their office and function should be . . . they think that their only duty is to sing the Gospel and Epistle at Mass.' In his commentary on Ephesians 4, Butzer showed that *diakonia* relates specifically to serving others and has nothing to do with

[24] Ibid., p. 65.

[25] Cited in Robert M. Kingdon's *Geneva and the Consolidation of the French Protestant Movement, 1564-1572* (Madison, WI: Univ. of Wisconsin Press, 1967), p. 56.

[26] Basil Hall, "Diaconia in Martin Butzer," *Service in Christ* (London: Epworth Press, 1966), p. 94.

'otiose and vain titles of dignity' whose holders despoil the goods of the Church to ignoble ends.[27]

Bucer went so far as to say of the diaconate that "without it there can be no true communion of saints,"[28] while simultaneously believing that, "The first duty of the deacons is to distinguish between the deserving and undeserving poor, for the former to inquire carefully into their needs; the latter, if they lead disorderly lives at the expense of others, to expel them from the community of the faithful. Care, next, is to be taken for needy widows. The second duty of deacons is to keep a written record of accounts, having sought diligently for the proper collecting of funds from all the parishioners according to their capacity."[29]

In the British Isles, almsgiving was emphasized as one means for poverty relief. King Edward VI would assert that, "to relieve the poor is . . . a true worshiping of God."[30]

John Knox continued this Reformation tradition of ministry to the poor in Scotland. In the Second Book of Discipline (1578), the Scottish emphasis can be seen from the following stipulations, codified in the Scottish book of government:

"Of Deacons and Their Office, the Last Ordinary Function [Office] of the Church. (chapter VIII)
1. The word *diakonos* sometimes is largely taken comprehending all them that bear office in the ministry and spiritual function [office] of the church.
2. But now as we speak, it is taken only for them to whom the collection and distribution of the alms of the faithful and the ecclesiastical goods does appertain.
3. The office of the deacon so taken is an ordinary and perpetual ecclesiastical function [office] of the church of Christ. . . .
6. Their office and power is to collect and distribute the whole ecclesiastical goods unto those to whom they are appointed."[31]

Earlier the Scots Confession (1560) in chapter 28 stipulated: "Now the true use of the ecclesiastical goods was, and now is, to maintain learning in schools and in holy assemblies, with all the service, rites, and buildings of the Church; finally, to maintain teachers, scholars, and ministers, with other necessary things, and *chiefly for the succor and relief of the poor* (emphasis added) . . . Therefore, we teach that schools and colleges whereunto corruption is crept in doctrine, in the

---

[27] Ibid, p. 98.
[28] Ibid, p. 99.
[29] Idem.
[30] Cited by Geoffrey Bromiley in "The English Reformers and Diaconate," *Service in Christ*, (London: Epworth Press, 1966), p. 120.
[31] Cf. David Hall, "The Second Book of Discipline, 1578," David W. Hall and Joseph H. Hall, *Paradigms in Polity* (Grand Rapids: Eerdmans, 1994), p. 243 for a modern translation.

service of God, and in manners, must be reformed; and that there provision should
be made, piously, faithfully, and wisely for the relief of the poor."

Hence the Calvinistic tradition was settled and fairly uniform in their institutionalization of the care for the poor. It was an ecclesiological function to be carried
out by spiritual officers according to biblical standards and principles. As it was
carried out well, it cared for the poor, employed the church's gifts, encouraged a
productive work ethic, and relieved governmental stewardship in this area. As
Bromiley summarizes, "the able-bodied should work and support themselves . . .
The answer to poverty was still found in individual benevolence exercised either
privately or through the Church."[32]

Luther in Germany

Nor did the other magisterial reformer Martin Luther fail to translate his faith into
practice in the area of poverty relief. As early as 1520, in his *Address to the
German Nobility*, Luther "strongly disapproved of any and every kind of
mendicancy and beggary and advised every town to assume responsibility for its
own poor and needy by appointing an official to advise the pastor."[33] Begging was
to be eliminated as its erstwhile theological foundation crumbled under Dr.
Martin's *sola fides* theology. Begging could no longer be viewed as a monastic
ideal, as a meritorious work, nor as Christian perfection. Instead, it was to be
curtailed as much as possible by a proper theological correction. Begging would be
eradicated with the care for the poor assigned to each small unit of governing—the
individual city. In his *Babylonian Captivity* (1520), Luther saw the church through
its diaconate as the agency to minister to the poor, in contrast to the role of deacons
within Roman Catholicism: "The diaconate . . . is a ministry, not for reading the
Gospel and the Epistle, as the practice is nowadays, but for distributing the
Church's bounty to the poor, in order that the priests might be relieved of the
burden of temporal concerns and give themselves more freely to prayer and the
Word."[34] In Strassburg, "we find as early as 1523 a thorough evangelical organization under the care of a director, four assistant directors, nine church workers
with twenty-one helpers. Here it was stipulated that the poor were not only to be
helped materially but to be visited as persons at least four times in a year."[35]
Ministry to the poor by the church was not a later development for the reformers.

A few outstanding cities are both exemplary and reflective of the value of
Lutheran welfare. In 1522 in Wittenberg, Luther helped sponsor a church
ordinance that provided for a common chest to assist the poor. It would, however,
be a gross error to fail to comprehend the theological rooting of the practice of

---

[32] Bromiley, op. cit., p. 113.

[33] James Atkinson, "Diaconia at the Time of the Reformation," *Service in Christ* (London:
Epworth Press, 1966), p. 84.

[34] Ibid., p. 86.

[35] Idem.

diakonia imbedded firmly in Luther's conception of justification by faith. As James Atkinson has observed:

> It is important to bear in mind that Luther's teaching on *diaconia* was the sequel of a precise theological formulation. It was neither a return to the ways of the primitive Church of Acts, nor was it an attempt to cope with the immense social problem of beggary maintained by catholic merit-earning practice. In effect it did restore primitive convictions and practice, and it also, by its teaching on justification by faith, caused works as a means of grace to wither away and work as a means of grace to rehabilitate itself. Nevertheless these were only fruits of a profound theological revolution.[36]

These poverty relief ministries were consistent outgrowths of theoretical bases. Shortly thereafter, Luther also helped establish a form of diaconal welfare through Karlstadt as Wittenberg drew up an "Ordinance for a common purse" dividing the cities into four quarters each with a trusted citizen disbursing the welfare in those quarters.[37] By 1533, the ecclesiastical protocol for the diaconate was more developed. In Leiznig, "The common chest supported the poor living in their homes, cared for and fed orphans, apprenticed and educated children, provided dowries for marriageable girls, and lent money to worthy artisans and merchants. Luther also suggested that the citizens of Leiznig establish schools for boys and girls in monastery buildings."[38]

In the *Church Order of Brunswick* (1528), Luther stressed the following:

> Before all things, it is necessary to provide for three things: first, to set up good schools for the children; next, to appoint preachers who shall deliver God's word pure to the people, and to secure the teaching of Latin and the exposition of holy Scripture for the learned; thirdly, to furnish Common Chests with the Church good and other offerings from which the service of the church may be kept up and the needs of the poor relieved. . . How necessary these first three things are, to set up schools, to ordain preachers, and to maintain them and the poor out of the Common Chests in hereinafter set forth; . . .
>
> First, of the Poor-Chests. In all large parishes there shall openly stand a Common Chest for the indigent, the poor, and others in need. To it shall come all free-will offerings which men shall put therein throughout the year, as each is disposed; item, all bequests and benefactions: item, the customary offerings on St. Auctor's day . . . ; item, if any one wishes to have the bells rung at a death . . . the money for the ringing (save what is due the sexton) shall be put into the Poor-Chest; item, whatever pious Christian people can devise for the help of these chests shall belong thereto; item, the Deacons of the Poor shall . . . go round on holydays before and after the sermon in church with bags whereon shall be a little bell so that they need not ask but that the people shall hear that they are there . . .

---

[36] James Atkinson, *Diaconia at the Time of the Reformation, Service in Christ supra*, 81.

[37] Jeannine Olson, op. cit., p. 162.

[38] Ibid., p. 163.

and preachers shall in their sermons recommend such service of the poor as Divine Service . . . For these chests there shall be chosen three Deacons by the Council and by the members of the Commune in the district . . . The Deacons shall keep an account of their receipts and expenditure, and a list of the names and houses of those who from week to week are in need of assistance, so that their reckoning may be the simpler and clearer. . . . Every Sunday, or other appointed day in the week, the Deacons shall meet together in each parish to distribute to the poor according to need, and to consider what is necessary for each sick or poor man. And when there is no money there, or too little, the preacher shall warn the people to come to the assistance of the Common Chest . . .

Of the Church-Chest. In each large parish there shall also stand a Church-Chest in the sacristy, wherein the overseers of Treasurers shall place the alms of their church, as follows . . . [These funds were to pay for the ministry] [39]

In another part of Luther's Germany (Nuremberg) perhaps the most famous system of Lutheran welfare systems was developed. Nuremberg was so notorious for its social advances that even the Catholic humanist Juan Louis Vives sought to imitate many of their principles. Even Charles V wished to consult Luther's Nuremberg social structure as he devised his own plans.[40] Reform in Nuremberg actually commenced as early as 1522 with a complete system of relief for the poor being enacted by ordinance on July 24, 1522. At Nuremberg, the typically Lutheran collection boxes or cauldrons were then put in places quite visible and near the church with their funds to be distributed by the leaders of the respective communities.

Zurich also was a model for social welfare. The city began its reform and its diaconal ministry as early as 1520. The same may be said for Strassburg and other cities in Lutheran territory. For example, "[i]n Strassburg, preaching of welfare reform began before the Protestant Reformation. Geiler Von Kaysersberg urged a new system of poor relief that included a suggestion that able-bodied people should work. Only those incapable of work, he argued, should receive relief."[41] Remembering that when exiled from Geneva, Calvin spent two years in the late 1530s in Strassburg, it is possible that these other Swiss reformed models could have indeed shaped, in no small part, the welfare relief model of Geneva. Luther, it should also be remembered, was opposed to hand-outs without responsibility or true demonstration of need. He earthily quipped, "Do not spoonfeed the masses. If we were to support Mr. Everybody, he would turn too wanton and go dancing on the ice."[42] According to Luther, the "poor by their own folly" were not deserving of help.

---

[39] B. J. Kidd, *Documents Illustrating the Continental Reformation* (Oxford: Clarendon Press, 1911) pp. 230-233.

[40] Olson, op. cit., p. 163.

[41] Ibid., p. 165.

[42] Cited by Geoffrey Bromiley in "The English Reformers and Diaconate" in *Service in Christ* (London: Epworth Press, 1966), p. 112.

Besides requiring careful safeguards and an annual audit, Atkinson summarizes the biblical principles in Martin Luther's welfare reform:

> Vagrant scroungers, the workshy, and ne'er-do-wells were treated with firmness: help was given, but only at minimum levels with the maximum of good counsel! The deacons were always predisposed to help or even to re-establish a genuine worker. There was always a remedial touch to their activities, and where a man was the victim of his own sin, careful consideration was given as to the reformation of his character and habits. Deacons were expected to know all their needy personally, and the unknown poor needed very respectable credentials to be helped. Poor folk genuinely traveling were helped (as residents), and were not classed as vagrants. It was generally accepted as normal practice that relatives should help their own, and each had a Christian responsibility to his own neighbour, apart from the official responsibility of the deacons.[43]

Lest the Lutheran approach be thought of as stingy, it has been noted,

> What is particularly impressive about this work is the real concern for the genuinely sick, particularly to women in childbirth. Careful allowances are given to midwives and to home help for the mother. Genuine solicitude is shown for the young, especially the neglected or orphaned. These children were schooled and trained for a trade. There is evidence of deacons asking the wealthy to pay school fees or further education fees for bright boys, and of this being considered an honourable and Christian request. The deacons helped the girls to an honourable marriage. Prisoners and delinquents, too, were given special care, and were visited and helped by the clergy: condemned prisoners were to be given spiritual comfort and the sacrament offered them.[44]

From this we can see that a number of welfare agencies began to blossom in the countryside of Western Europe following the Protestant Reformation. Indeed, the Calvinistic diaconate was a leader in its manifestation of consistent reformation of faith and life. Olson concludes: "Within the first generation of its founding, similar deacons funds were created by Reformed churches across the continent and in England. The parent institution in Geneva provided a model and an inspiration, keeping morale alive and offering a place of refuge to Reformed Christians faced with persecution and war and the increasingly foreboding world. The Bourse Francaise was a linchpin in the organizational structure of Reformed Churches providing financial links and strengthening the survival skills of that persistent minority the Reformed Church of early modern Europe."[45] Thus did these Reformation prototypes spread and become leaders in the sixteenth century welfare reform. Indeed, the Reformation "left stamped upon Christendom its idea of a properly coordinated and managed care of the poor and needy as the concern of the Church and as the responsibility of the Christian community."[46]

---

[43] Atkinson, op. cit., p. 87.

[44] Ibid., pp. 87-88.

[45] Olson, op. cit., p. 182.

[46] Atkinson, op. cit., p. 88.

Vives: An Example of Late-Medieval Roman Catholic Welfare

One can also profit by the example of the Roman Catholic humanist, Juan Luis Vives.[47] The major source of his views on social welfare may be found in his 1526 *On the Help of the Poor*. Vives, a product of renaissance humanism, offered a state-of-the-art version of welfare. In that both Vives and the Protestant reformers had drunk deeply from the pedagogy of humanism, in some ways their systems resembled each other's.[48]

Vives, respected in his day for a range of expertise, applied his talents to the remediation of poverty. He maintained views that may stand out in our own time, but to his contemporaries he was putting forth 'mere' Christian charity. Vives wrote, "I will not have as a Christian he who, within his means, gives no help to an indigent brother."[49] For Vives, "[t]he Christian society, the society which strives for earthly justice, looks to the divine law to be reconstituted as just, thus imitating the self's interaction with grace."[50] Alves and others even trace many of the poverty relief laws enacted in Spain in the 1520s and 1530s to the influence of Vives on these matters. So decidedly Christian was Vives' method that he drew attack from the rival secularists who preferred to follow Machiavelli. Vives advocated the impact of the principles of Christian morality on welfare and believed that the "'lay' urban social organism was to be a reflection of Christian morality."[51] Along with Loyola he affirmed the propriety of catechetical instruction as a part of any Christian-based welfare, along with the administration of fines to punish

---

[47] Cf. Abel Athouguia Alves, "The Christian Social Organism and Social Welfare: The Case of Vives, Calvin, and Loyola," *Sixteenth Century Journal*, XX, no. 1, 1989, pp 3-21.

[48] McKee is in slight disagreement with an aspect of the following study as to the importance of Vives. In her discussion of the origins of social welfare in the Reformation era, she confirms what we have seen above, although she disputes the original contributions of Vives:

"Where did the welfare reform begin and who influenced whom? The two major contenders for priority are certain cities of Germany and the Netherlands. A third suggestion which has called forth heated argument is that of the humanist Juan L. Vives, whose book *De subventione pauperum* (1526) was thought to have been the model for many cities. It has been fairly conclusively proved that Vives was not the father of sixteenth-century welfare reform though he was a popular and able exponent of the new movement. Having eliminated Vives, the chief candidates for first place are the German city of Nuremberg and the Flemish city of Ypres. The case for the latter is weakened by the elimination of Vives, who was thought to have outlined the Ypres reform. In fact, as the majority of scholars now affirm, Ypres is more like Nuremberg than like Vives' model, and the chronology of the wave of reform spreading across France, Italy, Spain, and England, lends weight to the claim that South Germany was the point of origin" (101, *John Calvin on the Diaconate and Liturgical Almsgiving, supra*).

[49] Cited by Alves, op. cit., p. 8.

[50] Ibid.

[51] Ibid., p. 14.

professional beggars.[52]   He may even have predated by four and a half centuries Pope John XXIII, who stressed the family basis of welfare.

> The family, grounded on marriage freely contracted, monogamous and indissoluble, must be considered the first and essential cell of human society. To it must be given, therefore, every consideration of an economic, social, cultural, and moral nature which will strengthen its stability and facilitate the fulfillment of its specific mission.[53]

Vives' method is summarized by Alves:

> The methods of his proposed system included a division of the poor into deserving native elements and undeserving foreign beggars; the establishment of work programs; and the generation of relief revenue through donations, the earnings of the poor's labor, and the use of money previously spent by the city on frivolous festivals. . . . poor relief necessarily resulted from the Christian organic concept, but the Christian social thinker knew in advance that the ideal would never function perfectly on earth . . . Vives desired vocational training for young paupers so that they would not always remain impoverished, but he wanted to keep both able-bodied and handicapped adults actively employed at all times to prevent idleness, the devil's playground. Those who were so morally corrupt that they refused to work were to be given just enough food to stay alive; but they were still to be given food.[54]

Vives shared with Calvin and other Protestants the view of depravity that maintained both that the charity-dispensers and the charity-recipients were sinful and therefore must be constrained by order and accountability. Furthermore, "Vives, Calvin, and Loyola all recognized the importance of planned relief. They distinguished between deserving and undeserving poor, and they all accepted the occasional confinement of the poor to hospitals as a given."[55]

Calvin, and later Beza, "condemned the unwillingness of the wealthy to aid the poor; with Calvin quite clearly stating that reluctance to work tried God's power and patience."[56] Loyola went so far as to construct a scale of punishments for able-bodied beggars, and as an example of the Roman Catholic approach of the time he maintained that "[k]ndness and harsh discipline both [were needed] in actual Christian practices," and that based on the separation of the sheep from the goats in Matthew 25:40, "[t]here had to be deserving and undeserving poor to explain this dichotomy. The sick, disabled, widowed, and orphaned were separated from the

---

[52] Ibid., p. 15.

[53] Cited by Michael Novak in *Gaining Ground* (Washington, DC: Ethics and Public Policy Center, 1986), p. 65.

[54] Alves, op. cit., pp. 12-13.

[55] Ibid., p. 12.

[56] Ibid., p. 13.

sturdy and lazy."[57] In sum, "Social control and social responsibility were inter-woven."

In line with the above two leading puritans made similar comments. William Ames, describing idlesess as the mother of many vices, spoke of:

> the lusty beggards and vagabonds are not to be suffered. Firstly, because they openly oppose themselves to the Divine Ordinance. Secondly, they are a burden to others without necessity. Thirdly because they defraud those who are poor indeed of some part of the alms they would receive if they had not been prevented by such. Fourthly, they do not carry themselves as members of any church or commonwealth. Fifthly, they directly set themselves to many kinds of wickedness.[58]

The views of William Perkins, the leading puritan theologian of the time, were similar to this Reformation tradition:

> . . . rogues, beggars, and vagabonds . . . commonly are of no civil society or corporation; they join not themselves to any settled congregation for the obtaining of God's kingdom; they are (for the most part) a cursed generation.' But as the author of this view, Mr. Christopher Hill, freely admits, there are countless places in Perkins' works which attack covetousness, usury, unjust dealing, and these could hardly be acceptable to the grasping bourgeois members of the congregation which, we are told, heard Perkins preach with avidity. Hill gets over this difficulty by saying that they just did not listen to those bits. Self-deception does indeed go to great lengths, but this particular version of it is incapable of proof or disproof, and Perkins' undoubtedly very great influence must surely have exercised itself in a more plausible, if more subtle way. Those, for example who hoarded grain to sell at a higher price in times of scarcity must have been singularly deaf if they fancied Perkins was bolstering common trade practices.[59]

The farthest thing from the minds of these social and religious reformers was the isolation of faith from practice. They believed that faith had every right to advo-cate its own structure and discipline—even method—on religiously-administered welfare. It was, after all, non-public and religious. For as Alves points out, "social control was still based on principles of charity . . . Thus, poor relief and the reform of personal morals were never far from [their] minds as proper activities for the Christian in the world."[60] About the only difference between Catholic and Protes-tant welfare at the time was the philosophic difference of approach: whether, with Calvin, the secular world was to be converted into a godly kingdom, or, with Catholicism, that a disciplined religious order should be the body of Christ in the secular world.

---

[57] Idem..

[58] Cf. George Rule, "The Puritans" in *Service in Christ* (London: Epworth Press, 1966), p. 129.

[59] Ibid., p. 127.

[60] Alves, op. cit., p. 15.

Vives, Calvin, Luther, Bucer, and Knox coalesced to form a surprisingly consensual approach to the church's role in social welfare. They gave great credence to the metaphor of the body being organically related (1 Cor. 12), both poor and non-poor. They reasoned, "Just as injury to the extremities can eventually harm the entire organism, so too prolonged hardship among the poor can feed the flames of civil disorder. When ignored, the poor generally rise up to demand satisfaction of their needs. Thus, *On the Help of the Poor* portrays relief for the poor as an important tool for the maintenance of social order and control, but it is also presented as a Christian duty with antecedents in classical thought."[61]

For the reformers of nearly five centuries ago, "The moral and spiritual health of the community was thus linked to such practical material concerns as poor relief. For Vives, Calvin, and Loyola, the obsession with the social organism myth and practical poor relief was not accidental. It was *mimesis*."[62] These welfare reformers looked to the past, specifically the canon of Scripture to find the broad principles of social welfare. True, they did not expect that every issue would be addressed by Scripture, but they did expect and did find the broad brushstrokes necessary for erecting a consistent and distinct biblical approach to welfare. The Christian religion, then, established the most powerful and longest lasting welfare model of any in modern western civilization. Only conceit or bias would fail to consult this eminently successful model to glean its enduring principles for our own time.

These consensual policy principles from the Reformation era are summarized below:

1. Theology guided practice.
2. If one did not work, he was not assisted (2 Thess. 3:10).
3. Each church was to administer a 'common chest.'
4. Welfare relief was temporary, with a long term goal of industriousness.
5. The family was the first rung of relief.
6. A distinction between the deserving and the non-deserving poor was maintained.

Over the centuries much of the ministry to the poor has been surrendered by the church. There are several possible reasons for this. Among them are changes in polity, the influence of pietism, and the expectations of statism. On the eclipse of the diaconate from the foreground, McKee provides a helpful explanation.

By the early eighteenth century, Cotton Mather in New England saw the diaconate as redundant and practically speaking unnecessary. Many early Presbyterian churches in North America were organized without diaconates, although problems with the officers of deacon and elder were a matter of concern to some people. Contributing to the difficulties with the diaconate was a growing

---

[61] Ibid., p. 7.
[62] Idem.

confusion about the precise nature and function of this office. Not a few Reformed groups in North America, especially those of Puritan background, retained either the Reformed elders' office or the deacons' office, but not both. Even more than in the earlier French Reformed tradition, the distinction between the two offices was blurred. Particularly those with a congregationalist polity tended to reject the office of elder but allocate to deacons some of the duties Calvin had assigned to elders. Sometimes the church's concern for the poor and needy thus became muted or overwhelmed in a host of other important duties of communal care.

One frequent result of the general ambiguity about the duties of the diaconate was the development of church trustees to handle finances. Whether or not some theological basis was found for these boards of trustees (my limited reading has turned up only pragmatic justifications), the introduction of these church servants further complicated the situation. Trustees usually managed financial matters, especially support for the pastors and church upkeep, which had once been part of the deacons' task."[63]

Elsie McKee reminds us:

In the late twentieth-century church the diaconate and diaconal ministries may and should differ in notable ways from the classical Reformed tradition, but the latter still serves as one useful touchstone. No changes of time or space can alter the crucial importance of having a special, permanent, ecclesiastical office charged with leading the congregation in the corporate expression of love for the neighbor, provided that church members do not assume everything can be left to the official deacons. An ecclesiastical diaconate is not the only way Christians publicly act on their conviction that the worship of God is necessarily followed by service of the neighbor. It is perhaps the key institutional witness to, and guide for, the commitment of the church as a body to God's suffering people, wherever and whoever they may be.[64]

Previous ecclesiastical practice provides a historical backdrop to which contemporaries may compare their present programs and from which they may construct future welfare reform. If *mimesis* was helpful for these reformers five centuries ago, surely it is indispensable for reformers today and tomorrow.

---

[63] Elsie McKee, *Diakonia supra* pp. 86-87.

[64] McKee, *Diaconia*, p. 119.

Groen Van Prinsterer: Political Paradigm from the Past

In the final decade of the Second Millennium, numerous evangelicals turned to Scripture, to other Christians, and to the history of the church for possible direction regarding political practices. In such searches, many Christians discovered that their spiritual fathers were the likes of Francis Schaeffer, Carl Henry, and others. They, in turn, had spiritual fathers of their own, acknowledging on occasion their indebtedness to Abraham Kuyper, an earlier evangelical.

Abraham Kuyper, the Dutch statesman (Prime Minister in 1900) who combined principles and politics par excellence, thought that no aspect of life (even politics) "should remain untouched by the Christian. There is no important question of life in which the believer should refrain from seeking an answer from the Lord."[1] For Kuyper and later for Schaeffer, "the believer has a divine mandate to be the servant of Christ in every aspect of life . . . The Christian must seek to integrate scriptural norms with the realities of public life. The result must be the articulation of Christian political principles applied in a concrete national situation."[2] Kuyper saw the major political options in his own day as a choice between the "Liberty Tree" or the "Cross," and protested "Christ, not Voltaire, is the Lord Messiah over the nations."[3] Kuyper's counsel to evangelicals in his own day was as perceptive as it is for ours: "The question is not if the candidate's heart is favorable to Christianity, but if he has Christ as his starting-point *even for politics*, and will speak out for his name."[4] In that light, Kuyper criticized his own theological family:

---

[1] McKendree Langley, "The Political Spirituality of Abraham Kuyper," *Pro Rege*, June 1980, p. 5.

[2] Ibid., p. 5.

[3] Ibid., p. 7.

[4] Ibid., p. 6.

"[T]he Evangelical Awakening as a spiritual movement was naively unaware of the titanic struggle between belief and unbelieving secularity, [and was] unhistoric in its ignorance of its own ties with the Christian past and lacking in theological substance."[5] Further, when Kuyper exhorted, "As for us and our children, we will no longer kneel before the idol of the French Revolution; for the God of our fathers will again be our God,"[6] the spiritual genetic code linking the likes of Kuyper and Schaeffer is all the clearer. Yet, this spiritual gene pool extends backwards at least one more generation from Kuyper. Much of Kuyper's thought was shaped by a previous generation's evangelical leader, William Groen Van Prinsterer (1801-1876), the subject of this examination.

In this discussion,[7] I shall draw heavily upon his primary work, *Lectures On Unbelief and Revolution* (1847). Heretofore, except for a few aphorisms, no English translation of Groen Van Prinsterer's work has been available until very recently, despite the fact that at least 12 Dutch editions were published.[8] This great gap led Henry Donald Morton to remark that a Calvinist (or any evangelical for that matter), "deprived of access to the writings of Groen Van Prinsterer is like any American deprived of access to the thought of John Adams or Abraham Lincoln, like any Englishman unable to read Lord Acton or Edmund Burke!"[9] To help remedy this, Harry Van Dyke undertook an English translation of *Unbelief and Revolution* in 1974. In 1989, the first major English translation was completed.[10]

This essay will not concentrate on the full scope of Groen Van Prinsterer's thought, but on the narrower question of Christian political principles, seeking to distill his major tenets for use in our own day. This discussion will highlight and extract seven political notions from Groen Van Prinsterer's seminal and largely-unknown work in order to guide modern Christians in their efforts to pursue righteousness and morality in social policy. From this discussion, the following political principles emerge:

---

[5] Ibid., p. 7.

[6] Idem.

[7] This is a fuller version of the essay that appeared in *Premise*, vol. 3, no. 9, Oct. 1996), p. 4 (http://capo.org/premise/96/Oct/); used with permission.

[8] A brief summary of Groen's thought is provided by McKendree Langley in "The Witness of a World View" in *Pro Rege*, Dec. 1979, vol. viii, no. 2., pp. 3-6. Also in 1976, Lectures XI and VIII-IX were published as separate monographs by the Christian Studies Center (Memphis, TN). Prior to the 1976 centennial, which revived efforts to publish Groen in English, mere summaries were available (see Van Dyke below, pp. 206-207). W. Robert Godfrey in "Church and State in Dutch Calvinism," *Through Christ's Word,* ed. by Godfrey and Jesse L. Boyd III (Phillipsburg, NJ: Presbyterian and Reformed, 1985) gives a succinct summary of the thought and importance of Groen. He also refers to a 1956 translation of Groen Van Prinsterer by J. Faber.

[9] *Guillaume Groen Van Prinsterer: Selected Studies* by J. L. Van Essen and H. D. Morton (Ontario: Wedge, 1989), p. 8.

[10] *Lectures in Unbelief and Revolution*, Harry Van Dyke, ed., (Ontario: Wedge, 1989. The references in parentheses in the remainder of this essay are to the original pagination preserved in the 1989 Van Dyke version.

1) Political programs are inescapably value-laden or based on ultimate philosophical principles.
2) Antithetical and irreconcilable ideologies are at war.
3) The dangers of rights-ism must be analyzed and exposed.
4) The limiting of pure democracy is necessary to honor the sovereignty of God.
5) The fruit of systemic unbelief is seen in our modern Western governments.
6) Theology is necessary both for a correct ethic and a correct politic.
7) An analysis of systemic unbelief is a starting point for evangelical political involvement.

Biography of the Grandfather of Evangelical Political Action

Born in Voorburg on August 21, 1801, Groen (whose Christian name given at baptism, Guillaume, was reserved only for official use) was the oldest child of a physician. His father was a progressive and a descendent from a line of preachers, while his mother was an aristocratic heiress from a prestigious banking family in Rotterdam. Such parentage afforded Groen many benefits and privileges; it also acquainted him with the tradition of the bourgeois. Receiving an excellent education in the classics, Groen was also catechized at his father's behest, making a formal profession of faith at age 17.[11]

At age 16 he entered college at Leyden, studying law and the classics. After six years of study he submitted and defended *two* doctoral dissertations on the same day, one on the Justinian Code and the second on Plato. Following his academic work at Leyden, he practiced law in The Hague and continued his historical studies. In 1827, he became engaged to Elisabeth van der Hoop, a pious young lady who would later introduce Groen to J. H. Merle d'Aubigne whose reformational preaching led in large measure to Groen's conversion. Groen and Elisabeth were married in the spring of 1828. She was a god-send in many ways, even assisting Groen and others in establishing nursery schools and other diaconal ministries near The Hague by 1832.[12]

In late 1827, Groen began a series of government clerical appointments and gained access to the House of Orange family archives. During these years his reading of Burke, Haller, and Lamennais wrought a lasting influence on his thought. He also underwent a gradual but forceful conversion, likely around 1831-1832. D'Aubigne had become the court preacher in 1828, and through his regular Bible exposition, Groen came to understand the Lordship of Christ—not only over

---

[11] Harry Van Dyke includes a readable and thorough biographical sketch in *Lectures on Unbelief and Revolution* (Ontario: Wedge, 1989), pp. 39-83, from which most of this summary is taken.
[12] Van Dyke, op cit., p. 27.

the individual soul but over politics and society as well. Although the specifics of his conversion can only be inferred, by early 1832 Groen is writing of his hope "that by God's grace that purely intellectual conviction may soon be personally applied to myself and genuinely appropriated."[13] Shortly thereafter, this thirst for righteousness seems to have been satisfied. The consistent witness to this conversion was confirmed without interruption from 1833 to his death in 1876. The role of d'Aubigne both in expounding the Scriptures and in impressing this new disciple with the applicability of Reformation thought to current issues is undisputed. So close were the families, that d'Aubigne named his own son Willem after Groen.[14]

What would become *Lectures on Unbelief and Revolution* was begun as early as 1831, but Groen's first post-conversion writing was his *Essay on the Means by Which Truth is Known and Confirmed* (Leyden, 1834). During the balance of the 1830s Groen devoted himself to archival research from the papers of the House of Orange, and accordingly has been dubbed the "father of modern Dutch historical research."[15] By the early 1840s, Groen had begun an overtly Calvinistic interpretation of Dutch history, *A Handbook of the History of the Fatherland* (completed in 1846). Groen was also an active churchman and an advocate for freedom in education.

By the late 1840s, Groen had established a reputation as an insightful social analyst. He gathered a group of approximately twenty influential thinkers to audit the series of lectures that formed his *magnum opus*. During 1847, these lectures were given, and later published with little revision by Luchtmans in Leyden. Carrying a wide influence (particularly on Kuyper and the next generation), Groen's *Lectures* have gone through five revisions (and twelve separate editions, with theologian J. H. Bavinck writing the Preface to the 1904 edition). Finally, an English version was released in 1989, for the first time delivering Groen van Prinsterer directly to English speaking readers.

Groen served in the Second Chamber of government from 1849-1865, only voluntarily interrupting his service from 1857-1861 in order to complete a second series (five volumes) of *Archives*. From 1850-1855, he was Editor-in-chief of the daily *De Nederlander* while serving in Parliament. Throughout the 1850s and 1860s, Groen was a vocal, if not always effective, advocate for anti-revolutionary principles in Dutch politics, repeatedly pleading for an educational system based on competitiveness, with Christian schools being allowed to compete on equal footing with secular schools. His death on May 19, 1876 occurred three years prior to the establishment of the first organized political party of the Netherlands, aptly named for Groen van Prinsterer's thought, the Anti-revolutionary Party.

---

[13] Ibid., p. 48.
[14] Ibid., p. 56.
[15] Ibid., p. 54.

Among his other writings[16] were: *Oration on the Reasons for Making Known the Nation's History* (Brussells, 1829); *The Measures Against the Seceders Tested Against Constitutional Law* (Leyden, 1837), a defense of ecclesiastical separatists; *Documents Relative to the Refusal of a Privately Endowed School in The Hague* (The Hague, 1844); *Constitutional Revision and National Concord* (1849); and *Selected Writings* (1859), various short essays from periodicals and journals. In addition, various unpublished treatises and essays (e.g., *Essay on the History and Consequences of the Growing Unity of Civilised Nations*) still await translation.

Political Principles Derived from our Paradigm

The seven central tenets of Groen's thought (cf. p. 205) are summarized below. Full citations are provided since this material has been difficult to access.

(1) Political programs are inescapably value-laden or based on ultimate philosophical principles. In other words, ultimate ideas have practical consequence.

Groen, unlike many evangelicals today, did not divide theology from politics. He realized that in politics, as in other endeavors, there was no true neutrality. The practical programs and policies that are adopted invariably have philosophical and ethical roots. If one begins with an agnostic or man-centered approach, that notion will infiltrate not only the ideas and macroscopic goals, but also the individual political implementations. There is an unavoidable connection between ultimate principles and their outworking in policy. Christians involved in politics need to recognize this inseparability and analyze accordingly.

In a cultural situation similar to our own, he began by noting his agreement with Lamennais that "everything proceeds from doctrines; manners, literature, constitutions, laws, the happiness of nations and the misfortunes, cultural barbarism, and those terrible crises that sweep nations away or else remove them, depending on their level of vitality." (5) Adopting a historical approach from the outset, he noted that historical events "are nothing other than the shapes and contours that reveal the sustained action of the spirit of an age." (5) Thus he sought to demonstrate that events are the historical unfoldings of philosophical principles.

To politically-active evangelicals who have learned the hard way that all politics are value-laden (local or not), Groen will fortify their resolve to maintain their principles. To those who still pine for the idealistic mirage that imagines citizens acting apart from their base-values, Groen is a needed corrective. Of all citizens, evangelicals should embrace the political doctrine that not only do ultimate ideas have ultimate consequences, but moreover, ultimate ideas also spawn very practical consequences.

The two primary ideologies that Groen observed at work in Western civilization in his time were the principles of the Revolution and the principles of

---

[16] According to Van Essen (op. cit., p. 44), 152 writings of Groen were annotated in a 1973 doctoral dissertation.

the Reformation. By the "Revolutionary Principles" Groen referred to the French Revolution of 1789 and to the "general spirit and mode of thinking that is now manifest." (6) For Groen, the event of the 1789 Revolution was singularly symbolic, signifying far more than an isolated coup. It represented an entire vein of philosophic thought that was man-centered and opposed to God's sovereignty. Revolutionary ideas, although associated with the French Revolution, were much more than tools for that one revolt alone. These revolutionary ideas became the philosophic program for western humanism expressed in government.

Groen exposed the humanistic offspring of those who ultimately value *libertas, egalitas et fraternitas,* finding in these Revolutionary ideas "the basic maxims of liberty and equality, popular sovereignty, social contract, the artificial reconstruction of society by common consent—notions which today are venerated as the cornerstone[s] of constitutional law and the political order." (6) American evangelicals who seem inclined to embrace democracy as a sacred and inviolable rule may wish to reconsider in light of Groen Van Prinsterer's critique and our own moral vacuum.

Moreover, Groen observed that wherever those particular theories and principles gained a foothold the people are "led about in a circle of misery and grief . . . a strict, consistent application of the Revolution doctrine will bring men to the most excessive absurdities and the worst atrocities." (6) Groen Van Prinsterer cites Bonald's putative pathology: "The Revolution began with a declaration of the rights of man; it will end only with the declaration of the rights of God." (7) He called Revolutionary doctrine "unbelief applied to politics. A life and death struggle is raging between the Gospel and this practical atheism. To contemplate a *rapprochement* between the two would be nonsense. It is a battle which embraces everything we cherish and hold sacred."(8) Groen spoke of the battle over Revolutionary or unbelieving political principles more than 150 years ago in terms that sound similar to the cultural war terminology frequently invoked recently. Groen urged Christians to become knowledgeable about the nature and direction of political philosophy in their time. He not only advocated a general statement of Christian principles, but also insisted that a Christian worldview penetrate "into the inner recesses of science and the maze of historical events; it is our duty to learn to adore and revere the Lord even here in these his works." (10) Groen was keenly aware that evangelicals' ignorance of history and constitutional law led them to "advocate very dubious opinions as soon as they enter upon the political terrain." (12)

Groen charged Christians to be involved in politics. He said that the church, "has been torn from the State only to be turned over to the State. Seceders have been persecuted in the name of modern justice. The Government holds itself entitled to hamper Christian education if not to prevent it outright by controlling the public school and obstructing private initiatives towards an alternative." (13) Rightly therefore, many evangelicals experience *de ja vu* when they read these words at the end of the twentieth century. Inevitably the ideas of either the Revolution or the Reformation work themselves out in practice according to their ideologies: "As the fruit is known by the tree, so shall the tree be known by its fruit." (15)

(2) Antithetical and irreconcilable ideologies are at war.

Groen Van Prinsterer previews this major distinction by contrasting the animating principle of the Revolution and the Reformation. He said:

> The [French] Revolution ought to be viewed in the context of world history. Its significance for Christendom equals that of the Reformation, but then in reverse. The Reformation rescued Europe from superstition; the Revolution has flung the civilized world into an abyss of unbelief. Like the Reformation, the Revolution touches every field of action and learning. In the days of the Reformation the principle was submission to God; these days it is a revolt against God. . . . The Revolution proceeds from the sovereignty of man, the Reformation proceeds from the Sovereignty of God. The one has revelation judged by reason; the other submits reason to revealed truths. The one unleashes individual opinions; the other leads to unity of faith. The one loosens social bonds, even family ties; the other strengthens and sanctifies them. The latter triumphs through martyrs; the former maintains itself by massacres. The one ascends out of the bottomless pit and the other comes down out of heaven. (14)

Groen was convinced that just as the underlying premises of any argument determined its outcome, so the underlying premises of social movements could be evaluated as to their validity in light of Scripture. Underpinning all social movement is one ideology or another. At their base, all social and political programs were founded either on God's prescriptions for society or on man's. Whether or not a movement is founded on theocentric or anthropocentric ordering determines its outcome. In the interim, these two base ideologies are at war.

On the advantage of the Christian ideology, Groen noted, "The Christian knows a principle which gives steadiness to political thought and which, if followed, would be sufficient to restore the tottery political structures on unshakable foundations." (18) He noted the antiquity of the Christian politic: "The anti-revolutionary or Christian-historical position finds unequivocal confirmation in the unanimous testimony of former times." (22) So, said Groen Van Prinsterer, the written Word of God becomes the "ax that cuts off every root of revolutionary misgrowth." (23) As historian, he chronicled at length the notion that the church and its orthodox theology have contended in matters of politics (throughout the ages) with theology in a prominent public role; theological values were not always closeted away like awkward step-children.

Groen asserted that when the Revolution came about, modern secularists had to change not only theology but history as well. This newer torch of wisdom, this post-1789 history, "projected onto peoples and periods ideas that were wholly foreign to them . . . history became a false witness, and this false witness became yet another powerful means of pressing public opinion into the harness of the

revolutionary school. History became a pantheon lined with revolutionary para-
gons, an arsenal filled with revolutionary weapons for murdering the truth." (24)

A knowledgeable historian, Groen spoke of historical figures like Grotius and
others (28), noting their downfall as emblematic of a faulty foundational ideology.
The key, according to Groen Van Prinsterer, was this: "Once and for all disposed
of the dangerous doctrines of popular sovereignty and an original social contract . . .
the newer theories rested on a single untrue assumption: that the state arose from
human consent which put an end to the state of nature." (37) This human-oriented
consent lies at the heart of the Revolutionary principle. The result of the principle
is that an unavoidable and unresolvable conflict arises among these presuppositional ideologies.

(3) The dangers of Rights-ism must be analyzed and exposed.

One of the most dangerous expressions of revolutionary ideas is the preferred
status awarded to the notion of individual rights. As modern societies search for a
rights-centered ethic to guarantee homosexual service in the military, health-
insurance for all, and the explosion of rights claims for nearly everything, one can
acknowledge Groen's foresight. He predicted the errors of this approach a century
and a half ago. Most perceptively he identified the totalitarian expansionism of
Rights-ism that unravels the social fabric if it is allowed to flourish in a body
politic. The claimants to rights-for-everything are the genetic offspring of Revolutionary ideas, not the biblical *ethos*. A first step to recovering a Christian polity is
to refute Rights-ism. In our own time, when justice has become hostage to radical
notions of individual rights, the Christian must often return to this theme.

Reminding his readers that "rights" had become more important than justice
(45), Groen said that formerly, "Justice, in a philosophical sense essential and
historical par excellence, was placed above History. It was this dominion of Right
over fact that gave rise to a whole series of acquired rights." (46) Whereas formerly
respect "for acquired rights meant . . . respect for the highest principles of justice"
(47), this was not so after the French Revolution, when a dangerous dogma was
created in which men used the desirability of centralization "to demand passivity
for subordination, to mistake autonomy for independence, to regard free activity as
rebellion, in every respect to subject everything found within the state's territory to
the arbitrary will of the state, to oppose on principle any self-government of private
persons or corporations. . ." (47)

In sum, Groen alleged that in the revolutionary reconstruction, "Too much
attention was paid to questionable historic rights, to the detriment of general
principles of justice. (44) At the heart of his criticism is the extension of alleged
rights and privileges into nearly every domain. Observing that "Rights have been
represented as limitless when in fact they did have limits" (98), he noted that in the
very theoretical concepts and definition of the state after the Revolutionary idea
took hold, commonwealths were superimposed backwards onto monarchies, thus a
"false idea arose that the state must be viewed as an association." (130) Groen

diagnosed the historical obfuscation: "[M]onarchical unity was confused with republican union; aggregation was held to be association; every state was made over into a society, a community of citizens; monarchy was reasoned away, and the kingdoms of Europe were delivered up to discord and dissolution." (130)

A contemporary critic of rights as an underlying and absolute sub-strata of modern thought has similarly enunciated the failure to grasp responsibility—the counterpart to rights—as "the other half of the democratic equation." The echo is striking:

> The American rights dialect is distinguished not only by what we say and how we say it, but also by what we leave unsaid. Each day's newspapers, radio broadcast and television programs attest to our tendency to speak of whatever is most important to us in terms of rights, and to our predilection for overstating the absoluteness of the rights we claim. . . . The strident rights rhetoric that currently dominates American political discourse poorly serves the strong tradition of protection for individual freedom for which the United States is justly renowned. Our stark simple rights dialect puts a damper on the processes of public justification, communication, and deliberation upon which the continuing vitality of the democratic regime depends.[17]

Groen's primary goal was to convince his audience that all real power is ordained by God: "The powers that be are not just tolerated. They are willed, instituted, sanctified by God himself." (51) While not arguing for absolute divine right ("We do not identify the will of any sovereign with the will of God." [50]), Groen noted a distinction between power and might or force: "All true legislation emanates from God. . . . Depart from this, and I see only arbitrary wills and a degrading rule of force, I see only men insolently lording it over other men, I see only slaves and tyrants." (56) If evangelicals recognize this fruit in their own civil government, perhaps it is time to consider Groen's analysis of the alternatives.

(4) The limiting of pure democracy necessarily honors the sovereignty of God.

Groen Van Prinsterer was also prescient in warning westerners that democracy *per se* was not a political panacea. Democracy, although one of the greatest blessings to human freedom in our time, was not the *deus ex machina* mandated by revelation. Many evangelicals confuse cause and effect, thereby in practice, elevating democracy to an absolute. Although it has brought much prosperity and liberty, democracy must not—unless Scripture sanctions—be raised to a political *summa*. To do so risks elevating corporate human sovereignty above God's sovereignty. Surely the Christian may support a limited democracy, ideally one characterized by loyalty to God's rule, even above human plebiscite. Jesus's own teaching is applicable to the conflict between competing political systems: "No one

---

[17] Mary Ann Glendon, *Rights Talk: The Impoverishment of Political Discourse* (New York: The Free Press, 1991), pp. 76, 171.

can serve two masters. Either he will hate the one and love the other, or he will be devoted to the one and despise the other." In political options, such bifurcation may oblige the choice between human sovereignty via democracy, or God's sovereignty. To further support this, merely watch an unrighteous official be chosen by a plurality of voters, and take note of how democracy can be less than felicitous at times.

Groen consistently warned of the danger of a pure democracy. It is unable to deliver righteousness if founded upon the will of unregenerate people. He said, "[I]t follows that there neither is, nor can be, any fundamental law that is binding upon the body of the People, not even the Social Contract itself." (207) He called the systems of Rousseau and Hobbes monstrous, looking to government as possessing a "provisional mandate, subject to cancellation or modification at the people's pleasure." (208) The result was that "any real distinction between democracy, aristocracy, or monarchy no longer exists" (209). When the "elections are over, they are slaves, they are nothing." (210)

Groen cautioned against the danger of unbridled majority rule, reminding that freedom is founded only in submission to the law and not in submission to the "detestable despotism of the majority." (210) "If freedom means unconditional obedience to the good pleasure of men," he said, "then freedom is a fiction." (212)

Groen then reviewed the basic historic forms of government, and had as the chief focus of his criticism the absolutization of the consent of the people. He noted that democracy depended upon an election or mandate of the people for its success. When "the law is made with the consent of the people and by the declaration of the King," proper power begins to diminish. Hence, according to Groen, historians who supported the Revolution necessarily had to reconstrue ancient history in order to democratize the ancient monarchs with a strong dose of revisionism.

In chapter six, Groen spoke at length of the perversion of constitutional law. The very vocabulary of politics had become corrupt. The etymological meaning of words was gradually driven out by revisionist meanings. (126) By such linguistic subterfuge, Groen showed how "monarchies" were transformed into "republics," and "subjects" were translated into "citizens."[18] Recognizing language as an important indicator and current of value, he noted that "men lived in monarchies and dreamt of republics . . . [and] since it is a basic need of the human mind to reconcile fancy with reality there was only one solution—to decide that every monarchy too, is a republic in origin." (129) Thus, Groen Van Prinsterer suggested that the beginning decline into democratism was well underway by his own time.

Groen noted that this was not merely the idea of one Revolution, but that the Revolution of 1789 illustrated that the "theoretic unfolding on every page of its history must have had a theoretic origin." (119) He believed that even the philosophic theory of liberty that has swept western civilization since 1789 was "born of

---

[18] For a thorough treatise on this idea, see *Citizens: A Chronicle of the French Revolution* by Simon Schama (New York: Knopf, 1989).

doctrine," (120) and specifically the doctrine of the rights of man. So he catechized, "If the king is an autocrat within a republic, whence his authority? By delegation. On the part of whom? The majority of citizens. In what manner? By convention and social contract. To what end? To look after the public interest. On what terms? Joint consultation and responsibility. For how long? Till the favor is forfeited or the mandate revoked." (130) Thus he saw a universal error in which post-revolutionary humanists "accepted a social pact as the precondition of the state" (131), and commented that even the best of scholars have "been sucked into the maelstrom." (131) A false notion "of the state was found everywhere," said Groen, as the social contract thoughts of non-Christian philosophers began to rule the day (135). He noted that whatever one's view of the state in a post-revolu-tionary construction, the social contract "leaves but two avenues: anarchy or tyranny, depending on personal inclination, character, and circumstances." (136) Oddly, many evangelical prognosticators are sounding the self-same alarm, warning against these two paths in our own day, for example: "Without God society can be constituted only by the artificial authority of the special interests or the passions of the moment."[19]

If Groen Van Prinsterer has begun to sound like Burke it is no wonder. He acknowledged his indebtedness to Burke who similarly had denounced:

> If I recollect rightly, Aristotle observes that a democracy has many striking points of resemblance with a tyranny. Of this I am certain, that in a democracy the majority of the citizens is capable of exercising the most cruel oppressions upon the minority whenever strong divisions prevail in that kind of polity, as they often must; and that oppression of the minority will extend to far greater numbers and will be carried on with much greater fury than can almost ever be apprehended from the dominion of a single scepter. In such a popular persecution, individual sufferers are in a much more deplorable condition than in any other . . . those who are subjected to wrong under multitudes are deprived of all external consolation. They seem deserted by mankind, overpowered by a conspiracy of their whole species.[20]

Burke also recognized that Aristotle (cf. *Politics*, book iv., chap. 4) realized the same dangers:

> The ethical character is the same; both exercise despotism over the better class of citizens; and decrees are in the one, what ordinances and arrets are in the other: the demagogue, too, and the court favorite are not infrequently the same identical men, and always bear a close analogy; and these have the principal power, each in

---

[19] McKendree Langley paraphrasing Lamennais in "God and Liberty" *supra*, p. 16.
[20] Edmund Burke, *Reflections on the Revolution in France*, ed. by J. G. A. Pocock (Indianapolis: Hackett, 1987), pp. 109-110. For the latest in modern revisionism, one might consult *The Great Melody: A Thematic Biography and Commented Anthology of Edmund Burke* by Conor Cruise O'Brien (Chicago: University of Chicago Press, 1993) to see an argument that Burke was not really very conservative.

their respective forms of government, favorites with the absolute monarch, and demagogues with a people such as I have described.[21]

After discussing Thomas Hobbes's view of the social contract, Groen criticized the government that becomes the tool of arbitrary will as a devouring Leviathan. So he found that various acts, including criminal acts and ownership of property, become beholden to common consent. On the other hand, he noted Algernon Sidney's view that the association "is and remains the true Sovereign," (138) illustrating Groen's point that once the Revolutionary principles are assumed there are two and only two options: the options of statism under the control of a tyrant or rank anarchism. Groen Van Prinsterer consistently maintained that the Revolution was the result of the perversion of constitutional law. The attendant Revolutionary theories flow from that font of perversion. He meant that Revolutionary theories such as "popular sovereignty, social contract, responsible government, and, as soon as there is popular displeasure, a sacred right to revolt" (142) inescapably ferment: "The Revolution simply realized the republican ideas under constitutional forms, while eliminating whatever used to stop them from being implemented in full." (143)

A profound misconception—that the blame for this non-authoritarianism derived from Calvinism's spread—had taken root in post-Enlightenment thought. Groen carefully pointed out that this blame cannot be laid at the feet of reformational Calvinists. In Lecture Six he defended the Reformation from culpability for this newfound freedom: "Calvinism assuredly never led to any sort of republicanism. . . . Calvinists evinced the opposite" (148) in calling for submission. Rather than rebellion, the Reformation principle called for order, submission, and an embrace of divine schemes of authority.   Repeatedly, Groen defends the Reformation principle.   He said that its basic premise was not unrestricted liberty, but a "liberty that is grounded in submission." (156) Furthermore, Groen noted: "A doctrine that points to the total depravity of man is little suited to foster self-exaltation." (158) A theologically informed view of civil government will heed Groen Van Prinsterer's warnings concerning the effect of human depravity.

According to Groen, "the Reformation . . . stemmed the tide of revolutionary unbelief in the sixteenth century . . . only through the flagging of the spirit of the Reformation did revolutionary unbelief gain the upper hand, in the eighteenth century." (165) The germ of unbelief was strong and continued to grow. Groen spoke of this unbelief as "political atheism." He extolled the virtue of the Reformation: "Into the midst of unbelief and insurrection it flung the principle of faith and obedience, so conducive to wholesome order through the marriage of freedom and submission. . . . The fundamental principle of submission to God both shored up the tottering authority of governments and shielded the liberties of subjects, thereby arresting the advance of the republican theories with their revolutionary

---

[21] Burke, op. cit., p. 110.

leaven." (168-169) He argued that the Reformation could not possibly be the cause of the Revolution, "since it sprang from an antithetical principle: from objective unity of faith rather than diversity of subjective opinions; from the infallibility of Revelation rather than the supremacy of Reason; from the sovereignty of God rather than the sovereignty of man." (176) Groen noted that once faith departed, Christian Europe was dechristianized (178): "Indeed, the last state was worse than the first. The reign of unbelief had arrived. Revolution was now inevitable. For the principle of unbelief, once admitted, propels men from consequence to consequence, ever further down the path of ruin. Once the bond is cut asunder that ties mankind to heaven, none can stop the rush to the abyss." (179) A century and a half later, many American evangelicals utter the "amen" to that in our own country.

Even earlier, Richard Baxter, for example, had sensed the possible incongruity between pure democracy and honor to God's sovereignty. Baxter, in opposition to the Ranters, Seekers, Levellers, and other sects of the seventeenth century, warned that pure democracy would invariably lead to heresy (as well as political disaster): "That the major[ity] vote of the people should ordinarily be just and good is next to an impossibility . . . All this stir of the Republicans is but to make the seed of the Serpent to be the sovereign rulers of the earth . . . The greatest heresy of all was that . . . all [men] had a spark of the divine in them, and so, that all men were equal."[22] Unlimited democracy is incompatible with a Christian allegiance to the sovereignty of God. Thus, evangelicals involved in politics must necessarily place limited trust in democracy alone as a cure for the ills of society.

(5) The fruit of systemic unbelief is seen in modern Western governments.

In Lecture Eight, Groen described unbelief as "the force of an irresistible march of events" (181) founded upon the Revolutionary principles. He said that the "real formative power throughout the revolutionary era, right up to our own time, has been atheism, godlessness, being without God . . . From the unbelieving nature of the Revolution one can predict its history. Conversely, in the facts of its history one can discern the constant tokens of its unbelieving origin." (182) That Revolution would stem from atheism and return to it, Groen warned, was a "necessary consequence" (182), "a matter of plain logic . . . atheism in religion and radicalism in politics are not only not the exaggeration, misuse or distortion, but in fact the consistent and faithful application, of a principle which sets aside the God of Revelation in favor of the supremacy of Reason." (183)

Groen's argument is that "where unbelief is free to run its natural course in religion and politics, it cannot but lead to the most radical doctrines." (183) The basic credo of the Revolution is "the sovereignty of man, independent of the sovereignty of God," which Groen considered radically false: "Once orthodoxy

---

[22] Cited in *The Century of Revolution* by Christopher Hill (Edinburgh: Thomas Nelson, 1961), p. 167.

failed to preserve this rich heritage, it fell into the hands of the philosophers." (187) Moreover, said Groen,

> Revolution is in its entirety nothing other than the logical outcome of systematic unbelief, the outworking of apostasy from the Gospel. . . . Since religion and society have the same origin, God, and the same end, man, a fundamental error in religion is also a fundamental error in politics . . . the Revolution doctrine is the religion, as it were, of unbelief. It is the negation of everything resting upon belief . . . The principle of this vaunted philosophy was Reason, and the outcome was apostasy from God and materialism.

Painfully, evangelicals have come to recognize that indeed while there is organizational separation of church and state, there can be no divorce between religious belief and the values of civil government. The predominant religion of our age is still that of systematic unbelief and, if unrestrained, atheism does intrude and impose itself in government. Recognizing that these various political values stem from the humanist revolution may be the beginning of political wisdom.

(6)   Theology is necessary both for a correct ethic and a correct politic.

Evangelicals, of all groups, should realize the unavoidable theological foundation for ethics and politics. In the latter twentieth century as humanism has blossomed in governments, it is indubitable that the debate should cease over whether or not all politics are theological in both root and fruit. One can certainly analyze various political ideas and programs in light of their ultimate principles, which are hardly theologically neutral. Religious belief is inseparably connected to social and political proposals.

Groen Van Prinsterer argued that, "Without belief in God there is no basis for morality." (195) Later he said, "Atheism cannot tolerate the truth, because it cannot be tolerated by the truth. It recognizes a mortal enemy in every belief. It puts up with the least hint of that religion only that keeps silent, that bends its neck, that submits to the rules and regulations of unbelief. Atheism equalizes all religions all right—provided all are equally destitute of the signs of vigor and life." (199) In addition he cited Burke approvingly: "They who do not love religion, hate it. The rebels to God perfectly abhor the author of their being. They hate him 'with all their heart, with all their mind, with all their soul, and with all their strength.'" "Indeed," commented Groen, "the defining feature of the Revolution is its hatred of the Gospel, its anti-Christian nature. This feature marks the Revolution, not when it 'deviates from its course' and 'lapses into excesses,' but precisely when it holds to its course and reaches the conclusion of its system, . . . the Revolution will never be able to shake it off." (200) Revolutionary humanism does have a religious root, a root embedded in the ancient soil of hideous rebellion and repudiation of God. The theology of a politician or advocacy group is detectable. According to Groen, they all grow from one root or the other, from systematic belief or unbelief.

The same principle of unbelief, Groen said, operates in philosophy proper, elevating the supremacy of reason that "culminates in atheism and materialism." (201) The mainstays of this philosophy are revolutionary liberty, or the sovereignty of the human will [that] dissipates itself in the depths of radicalism." (201) Groen Van Prinsterer argued that it is an inevitable step from "the chimerical idea of making every man's reason independent of all authority, or of destroying all faith completely, to the no less ridiculous project of emancipating men from every temporal ruler." (202) Thus the foundation of all rights and duties lies in the sovereignty of God, he said, and "[w]hen that Sovereignty is denied, what becomes of the fountain of authority, of law, of every sacred and dutiful relation in state, society, and family?" (203) Groen Van Prinsterer's answer is that they all deteriorate, noting that:

> There can be, despite all social diversities, no real difference among men. Eliminate God, and it can no longer be denied that all men are, in the revolutionary sense of the words, free and equal . . . Henceforward the state is conceived as a multitude of indivisible particles, of atoms . . . From the standpoint of unbelief, to liquidate every form of independent authority means to remove an abuse that is degrading to humanity. And from that standpoint the judgment is correct, since unbelief knows only human authority. It is in the denial of the divine right of authority that we find the source, not only of liberalism, but of the perfervour which it generates. (203)

In contrast to the Christian emphasis on historical continuity, the neophilic Revolution holds that "innovation is the only wisdom available" (205), and furthermore, "[t]hrough mutual consent alone" is the state founded.

(7) An anatomy of the conquest of systemic unbelief is a starting point for evangelical political involvement.

Groen gave hope by arguing that an ill-founded politic will inevitably run its course because there is an "unavoidable collision of truth and law." (223) He sounded similar to one recent observer who, when speaking of the communist collapse, noted that "Reality is resilient."[23] Groen advised that despite attempts to modify these reality-induced correctives, even when the logical extension of ideas are not clear, nonetheless the ideas will bear fruit. Groen listed the following: "First it will try as much as possible to get rid of every notion of the Divine," (226); it will turn to "superstition and idolatry" (228); and it will falsely conclude that it will be as ridiculous to believe in God as it is today to believe in ghosts; the day will come when we shall believe only in ghosts." (228)

Groen Van Prinsterer then identified the five stages of this unfolding Revolution: (1) a preparation period; (2) a time of development, in which the champions of progress are compelled to move forward with their reformation and are largely successful; (3) a period of reaction; (4) a period of renewed experimentation when

---

[23] Michael Bauman, *Man and Marxism* (Hillsdale, MI: Hillsdale College Press, 1991), 4.

the reaction ends; and (5) a period of despair regarding liberty and indifference about justice. This phase, Groen called "despondent resignation."

Thus, the French Revolution in its declaration of the rights of man destroys civil liberty, property, political liberty, freedom of religion and a number of basic values which are necessary for a sturdy civilization. Any system founded on that same philosophical root will yield similar results.[24]

In the next three Lectures Groen Van Prinsterer sought to chronicle historically his earlier enunciated thesis about the phases inherent in the Revolution. In Lecture Eleven he argued that "the germ of error and corruption, must in theory and practice culminate in atheism and radicalism." (260) He noted that he found this confirmed in practice and that the Revolution was a major idea which develops into "a systematic rebellion against the revealed God." (262) He believed the Revolution was a European Revolution that had as one of its outcomes the overturning of Christendom (263), while at the same time destroying the foundations of law (264). Moreover, he noted that the Revolutionary principle had an organic relationship connecting Jacobinism, Bonapartism, and Constitutionalism all as branches of the same tree. He asserted again that the only remedy for this is that those citizens must "turn to God whose truth alone can resist the power of the lie." (271)

Groen depicted the Revolution as the "systematic application of the philosophy of unbelief; with its crimes and massacres and devastation; with its self-deification and its adoration of Reason on the ruins of the ancient state." (293) Further, he said: "What happened in 1789 had to happen" (294), a clear example of the ideological determinism apparent in his work. Groen said that once the Revolution has begun, "ceaseless forward movement, amid a progressively more vehement struggle; release of every moral and legal bond; compulsory unity under the iron yoke of an increasingly more violent centralized government" (296) is unleashed. The Revolution, then, was not an anomaly but a typical analogy (321), characterized as a "symphony of hell, a harmonious chord and a most worthy finale . . . [a] political descent into Inferno." (329-330)

Groen concluded: "Such is the final fruit of liberalism, that men, having lost liberty, also lose the love of liberty and the belief in liberty!" (394). He recommended a genuine renewal: "Only from a revival of Christian charity and Evangelical spirit can we draw strength to match unbelief and derive the confidence without which no self-sacrifice, no progress, no improvement is possible. Only through faith in the Son of the living God can the Revolution be vanquished." (396)

Groen characterized the life of post-revolutionary Europe as dominated by "revolutionary autocracy." He noted the totalitarian impulse of the modern democratic state: "We do not really live in a monarchy, nor in a republic, but under a

---

[24] Rousas Rushdoony views the French Revolution as the confluence of the Enlightenment, secret societies, and statism. Furthermore, he dissects 15 philosophical differences between the French Revolution and the American Revolution. Cf. his *This Independent Republic* (Fairfax, VA: Thoburn Press, 1978), pp. 136-143.

centralizing, all-controlling government which is either exercised personally or else conveniently distributed among high state officials. We are living under the almighty power of a revolutionary government under one head, a government limited *de jure* in a variety of ways, *de facto* in no way whatsoever." (414)

In many ways, Groen Van Prinsterer was a precursor of things to come over the next 150 years. He predicted trends such as the rise of socialism, the dominance of rights-centeredness, and the ills of relativism in political ideals. If the governmental system advocated by Groen (culminating with Abraham Kuyper) is compared with our present system, and if Jesus' standard, "By their fruit ye shall know them" is applied, evangelicals cannot help but embrace this anti-revolutionary principle. To do so is to link arms across space and time with the reformers, and to pursue reformation according to Scripture once again. Such might even contain unifying promise for those of disparate backgrounds who are united in their disdain of humanism in its political manifestations.

Certainly Groen himself did not escape criticism. His major work was criticized by his contemporaries as one-sided, immoderate, derivative, internally contradictory, and selective. Later critics have attacked his method as aprioristic and partisan. He is also open to criticism for style, but more substantively for his apparent identification of the Kingdom of God too closely with a particular movement. Certainly specific historical conclusions may be challenged, Groen's monarchical bias may be questioned, and his methodology scrutinized. Indeed, criticism of Groen's work is now possible and will certainly be profitable. Yet, along with such criticism will also come a familiarity that will be beneficial.

It is imperative that we also take stock of potential evangelical forays into politics in our own times. Have we been very successful without the counsel of the likes of Groen Van Prinsterer? It is hard at this time to show empirically much advance for all the evangelical efforts in the past two decades. If we see that even tenuous gains can lapse in a few months, we must wonder about our foundation. If we have failed, then "Whither?" In light of the recent exhibitions of Rights-ism run amok, it may be an opportune time to review Groen Van Prinsterer and begin to reconstruct a more enduring form of evangelical politics on some other basis.

Moreover, a proper acquaintance with Groen can serve as a proper hermeneutic to clarify much of the intrinsic thought of Abraham Kuyper. And this instructive model from the past is equally capable of serving as a predictive model for the future. Will evangelicals continue to build on sandy foundations? Or are we ready to reconstruct a new and more viable Christian political platform? It may depend on how desperate we become. In any of these scenarios a familiarity with Groen Van Prinsterer is long overdue. As a leading Kuyper student, McKendree Langley predicted, "If evangelicals neglect to concern themselves with this political aspect of sanctification, they will increasingly find themselves socially impotent to bring a healing influence upon American life."[25]

---

[25] McKendree Langley, "The Political Spirituality of Abraham Kuyper," op cit., p. 9.

Westminster Spirituality

The claim that the authors of the Westminster Confession were spiritual giants may be met either with looks of horror, disbelief, shock, or bursts of laughter. Sadly, few moderns are aware of the depth and breadth of spirituality in these divines. Our unawareness of this is both our own loss and due to no fault of the divines. The footprints of their spirituality are not beyond tracing out.

Perhaps only an age like our own—which so loathes so much of the past—would make this mistake. However, Christians should have broader horizons than the narrow confines of any single age, and saints should desire to benefit from the examples of those who have gone before them. Indeed, a perennial challenge is to identify mentors or to emulate those whose spirituality surpasses our own. I modestly suggest that we begin our search for such spiritual role models, not so much with our own contemporaries as we are inclined to do but with some who may have superseded our own spirituality. It may be put this way: If we desire to imitate the best of orthodox spirituality, why not study the lives and practices of the best of Christians? Until we surpass the divines of Westminster in spirituality, until our age on the whole possesses more innate spiritual vitality, until we find deeper and cooler wells of spiritual refreshment, why not draw the contours of spirituality from the lives and spiritual disciplines of these divines?

If we have ears to hear we can garner some of the richest testimonies from real Christians of an earlier age. In fact, these testimonies are more God-centered and dripping with grace-filled piety than many of the standard testimonies we hear today. Not to disparage any modern testimonies, but the truth of the matter is that those Puritans on the average were more—not less—advanced than the average evangelical today.

Critics of Westminster Spirituality

Critics, of course, would be hesitant to agree with our study. Certain persons and images from the past sometimes stand in dire need of rehabilitation. The divines, too, suffer outside the camp as some of the most maligned in history, being ranked with the likes of Calvin, Beza, Turretin, and a few others. Sadly, most of the modern world (and it should not be so in an informed church) think of these divines as machine-tooled, robo-theologians, bereft of heart, passion, emotion, and maybe even soul. That is a caricature underivable from the best historical review.

Images accumulated through history are often hard to jettison, even if those accrued images are not in accord with actual history. Unfortunately the divines of Westminster have been tarred and feathered (normally by opponents) to the point that they are seldom recommended as worthwhile models of spiritual fervor or compassion. They have frequently been caricatured as "black hats" by those who did not understand or agree with them. With even the slightest archaeological digging, however, one can see that these men—far from being spiritually sterile—evinced a spirituality of the highest order. It is not the case that these divines were spiritual pygmies. It is time to help rehabilitate these saints. Any who slander them without reviewing the record first are guilty of false witness not to mention ignorance. These divines were deeply spiritual; most of us could learn from them.

Of the Westminster Confession of Faith as an accurate and vital compilation of Christian truth, B. B. Warfield contended that its influence could not "lack in spiritual quality. . . . [Its] authors were men of learning and philosophic grasp; but above all of piety. Their interest was not in speculative construction, but in the protection of their flocks from deadly error."[1]

On the group as a whole, biographer James Reid commented:

> There were never, perhaps, men of holier lives than the generality of the Puritans and Nonconformists of this period. Their piety and devotedness to God were very remarkable. Their ministers made considerable sacrifices for God and religion. They spent their lives, in sufferings, in fastings, in prayers, in walking closely with God in their families, and among their people who were under their pastoral care, in a firm adherence to their principles, and in a series of unremitted labors for the good of mankind. They were indefatigably zealous in their Master's service.[2]

Many of the critics' barbs must first be dismissed if we are to benefit from the example of these saints. For example, Sidney Ahlstrom marveled, "That so many learned and contentious men in an age of so much theological hair-splitting could

---

[1] Cited in W. G. T. Shedd, *Calvinism: Pure and Mixed* (rpr. Edinburgh: Banner of Truth Trust, 1986), p. 161.

[2] James Reid, *Memoirs of the Westminster Assembly of Divines* (Edinburgh: Banner of Truth Trust, 1982), p. 130.

with so little coercion establish so resounding a consensus on so detailed a doctrinal statement is one of the marvels of the century."[3] Criticism of the divines as precisionists is certainly not exclusively a twentieth century sport.

A great tradition of slandering the divines exists. In his 1647 burlesque, *The Assembly-Man*,[4] John Birkenhead (1616-1679) illustrates the accusation of the divines for intolerance: "The only difference 'twixt the Assembler and a Turk, is, that one plants Religion by the power of the Sword, and the other by the power of the scimitar." He proceeded to allege, "Nay, the greatest strife in their whole Conventicle, is who shall do worst; for they all intend to make the Church but a Sepulchre, having not onely plundered, but anatomized all the true Clergy."[5]

Thus, these godly men were unfortunately but frequently accused of intolerance and the desire to seize power to persecute their opponents. In response, Hetherington wisely noted "that both the principles and the constitution of a rightly formed Presbyterian Church render the usurpation of power and the exercise of tyranny on its part wholly impossible."

Fairborn alleged that "to the Presbyterians, toleration was the very man of sin" and Masson, Milton's biographer, accused the Assembly as follows: "Toleration to them was a demon, a chimera, the Great Diana of the Independents."[6] They were also accused of immoderation in their pursuit to elucidate so many biblical truths. However, the Confession of Faith is quite moderate and non-inventive in its formulation of biblical truth.

The Assembly's moderation is evident in its refusal to settle the speculative controversy about the order of God's decrees in salvation (lapsarianism), instead allowing those debatable matters to be settled in other forums. Although the moderator (Twisse) had well-formed opinions on this subject, such specificity is not reflected in the Confession. Rather than taking out absolutist positions on every subject, this Assembly was guided by the biblical mandate of moderation. The Confession does not lay out an elaborate end-time scheme nor treat complex ethical issues. Neither does it attempt to settle all conceivable issues. It is restrained and moderate in scope. Still, criticisms endure.

John Milton even roasted the divines in his most famous epic. One scene from *Paradise Lost* was based on the sitting of the Assembly, as angry Milton compared the divines with the fallen angels in the infernal world. Milton likely had the Assembly in mind when he wrote:

> Others, apart, sat on a hill retired,
> In thought more elevate, and reasoned high

---

[3] Sydney Ahlstrom, *A Religious History of the American People* (New York: Doubleday, 1975), vol. I, p. 136.

[4] Found in *Journal of Presbyterian History*, vol. xxi, nos. 2 and 3, June and September, 1943, pp. 133-147.

[5] *Journal of Presbyterian History*, vol. xxi, nos. 2 and 3, p. 140.

[6] William Beveridge, *A Short History of the Westminster Assembly* (1904; rpr. Greenville, SC: A Press, 1991), p. 86.

Of Providence, foreknowledge, will and fate;
Fixed fate, free will, foreknowledge absolute;
And found no end, in wandering mazes lost[7]

Similar doggerl was composed for the Synod as well:

Pretty Synod doth it sit,
Void of grace, as well of wit, . . .
Thereby to end us;
From Synod's nonsense and their treason,
And from their catechistic reason,
Good heaven, defend us![8]

Birkenhead the Royalist sympathizer was one of the most stinging critics of the Assembly. While the Assembly was sitting, his anonymously published tract, *The Assembly-Man*, broadcast vitriolic contempt for the Assembly. Birkenhead alleged that they sat "four years towards a new Religion, but in the interim left none at all."[9] Moreover, he esteemed the divines as "[a]toms; petty small Levites, whose parts are not perceptible . . . [who] follow the Geneva Margin, as those Seamen who understand not the Compass crept along the shore."[10]

Birkenhead assessed the Shorter Catechism as "paultry," accused the divines of being materially motivated, only interested in "silver chains," and satirized that "though the Assembler's Brains are Lead, his Countenance is Brass; for he condemned such as held two Benefices, while he himself has four or five, besides his Concubin-Lecture."[11] Contemporary critics did not avoid personal criticism. Assembly divine John Arrowsmith, an eminent Professor at Cambridge, along with his fellow-assemblymen, was castigated as follows: "So that Learning now is so much advanced, as Arrowsmith's Glass-eye sees more than his Natural."[12]

The Puritan traits of the divines were mocked, and they were charged with effeminacy: "His [a divine] two longest things are his Nails and his Prayer. But the cleanest thing about him is his Pulpit cushion, for he still beats the dust out of it."[13] Of the Puritan long-windedness, Birkenhead ridiculed a divine: "Yet though you heard him three hours, he'll ask a fourth, . . . If he has got any new Tale or Expression, 'tis easier to make Stones speak than him to hold his peace. He hates a Church where there is an Echo for it robs him of his dear Repetition, and confounds

---

[7] Cited in *Memorial Volume of the Westminster Assembly, 1647-1897*, ed. by Francis Beattie, Charles Hemphill, and Henry Escott (Richmond: Presbyterian Committee for Publication, 1897), p. 81.

[8] Cited in *Memorial Volume*, p. 81.

[9] Cf. *Journal of Presbyterian History*, vol. xxi, nos. 2 and 3, p. 137.

[10] Ibid., p. 138.

[11] Ibid., p. 139.

[12] Ibid., p. 141.

[13] Ibid., p. 142.

the Auditory as well as he." Of their sermons Birkenhead alleged that "had they the art to shorten it into Sense, they might write his whole Sermon on the back of their Nail."[14] Bitter criticisms were often set forth, citing the divines as the dupes of Parliament: "At Fasts and Thanksgivings the Assembler is the States' Trumpet; . . . proclaim News, very loud, the Trumpet and his Forehead both of one metal."[15]

Birkenhead's summation of the character of the divines was that they had "the Pride of three Tyrants, the Forehead of six Gaolers, and the Fraud of twelve Brokers. Or take him in the Bunch, and their whole Assembly is a Club of Hypocrites, where six dozen schismatics spend two hours for four shillings apiece."[16]

Is this an accurate description of their spirituality or is it a caricature? If accurate, then by all means these lives should not be spiritual guides. But if inaccurate, we ought to learn from these. Whatever the conclusion, it is important for anyone claiming the heritage of Westminster to do so without naiveté. While exposure to criticism can help us avoid idolizing Westminster, exposure to history can help us avoid the groundless presumption that we are superior.

The Spirituality of the Westminster Assembly

This survey briefly considers the following: fasting, spiritual warfare, preaching, confession of sins, testimonies about the family's nurture of children, as well as missionary zeal, reliance on Scripture, and last breath testimonies of faith from the lips of these seventeenth century saints.

Beecher never spoke more truly than when he said of Calvinism: "There never was a system since the world stood which put upon man such motives to holiness, or which builds batteries which sweep the whole ground of sin with such terrible artillery. As a matter of fact, wherever this system of truth has been embraced it has produced a noble and distinct type of character—a type so clearly marked that secular historians, with no religious bias, have recognized it, and pointed to it as a remarkable illustration of the power of religious training in the formation of character."[17] At the 250th anniversary of this Assembly it was noted: "We claim, then, for our venerable creed, that whatever the world may say of it, it is fitted to be, and according to the testimony of impartial history, has proved itself to be a *character-making* creed."[18]

From the outset of the Assembly these participants saw themselves as unworthy and consequently wanted it known how much they depended on the grace of God from first to last. In the wording of the Solemn League and Covenant,

---

[14] Ibid., p. 145.

[15] Ibid., p. 146.

[16] Ibid., p. 147.

[17] *Memorial Volume of the Westminster Assembly, 1647-1897*, ed. by Francis Beattie, Charles Hemphill, and Henry Escott (Richmond, VA: Presbyterian Committee for Publication, 1897), pp. 261-262.

[18] *Memorial Volume*, p. 265.

adopted first in Scotland and later introduced on August 17th, 1643 to the Assembly, they expressed their inner longings in these words: "we profess . . . our unfeigned [sincere] desire to be humbled for our own sins . . . especially that we have not as we ought valued the inestimable benefit of the gospel; that we have not labored for the purity and power thereof; and that we have not endeavored to receive Christ in our hearts, nor to walk worthy of him in our lives; which are the cause of other sins and transgressions so much abounding amongst us; and our true and unfeigned purpose, desire, and endeavor for ourselves, and all others under our charge . . . to amend our lives, and each one to go before another in the example of a real reformation; that the Lord may turn away his wrath and heavy indignation, and establish these churches and kingdoms in truth and peace."[19]

The genuine piety of the membership of the Assembly is exemplified in a speech by Philip Nye. While urging adoption of the Solemn League and Covenant, he spoke of the fear of the Lord, the humility requisite for their task, and the necessary simplicity of spirit. Nye called for "courage, spirits that are bold and resolute . . . not amazed amidst much stirs . . . wise statesmen, like an experienced seaman, [who] knows the compass of this vessel, and though it heave and toss, and the passengers cry out about him, yet in the midst of its all, he is himself, turning not aside from his work, but steering on his course."[20] As a prototype of the *pathos* and piety of this group. Nye urged:

> I beseech you, let it be seriously considered, if you mean to do any such work in the house of God as this is; if you mean to pluck up what many years ago was planted, or to build up what so long ago was pulled down, and to go through with this work, and not be discouraged, you must beg of the Lord this excellent spirit, this resolute stirring spirit, otherwise you will be outspirited, and both you and your cause slighted and dishonored.[21]

Nye also went on immediately to charge: "On the other hand, we must labor for humility, prudence, gentleness, meekness. A man may be very much zealous and resolute, and yet very meek and merciful: Jesus Christ was a Lion and yet a Lamb also."[22] He concluded his exhortation to adopt the Solemn League and Covenant in a fashion indicative of the Assembly's goal:

> Grant unto us also, that when this life is finished, and we gathered to our fathers, there may be a generation out of our loins to stand up in this cause, that his great, and reverend name may be exalted from one generation to another, until he himself shall come, and perfect all with his own wisdom: even so come Lord Jesus, come quickly. Amen.[23]

---

[19] Anon., *A History of the Westminster Assembly of Divines* (Philadelphia, 1841), p. 38.
[20] Reid, op. cit., p. 379.
[21] Ibid., p. 380.
[22] Ibid., p. 380.
[23] Ibid., p. 381.

These were hearts held out sincerely and promptly to serve God, just as aflame with zeal for the Lord and his house as Calvin and other fathers of the faith had been. These were not sterile academicians; they possessed a passionate zeal for the Lord's honor.

At the covenanting service , the following expressions of prayer and worship were evident: Mr. Wilson expounded verses in the Psalms, with Mr. White praying nearly an hour, followed by another hour-long exhortation by Nye. The commissioners raised their hands as in pledging, after each clause of the Covenant was read. This was followed by another prayer by Dr. Gouge, finalized by adjournment to observe the fast.[24]

Another historian commented on another characteristic of the spirituality of the divines in terms of:

> . . . the sense of humble dependence on God, as seen in the prominence given to prayer. Not only were the daily sessions opened and closed with prayer, and often interspersed with prayer for specific objects, but once a month all business was regularly suspended, that a day of fasting and prayer might be observed in concert with the two houses of Parliament. And what days they were! We read, for instance, in Lightfoot's Journal, that on Friday, October 13, 1643, the order is taken for the fast on the following Monday in these words: 'The time to be from nine to four, the exercises to be the word and prayer, three to pray and two to preach. Dr. Burgess, Mr. Goodwin, and Dr. Stanton to pray, and Mr. Palmer and Mr. Whittacre to preach.'[25]

Fasting

A frequent staple of spiritual rejuvenation for the Assembly was the fast. While in the heat of the debate on the form of government, this Assembly was neither oblivious to prayer concerns nor unmindful of the prayers of the saints poured out on the altar. On May 17, 1644, the Assembly adjourned this controversy to fast and pray for the needs of the nation and the army. According to Baillie, the "sweetest day ever seen in England" saw the divines begin a day of prayer with Dr. Twisse leading, followed by two hours of prayers by Mr. Marshall, confessing the sins of the Assembly in a passionate yet prudent manner. Two hours! The fast continued with preaching by John Arrowsmith, succeeded by another two hour prayer by Mr. Vines. Another sermon was offered, and yet another two-hour prayer was offered by Mr. Seaman. This particular fast led Baillie to say, "God was so evidently in all this exercise, that we expect certainly a blessing both in our matter . . . and in the whole kingdom."[26]

---

[24] Summarized from Beveridge [1904], p. 47.

[25] *Memorial Volume*, pp. 82-83.

[26] Beveridge [1904], pp. 81-82.

Immediately prior to collecting the Scripture proofs, the Assembly felt an ominous pressure from Parliament. When asked to present their final versions with Scripture references, the Assembly hastily "appointed a day of fasting and humiliation for themselves . . . The fast was observed within their own walls on the 6th of May."[27] This Assembly did not trust in their own strength. Rather, they frequently resorted to prayer and fasting. The Scottish ambassadors, keenly aware of the impending storm in England, were "deeply sensible of their own defects . . . [and] the first thing which they did after returning home was to hold a solemn fast to lament their own defection from the solemn league and covenant."[28]

On one occasion, Henry Hall led a solemn fast just prior to the convening of the Assembly (May 29, 1643). On that opportunity he preached on suffering, difficult though it be, as an aid to sanctification. Said Hall, "A Christian is never so glorious, as when he suffers most reproach and ignominy for Christ's sake . . . keep alive this sacred fire, upon the altar of our hearts, that it may inflame our devotion toward God, kindle our love toward men, and burn out all our corruptions."[29]

An early historian said:

> We often find this Assembly engaging in the self-denying duty of fasting; and once a month regularly, they united with the Parliament in observing a solemn fast. On these occasions, nearly the whole day was spent in the public exercises of religion. It is noted by Baillie, that on these solemn occasions, one minister would sometimes pray, without ceasing, for two whole hours. The godly men of that day seem to have been mighty in prayer, and to have known what it was to pray without fainting. Their preaching too, we have reason to believe, from the specimens which have come down to us, was solemn, searching, evangelical, pungent, and powerful. Mr. Baillie incidentally observes, in one of his letters, that Mr. Marshall was reckoned to be the best preacher, and Mr. Palmer the best catechist, in England.[30]

Most of the sermons preached before the Parliament on these fast days were printed later.

Furthermore, the very *Directory for Worship* produced by this Assembly included separate chapters on fasting and thanksgiving, so important were they as spiritual basics. The original drafts of these were drawn up by the pious Goodwin (fasting) and the moderator, Herle (thanksgiving). Samuel Carruthers described one fast:

> The first of these [fasts] was Monday, 25 September, the day when the Commons and the Divines took the Covenant; they met in St. Margaret's Church, White leading in prayer, Nye speaking a word of exhortation, and Gouge concluding with prayer. Three weeks later (16 October) there was again a day of fasting and

---

[27] Anon., *A History of the Westminster Assembly of Divines* (Philadelphia, 1841), p. 124.

[28] Ibid., p. 165.

[29] Reid, Vol. II, p. 6.

[30] Anon., *A History of the Westminster Assembly of Divines* (Philadelphia, 1841), 177-78.

prayer, this time in their usual meeting place. It was from nine till four, and during these seven hours (probably not actually continuous) three men (Burges, Goodwin, and Staunton) prayed, and two (Palmer and Whitaker) preached. Lightfoot records that Burges' prayer took an hour, as did also Staunton's. There were four intervals of psalm-singing, but it is not recorded that Scripture was read; and Twisse concluded with prayer. There was a collection (£3 15s.) for maimed soldiers; but next day it was voted to be given to Mrs. Rood, widow of a minister, in straitened circumstances.[31]

The leading historian in the early twentieth century of the Assembly noted:

On 14 May, 1644, the Lord General, Essex, informed the Divines that he had appointed a fast for the army to be held three days later, and asked them to appoint preachers. They resolved, also at his request, to keep that day as an Assembly fast. Accordingly, Twisse opened with a brief prayer. Then, after singing part of Psalm xxvii, Marshall said, 'Let me speak a few words.' He declared that the nation 'had not had so troublous times for many hundred years;' reminded them that they had been preserved in safety, and that upon them 'the eyes, not only of the kingdom, but of all the churches in Christendom' were fixed. They had expected that much would have been done by now; but 'for some cause or other it pleaseth God that we have had many a sad breach that we cannot drive on so cheerfully.' That was reason enough for humiliation; let each one look into his own heart and see whether he were to blame. Then there was 'common and almost general apostasy in the kingdom;' had they done enough about that? If they did some heart-searching, then, said he, 'we shall find more fruit of one day's musing than of many days' disputing.' He then led in prayer 'for two hours, most divinely, confessing the sins of the members of Assembly in a wonderfully pathetic and prudent way.'[32]

At one fast John Arrowsmith preached for an hour from Haggai 2:4-5, and Richard Vines led in prayer for nearly two hours, followed by a second sermon that also lasted an hour. Samuel Carruthers' details are worth hearing again to capture partially some of the three century old Westminster spirituality.

On 30 June, 1645, the Commons asked the Divines to make the next day a day of prayer. There was no session of the Assembly the next day. Once more ten churches were named, the occasion being made a public one. On 26 September, 1645, the Divines once more resolved to have a day of humiliation for themselves. This was prompted more by the condition of their own business than by that of public affairs. They appointed Wednesday, 1 October, from 9 a.m. to 4 p.m., and appointed two members 'for exhortation' and three 'for prayer.'[33]

---

[31] Samuel Carruthers, *The Everyday Work of the Westminster Assembly* (London: Presbyterian Historical Society, 1943), p. 65.
[32] Ibid., pp. 65-66.
[33] Ibid., pp. 69-70.

The scope and manner of keeping theses fasts is also interesting. "In addition to the regular monthly fast, established by Parliament before the Assembly met, special fasts and thanksgivings were held. The suggestion for these came sometimes from Parliament and sometimes from the Assembly; they were sometimes country-wide (so far at least as the authority of the Parliament might at the time extend), usually a week or more later in the provinces than in London, to allow the instructions to be forwarded; at other times only in certain districts or in certain churches." For example, "[o]n 18 July, 1643, the Assembly suggested a fast 'for the two late disasters in the North and in the West,' but the next day, before they communicated with the Houses, they were informed that one had been fixed for the 21st, and certain divines were asked to preach."[34]

If critics of the Assembly knew more about the prayer lives and fasting of these divines, most criticisms might be delayed until critics exceed the divines' godliness.

Spiritual Battle

In one letter, these divines disclosed their hearts' passion in terms of spiritual warfare: "We doubt not, but the sad reports of the miseries under which the church and kingdom of England do bleed, and wherewith we are ready to be swallowed up, is long since come to your ears; and it is probable, the same instruments of Satan and Antichrist have, by their emissaries, endeavored to present us as black as may be among yourselves."[35]

Their cognizance of the Satanic and the presence of antichristian opposition is apparent from a portion of a letter to Belgic, French, and Swiss churches at the time. The authors' spirituality is seen when they say,

> But though we hoped through the goodness of God, and his blessing . . . that our winter had been past, yet alas! we find it to be quite otherwise. We know our sins have deserved all, and if we die and perish, the Lord is righteous; to his hand we submit, and to him alone we look for healing. The same antichristian faction not being discouraged, by their want of success in Scotland, have stirred up a bloody rebellion in Ireland, wherein above one hundred thousand Protestants have been destroyed in one province . . .[36]

This was an Assembly not only of pious men but one acquainted with persecution, loss, and the peril of death. They concluded this appeal by importunately craving,

> your fervent prayers, both public and private, that God would bring salvation to us; that the blessings of truth and peace may rest upon us; that these three nations may be joined as one stick in the hands of the Lord, and that we ourselves,

---

[34] Ibid., p. 73.

[35] Anon., *A History of the Westminster Assembly of Divines* (Philadelphia, 1841), p. 54.

[36] Ibid., p. 56.

contemptible builders, called to repair the house of God . . . may see the pattern of this house, and commend such a platform of Zerubbabels as may . . . establish uniformity among ourselves; that all mountains may become plains before them and us; that then all who now see the plummet in our hands, may also behold the top-stone set upon the head of the Lord's house among us, and may help us with shouting to cry Grace, grace, to it.[37]

It had also become the practice of the ministers to meet together every Monday to consult together how they might best promote the spread of the gospel. One historian noted that so widespread was the dispersion of piety, that even the military was effected with the result that, "never was an army in which religious feeling, of one kind or another, so predominated. Frequently their commanding officers preached and prayed in public, and the soldiers were deeply imbued with the same spirit, and spent much of their time, when in quarters, in disputing, or praying."[38] This spirit endowed them with invincible courage and admirable piety.

Preaching and Suffering

Experiential Christianity was a forté of these divines. It almost appears that in some way there was a connection between their suffering and their passionate preaching. For example, one unsympathetic poet described Assembly member Edmund Calamy's imprisonment for the faith at Newgate and his preaching style as follows:

Dead, and yet preach! these Presbyterian slaves
Will not give over preaching in their graves . . . .
What can't you Nonconformists be content
Sermons to make, except you preach them too?[39]

Thus, according to opponents, it was one thing for the Westminster men to believe, but critics detested their spreading the tidings even in jail.

Samuel Rutherford, a participant of the Assembly and author of *Lex Rex*, put it well: "The preaching of the word only, if alone without the Spirit, can no more make an hair white or black, or draw us to the Son, or work repentance in sinners, than the sword of the Magistrate can work repentance. . . . What can preaching of man or angel do without God; is it not God and God only who can open the heart?"[40] This same Rutherford, when preaching on Matthew 9:27-31, proclaimed: "As you have need of Christ in your poverty, by faith you accept of him as a Surety to pay your debts when you are broken and cannot pay them yourselves."[41]

---

[37] Ibid., p. 58.

[38] Ibid., p. 143.

[39] Reid, pp. 182-183.

[40] Samuel Rutherford, *A Free Disputation* . . ., p. 351 as cited in Warfield, *The Westminster Assembly and Its Work* (rpr. Edmonton: Still Waters Revival Books, 1992), p. 221.

[41] Samuel Rutherford, *The Power of Faith and Prayer* (1713 rpr. Isle of Lewis: Reformation Press, 1991), p. 51

Robert Harris was a divine who was familiar with the pulpit axiom: "I preach, as if I ne'er should preach again; And, as a dying man, to dying men." This same Harris, both a pastor and the President of Trinity College, Oxford, was known for excellent order in nurturing his own children in the faith. In his last will, he stated: "Also, I bequeath to all my children and their children's children, to each of them a Bible with this inscription, *None but Christ*."[42]

His illnesses were public knowledge, and yet he found sweet delight in the Lord accounting as his best days those in which he "enjoyed most intercourse with Heaven." After a long testimony to the power of the fellowship of sufferings with Christ, James Reid commented that Harris "did not expect much from any man, were his parts ever so great, until he was broken by afflictions and temptations."[43] Harris observed with a keen spiritual eye, "[t]hat it was just for God to deny us the comforts of our graces, when we deny him the glory of them," and "[t]hat the humblest preachers converted the greatest number of souls, not the most choice scholars while unbroken."[44] Harris had the insight to say, "[t]hat a preacher has three books to study: the Bible, himself, and the people . . . [and] that preaching to the people was but one part of the pastor's duty: he was to live and die in them, as well as for them."[45] In sickness he said, "I never in all my life saw the worth of Christ, nor tasted the sweetness of God's love, in so great a measure as I now do."

The lesson has been well stated: "The heroism of these great men was sublime, their self-abnegation, Christ-like. Not for glory did they brave death, not for honors did they toil, but because they were constrained by the love of Christ and of their fellow-men. I would that you, my spiritual fathers, would read more of these 'living epistles' to your people from your pulpits."[46]

Matthew Newcomen, one of the divines, spoke of preaching as "the greater light of heaven," when he charged the Assembly at its outset to have courage:

> Keep no silence, give the Lord no rest until He establish the house . . . except the Lord build the house, reform the Church, it is to no purpose to go about to reform it. . . . I need not tell you how many eyes and expectations there are upon this Assembly. . . . what you pray for, contend for: . . . as you pray that God would establish his Church in peace, so labor to work out the Church's peace. And lastly, as you pray that God would make the Church a praise, so endeavor that also; endeavoring . . . that all her ways may be ordered according to the rule of God's Word: that the Gospel may run and be glorified: that those two great illuminating ordinances of Preaching and Catechizing, which are as the greater and lesser lights of heaven, may have such liberty, encouragement, maintenance, that all the earth may be filled with the knowledge of the Lord.[47]

---

[42] Reid, Vol. II, op. cit., 21.

[43] Ibid., p. 23.

[44] Ibid., 23.

[45] Idem.

[46] *Anniversary Addresses*, p. 40.

[47] Cited in *Journal of Presbyterian History*, vol. xxi, nos. 2 and 3, pp. 126-127.

Many have estimated that the Puritan preaching of the 1640s was among the most influential in history. During that decade, over 240 sermons (185 of which were on OT texts and very few were from the Pauline Epistles[48]) were preached to Parliament, and "[e]very facet of individual and social life was informed and understood by a faith that was subject to Scripture."[49] Rather than utilizing modern features of pulpit ministry such as attempts at humor, levity, drama, and entertainment, these Puritans knew the power of the pulpit to be the dominant medium. Robert Norris reminds us that:

> Any philosophy of preaching that forgets the gravity of the task and neglects the lessons of Westminster will forgo the powerful effects produced by the preaching of those times. We will not serve the present generation by neglecting the lessons of the past. And while sacred eloquence assumes different forms in different generations, and while no time or church can claim perfection in the manner of presenting the truth, rarely has any one Christian assembly produced better counsel backed with the testimony of proven result than the divines assembled at Westminster.[50]

Another glimpse into the Westminster divines' use of the pulpit for spiritual formation may be seen in a typical (and excellent) ongoing series of "exhortations." A decade after the adjournment of the Assembly, several of the divines united to give sermons at "The Morning Exercises at Cripplegate, St. Giles in the Fields, and in Southwark." These exhortations or practical sermons were given by the presbyters near London, many of whom had been supportive of the aims of the Assembly. Even if all of the "Morning Exercise" preachers were not actually involved in the Assembly, there is no evidence that they differed with the *ethos* of the Assembly. A glance at their topics illumines the practical emphasis on spirituality, as well as the priority of preaching. A sample of the sermons (from Westminster divines) below highlights the spiritual thrust of the preaching: "What Must and Can Persons do Toward Their Own Conversion?" (Ez. 18:32) by William Greenhill; "Now is the Time: Or, Instructions for the Present improving the Season of Grace" (2 Cor. 6:1-2) by William Jenkin; "On Sabbath Sanctification" (Is. 63:13-14) by Thomas Case; and "How Ought We to Bewail the Sins of the Places where we Live?" (2 Pet. 2:7-8) by William Jenkin.[51]

---

[48] Cf. Robert M. Norris, "The Preaching of the Assembly," *To Glorify and Enjoy God: A Commemoration of the Westminster Assembly*, John L. Carson and David W. Hall, eds. (Edinburgh: Banner of Truth Trust, 1994), pp. 65, 73.

[49] Ibid., p. 66.

[50] Ibid., p. 81.

[51] Taken from *Puritan Sermons, 1659-1689*, (Wheaton, IL: Richard Owen Roberts, 1981), vols. 1-6. Many other sermons and "cases of conscience" were addressed by the likes of John Owen, Thomas Manton, Robert Trail, Thomas Watson, Richard Baxter, and Stephen Charnock at these preaching sessions.

Confession of Sins

As noted above, these divines were not afraid to confess their sins. On one occasion "Palmer rose with the words, 'I desire to begin there,' and opened with the fault of slack attendance, coming late and going early, especially the sparse attendance at committees. It throws a curious light upon their proceedings that he said that during the meetings there was 'reading of news,' 'talking and in confusion; we do not attend at the beginning nor ending for prayer as we ought to do.' His next complaint is also a perennial one: 'On the one hand, some of us are too forward to speak, and some are, I fear too backward.' Finally, he referred to 'unhappy differences and unbeseeming phrases.'"[52]

Charles Herle was not afraid to admit the sins of the Assembly publicly and arranged a list of offenses of the Assembly in order to expedite confession (below):

I. *The sins of the Assembly.* 1. Neglect of the service, in slackness in coming and departing at pleasure; 2. By abstaining from prayers; 3. Manifesting a neglect in the time of debate, and neglecting committees; 4. Some speaking too much, and others too little; 5. By irreverent carriage; 6. By haste in debating; 7. Driving on parties; 8. Not serious examination of ministers.

II. *Of the armies.* 1. Emulation among the officers, causing the loss of many opportunities; 2. Want of ministers; 3. Swearing, drinking, etc., 4. Want of discipline in the army.

III. *Of the people.* 1. Profaneness, scorn of God's hand upon us; 2. Duties of humiliation 'disfigurated'; 3. Our hearts not humbled upon humiliation; there was 'curling of hair, patching, bare breasts, and painting'; 4. Divisions in opinion and affection among professors; 5. Jealousies, sidings, and tale-bearings; 6. Unthankfulness for God's mercies; 7. Neglect of personal and family reformation; 8. Carnal confidence and general security.

IV. *Of Parliament.* 1. Not tendering the Covenant to all in their power; 2. Not active in suppressing Anabaptists and Antinomians; 3. Not seeking religion in the first place; 4. Not suppressing state plays, taverns, profaneness, and scoffing of ministers, and even incest itself; 5. Not a free publishing of truths, for fear of losing a party; 6. Oppression by committees, with intolerable fees; 7. Not debts paid; 8. Remissness in punishing delinquents; 9. Private ends aimed at, 'the great incomes of some new invented offices'; 10. Delays in relieving the army; 11. Church lands sold, but not for the maintenance of ministers. [53]

Spiritual Formation of the Family

Another aspect of spirituality was the undying commitment of these Assembly-men to the spiritual nurture of children, the family, the sabbath, and character formation. As observed at the 250th anniversary of the Westminster Assembly:

---

[52] Carruthers, op. cit., p. 76.

[53] Ibid., p. 80.

There is a most real and vital connection between belief and conduct, between creed and character. What men believe, that they become. As Bacon says: 'Truth and goodness differ but as the seal and the print; for truth prints goodness.' The same may be said of error and evil. Evil in conduct and character is ever the imprint of error. . . . Today we are to inquire how the Standards, framed by the Westminster Assembly, abide this test. How have they stood translation into real life or incarnation in living men and women? Have their practical effects been such as to vindicate their right to survive among the creeds of Christendom? What influence have they exerted upon 'the individual, the family, and society,' where they have been embraced? . . . The Westminster divines well understood the necessity of training up a child in the way he should go in order to insure against his departing from it in age. They heard and heeded the risen Master's commission to Simon Peter, 'Feed my *lambs*.' Their very best work, in the judgment of many, is found in the provision which they made for the lambs of the flock. Richard Baxter is quoted as saying: 'If the Westminster Assembly had done nothing more than produce the Shorter Catechism they would be entitled to the everlasting gratitude of the Christian church.' He further expressed the opinion that, next to the Bible, it was probably the best book in the world. Hence, wherever these doctrines have been received they have brought forth the fruits of righteousness. What Dr. Chalmers said of Scotland is true the world over: 'Wherever there has been most Calvinism, men have been most moral.'[54]

The beliefs and the practiced spirituality were two sides of the same coin for the Westminster fathers. The "character developed among them was as pure and noble as it was distinct. It is safe to say it has seldom been surpassed in the history of the world. That they had their faults goes without saying. But even their 'failings,' as Burns said of his father's, were such as 'leaned to virtue's side.'"[55]

One of the tell-tale emblems of Westminster spirituality was the honoring and loving of God on a regular, sabbatical basis. Scottish commissioner to the Westminster Assembly, Archibald Johnston, exemplified the spiritual thrust of the Sabbath as he prayed in 1655: "O Lord Jesus, woo Thou their hearts, warme their affections, revive their spirits, gayne their loves; let it be as a resurrection from the dead."[56] On another fast-day,[57] Johnston recorded, "I got several tymes teares in the church prayers, and between sermons with my wyfe, and then in privat with great freedom."[58] The pitch of spirituality is seen in this prayer and memoir by Lord Wariston: "O Lord, speak graciously to the remnant, and cause our ears to hear

---

[54] *Memorial Volume*, pp. 257-258, 260.

[55] *Memorial Volume*, p. 262.

[56] *The Diary of Sir Archibald Johnston of Wariston* (Edinburgh: Scottish Historical Society, 1940) Third Series, vol. XXXIV, p. 9.

[57] Johnston frequently refers to fasts (*The Diary of Sir Archibald Johnston of Wariston* (Edinburgh: Scottish Historical Society, 1919) Second Series, vol. XVIII, pp. 139, 302, 303) and the Lord's Day (Ibid., pp. 43, 130, 303).

[58] *The Diary of Sir Archibald Johnston of Wariston* (Edinburgh: Scottish Historical Society, 1919) Second Series, vol. XVIII, p. 16.

Thee. Oh, I feared our abusing the Lord's patience, who has restrayned the rod now from overflowing . . . and has delayed His anger to see if wee would repent and returne."[59] Historian William H. Roberts, commemorating the spiritual disciplines of the divines a hundred years ago, made this correlation:

> The family and the Sabbath! The two institutions of Eden which survived the wreck of the fall! They are the two strong supports of all social order, the Jachin and Boaz upon which human society rests. Let them be disintegrated and social chaos inevitably follows. These two institutions our venerable Standards exalt as no others do. For their maintenance the Presbyterian Church has always stood. . . . they have been handed down to us as a precious legacy from God-fearing ancestors . . . a high trust, to be passed on in unimpaired integrity to generations yet to come. . . . These two springs of blessing have been opened for us, at unspeakable cost, by hearts and hands long stilled in death. We have drunk from them and been refreshed. . . . There are no institutions of our holy religion which the great enemy of all good is attacking today with more persistent or subtle malignity and zeal.[60]

We also observe the great emphasis on the family as a primary sphere in which the Westminster faith was propagated. One fruit of Westminster is its influence on discipling the family. The role of the family as the chief propagator of the faith can be seen by the extensive use among Westminster adherents of catechism for instructing the young. The Westminster tradition placed a premium on godly parents instructing their covenant children in the principles of the true religion through the catechism. Moreover, family devotionals were a staple for the piety of the Westminster Assembly and great use of family nurture was evident. These made the most of the proverb: "As the twig is bent, the tree is inclined."[61]

On the value of the catechisms and early memorization, a century ago the potential for the influence of the Catechism on youth was estimated as follows:

> 1. Unless they are learned in childhood and youth, the strong probability is that they will never be learned at all. Not one in five hundred of our people, perhaps, learns them later in life. They must be learned, then, early in life, or never. Are we willing for the latter alternative? Are we willing that our children shall never *accurately* know the great truths of religion? Are we willing that they shall never accurately know what is meant by such doctrines as faith, and repentance, and justification, and sanctification? Would that be wise? Would that be safe?
> 2. We cannot too early impress the great truths of the Catechisms on their minds and hearts . . . in childhood and youth the soul is most susceptible of deep and lasting impressions. In our great museums we sometimes see stone slabs with

---

[59] *The Diary of Sir Archibald Johnston of Wariston* (Edinburgh: Scottish Historical Society, 1919) Second Series, vol. XVIII, p. 56.

[60] *Memorial Volume*, pp. 268-269.

[61] *Anniversary Addresses*, p. 230.

the marks of raindrops on them that fell before man had any existence, and the impressions of the feet of tiny birds. . . . So, in childhood and youth, the souls of our children are most susceptible of impressions for good or evil; and then, as the years elapse, those souls, with those impressions on them, indurate; and thus those impressions become as lasting, as everlasting, it may be, as the souls themselves. How important it is, then, that these earliest and most enduring impressions should be made in behalf of right and truth and God by the inculcation of the great truths of our Catechisms!

3. It is necessary to our success as a denomination that our Catechisms be intelligently and faithfully taught. Our doctrines are constantly and bitterly assailed. In much of the literature of the day, especially in that kind which, unfortunately, our children too much read, they are caricatured as severe, harsh, unreasonable, antiquated; as belonging to a remote and ignorant past; as being entirely out of harmony with the progress that has been made in better views of the benevolence, of the divine nature, of the dignity of man, and of the vastness and freeness of redeeming love.[62]

A document written contemporaneous with the drafting of the Westminster Confession also exhibits the strong views of the family held by the Scottish commissioners. In 1647, the Scottish General Assembly approved a *Directory for Family Worship*. This document reflected the views as well as the sentiments of many of the members of the Westminster Assembly on the importance of family worship. So essential was family worship—not only as a supplement to regular worship on the Lord's Day—that the Scottish presbyters laid out directions that were to be used to augment building up of faith, cherishing piety, maintaining of unity, and deterring schism among godly families. So important was this family faith that the Scottish General Assembly even called upon presbyteries to require those within their bounds to carry these things out at the threat of discipline and moreover that every individual family was to practice family worship. "And if any such family be found, the head of the family is to be first admonished privately to amend his fault; and, in case of his continuing therein, he is to be gravely and sadly reproved by the session; after which reproof, if he be found still to neglect Family-worship, let him be, for his obstinacy in such an offence, suspended and debarred from the Lord's supper, as being justly esteemed unworthy to communicate therein, till he amend."

Missionary Zeal

Another mistake of those who are not thoroughly familiar with the Westminster divines is to allege that they had little or no interest in foreign missions. As early as John Calvin there was interest in evangelizing the Villegagnon Colony (Brazil).[63]

---

[62] *Memorial Volume*, pp. 136-137.

[63] "The Westminster Divines and Foreign Missions," *Journal of the Presbyterian Historical Society*, vol. xxi, June and September, 1943, nos. 2 and 3, p. 148.

By 1641, fifteen divines who would become commissioners to the Westminster Assembly joined William Castell in a petition calling for the evangelization of the New World. In addition to these, two of the Scottish divines, Alexander Henderson and Robert Baillie, joined their names to the petition that had seventy signatories. The petition began with a lament about "the great and general neglect of this kingdome, in not propagating the glorious Gospel in America, a maine part of the world."[64] The petition continued:

> Although some of the reformed religion, English, Scotch, French, and Dutch, have already taken up their habitations in those parts, yet both their going thither (as yet) has been to small purpose, for the converting of those nations, either for that they have placed themselves but in the skirts of America, where there are but few natives (as those in New England), or else for want of able and conscionable ministers (as in Virginia) they themselves are become exceeding rude, more likely to turn Heathen, than to turn others to the Christian faith.[65]

The petitioners noted that "there is no great difficulty in the preparation here, or tediousnesse in the passage thither, or hazard when wee come there. . . . It being ordinarily by six weeks sayle, in a sea much more secure for Pirats . . . And as for our good successe there, wee need not fear it. The natives being now every where more than ever, out of an inveterate hatred to the Spaniard, ready and glad to entertained us."[66]

Signed by Westminster divines R. Brownricke, R. Sanderson, D. Featly, M. Styles, E. Stanton, G. Walker, J. Caryl, E. Calamy, A. Byfield, W. Price, J. White, H. Paynter, S. Marshall, J. Burroughes, and J. Whittaker, this petition to Parliament concluded:

> And which is much more our going with a generall consent in Gods cause, for the promoting of the Gospel, and inlarging of his church, may assure us of a more than ordinary protection and direction. That hitherto, wee have been lesse successfull in our voyage that way, wee may justly impute it to this, that as yet they have not beene undertaken with such a generall consent, and with such a full reference to Gods glory as was requisite. And so your Petitioner having delivered his apprehension herein, more briefly, then so weighty a matter might well require, he submits all the premises to your more full deliberation and conclusion, which hee humbly prayeth, may bee with all convenient speed; the onely best way under God to make it the better successfull . . . concerning the propagation of the glorious Gospel of Christ in America.[67]

[64] Idem.
[65] Ibid., p. 149.
[66] Ibid., p. 156.
[67] Ibid., p. 157.

The Scottish Parliament also received a similar bill, signed by Henderson and Baillie:

> The motion made by Master William Castell, Minister of the Gospel, for propagating of the blessed Evangell of Christ our Lord and Savior in America, wee conceive in the generall to bee most pious, Christian and charitable. And therefore worthy to be seriously considered, of all that love the glorious name of Christ, and are zealous of the salvation of soules, which are without Christ, and without God in the world, wishing the opportunity and fit season: the instruments and means. And all things necessary for the prosecution of so pious a worke, to bee considered by the wisedomes of Churches and civil powers, whom God hath called, and enables with Piety, Prudence, and Peace, for matters of publicke concernment, and of so great Importance, And beseeching the Lord to blesse all their consultations and proceedings for the advancing and establishing the Kingdome of Jesus Christ.[68]

In addition, the work of John Eliot to the American missionaries illustrates that these divines were neither narrow in their concerns nor sterile in their spiritual impulses. About the time of the conclusion of the Assembly, the following pamphlets were published in London: *The Day-Breaking, if not the Sun-rising of the Gospel with the Indians in New-England* (1647); *The Clear Sun-shine of the Gospel, etc.* (1648); *The Glorious Progress of the Gospel, etc.* (1649); *The Light appearing more and more towards the perfect Day, etc.* (1651); *Strength out of Weaknesse* (1652); and *Tears of Repentance* (1653). These demonstrate a devout concern for missions.

Scripture

No survey of Westminster spirituality would be complete without reference to the admiration of the divines for Scripture, which they viewed as both the authority for life and a devotional staple. The Assembly was so emphatically tied to the Bible that they even proposed a study Bible. A committee was commissioned to make "[t]he Annotations of the Westminster Assembly." Annotations to the Pentateuch, the OT historical books, Psalms, Proverbs, the major prophets, the Gospels, and Paul's Epistles were compiled. However, these were never published with the sanction of Parliament.

On the views of Assembly members and the Bible, Calamy, one of the most astute professors also commented,

> There are two great Gifts that God hath given to his people. The *Word Christ*, and the *Word of Christ*; Both are unspeakably great; but the first will do us no good without the second. . . . Blessed be God who hath not only given us the book of the Creatures, and the book of Nature to know himself and his will by; but also, and especially the book of Scriptures, whereby we come to know those things of

---

[68] Ibid., pp. 158-159.

God, and of Christ, which neither the book of Nature nor of the Creatures can reveal unto us. Let us bless God, not only for revealing his Will in his Word, but for revealing it by writing.[69]

One of the participants of the Assembly, Anthony Burgess, wrote in another place on this same topic: "As for that dangerous opinion, that makes God's calling of man to repentance by the Creatures, to be enough and sufficient, we reject, as that which cuts at the very root of free grace: A voice, indeed, we grant they have, but yet they make Paul's trumpet, an uncertain sound; men cannot by them [creational revelation] know the nature of God and his Worship, and wherein our Justification doth consist."[70] John Arrowsmith, another member of the Assembly and one of the leading theological professors of the time, said similarly, "For to maintain (as some do) that a man may be saved in an ordinary course . . . by any religion whatsoever, provided he live according to the principles of it, is to turn the whole world into an Eden; and to find a Tree of Life in every garden, as well as in the paradise of God."[71]

Even more to the point, Assembly member William Bridge stated, "Though Human Reason be a Beam of Divine Wisdom, yet if it be not enlightened with an higher Light of the Gospel, it cannot reach unto the things of God as it should. . . . For though reason be the Gift of God, yet it doth proceed from God as he is God, and General Ruler of the World."[72]

The Scotsman George Gillespie wrote: "The Scripture is known to be indeed the word of God by the beams of divine authority it hath in itself . . . such as the heavenliness of the matter; the majesty of the style; the irresistible power over the conscience; the general scope, to abase man and to exalt God; nothing driven at but God's glory and man's salvation . . . the supernatural mysteries revealed therein, which could never have entered the reason of men; the marvelous consent of all parts and passages (though written by divers and several penmen), even where there is some appearance of difference . . . these, and the like, are characters and marks which evidence the Scriptures to be the word of God."[73]

Calamy attested,

It is certain that all Scripture is of Divine inspiration, and that the holy men of God spake as they were guided by the Holy Ghost. . . . It transcribes the mind and heart of God. A true Saint loveth the Name, Authority, Power, Wisdom, and Goodness

---

[69] Edward Calamy, *The Godly Man's Ark*. London, 1672, pp. 55-56, and 90 as cited in Warfield, *The Westminster Assembly and Its Work*, p. 198.

[70] Anthony Burgess in *Spiritual Refining*, London, 1652, p. 588 as cited in Warfield *supra*, p. 197.

[71] John Arrowsmith in *A Chain of Principles*, Cambridge, 1659, p. 128 as cited in Warfield *supra*, pp. 197-198.

[72] William Bridge, *Scripture-Light, the Most Sure Light*, London, 1656, pp. 32-33, as cited in Warfield, p. 199.

[73] Cf. Gillespie's *Miscellaneous Questions*, p. 105-106 of the Presbyterian's Armory edition, cited by Warfield, p. 176.

of God in every letter of it, and therefore cannot but take pleasure in it. It is an Epistle sent down to him from the God of heaven . . . The Word of God hath God for its Author, and therefore must needs be full of Infinite Wisdom and Eloquence, even the Wisdom and Eloquence of God. There is not a word in it, but breathes out God, and is breathed out by God. It is . . . an invariable rule of Faith, an *unerring* (emphasis added) and infallible guide to heaven.[74]

All the Scriptures are *theopneustoi* ["God-breathed" as in 2 Tim. 3:16] by Divine inspiration; and therefore the breathings of God's spirit, are to be expected in this Garden: and those commands of attending to the Scripture only, and to observe what is written, is a plain demonstration that God hath tied us to the Scriptures only: so that as the child in the womb liveth upon nourishment conveyed by the Navel cleaving to it, so doth the Church live only upon Christ by the Navel of the scripture, through which all nourishment is conveyed.[75]

Of the autographs as the authority and without error, Daniel Featly said, "If you will dispute in Divinity, you must be able to produce the Scriptures in the Original Languages. For no Translation is simply Authentical, or the undoubted word of God. In the undoubted word of God there can be no error. But in Translations there may be, and are errors. The Bible translated therefore is not the undoubted Word of God, but so far only as it agreeth with the Original."[76]

Edward Reynolds wrote, "The scriptures . . . are the alone rule of all controversies . . . So then the only light by which differences are to be decided, is the word, being a full canon of God's revealed will."[77] Samuel Rutherford was of the opinion that, "The Scripture makes it self the judge and determiner of all questions and controversies in religion."[78] Youthful George Gillespie spoke of "the written word of God [as] surer than any voice which can speak in the soul of a man, and an inward testimony may sooner deceive us than the written word can; which being so, we may and ought to try the voice which speaks in the soul by the voice of the Lord which speaks in the Scripture."[79]

The leading scholar at the Assembly of the Bible in its original languages, John Lightfoot, clarified the importance of the Scripture this way: "How may Christians inquire of God in their doubtings, as Israel did . . . in theirs? I answer briefly, . . . to the written word of God, Search the Scriptures. . . . There is now no other way to inquire of God, but only from his word."[80]

As to the modern question of whether or not the Westminster Confession of Faith advocated the inerrancy of Scripture, the above citations should be sufficient.

---

[74] *The Godly Man's Ark*, pp. 55, 80 as cited in Warfield, pp. 208-209.

[75] Anthony Burgess in *Spiritual Refining*, p. 152 as cited in Warfield, p. 208.

[76] Cited by Warfield, p. 242.

[77] *Works*, v., pp. 152-153, 1826 as cited in Warfield, p. 256.

[78] *A Free Disputation*, London, 1649, p. 361 as cited in Warfield, p. 256.

[79] *Miscellaneous Questions*, 1649 as cited by Warfield, p. 256.

[80] *Works of John Lightfoot*, vi, p. 286 as cited in Warfield, p. 256.

Other contemporaries of the Westminster Assembly, such as Richard Baxter, a leading Puritan of the day, uttered the following.

> May one be saved who believeth that the Scripture hath any mistake of error, and believeth it not all? . . . He that thinketh that the prophets, sacred historians, evangelists, and apostles, were guided to an infallible delivery and recording of all the great, substantial, necessary points of the gospel, but not to an infallibility in every by-expression, phrase, citation, or circumstance, doth disadvantage his own faith as to all the rest; but yet may be saved, if he believe the substance with a sound and practical belief.[81]

Samuel Rutherford wrote:

> Whereas the means of conveying the things believed may be fallible, as writing, printing, translating, speaking, are all fallible means of conveying the truth of old and new Testament to us, and yet the Word of God in that which is delivered to us is infallible, 1. For let the Printer be fallible. 2. The translation fallible. 3. The grammar fallible. 4. The man that readeth the word or publisheth it fallible, yet this hindereth not but the truth itself in the written word of God is infallible.[82]

Edward Reynolds, a member of the Assembly, tied the unfailingness of Scripture to the attributes of God. Reynolds wrote:

> 1. That God in his authority is infallible, who neither can be deceived, nor can deceive. 2. That the things, delivered in holy Scriptures are the dictates and truths, which that infallible authority hath delivered unto the church to be believed; and therefore that every supernatural truth, there plainly set down . . . in an unquestionable principle; and everything, but evident consequence and deduction from thence derived, is therefore an undoubted conclusion in theological and divine knowledge.[83]

Furthermore, Reynolds was clear when he said,

> First, That God is of infallible authority, and cannot lie nor deceive: which thing is a principle, . . . And, secondly, That this authority, which in faith I thus rely upon, is, indeed and infallibly, God's own authority. . . . in regard to our weakness and distrust, we are often subject to stagger, yet, in the thing itself, it dependeth upon the infallibility of God's own Word, who hath said it, and is, by consequence, nearer unto Him who is the fountain of all truth; and therefore must need more share in the properties of truth, which are certainty and evidence . . . [84]

---

[81] An excellent summary of these contemporaneous views is set forth in the article, "Inerrancy, Infallibility, and Scripture in the Westminster Confession of Faith" by John Delivuk in the *Westminster Theological Journal*, Fall 1992, vol. 54, no. 2, pp. 349-355.

[82] Ibid., p. 352.

[83] Ibid., p. 353.

[84] Ibid., p. 354.

John Delivuk concludes,

> Edward Reynolds and the other authors of the WCF believed that the Bible was inerrant. This was shown above by the seventeenth-century meaning of the word infallible, the confession writers' use of infallible in contexts where it could be used interchangeably with inerrant, and by their view of Scripture as the product of a perfect God, who had given some his attributes, such as truth and perfection, to his word. The combined evidence of these three points leads one to conclude that the authors of the confession believed strongly in the inerrancy of the Bible. . . . The authors of the confession believed that the Bible is reliable and true in all matters which it addresses, that it is completely free from all errors, falsehoods, or deceits, and that this truthfulness extends to all matters religious and secular.[85]

Final Spirituality

A final attribute of this sophisticated spirituality is bravery. "Courage is another trait which to a marked degree has characterized such as are moulded by this creed. . . . He who believes in an Almighty Father, who has foreordained whatsoever comes to pass, and who through his overruling providence is preserving and governing all his creatures, and all their actions, is made superior to those experiences of life which cause others to quake and fear. Hence, Bancroft says, 'A coward and a Puritan never went together.'" [86]

Such bravery is evident in the death-bed testimonies of some of these divines. On dying in a manner worthy of our Lord, Jeremiah Whittaker put it this way:

> 'O, my God, break open the prison door, and set my poor captive soul free: but enable me to wait willingly thy time. I desire to be dissolved. Never was any man more desirous of life, than I am of death. When will that time come, when I shall neither sin nor sorrow any more? When shall mortality put on immortality? . . . The soul that would be truly wise, And taste substantial joys, Must rise above this giddy world, And all its trifling toys. Our treasure and hearts with God, We die to all on earth.'[87]

Often the truest measure of Christian vitality is weighed at the conclusion of life. When all was completed, when the fruit was harvested, these divines were some of the most excellent Christians ever, certainly enough to induce us to give a respectful consideration of their words and works. Joseph Caryl was one such member of this Assembly who though dead still speaks. About him, as an example of piety, it was elegized,

---

[85] Ibid., p. 355. Cf. also John Delivuk, "Some Hermeneutical Principles of the Westminster Confession" in *Evangelical Hermeneutics*, Michael Bauman and David W. Hall, eds. (Camp Hill, PA: Christian Publications, 1995).

[86] *Memorial Volume*, pp. 263-264.

[87] Reid, Vol. II, pp. 232-234.

His pious sermons did declare his worth,
His expositions set his learning forth; . . .
As in some mirror you might clearly see
In him, a perfect map of Piety;[88]

Samuel Rutherford was known as an ardent defender of the faith. Flavel commended him for contending against the sectarians of the day, while Robert Baillie extolled Rutherford as a champion against diverse enemies and specifically against the antinomians. Piety was one of his greatest attributes. As he was dying, Rutherford uttered, "I feed upon manna, I have angels' food, my eyes shall see my Redeemer, I know that He shall stand at the latter day on the earth, and I shall be caught up in the clouds to meet Him in the air . . . I sleep in Christ, and when I awake I shall be satisfied with his likeness. O for arms to embrace him."[89] His final words were, "Glory, glory dwells in Emmanuel's land." In the hymn "The Sands of Time are Sinking," Annie Cousins paraphrased the dying words of pious Rutherford, exhibiting the final level of this man's convictions. Perhaps many have sung this hymn without knowing it originated from the sentiments of one of the members of the Westminster Assembly.

Oh! Christ, he is the fountain,
The deep, sweet well of love;
The streams on earth I've tasted,
I'll drink more deep above.
There to an ocean fullness
His mercy doth expand,
And glory, glory dwelleth
In Immanuel's land.[90]

Conclusion

These lives are full of piety and well worth knowing. They are examples of timeless spirituality, well-rounded, balanced, and stable. Most will be spurred on to greater faithfulness in Christian living by studying the men of Westminster. Reflecting on the value of familiarity with these divines, James Reid noted:

a brilliant constellation at Westminster. . . [of] sound principles, Christian dispositions, and conversation becoming the gospel of Christ. In these, we may clearly see the power of divine grace shining forth in all its glory in real life, subduing the inbred corruptions of our fallen nature, and animating to every good

---

[88] Reid, pp. 198-199.

[89] Reid, II, p. 357.

[90] Many other biographical sketches are available to further these and other lessons in spirituality. For a particularly helpful recent work, cf. William S. Barker, *Puritan Profiles* (Geanies House, Fearn, Ross-shire, Scotland: Christian Focus Publications, 1996).

word and work. In these, we may see pious and learned men eminently zealous in the advancement of true religion, and earnestly contending for the faith which was once delivered unto the saints.[91]

On the benefit of reviving the influence of this spiritual vitality, one hundred years ago Robert Coyle urged:

> What we need to multiply conversions, to make our preaching mighty, to kindle our missionary fires, to set every Board free from the incubus of debt, to bring us together, North and South, to unite the entire Presbyterian family, and send us forth upon a new career of conquest and glory, is a revival of loyalty to our King. What is needed is to get away from side issues, away from the catching themes of the hour, away from themes literary, and themes political, and themes social, and themes exploited by the daily press, and lift up the name of our King, and make it pre-eminent above every name. Unless this is done, agnosticism and materialism will win the day. Unless this is done, the pulpit will go into eclipse.[92]

Often overlooked is the fact that these Westminster standards also have influence and potential for unity.

> Some do not like creeds; but our Church has always thought it fair and honorable to state explicitly what it understands the Word of God to teach. Our Creed then is our witness-bearer to the whole world. Indeed, no man can write or preach a sermon without stating in part his creed, and we are bound to contend earnestly for the faith once delivered to the saints. At the same time our Creed is pre-eminently an irenical document, and we believe the clear, definite statement by the Christian denominations of what they believe, is the very best road to an ultimate agreement of the churches on the fundamental and essential doctrines of our holy religion.[93]

The examples of these divines are of enduring value and in no way out-dated for they represent God's eternal truths. Of existing resources among Christians, these practices are still among the best, although they are frequently ignored. Rather than being so dismissive, we should know something of the inner lives of those divines at Westminster. It helps to know what spiritual disciplines were used by Christians three and a half centuries ago.

Many Christians have already plowed the furrows of spiritual formation. In this discipline, we do not unearth much that is radically new. In the main, we merely dust off a great chapter of history that is not so different from our own times. Since the faith is the same in 1643 as in 1993 (cf. Jude 3), we find some agreement with Chesterton who called the church, a "democracy of the dead," meaning that if we truly understand the unity of the church—both militant and triumphant—we will not want to disenfranchise those in our church who have gone home to be with the Lord. They, too, have much to say in the referenda of today.

---

[91] Reid, Vol. II, p. 3.

[92] *Anniversary Addresses,* 1898, p. 145. Note, and it did!!

[93] *Anniversary Addresses,* p. 176.

Measuring the influence of Westminster by its ability to inspire extraordinary spiritual courage and loyalty, the comment was made a century ago that, "Rather than yield their rights of conscience, 2000 English Presbyterian ministers, on St. Bartholomew's Day, 1662, showed the stuff they were made of by leaving their churches, their support, their homes, their weeping flocks, and becoming strangers and wanderers in their native land. It was this doctrine that put into the Presbyterians of Scotland the strength and stability of their own granite hills. . . . Happy will it be for our denomination if this day shall kindle something more of that spirit in us, and send us to our homes and our people to pass it along."[94]

Nor are these merely past sentiments, true only for an earlier age. At a commemoration of the Assembly one century ago, the record was set straight:

> The accusations which their opponents have made against them have, in most instances, been encomiums. They have been criticized for being too strict and uncompromising in their views of life and duty. But all excellence is marked by strictness. Strictness certainly characterizes everything which truly represents God. The laws of nature are all strict; the laws of hygiene are strict; and the life which would secure their benediction must be a strict life. So with the laws of morals. Like him who ordained them they know 'no variableness nor shadow of turning.' Any pretended exposition of the moral nature and claims of God which is characterized by looseness, by that very tact brands itself as false. Their narrowness has been unctuously deplored. But after all is it not the narrowness of truth? The Master himself said, 'Strait is the gate and narrow is the way which leadeth unto life, and few there be that find it.' 'Narrowness,' it has been said, 'is often the badge of usefulness.' Great leaders of men have been narrow. Elijah was too narrow to adopt the worship of Baal. Martin Luther was too narrow to include in his creed the errors of the Papacy. Wesley was too narrow to sympathize with the cold ritualism of his age. William Carey was so narrow that he had no sympathy with the anti-mission spirit of his age. Gideon was so narrow that he could not tolerate the idols in his father's house, but rose in his might and tore them down. The narrowness of Calvinists has usually been of the same sort.[95]

---

[94] *Anniversary Addresses*, pp. 140-141.
[95] *Memorial Volume*, pp. 262-263.

A Brief Tutorial on the Value
of Religion for Politics

Many journalists, certain political pundits, and even some Christians do not believe that Christianity or its influence is salutary in its effect on politics. To read some reports, the rise of the religious right may be the biggest threat to Western civilization since the Huns. Biblical religion, however, has not always been viewed as a threat to political health. In many ages it has been seen as positively beneficial. Following a generation of widespread mythology about the ills of religion's effect on politics, a brief tutorial on the benefit of religion may be in order.

In early biblical times, Joseph took his faith into the political theater, rising to become a trusted official in the administration of an Egyptian king. Centuries later, Moses (and Jethro) would contribute the earliest known republican structure. A seventeenth century political theorist, Johannes Althusius, extolled the virtues of this original political structure: "I consider that no polity from the beginning of the world has been more wisely and perfectly constructed than the polity of the Jews. We err, I believe, whenever in similar circumstances we depart from it." Part of what he had in mind as unimproveable was an early form of republican-federal government. Both American Christians and secularists would do well to review the origins of our own form of government to realize its biblical moorings.

Religion: The Origin of the Republican Form

Exodus 18 provides an early example of the federal-republican structure that became the basis for our American republic. Thus, our government structure is inherently and originally religious in nature and root. Accordingly, *the best government in the world models and follows the best government in the Bible.*

By the time of Moses, a consistent tradition of government prevailed. In earlier times, however, small social units were governed by patriarchs or elders. A century before Moses, most governments were either small tribal units or, if large, monarchies. The pinnacle of Egyptian culture saw monarch after monarch follow one another in dynastic succession. The great Pharaohs—Rameses, Thutmoses, and Tutankhamon—were authoritarian monarchs, pure and simple. In the half century preceding Moses, institutions resembling a senate, a council, or other checking branches of government did not exist. Unilateral power was located in the monarch, both in the Middle East and the Far East.

Moreover, all that the people of Israel knew—four centuries after the time of Jacob—was the monarchical pattern of government. Ideas or notions about government by any pattern other than hierarchical were not evidenced. Other schemes were forgotten, unknown, or at least not practiced anywhere around them. Thus, the republican-type plan suggested by Jethro came as an innovation and did not have its origin in the mind of man or the will of the flesh.

A form of governing was introduced during Moses' leadership. Rather than instituting either a democracy or a monarchy, leadership was by a plurality of prudent representative leaders who were to have wisdom, the fear of the Lord, trustworthiness, and hatred of graft (Ex. 18:21). This early form of a representative government indicates that layers of accountability (Ex. 18:21) are warranted, with differing levels of leadership hearing appeals and acting on matters as they arise (Dt. 1:15-18). In contrast to the predominance of monarchs at the time, Jethro advised Moses to institute a graduated series of administrations. This early pattern permits problems to be handled first by those closest to the issues. Then, if not satisfactory, they may proceed to the next level of administration (appeal). This federal structure preserves a blend of grass-rootedness with a modicum of unity. The earliest American constitutional documents sought to preserve and perpetuate this delicate balance between unity and independence. It seems that the earliest republican form of government came from the mind of God through Jethro, a non-Israeli priest, long before either the Golden Age of Greco-Roman governance or the Enlightenment or modern revolutions.

Both the biblical mooring and the superiority of this system seemed obvious to those in the founding era of America. Indeed, many theorists, ranging from Aquinas and Machiavelli to Althusius and Thielicke, see Jethro's advice as a pristine example of federalism or republicanism. Commenting on the parallel passage in Deuteronomy 1:14-16, Calvin stated: "Hence it more plainly appears that those who were to preside in judgment were not appointed only by the will of Moses, but elected by the votes of the people. And this is the most desirable kind of liberty, that we should not be compelled to obey every person who may be tyrannically put over our heads; but which allows of election, so that no one should rule except he be approved by us. And this is further confirmed in the next verse, wherein Moses recounts that he awaited the consent of the people, and that nothing was attempted which did not please them all." Thus, Calvin viewed this distinctive religious benefit as a republican form.

Thomas Aquinas viewed the Mosaic government as an early incarnation of republican democracy: "Such was the form of government established by the Divine Law. For Moses and his successors governed the people in such a way that each of them was ruler over all . . . Moreover, seventy-two men were chosen, who were elders in virtue . . . so that there was an element of aristocracy. But it was a democratical government in so far as the rulers were chosen from all the people . . ."

Other biblical commentators have interpreted similarly. Samuel Rutherford in *Lex Rex* used the Mosaic pattern to argue for a republican or at least an anti-monarchical form of civil polity. Indeed, most of the Reformation era political tracts (e. g., by Calvin, Beza, Bucer, Knox, Buchanan, Ponet, Althusius, etc.) devoted extensive commentary to the OT patterns of government. These reformers viewed the canon of Scripture as applicable for their own politics.

This origin of the federal or republican form of government contained correction for maladministration and provided a decentralized form. With no other prior examples, and with this innovation coming from a spiritual man, the question begs itself: What was the origin of this idea since it was so unusual?

Since this pattern can hardly be ascribed to the surrounding nations or to earlier precedent, and since it is not the most efficient form of government, the origin of the idea of republicanism may be inexplicable apart from divine revelation. Indeed, no ruling class—apart from thoroughly Christian virtue—would dream up such power sharing. Nor would any except the most distrustful of human ability concoct such balance of power. It seems that the only likely explanations for the origin of this republicanism lie in (1) the divine revelation from God through Jethro, or (2) the logical extension of the doctrine of human depravity. Of course, these two together provide a satisfactory rationale for the beginning of republican government.

Perhaps the best reason for viewing Moses' government as early republicanism is the NT phrase, *politeia* (cf. Eph. 2:12), which clarifies the meaning of the "citizenship" of Israel. By inference we may understand that the *politeia* of Israel denoted a free, constitutional government, since the word *politeia* was thus employed by Plato, Aristotle, Cicero and others in pre-Christian eras. In Aristotle's writings, the four major options for forms of government were: monarchy, polity (*politeia*, republic), democracy, or tyranny. The word "*politeia*" as used in Ephesians 2:12 was consistently used of a republican government. In this case, it illuminates what was meant by the Mosaic form of government. The NT frequently adopted useful political concepts of its day.

Rather than eschewing political variables, the NT actually empolys many political concepts. "Governments" is listed as a charismatic gift (Rom. 12:8; 1 Cor. 12:28), and the Apostle urges for sin not to be allowed to "reign" (Rom. 6:12). The NT word for church, *ekklesia*, itself doubles as the term for the meeting of the citizen assembly (Acts 19:23). One early church theologian, Origen, even seems to draw a conscious parallel between the *ekklesia* of God in Athens and Corinth and the civil *ekklesia* is those same municipalities. If political categories such as these were inherently evil, the NT would have avoided them as pervasive metaphors.

The NT frequently invokes governmental terminology, such as: principalities (Col. 1:16), rulers (1 Cor. 2:8; 15:24; Eph. 1:21; Eph. 2:2; Eph. 3:10; Eph. 6:12; Col. 1:16), kings (1 Cor. 4:8), ambassadors (2 Cor. 5:20), authorities (Eph. 1:21; Col. 1:16; 2:15), and dominions (Eph. 1:21; Col. 1:13; Tit. 3:2). These metaphors are no more improper than metaphors from athletics, farming, or other images. The categories themselves are not evil or sub-Christian. Christians are members, political citizens (*politeia*; Eph. 2:19), of the new Israel. Ruben Alvarado concludes his study of NT political terminology: "[T]he New Testament's adoption of the language of the *polis* to describe the nature and ministry of the church means that the contemporary privatized view of the church is erroneous. From the beginning the church's ministry has been public, even when it has gone unrecognized. We moderns have accepted the lie that the church is not and cannot be a public institution. But like it or not, that is what she is." The NT does not avoid governmental matters; it seeks to transform them and "take every thought captive" to Christ (2 Cor. 10:5). The Bible has an unmistakably political emphasis in certain of its teachings.

From the earliest of biblical episodes, believers have salted (not assaulted) society and politics. In most cases, religious influence—such as in the origination of republicanism—has been decidedly positive.

Examples of Salt and Light

A few other examples of biblical Christianity ushering virtues into the public square will support the notion that biblical insights benefit politics. Many could be mentioned, but we will restrain ourselves to mention only a few highpoints of religious contribution to politics. To answer the question: "Is religion of any benefit to civil society?" consider the following.

Early Christians left behind a clear tradition of praying for political leaders. The apostolic church proved its salutary effect and positive posture toward governors when they prayed as follows.

Justin Martyr (ca. AD 150) wrote: "And everywhere, we, more readily than all men, endeavor to pay those appointed by you the taxes, both ordinary and extraordinary, as we have been taught by him . . . Whence to God alone we render worship, but in other things we will gladly serve you, acknowledging you as kings and rulers of men, and praying that with your kingly power you may be found to possess also sound judgment. But if you pay no regard to our prayers and frank explanations, we shall suffer no loss, since we believe . . . that every man will suffer punishment in eternal fire according to the merit of his deed, and will render account according to the power he has received from God . . ."[1]

Once while pleading for peace, Athenagoras, another early Christian teacher and writer, stated: "We deserve favor because we pray for your government, that you may, as is most equitable, receive increase and addition, until all men become subject to your sway."[2]

Tertullian (*Apology* 30, ca. AD 200) reported that Christians offered prayer:

> for the safety of our princes to the eternal, the true, the living God, whose favor beyond all other things, they must themselves desire. They know from whom they have obtained their power . . . They reflect upon the extent of their power and so they come to understand the highest; they acknowledge that they have all their might from him against whom their might is nought. Let the emperor make war on heaven; let him lead heaven captive in his triumph; let him put guards on heaven; let him impose taxes on heaven! He cannot. . . . He gets his scepter where he first got his humanity; his power where he got the breath of life. . . . Without ceasing, for all our emperors we offer prayer. We pray for life prolonged; for security to the empire; for protection for the imperial house; for brave armies, a faithful senate, a virtuous people, the world at rest, whatever, as man or Caesar, and emperor would wish . . . [because the emperor] is called by our Lord to his office . . . on valid grounds I might say Caesar is more ours than yours because our God appointed him. Therefore, as having this propriety in him, I do more than you for his welfare, not merely because I ask of him who can give it, or because I ask it as one who deserves to get it, but also because, in keeping the majesty of Caesar within due limits, and putting it under the Most High, and making it less than divine, I commend him the more to the favor of Deity, to whom I make him alone inferior. But I place him in subjection to one I regard as more glorious than himself.[3]

Clement of Rome offered this prayer which illustrates a proper attitude toward civil authority: "Grant to them, Lord, health, peace, concord, and stability, so that they may exercise without offense the sovereignty that you have given them. Master, heavenly King of the ages, you give glory, honor, and power over the things of earth to the sons of men. Direct, Lord, their counsel, following what is pleasing and acceptable in your sight, so that by exercising with devotion and in

---

[1] Justin Martyr, "First Apology," 1:17 *Ante-Nicene Fathers*, Alexander Roberts and James Donaldson, eds. (1885, rpr. Peabody, MA: Hendrickson Publishers, 1995), vol. 1, p. 168. In Justin Martyr's "The Sole Government of God," (Ibid., pp. 290-293), the early apologist compiles various pre-Christian poets' comments on God as administrator (governor) of the universe to refute idolatry.

[2] Cited by William Barclay, *Daily Study Bible* (Romans) (Philadelphia: Westminster, 1971) in loc.

[3] Tertullian, "Apology," *Ante-Nicene Fathers*, Alexander Roberts and James Donaldson, eds. (1885, rpr. Peabody, MA: Hendrickson Publishers, 1995), vol. 3, pp. 42-43.

peace and gentleness the power that you have given to them, they may find favor with you."[4]

Justinian (483-565) advanced an early law code, providing a primitive standard of international justice. After finding the Roman laws in chaos, Justinian I assembled the *Codex Constitutionum* in 529. This Justinian Code proved to be an enduring contribution to the stability of government and Western law. Such orderly and expert matrixes were definite advances in human government, nurtured by the soil of a Christian value system. Christian beliefs in impartial justice and lawful orderliness began to be implemented in the Holy Roman Empire. Where barbarity, incivility, caprice, and sheer power once had reigned, early forms of *Lex Rex* were exhibited. It was religion that fostered civility and order, not irreligion.

Paul Sigmund summarizes some of the developments introduced by the church prior to the twelfth century: "Gratian's canon law collection (1139) provided the texts for the use by canon lawyers in the service of the papal centralization . . . The twelfth-century revival of the study of Roman law at Bologna helped to give the emergent states of Western Europe a legal foundation . . . In England a 'common law' had been forged by the king's justices . . . The first representative institutions were beginning to meet in inchoate form . . ."[5]

The Middle Ages were actually full of growth and development in political theology. M. Stanton Evans and others lament that historical revisionism is frequently deceptive "in its portrayal of medieval clerics as agents of repression." He asserts that not only the proto-Protestants, but also *"the Catholic Church of the Middle Ages was the institution in Western history that did the most to advance the cause of constitutional statecraft.* This resulted from its constant readiness, in the spirit of the Hebrew prophets, to challenge the might of kings and emperors if they transgressed the teachings of religion."[6] Evans champions the contributions of Roman Catholic theologians of state:

> St. Ambrose states that 'the emperor is within the church, not above it . . . things that are divine are not subject to imperial power,' when St Augustine says, 'it is not for judges to judge of the law but according to the law;' or when St. Isidore asserts that 'the title of kings is held by proper administration, by wrongdoing it is lost.'. . . These sentiments, obviously, are light years from the ideas of Plato and Aristotle, and also from the words of humble deference to princes that would become the norm in absolutist kingdoms. Their impact in proclaiming limits on the scope of secular power, in posing a check to royal pride, and in advancing the Western concept of separate spheres allotted to church and state, is manifest. The

---

[4] *Catechism of the Catholic Church* (Liguori, MO: Liguori Publications, 1995), p. 463.

[5] Paul Sigmund, *St. Thomas Aquinas on Politics and Ethics* (New York: W. W. Norton, 1988), p. xiv.

[6] M. Stanton Evans, *The Theme is Liberty: Religion, Politics, and the American Tradition* (Washington, DC: Regnery, 1994), pp. 150-151.

implications were apparent all over Europe, but the developments of special interest to our story are those occurring in medieval England.[7]

The Magna Carta: *Medieval Contributions*

Although it is seldom admitted by secularists in the twentieth century, medieval views were actually fairly well-developed and robust. One of the best known highlights of medieval government was the *Magna Carta*. This signal event— rather than indicating the crudity of unenlightened people—was actually a sign of maturity in political thought, squarely founded on articles of Christian belief. In contrast to the other contemporary forms of government, this British landmark (1215) was an example of the impact of Christian teaching on matters of state.

Evans corrects a common misperception: "We are used to thinking of England as the home of representative government; less familiar is the idea that England enjoyed free institutions at the on-set of the modern age because it had retained them from the preceding era."[8] Contrary to modern myths, "It was the era of the Middle Ages that nourished the institutions of free government, in contrast to the ideas and customs of the ancients. Conversely, it was the rejection of medieval doctrine at the Renaissance that put all Western liberties at hazard, leading to autocracy in Europe and despotic practice in the modern era."[9]

One may legitimately ask if religion aided freedom and benefited political advance? Or was evangelical Christianity a retardant in this instance? The preamble of the *Magna Carta* explicitly referred to the counsel of the clergy, including Stephen, Archbishop of Canterbury, and other bishops. It began with an overt religious affirmation: "John, by the Grace of God, King of England . . ." The preamble alluded to its ends: "We, in the presence of God, and for the salvation of our own soul, and the souls of all our ancestors . . . to the honor of God, and the exaltation of the Holy Church and amendment of our Kingdom . . ." The purpose of this "present Charter" was to confirm certain essential constitutional agreements for posterity. Civic instability and flux was to be avoided by setting forth clear constitutional covenants in writing. One of the first mentioned was that "the English church shall be free" and have freedom of elections. Resistance of hier-archical imposition was clear. That the church was to have a prominent role in politics, one of the clauses even guaranteed that the King could summon "the Archbishops, Bishops, Abbots" and other nobles for counsel. Further, the *Magna Carta* made it plain that trials were to be fair, fines were not to be levied for inconsequential matters (as if the state were all important), personal property was

---

[7] Ibid., pp. 152-153.

[8] Ibid., p. 32.

[9] Ibid., p. 150. Another important force in undermining hierarchical and centralized govern-ments was the Conciliar movement. Beginning with the Council of Constance (1415) and leading up to the Reformation, various ecclesiastical trends—such as the Conciliar movement— either reflected or led the incipient de-centralizing tendencies.

not to be confiscated without remuneration, and imprisonment was not allowed without "legal judgment of his peers or by the laws of the land." Moreover, previous unjust fines or confiscations of property were to be remitted and a representative council of 25 Barons was to be created "for GOD and for the amendment or our kingdom." This revolutionary document was fully supported by the church. Furthermore, most constitutional scholars recognize that without the support of the church and without this uprising *pro libertas*, the monarchical form of government likely would have had a much longer life-expectancy. In this case at least, the involvement of believers in politics benefited society.

As a pre-modern document, the *Magna Carta* was a catalogue of liberties, rights, and safeguards from statist intrusion. Expressive of the medieval theology of its time, this document was a benchmark of civic liberties, and owed its origin to Christianity: "Only with the advent of biblical religion and its distinctive views of Deity, nature, man, and government, did people begin to grasp the idea of limited power in the state. . . . It was in this period that biblical attitudes toward secular power, and many other things, suffused the whole of European culture, and thereby created the institutions of the free society."[10] Evans surmises:

> The church lent its prestige to Magna Carta in other ways as well. . . . the clergy sought to strengthen its authority among the faithful. One archbishop ordered that it be posted in every cathedral, while another had it read out to the people both in Latin and in English. This considerable record of church involvement with the charter, again, is directly contrary to the standard treatment. . . . While the church was the principal influence in restraining monarchy in the medieval epoch, it was not alone in taking this position. Power in the Middle Ages was fragmented, not only as between church and state, but among competing secular interests, so that the monarchs of Europe were hedged about with many countervailing forces. It was this wide diffusion of authority that led to the rise of representative institutions, as well as to other distinctive features of the medieval order.[11]

By the time of the fourteenth century, weak institutions began to wear thin. Corruption in both civil and ecclesiastical affairs began to call out for reform. The early Renaissance was an expression, in part, of the needed reform in economics and politics. With the rise of guilds and with lurches toward free markets, the feudal system would eventually be terminated. Corresponding political changes would follow the economic revolutions of the fourteenth and fifteenth centuries. Pre-modernism would become characterized by open markets, a consistent trend away from monarchies, and an incipient egalitarianism.

The Council of Constance (1415) and other purely religious convocations in the early Renaissance were other instances of the church calling the civil ruler to improved standards of governance. The Conciliar movement gathered various

---

[10] Ibid., pp. 150-151.
[11] Ibid., p. 154.

clerics together to give what was unparalled at the time: advice or counsel to a hierarchical leader. In this case, the pope, similar to the experience of King John (above) in England, was summoned to meet as one among equals, at least in terms of advice. This was radical for the time, but it was a harbinger of the incipient decentralizing tendencies on the horizon. Many would not think of such isolated religious councils as so important, but the inner dynamic of the ruler meeting with the ruled, often depicted as a Reformation contribution, actually grew within the church prior to the Reformation.

The Protestant Reformation and Political Advance

The Protestant Reformation was a colossal boost to the growing influence of Scripture on democracy. Medieval sources contained precedents for rebellion, but Protestants became especially animated in their search for theological foundations for more democratic expressions.[12] Karl Holl summarized the major effects of Reformation thought as: "on the one hand, a deepening of the theory of the state; on the other, a definite limitations of its powers."[13]

It was the Protestant Reformation that eroded the principle of unqualified submission to the civil authority. In light of some of the abuses and excesses of civil rulers, most Protestants came to accept a modified resistance (passive) if the ruler mandated something explicitly opposed to revealed matters. Despite the Protestant unity on this issue, there was a division on the question of whether or not it was permissible *actively* to resist the civil magistrate. And if such active resistance was recognized, to whom was this responsibility entrusted: to the masses or to the lower magistrates? In any case, however, this evangelical faith fueled advances in civil government.

John Knox, for example, agreed that people should revolt against a tyrannical ruler, even going so far as to permit deposition and execution.[14] In 1558, Knox's co-pastor, Christopher Goodman, published *How Superior Powers ought to be obeyed of their subjects; and wherein they may lawfully by God's word be disobeyed and resisted*. This Reformation revolution affirmed that rulers could not be absolutized:

> When kings or rulers become blasphemers of God, oppressors and murderers of their subjects, they ought no more to be accounted kings or lawful magistrates, but as private men to be examined, accused, condemned and punished by the law of

---

[12] M. Stanton Evans believes that the movement from medieval to modern doctrine can be demonstrated by citing only Roman Catholic spokesmen. Cf. his *The Theme is Freedom: Religion, Politics, and the American Tradition* (Washington: Regnery, 1994), p. 173.

[13] Karl Holl, *The Cultural Significance of the Reformation* (Cleveland: Meridian, 1959), p. 45.

[14] Keith L. Griffin, op. cit., p. 4; cf. *The Works of John Knox*, David Laing, ed. (Edinburgh, 1895), vol. 4, pp. 415-416.

God, and being condemned and punished by that law, it is not man's but God's doing . . . When magistrates cease to do their duty, the people are as it were without magistrates . . . If princes do right and keep promise with you, then do you owe them all humble obedience. If not, ye are discharged and your study ought to be in this case how ye may depose and punish according to the law such rebels against God and oppressors of their country.[15]

The Protestant Reformation provided an ideological basis for politics that transcended any particular administration. Peter Martyr Vermigli (1499-1562) recognized the state as a lawful sphere ordained by God, but certainly not unlimited. A recent study summarizes Vermigli's views:

We must be subject to the civil ruler 'only as touching his function and office, which if he at any time goes beyond and commands anything that is repugnant unto piety, and unto the law of God, we ought to obey God rather than men. This resistance, however, is by way of exception to Scripture's general command. In a sinful society, we cannot do without authority, for we all want to be lords and anarchy would inevitably be the result. Authority comes from God to fathers, husband, masters, rulers. Without it, we have only 'infinite brawlings and endless contentions,' in church, state, work, and family.[16]

Vermigli wrote an influential commentary on the Book of Judges which quickened many to the basis of resistance to evil leadership. Vermigli's influence was long lasting in political matters.[17] Not only the European reformers but the American colonial clergy were also indebted to Peter Martyr's thought. John Cotton, a pastor in the Massachusetts Bay Colony, appreciated Martyr, echoing his view of limited government: "It is necessary, therefore, that all power that is on earth be limited, church power or other . . . It is therefore fit for every man to be studious of the bounds which the Lord hath set."[18]

Attributing to Luther a large role in the advance of civic freedom of conscience and the adoption of the view which viewed the state as superior to the will of the individual, Karl Holl noted: "at the same time it was the Reformation that first set a rigid limit to the absolute power of the state." Moreover, he conceded "to the

---

[15] Cf. Patrick Poole, ed., *Reformation Political Tracts* (forthcoming).

[16] Mariano Di Gangi, *Peter Martyr Vermigli: Renaissance Master* (Lanham, MD: University Press of America, 1993), p. 103.

[17] Mariano Di Gangi notes that Thomas Erastus studied under Vermigli in Heidelberg. He comments: "Understandably, Erastus appreciated Martyr's teaching on 1 Samuel 8 to the effect that ministers of religion are not exempt from the authority of the state, but subject to the civil magistrate. Incidentally, it should be noted that while the Genevan model of church government featured the exercise of discipline through the consistory or session of elders, the Zurich pattern functioned on the assumption that church courts derived their effective jurisdiction from the secular sovereign. That Zurich model rather than the Genevan was adopted in the Massachusetts Bay Colony." Ibid., p. 195.

[18] Ibid., p. 203.

Reformation respect . . . for being the first of all in modern times to have prepared the way for freedom of conscience in the state. All further victories with respect to tolerance rest on this first step . . ."[19] Civic freedom was a consequence of the religious freedom. In many cases, evangelicals were the best friends of political improvement.

John Calvin (1509-1564) is frequently credited with massive impact on political and economical matters in modern Europe.[20] The political impact of Calvin's view of God's sovereignty has been summarized aptly by Abraham Kuyper:

> [T]he Calvinistic confession of the sovereignty of God holds good for all the world, is true for all nations, and is of force in all authority which man exercises over man . . . It is therefore a political faith which may be summarily expressed in these three theses: 1. God only, and never any creature, is possessed of sovereign rights, in the destiny of nations, because God alone created them, maintains them by his Almighty power, and rules them by his ordinances. 2. Sin has, in the realm of politics, broken down the direct government of God, and therefore the exercise of authority, for the purpose of government, has subsequently been invested in men, as a mechanical remedy. And 3. In whatever form this authority may reveal itself, man never possesses power over his fellow man in any other way than by the authority which descends upon him from the majesty of God. Calvinism protests against State-omnicompetence, against the horrible conception that no right exists above and beyond existing laws, and against the pride of absolutism, which recognizes not constitutional rights, . . . Calvinism is to be praised for having built a dam across the absolutistic stream, not by appealing to popular force, nor to the hallucination of human greatness, but by deducing those rights and liberties of social life from the same source from which the high authority of government flows, even the absolute sovereignty of God[21]

Asserting that the state was not merely a necessary evil for Calvin, Karl Holl recognized that Calvinism, even more than Lutheranism, provided a theological basis to oppose unjust governments.[22] Everywhere Calvinism went, it "placed a solid barrier in the path of the spread of absolutism."[23] Holl claimed that even though precursors of human rights were found in the Middle Ages, nonetheless, "its formal acceptance into political theory is not completed until this period and only under the impact of religion. . . . The acceptance of universal human rights into the

---

[19] Holl, op. cit., pp. 53, 55.

[20] Ralph C. Hancock, *Calvin and The Foundations of Modern Politics* (Ithaca: Cornell University Press, 1989), says that the Protestant Reformation was "an essentially modern movement that in some way laid the foundations for our modern openness."

[21] Abraham Kuyper, *Lectures on Calvinism* (Grand Rapids: Eerdmans, 1953), p. 85.

[22] Karl Holl, op. cit., pp. 65-66.

[23] Ibid., p. 68.

constitution was, however, not just the modification of a single point; it included in itself the transformation of the whole concept of the state."[24]

Calvin's primary teaching on these matters is recorded in his *magnum opus, The Institutes of the Christian Religion.*[25] The Genevan reformer believed that civil government was a token of "how lovingly God has provided for mankind" (IV, xx, 1). Calvin believed that if there was no civil government and if depraved men perceived that they could go "scot-free" (IV, xx, 2), they surely would and society would deteriorate into anarchy. On one occasion, he likened such irresponsible anarchy to living "pell-mell, like rats in straw" (IV, xx, 5).

Calvin wrote that if civil rulers properly understood their callings, i.e., "that they are occupied not with profane affairs or those alien to a servant of God, but with a most holy office, since they are serving as God's deputies" (IV, xx, 6), they would serve with more equity. He queried rhetorically:

> For what great zeal for uprightness, for prudence, gentleness, self-control, and for innocence ought to be required of themselves by those who know that they have been ordained ministers of divine justice? How will they have the brazenness to admit injustice to their judgment seat, which they are told is the throne of the living God? How will they have the boldness to pronounce an unjust sentence, by that mouth which they know has been appointed an instrument of divine truth? With what conscience will they sign wicked decrees by that hand which they know has been appointed to record the acts of God? To sum up, if they remember that they are vicars of God, they should watch with all care, earnestness, and diligence, to represent in themselves to men some image of divine providence, protection, goodness, benevolence, and justice (IV, xx, 6).

This biblical view applied a transcendent perspective with which to evaluate rulers. Calvin gave impetus to post-Reformation political upheavals when he commented that even kings were not to "arrogate to themselves more than belongs to them." He commented on Psalm 82:

> It is unquestionably a very unbecoming thing for those whom God has been pleased to invest with the government of mankind for the common good, not to acknowledge the end for which they have been exalted above others . . . but instead of doing this, contemning every principle of equity, to rule just as their own unbridled passions dictate. So infatuated are they by their own splendor and magnificence as to imagine that the whole world was made only for them. Besides, they think it would derogate from their elevated rank were they to be governed by moderate counsels; . . . To correct this arrogance, the psalm opens by asserting that although men occupy thrones and judgment-seats, God nevertheless continues to hold the office of supreme ruler. . . . The more effectually to overthrow this irrational self-confidence with which they are intoxicated, civil

---

[24] Ibid., pp. 72-73.
[25] John Calvin, *The Institutes of the Christian Religion,* John T. McNeill, ed. (Philadelphia: Westminster, 1960). All chapter and section references are to this edition.

order is termed the assembly of God; for although the divine glory shines forth in every part of the world, yet when lawful government flourishes among men, it is reflected therefrom with pre-eminent luster.[26]

One of the earliest Protestant systematic treatises of matters of state was George Buchanan's *The Rights of the Crown in Scotland* (*De Jure Regni Apud Scotos*). This work, perhaps "the most influential political essay of the century,"[27] was an early (1579) integrated Protestant argument for limited government. Buchanan believed that lawful kings and tyrants were contraries.[28] With Cicero, Buchanan believed that nothing was more acceptable to the sovereign Deity than well-ordered states which were united in the principles of justice.[29] This early Protestant asserted that, "it was much safer to trust liberties to laws than to kings . . . confine them to narrow bounds, and thrust them, as it were, into cells of law . . . circumscribe [them] within a close prison."[30] That rulers were to be subordinate to a constitution is seen in Buchanan's statement: "Kings being accordingly left, in other respects free, found their power confined to prescribed limits only by the necessity of squaring their words and actions by directions of law."[31] Buchanan called it an egregious mistake to suppose that "nations created kings not for the maintenance of justice, but for the enjoyment of pleasure."[32] He maintained that, "the people from whom he [king] derived his power should have the liberty of prescribing its bounds; and I require that he should exercise over the people only those rights which he has received from their hands."[33] Buchanan noted: "The law then is paramount to the king, and serves to direct and moderate his passions and actions."[34]

According to this emerging Protestant consensus, a king exercised power on behalf of the people whereas a tyrant wielded authority on behalf of himself: "For to make everything bend to your own nod, and to center in your own person the whole force of the laws, has the same effect as if you should abrogate all the laws."[35] Further, Buchanan argued:

---

[26] John Calvin, *Calvin's Commentary on Psalms* (Grand Rapids: Baker Bookhouse, 1979), vol. v, pp. 329-330.
[27] Harold Laski, ed., *A Defense of Liberty Against Tyrants* (Gloucester, MA: Peter Smith, 1963), p. 5.
[28] George Buchanan, *The Rights of the Crown of Scotland* (1579, rpr. Harrisonburg, VA: Sprinkle, 1982), p. 241.
[29] Ibid., p. 243.
[30] Ibid., p. 247.
[31] Idem.
[32] Idem.
[33] Ibid., p. 252.
[34] Ibid., p. 276.
[35] Ibid., p. 261.

But those who openly exercise their power, not for their country, but for themselves, and pay no regard to the public interest, but to their own gratification; who reckon the weakness of their fellow-citizens the establishment of their own authority, and who imagine royalty to be, not a charge entrusted to them by God, but a prey offered to their rapacity, are not connected with us by any civil or human tie, but ought to be put under an interdict, as open enemies to God and man.[36]

Without these Reformation advances, western politics would have been impoverished. Some think of the pinnacle of Reformation political thought as the mature work of Johannes Althusius (1557-1638). Daniel Elazar sums up: "The road to modern democracy began with the Protestant Reformation in the sixteenth century, particularly among those exponents of Reformed Protestantism who developed a theology and politics that set the Western world back on the road to popular self-government, emphasizing liberty and equality."[37] Althusius's 1603 *Politica*, a digest of "politics methodically set forth and illustrated with Sacred and Profane Examples," recognized that the federal design was first exhibited in Scripture: "Moreover, . . . every aspect of the polity is to be informed by federal principles and arrangements in the manner of the network of biblical covenants. Also, it . . . is grounded in a realistic understanding of human nature, its limits and possibilities."[38]

One of the contributions of Reformation era thought was the value of limited governmental power. The reformers saw all institutions under the sovereign administration of Christ. Thus, the power of the state could never be ultimate, nor complete. It, too, was always *sub Deo*. Althusius and others spoke of the power of state as limited and qualified by some objective standards outside itself. The state, if it failed to heed these, forfeited its legitimacy. State legitimacy was always contingent, contingent upon conformity to an objective, supra-national, and unchanging standard. It was noted that rulers "do not themselves have such great power, for no one gave them the power and jurisdiction to commit sin. Nor did the commonwealth . . . deprive itself of the means of self-protection, and thus expose itself to the plundering of administrators. . . . Finally, the wickedness of administrators cannot abolish or diminish the imperium and might of God, nor release the administrators from the same."[39]

Althusius paved the way for other governmental developments, as can be observed from his teaching that sounds like a precursor to the 10th Amendment (whatever powers are not explicitly delegated to the federal government are reserved to the states) to the U. S. Constitution: "Besides, whatever power the

---

[36] Idem.

[37] Daniel Elazar, "Althusius' Grand Design for a Federal Commonwealth," in *Politica* (Indianapolis: Liberty Fund, 1995), p. xxxv.

[38] Johannes Althusius, *Politica* (1603, rpr. Indianapolis: Liberty Fund, 1995), p. xxxvii.

[39] Ibid., pp. 98-99.

people did not have it could not transfer to its administrators. Therefore, whatever power and right the administrators did not receive from the people, they do not have, they cannot exercise over the people, nor ought they to be able to do so."[40]

Lex Rex: *A Radical Concept*

Samuel Rutherford's *Lex Rex* (Law is king) is one of the earliest comprehensive religious discussions of the role of civil government. Rutherford began his well-informed treatise by proving that civil government has its root in God, not the church or other agencies. While admitting that civil government is voluntary as opposed to natural, Rutherford also recognized that political power flowed from God.

The ruler is always sworn by oath to objective and constitutional standards according to *Lex Rex*. Rather than being above the law, the prince is under the law and subservient to the ends of the state. Rutherford viewed civil governors not so much as dominating lords, but as ministerial fiduciaries analogous to tutors, husbands, patrons, ministers or fathers.[41]

The king was, according to Rutherford, a "life-renter, not a proprietor." Rutherford, at one point, set forth ten arguments to support that, "simply and absolutely the people are above and more excellent than the king, and the king in dignity inferior to the people."[42] Among these were that a pilot is less than the sum of the passengers; the death and destruction of a church is sadder than the death of a king; and nursing fathers are of less worth to God than those to whom they are to nurse. It is little wonder, therefore, that Rutherford's writing was seen as anti-monarchical and ordered to be burned.

Puritan theologies like these led to the colonization of the New World. The Mayflower Compact opened on an unadulterated religious note: "In the name of God. Amen. . . . Having undertaken for the Glory of God and Advancement of the Christian Faith, and the honor of our King and Country, a voyage to plant the first colony in the northern parts of Virginia . . ." Such civic purpose was rooted in Reformation beliefs. Similarly the 1639 *Fundamental Orders of Connecticut*, sometimes referred to as the first written constitution in the New World, began by affirming the providence of God, and continued to state that the confederation was commencing "to maintain and preserve the liberty and purity of the Gospel of our Lord Jesus" and also church discipline. Other safeguards that limited power were also included.

The Constitution of the United States was conceived in an *ethos* of skepticism about human ability. One result was that no human being would be given unlimited power. Another safeguard was that states were governed best with the input of the people, under

---

[40] Ibid., p. 99.
[41] Samuel Rutherford, *Lex Rex* (rpr. Harrisonburg, VA: Sprinkle Publications, 1984), 69.
[42] Ibid., p. 78.

fixed constitutional principles. At first, the American Constitution stood alone, rather unique. In time, many other nations came to follow aspects of this pattern that was so rooted in Scripture. Some would even imitate American democracy driven by human-centered populism; nevertheless, it is most difficult to ignore the God-centered principles at the base of American government. These were hardly evil intrusions of religion into politics. If anything, the religious *ethos* of the founding era expanded over the next century.

Religion was expressed publicly and persistently for over a century after the American Revolution. Religion and evangelical preaching buttressed—rather than repressed—the founding of the nation.[43] If it was beneficial once, what compelling empirical evidence has been offered to demonstrate that it is less necessary or less salutary today?

Clarifying the Separation of Church and State

Many contemporaries could benefit from the wisdom of earlier generations on the meaning of the separation of church and state. A proper view of this crucial distinction clarifies that the separation of church and state is actually a biblical contribution to civil politics. A division of labor is warranted by Scripture, while a total divorce of faith and politics is not sanctioned. During the American Civil War, James A. Lyon attempted to clarify the relationship of these two spheres. He called the total separation of religion and politics a "popular fallacy" and an "idol." He wrote: "Of the many popular fallacies that are generally afloat in society, there is perhaps none that is deeper rooted or more damaging in its effects than the one just stated. How it originated, and became so deeply implanted in the popular mind, it may be rather difficult to explain. It is, however, a modern notion."[44]

Warning against the "infidelity and atheism developed in the French Revolution," Lyon sought to clarify that neither the teaching of Jesus, nor a proper understanding of the separation of church and state implied that the Christian faith must abstain from a public role: "The clear and manifest idea, therefore, contained in the declaration that 'Christ's kingdom is not of this world,' is not that Christianity takes no interest in, and exerts no influence over the civil and political well-being of its followers and professors, but that the principles that govern Christ's kingdom are not to be confounded with, nor conformed to the principles that govern a wicked and apostatized world. . . . But the union of church and state is a very different thing from the union of religion and politics."[45] Similarly, William Archer Cocke

---

[43] For more on this, cf. my *Election Day Sermons* (Oak Ridge, TN: The Kuyper Institute, 1996).

[44] James A. Lyon, "Religion and Politics," *The Southern Presbyterian Review*, vol. 15 (April, 1863), p. 569. He also noted that, "the separation of religion and politics, as a cardinal maxim in the foundation and superstructure of civil society, is of recent growth, the birth of modern infidelity." Ibid., p. 570.

[45] Ibid., p. 570.

believed, "Pure religion never sighed for a union of Church and State, nor sanctioned the murdering of the martyrs, nor introduced the fagot and the fire."[46] Cocke went on to say, however, that "such religion as ought to exist in the citizen should also appear in the political and civil affairs of the country. We repudiate all alliance between Church and State; yet the virtue which should govern the State, ought to be reflected from the religion of the citizen.[47]

Lyon exposed several of the underlying fallacies related to the view of the absolute separation of church and state. One flaw of that view was that it assumed that "man's true temporal interest and his eternal welfare are incongruous, or rather, that they are diametrically opposed; whereas, in truth, they are, in a certain sense, identical. . . . Politics are to religion what the body is to the soul.[48] Another reason, according to Lyon, that religion and politics could not be separated was that politics was the corporate expression of the individual, and thus could not be religionless: "The grand design of politics is to develop the good and suppress the bad in humanity, to the advantage of the State. Religion does the same thing, to the advantage of the individual, the component element of the state. Strictly speaking, the state is but the individual multiplied. Or more properly, the state is the family enlarged. So that whatever is for the true interest of the individual or the family, becomes *mutatis mutandis*, the true interest of the state. It follows, therefore, that if religion and business may be united in the individual, and religion and domestic government in the family, so, on the same principles, religion and politics should be united in the government of the state. The popular fallacy, therefore, which would dissever religion from politics, would on the same principles divorce it from every pursuit, calling, and relation in life . . ."[49] Two other aspects of "the mistaken supposition that there is an intrinsic incongruity between" religion and politics are: (1) that when the Scripture calls kings "nursing fathers," that could not possibly indicate a divorce of religion from politics; and (2) an eschatological argument that, "The glorious vision of the future is called . . . the 'millennium.' Then, of course, there can be no separation between religion and politics. And if not then, there should not be now, since the principles that will characterize and predominate in the millennial state, are the very same that are at work now in bringing it about. It is a great mistake to suppose that one kind of principles will work in bringing about the millennium, and another kind will predominate during the millennium. This would be to imagine that like effects were not produced by like causes! Consequently, if religion and politics will be necessarily and legitimately united during the millennial state, they are, and must of necessity be, united in bringing it about."[50]

---

[46] William Archer Cocke, "The Religious Principle in the Life of the Nation," *The Southern Presbyterian Review*, vol. 22 (July, 1871), p. 350.

[47] Idem.

[48] Lyon, op. cit., p. 583.

[49] Ibid., p. 585.

[50] Ibid., p. 586.

Thomas Peck affirmed Lyon's thesis: "It is only in modern time, indeed, that the philosopher has undertaken to grapple with these relations, with a view to the practical separation of the spheres of the temporal and the spiritual, the civil and the ecclesiastical, the church and the state. In the ancient forms of civilization, in its leading types, the Oriental, the Greek, and the Roman, we look in vain for any discrimination between these powers."[51]

However, James Lyon and others did not call for a "union of church and state in formal bands, any more than by a union of church and commerce, the church and manufacturers, or church and law, or medicine, or any other calling or pursuit in life."[52] Instead of a constitutional union of church and state, these nineteenth century leaders called for a union of virtue and politics. William A. Cocke believed that undergirding any public virtue would be "the great principle, that religion is the life of a nation."[53] Further arguing that, "the very best forms of government are vain without public virtue," he asserted that "God designed that the religious principle, as we have defined it, should be the life of a nation."[54] He clarified the implications of this belief as follows: "This does not recognize the interference on the part of the state with the forms or creeds of religion; nor the recognition of any Church by the laws; but simply that the principle of religion, carried from the domestic circle, and intermingled with the pure and lofty ideas which give life and dignity to civil society, ought, and for the well-being of the nation, must direct and regulate the machinery of state along the paths of virtue."[55]

Cocke warned against abandoning religion as a buttress for virtue: "The history of every age assures us that nations have been drawn into the vortex of ruin whenever they have departed from the religious principle; and whenever it ceased to act as their chart and compass, the ship of state tossed and broken by angry winds has foundered and gone down as it were like the Spanish Armada . . ."[56] As to exactly how the religious principle will enter the life of the nation "so as to maintain civil purity, a purity which shall be reflected from every branch of the government" without a confusion of church and state, Cocke explained: "Our answer to this question is, it must start from the domestic circle, the very cradle of its nationality; there it must germinate, and spread from family to family until it pervades the entire community. And as we have endeavored to illustrate that from the domestic order arose the state, that is, the government or the civil order, so must its principles be derived from its original source."[57] Believing that, "[t]he

---

[51] Thomas Peck, "Church and State," *The Southern Presbyterian Review*, vol. 16 (October, 1863), p. 122.

[52] Lyon, op. cit., p. 590.

[53] William Cocke, op. cit., p. 351.

[54] Idem.

[55] Ibid., p. 353.

[56] Ibid., p. 358.

[57] Ibid., p. 360.

Bible is the only basis of moral philosophy, as it is of the principles of all good government,"[58] Cocke argued:

> In defending the principle that Christianity should be the basis of all human government, we ought also to defend the position that it is a destructive error to incorporate it in constitutions or laws; but to illustrate the beautiful, brilliant, and ever abiding truth, that the religious principle is the life of the nation, when it moves the moral faculties of the people to regulate the political machinery, not by mere codes of policy, but by the precepts and principles which true religion established for the regulation of human conduct.[59]

Another nineteenth century thinker, James H. Thornwell, also believed that virtue would not ensue unless connected to religion. He affirmed the interrelatedness of morality and religion.[60] Thornwell went so far as to assert that a religious foundation was essential for politics, writing that citizens who were religion-less were "incapable of law. . . . Every State, therefore, must have a religion, or it must cease to be a government of men. . . . no Commonwealth has ever existed without religious sanctions. . . . Everywhere, in all ages, in all countries, in ancient as in modern times, in civilized as well as in barbarian nations, we find [man] a worshiper at some altar, be it venerable, degraded, or bloodstained."[61] Thornwell and others recognized a proper separation of church and state, as well as a legitimate interaction between these two vital spheres.

With this understanding of the respective and non-confused roles of church and state, modern citizens need to hold no fear of religion as a benefit to politics. Many additional supporting arguments could be marshaled to support this case. But the hesitancy to embrace the benefit of religion is likely not due to an evidentiary deficit. Rather, it seems that a presuppositional bias blocks the interpretation of data. In view of all the past contributions, with all the histories citing the positivity of religion, and with various works over the past 30 years, one could at least admit that *good* religion has had *good* impact on politics. If adversaries wish to debate the relative merits of a particular religion, then such a discussion might well be profitable. However, in light of the above and many other studies, it is implausible to argue that evangelical religion has failed to benefit the political sector. To the contrary, when it has had a proper impact, nations have prospered.

---

[58] Ibid., p. 372.

[59] Ibid., p. 376.

[60] James Henley Thornwell, "Sermon on National Sins," *The Collected Works of James H. Thornwell* (Edinburgh: Banner of Truth, 1986), Vol. IV, p. 515.

[61] Ibid., pp. 515-516.

The Evangelical Classic Turn:
From House Church to Church-House

What do Jim Jones, Robert Webber, and Thomas Oden have in common? One was a homicidal cultist, another was a disgruntled Wheaton College evangelical who turned Romeward, and the third is a converted liberal. Few see any common thread among these, and most would be surprised to see them yoked together as three formative influences on the theology of ministry within American evangelicalism in the past decade. Nonetheless, they may in the end prove to be among the most determinative persons to mold evangelicalism in America during recent years, even if *via negativa*. These three were reactionary figures, each in his own way symbolic of the excesses of non-classic expressions of evangelicalism. Between 1978 and the present, each of these three figures crested in his revolt against a *status quo*. By their perceived or observed immoderation, they either led or by reaction caused a major part of the evangelical community to veer toward the historic, classic *praxis* of Christianity. Prior to their respective reaction formations, evangelicals seemed profoundly uninterested in the classical.

During the 1970s and 1980s, evangelicals were hardly known as having a yen for traditional or classic Christianity. Peculiarly American in its disdain for the past, the adolescent evangelicalism of the 1970s and 1980s was loath to place a high value on the classic expressions of Christianity. Yet by the latter decade's end, the classic was valued with a vigor unobserved for some time. As the evangelical movement in America emerged from its adolescence and moved toward adulthood in the 1980s, one of its most unnoticed developments was the turn to the classic. This trend, if I am correct, has and will contribute greatly to the shape of ministry and theology in the coming century.

This essay will seek to portray these three figures and others from the evangelical community as catalysts who forced those without disciplined theological matrixes to flee to the safety of classic Christian doctrine and practice.

There were certainly other members of this supporting cast, but these three are exemplars of the extremes that can result from a non-disciplined Christianity. One is a horrid reminder, another is not as painful, and at least one is serendipitous.

These and others from within recent American evangelicalism forced an undisciplined, rather raw, and youthful evangelicalism to mature. By their abuses and by their observation of wrongs, a powerful correction developed within the evangelical community, spurred by the likes of these. The correction, we may now see, was definitely a reactionary thrust, perhaps even a text-book illustration of reaction formation. The path of this development is similar to a stock-market correction, i.e., when excesses occur, the market will eventually react and, after the correction, arrive at realistic levels of value. In some ways we can only be thankful that the abuses were not more flagrant. This may be an opportune moment to affirm that in the providence of God these characters were used to call the community to maturity. Evangelicals were forced by these men's excesses to distance themselves from the errors identified in these (and other similar) ministries. In so doing, the evangelical community took a definite turn away from its independent and non-structured tradition. As the 1980s closed, a turn toward the historic in several areas could be perceived. Evangelicals would learn the painful but traditional lesson that if the biblical community was to have a lasting, multi-generational impact—both internally to the church and externally to the world—then it must of necessity seek shelter in some of the classical doctrines and practices of the historic church. This swerve toward the classic is detectable in at least four areas: leadership, worship, doctrine, and discipline.

First, consider the classic turn in the area of *leadership.* As the 1970s ended, most evangelicals placed inordinate trust in the unchecked dominance (usually through charisma) of their leaders. Few scandals since Elmer Gantry had occurred within this new generation of evangelical leadership. Following World War II, hardly any major scandals occurred in the 50s or 60s. The leadership of Billy Graham, Bill Bright and others was beyond moral reproach. With the explosion of the charismatic movement, a new unchecked dynamism entered the leadership corporate culture of evangelicalism. A number of neo-pentecostal leaders grew into positions of virtual unaccountability. Along with the invasion of TV ministries came an unparalleled rise in fund raising, revenues, and opportunities for abuse. Still, prior to 1978 no major scandal of leadership had rattled the evangelical movement. A bombshell in 1978 would prove to be a harbinger both of the excesses and of the reactive correction in evangelical leadership.

The Rev. Jim Jones and the Guyana tragedy awakened evangelicals to the destructive possibilities of undisciplined leadership. The Jones debacle taught the community that they must not depend on the visions of a charismatic leader. Jones was certainly a bad apple and could be dismissed as an aberration from good evangelical leadership. It would take other "falls" to convince evangelicals that they must provide a kind of classic discipline and accountability even for the best of leaders.

By mid-decade, other cracks would be seen in the armor of the non-classic style of leadership. Hal Lindsay, the favorite son of evangelicals in the 1970s, went through a divorce, as did evangelical leaders Tom Skinner and Keith Miller. New leaders such as Gordon MacDonald and Frank Tillipaugh would admit to adultery (albeit with repentance) by the end of the 1980s. However, it was several prominent TV ministers who forced a return to the classic in the area of leadership style which, in turn, would influence the theology of ministry.

By the late 1980s, evangelicals became ashamed of their leadership as the highly televised charismatic leaders Jim Bakker and Jimmy Swaggart were found wanting in numerous areas. Evangelicals were forced to face up to the need for ministerial accountability—which would eventually resemble old patterns like a presbytery or diocese—as Bakker and Swaggart became known as thieves, liars, adulterers, and deceivers. Roiled by these discoveries, evangelicalism was presented with the option of either legitimating these covert sins or finding a more stable structure of leadership. Most evangelicals would discover a partial solution in true ministerial accountability. Suddenly, evangelicals realized a need for discipline, structure, and even government. Freedom in Christ was fine, but it was rediscovered that without proper governing structures even the best of leaders could take that liberty or pervert it into license. Acton's "Power corrupts, and absolute power corrupts absolutely," could well be modified to: "Unchecked ecclesiastical power corrupts, and absolute unchecked ecclesiastical power corrupts absolutely." In response, the evangelical community resorted to more classic and biblical forms of accountability to protect itself and the reputation of its Lord.

The recent years witnessed the beginning of a renewal in ecclesiology, the heretofore ignored stepchild of the theological blue-bloods. Part of the correction was found in reintroducing church government, discipline, and defined structures as mechanisms to limit the possible corruption of leadership. This aspect of the return to the classic was evident in the rediscovery of ancient traditions and practices of government. Perhaps most symbolic was the rise of the Evangelical Council of Financial Accountability,[1] along with the increased attention given to church discipline in publications and other ministerial associations whose *raison d'etre* was to prevent the abuses of some of the above leaders. The coming-of-age evangelicalism was returning to the past for guidance and to avoid these excesses. Jim Jones and others forced us to change our theology of ministry. Accountability and government had become more important than either charismatic individuality or sheer spontaneity.

Worship also benefited from a distinct gravitation to the classic. Prior to the 1980s, there was little, if any, consensus about evangelical worship. Several strains of evangelical theology led to this menacing hydra. Obviously the Pentecostal and charismatic traditions of worship, which viewed order and structure as sure

---

[1] Even the ECFA proved inadequate in the 1995 New Era scandal, the largest boondoggle of the century for evangelicals.

inhibitors of true worship, defied prescribed order. Similarly, the Anabaptist and Brethren traditions despised form and structure in worship. Most independent churches worshiped in the style of the changing and prevalent tempers of its leaders. Prior to the 1980s, there was an almost doctrinaire rejection of any form, structure, or liturgy in worship. Evangelicals prided themselves in being non-formal and non-traditional in worship.

Yet, after several decades of experimentation, subjectivity, much emotion-alism and unpredictability, many in the evangelical world began to yearn for a more stable, less "blown by every wind of doctrine" practice or theology of worship. The focus on self and repeated testimonials would wear thin. Droves of evangelicals would shake off the dust of the novelties of the recent past and find richness in traditional forms of worship enlivened by the Spirit.

In the early 1980s several evangelicals began to show their dissatisfaction with the "free" liturgical tradition. Robert Webber, an erstwhile Wheaton College professor, startled the evangelical world when he joined the Roman Catholic Church. Former Jesus People musician John Michael Talbot filled his music with Roman liturgies. Peter Gilquist, a former Campus Crusade leader, would take a few other ex-Crusade staffers and start a denomination. Gilquist became a bishop, wore a clerical collar, and instituted high formality in worship, where hand-clapping and spontaneity had once reigned. A little later this denomination joined the Eastern Orthodox communion, eventually making its trek complete. Franky Schaeffer, son of stalwart evangelical apologist Francis Schaeffer, renounced the shallowness of evangelical worship and was confirmed in the Eastern Orthodox church in 1990. At first, these were thought to be eccentric deviations from evangelical worship.

However, others began to agree that in fact the vast majority of evangelical worship was unfortunately shallow, preoccupied with self-triumphalism, and exces-sively tilted toward the emotional-subjectivistic. A correction was in the offing.

Webber and others pointed out the superficiality of much evangelical worship. Their solution was not workable, although they served the community by requiring it to face up to its infancy in this most cardinal area. During the 1980s, evangelicals began to write and preach on the priority of worship again. A God-centeredness gradually began to challenge the man-centeredness of earlier evangelical liturgy. A revival of the Godward thrust of worship was pleasantly received, and some contemporary Christian music began to focus on worship-songs and God-oriented praise. Some even rediscovered the most classic worship music in the Psalter. A number of new hymnals were produced in the 1980s, a number of which were less pop-oriented and more appreciative of classic traditions.

Classic creedal statements and stately prayers began to sprout in evangelical worship services. At times evangelical Anglicans seemed to be envied for their doxological liturgy. Even Southern Baptists, among the most fiercely independent and non-liturgical of American evangelical denominations, were rediscovering the rich heritage in reformation liturgy.[2] Robert Rayburn's book, *O Come Let us Worship*, and others were widely received. All in all, a perceptible return to the classic elements and rubrics of worship could be noticed both in evangelical discussion and practice in ministry. No longer was worship the spontaneous, free-flowing, uninhibited chaos of some earlier times. The abuses had proven worship too essential to abandon to chance or human personality. A pivot toward the traditional was found in evangelical worship by the beginning of the 1990s. The previous errors in this area forced the evangelical community to mature in the realm of worship. The retreat to the historic was the prime indicator of this.

Another area significantly transformed in recent years is *doctrine*. Modern American evangelicalism was proud of its non-doctrinal, independent character. Yet, this would prove dangerous as well. Evangelicals were so committed to non-liberalism that they frequently confused causes with effects. As the twentieth century progressed, most evangelicals parted ways, either formally or informally, with the liberal mainline churches that historically had held to fixed doctrinal formularies. Post-World War II evangelicals brought this fiercely non-doctrinal independence with them. For a generation from 1940-1980, evangelicals' self-image was largely non-doctrinal. Yet the rise of cults, the emergence of a new generation of even more radical theology, the onslaughts of an invigorated secularism and other threats caused evangelicals of the 1980s to sense a need for doctrinal moorings of one kind or another.

Two main sources of tradition had rendered evangelicalism anti-doctrinal in its early stage. *One* was that evangelicals cherished an *ethos* of distrust for creedal *formulae*. In that the creedal churches had been the very ones opposing the newborn evangelicalism, evangelicals in reaction opted to have nothing to do with fixed doctrine. The freedom of the individual, soul-competence, and the priesthood of believers were elevated in importance over centuries of biblical doctrine. Although this was neither inherent to nor a long-standing part of the evangelical tradition, nonetheless, at the beginning of the twentieth century evangelicals began to eschew doctrine *per se*. Fixed doctrine came to be seen as largely evil, impractical, or divisive. Such hyper-individualism would prove to be more rooted in the Enlightenment and American democratic rights than in biblical warrant. Whether consciously more rooted in the Enlightenment than in the Scriptures or not, one source of evangelical paranoia over doctrine was its insistence on the priority of the individual over tradition.

A *second* source of evangelical aversion to doctrine was its strong (and longer-standing) rejection of Roman Catholicism. Roman Catholics and other confessional churches epitomized what evangelicals perceived as a "letter killeth" dynamic. Hence evangelicals reinforced their disavowal of fixed doctrine by frequent references to the numbing effect of Roman creeds, confessions, or hierarchies of hermeneutical infallibility.

---

[2] See *Review and Expositor*, Winter 1989, vol. 86, no. 1 on this rediscovery of liturgy.

With decades of over-reactions the evangelical movement in the late twentieth century was ripe for a correction. Enter Thomas Oden, Professor of Theology at Drew University. Oden, a convert from liberalism in doctrine, pointed out the bankruptcy of post-World War II liberalism and advocated a renewed interest in patristics and historic orthodoxy to fill the vacuum of an increasingly irrelevant liberalism. Of course, a sounder theological foundation had been begging for stronger doctrinal mooring for years, but by the end of the 1980s the evangelical community was finally listening. It seemed God was using a deprogrammed liberal to call us back to the importance of doctrine.

At the end of the decade, in "The Long Journey Home," Thomas Oden testified to his conversion from liberalism. In his conversion he rediscovered doctrine of the classic kind. Oden admits, "It is now time for my tradition to find its way back into classic Christian orthodoxy after some years of dubious experimentation and fitful wandering."[3] The distinguished professor from Drew wished to reaffirm the basics of the evangelical tradition. As a spokesman for the classic tradition, Oden said:

> Now toward the end of my journey of spelunking through the cavernous issues of systematic theology, I want to reaffirm solemn commitments made at its beginning: to make no new contribution to theology, and to resist the temptation to prefer modern writers less schooled in the whole counsel of God than the best ancient classic exegetes. I seek quite simply to express the one mind of the believing Church that has been ever attentive to that apostolic teaching to which consent has been given by Christian believers everywhere, always, and by all. This is what I mean by the Vincentian method . . . I have been passionately dedicated to unoriginality.
>
> My purpose has not been to survey the bewildering atonalities of dissent but to identify and plausibly set forth the cohesive central tradition of general lay consent to apostolic teaching, not its centrifugal variations but its centripetal centering. The focus is upon setting forth sound layers of argument traditionally employed in presenting in connected order the most commonly held points of Biblical teaching as classically exegeted by the leading teachers of its first five centuries. I am doggedly pledged to irrelevance insofar as relevance implies a corrupt indebtedness to modernity.[4]

Upon hearing this, one might be reminded of words over a century earlier by Charles Hodge who had boasted that at Princeton Seminary not a single original doctrine had been introduced in all his years of teaching. Championing the classic, Oden almost seems to endorse the well known proverb in his allergic reaction to modernity: "He who marries the science of today, is a widower tomorrow." The result is a detectable return to the classic that began to impact many evangelical theologies of ministry.

---

[3] Thomas Oden, "The Long Journey Home," *The Journal of the Evangelical Theological Society*, March 1991, vol. 34, no. 1, p. 77.

[4] Ibid., p. 79.

Further, Oden confessed his methodological priority for the classic approach:

I am pledged not to become fixated upon the ever-spawning species of current critical opinion but instead to focus single-mindedly upon early consensual assent to apostolic teaching of how God the Spirit works to fulfill the mission of God the Son on behalf of God the Father . . . The tested language of the Church speaks in its own unrelenting ways to modern minds struggling with the follies and limits of modern consciousness. Deteriorating modern ideologies must now catch up with the ever new forgings of classic Christianity, not the other way around . . . How? By seeking the shared rootage of early exegesis out of which each has grown.[5]

The unsensationally classic and non-novel approach of Oden was received with high approbation by evangelicals in the 1990s. It was without surprise, a classic and dusty paleo-orthodoxy that stood in stark contrast to the experimental and novel of the 1960s and 1970s. Moreover, Oden advised,

The weighting of references may be compared to a pyramid of sources with Scripture as the foundational base, then the early Christian writers, first pre-Nicene then post-Nicene, as the supporting mass or trunk, then the best of medieval followed by centrist Reformation writers at the narrowing center, and more recent interpreters at the smaller, tapering apex, but only those who grasp and express the anteceding mind of the believing historic Church. I am pledged not to try heroic-ally to turn that pyramid upside down, as have those guild theologians who most value only what is most recent or most outrageous. Earlier rather than later sources are cited where possible, not because older is sentimentally prized but because they have had longer to shape historic consensus. Consent-expressing exegetes are referenced more confidently than those whose work is characterized by individual creativity, controversial brilliance, stunning rhetoric, or speculative genius.[6]

In a section headed, "Whether creeping modern chauvinism also exists among evangelicals," Oden warned the maturing evangelical community,

Modern scholarly habits, fixated upon novelty, often betray an underlying value premise I call 'modern chauvinism'—the assumption that old ways are predictably oppressive and that new ways are intrinsically morally superior. This is a tragic shift that seems to be taking place throughout the evangelical community. Over and over again I have encountered evangelicals who are so enamored by the 'newness' of modern theological ideas that they abandon the real giants whose writing have stood for centuries . . . When I was attempting to describe modern chauvinism . . . I hardly had in mind evangelicals but rather the more obvious secular accommodators. Now I realize that the particular form that modern chauvinism takes among some evangelicals is the tendency compulsively to quote only or mostly recent 'historically informed' exegetes to the neglect of classic exegetes of the first five centuries, a hermeneutic just as oriented toward

---

[5] Ibid., p. 80.
[6] Ibid., p. 81.

modernity as the guild exegetes of fading liberalism. This is the special form of creeping modern chauvinism that has gained more than a toehold in evangelical institutions—a step backward toward a deteriorating modernity, not forward toward a postmodern inquiry into orthodoxy.[7]

Oden describes a personal turning point that parallels the ministry experience of many:

> I would remain densely uneducated until I had read deeply in patristic writers . . . where it at length dawned on me that ancient wisdom could be the basis for a deeper critique of modern narcissistic individualism than I had yet seen. Then I fancied that I was formulating unprecedented insights and ordering them in an original way. Later, while reading John of Damascus on the *oikonomia* ('arrangement, plan') of God (in *The Orthodox Faith*) I began belatedly to learn that all my supposed new questions were much-investigated amid the intergenerational wisdom of the *communio sanctorum* and that what I had imagined myself to be just recently inventing had been largely well understood as a received tradition in the eighth century.[8]

The repentant Oden now classifies himself as an adherent of paleo-orthodoxy: "Paleo-orthodoxy understands itself to be postlib, postmodern, post-postmodern, post-neo-anything theology, since the further one 'progresses' from ancient apostolic testimony to God's Word the more hopeless becomes the human condition."[9] Now when criticized with epithets like "fundy" or "byzantine," Oden feels "like [he] just got a badge of honor under fire." He continues,

> The shift from then to now is from a fixation on modernity to the steady flow of postmodern paleo-orthodox consciousness. The reason I am now trying to write almost nothing that is currently relevant is that tomorrow it will be less relevant. I am seeking to understand what is perennially true, not ephemerally relevant. The social and political events that are affecting my thinking are epic movements of despairing modernity, not discrete day-by-day scandal-sheet items like many of the supposed great media events of the last decade, which pale in significance in relation to the demise of modernity that is never reported or media-interpreted.[10]

Oden stated: "I have personally lived through a desperate game: the attempt to find some modern ideology, psychology, politics, or sociology that could conveniently substitute for Christianity. That game is for me all over. There is no way to think about modernity except amid the collapse of modernity." Soon many evangelicals found themselves in agreement with—and quoting—Oden, a convert from liberalism. There were other converts to classical Christian theology as well. Several evangelical denominations were boosted by real growth while holding firmly to classic and comprehensive Reformation creeds. The Southern Baptist

---

[7] Ibid., pp. 82-83.
[8] Ibid., pp. 83-84.
[9] Ibid., p. 85.
[10] Ibid., p. 86.

Convention, despite their denials of creedalism, grew to require an informal doctrinal adherence. These churches grew during these 1980s without this doctrinal adherence proving detrimental. With such emerging realities, theologies of ministry would inevitably be influenced.

The theonomic Reconstructionist movement, spawned in the 1980s, was quite emphatic about the need for doctrinal underpinnings. John MacArthur, one of the leading evangelical leaders of the 1970s and 1980s, parted company with those who exhibited less doctrinal rigor and revisited many of the puritan classics for strength. Evangelical publishers—like the Banner of Truth and others who were consciously committed to definite doctrinal views—actually grew and prospered in the 1980s, establishing a market for their wares. Evangelicals in droves were hungering for solid doctrinal anchors. It was becoming passé to be anti-doctrinal—a definite turn toward the classic.

Another evangelical who stressed the renaissance of doctrine and its need was Alister E. McGrath. By the late 1980s, McGrath was receiving plaudits for his mild mannered but thorough call for a return to historic doctrine. In some ways he was a voice for the newer, neo-evangelicalism of the future, an evangelicalism that was amicable to the past.

McGrath, a lecturer in Christian Doctrine and Ethics at Oxford, suggests that a recovery of Christian doctrine is fundamental to a recovery of Christian ethics. [11] "In other words," he asserted,

> Christian doctrine is what sets Christian ethics apart from the ethics of the world around us. It defines what is distinctive, what is Christian, about Christian ethics. To lose sight of the importance of doctrine is to lose the backbone of faith and to open the way to a spineless ethic. . . . Every movement that has ever competed for the loyalty of human beings has done so on the basis of a set of beliefs . . . The same is true of liberalism, whether in its religious or political forms. As Alasdair MacIntyre demonstrates so persuasively, liberalism is committed to a definite set of beliefs and hence to certain values. It is one of the many virtues of MacIntyre's important work that it mounts a devastating critique of the idea that liberalism represents some kind of privileged and neutral vantage point from which other doctrinal traditions (such as evangelicalism) may be evaluated. Rather, liberalism entails precommitment to liberal beliefs and values. Liberal beliefs (and thus values) affect liberal decisions—in ethics, religion and politics. [12]

Later, McGrath states, "In order for anyone—Christian, atheist, Marxist, Muslim—to make informed moral decisions, it is necessary to have a set of values concerning human life. Those values are determined by beliefs, and those beliefs are stated as doctrines. Christian doctrine thus provides a fundamental framework for Christian living." [13] Further, he observes, "Like every other form of morality,

---

[11] *The Journal of the Evangelical Theological Society*, June 1991, vol. 34, no. 2, 145-55.
[12] Ibid., p. 146.
[13] Idem.

Christian morality is something special and distinct, not just a subspecies of some nonexistent universal morality. With the passing of the myth of a universal morality, Christian writers have begun to write with much greater confidence on the theme 'Christian morality' in the knowledge that there is a distinctly Christian outlook on many matters. And this outlook, it is increasingly being stressed, is based upon Christian doctrine."[14]

He further comments, "Distinctive ethics (whether Marxist, Christian or Buddhist) are dependent upon worldviews, which are in turn shaped by doctrines, by understandings of human nature and destiny. Beliefs are important because they claim to describe the way things are. They assert that they declare the truth about reality. But beliefs are not just ideas that are absorbed by our minds and that have no further effect upon us. They affect what we do and what we feel. They influence our hopes and fears. They determine the way we behave."[15] Doctrine is important, as McGrath pointed out, and evangelicals were rediscovering the ineluctability of doctrine, especially the classic sort.

Additionally, McGrath exhorted:

Inattention to doctrine robs the Church of her reason for existence and opens the way to enslavement and oppression by the world . . . A Church that takes doctrine seriously is a Church that is obedient to and responsible for what God has entrusted to it. Doctrine gives substance and weight to what the Christian Church has to offer to the world. A Church that despises or neglects doctrine comes perilously close to losing its reason for existence and may simply lapse into a comfortable conformity with the world-or whatever part of the world it happens to feel most at home with. Its agenda is set by the world; its presuppositions are influenced by the world; its outlook mirrors that of the world. There are few more pathetic sights than a Church wandering aimlessly from one 'meaningful' issue to another in a desperate search for relevance in the eyes of the world.[16]

Had this not been part of the American evangelical experience—the endless wandering from meaningful to new meaning? Evangelicals were undergoing correction. The end of the decade of the 1980s revealed a marked contrast with the anti-classic corporate culture of the 1970s.

In a later discussion, McGrath provided an insightful diagnosis of error in several modern trends—once again championing the necessity of doctrine as determinative of practice. He disputes the claim that doctrine is "hopelessly irrelevant" as often asserted by ministers who "present it [doctrine] for consideration as though it were, and, in fact, by their faulty exposition of it make it so."[17] Citing Dorothy Sayers, McGrath affirms, "It is quite useless to say that it doesn't matter particularly who or what Christ was or by what authority he did those things, and

---

[14] Ibid., p. 147.

[15] Ibid., p. 149.

[16] Ibid.

[17] Alister McGrath, "In What Way Can Jesus Be a Moral Example for Christians," *The Journal of the Evangelical Theological Society*, Sept. 1991, vol. 34, no. 3, p. 289.

that even if he was only a man, he was a very nice man and we ought to live by his principles: for that is merely Humanism, and if the 'average man' in Germany chooses to think that Hitler is a nicer sort of man with still more attractive principles, the Christian Humanist has no answer to make."[18]

Further, McGrath points out the error of modern day liberal ethics, which he critiques as follows:

> According to some . . . Christianity enunciates no distinctive moral insights. Christians are free to (and expected to) echo prevailing secular ethical standards. A similar devaluation of the moral example of Jesus is the effect, if not necessarily the intention, of liberal Christianity. Jesus' example is approached through a filter of antecedent values and principles, derived from other sources (such as prevailing liberal middle-class values). It is these antecedent values and principles that are finally normative for liberal Anglicanism, with the example of Jesus being marginalized where he appears to contradict them and appropriated where he appears to endorse them. It is not the moral example of Jesus that is important but those preselected contemporary values that appeal to his liberal interpreters.[19]

Their error, McGrath points out, was in mistaking that Jesus' authority relies upon his moral excellence, which

> on closer inspection turns out actually to undermine that very authority. By what standards do we judge his teaching? The argument rests on knowing in advance what moral or religious teachings are to be regarded as outstanding. Jesus is then regarded as authoritative to the extent that he echoes these already existing standards. He is judged by a higher authority . . . For *classical* (emphasis added) Christian thought it is existing human religious and moral ideas that are to be challenged and judged by Jesus Christ; for these modern writers it is existing notions of morality and religion that are to judge Jesus Christ.[20]

McGrath correctly diagnoses that this is

> setting ourselves above [Christ] in judgment. It is our own concepts of morality, our own standards (wherever they come from), that are judging him. And all too often those standards are little more than the prejudices of our own culture . . . We are prisoners of our culture, unable to see its limitations . . . If Jesus echoes our own values and aspirations, we gladly accept his support; if Jesus should happen to challenge them, we dismiss them or choose to ignore the challenge . . . It is for this reason that doctrine is of central importance. Christianity does not assert that Christ has authority on account of the excellence or acceptability of his teaching. Rather, the teaching of Christ has authority and validity on account of who he is: God incarnate. The NT provides ample justification of this point. Throughout his

---

[18] Ibid., p. 289.
[19] Ibid., p. 290.
[20] Idem.

writings Paul begins by making doctrinal affirmations and then proceeds to draw moral conclusions. Doctrine comes first, moral and religious principles follow.[21]

Here is a stunning reversal in a relatively short period of time on the priority of doctrine. The doctrinal classics afforded more protection from abuse. With the advent of the millennial mania of the 1970s, the revival of cults, and surrounded by an age of abuses, idiosyncrasies and purported extra-biblical revelations, the classics were welcomed.

Evangelicals began the decade: (1) pietistic, individualistic, and uninvolved in society, (2) averse to any "Creed except Christ," (3) emphasizing the experiential and personalistic in worship, (4) independent and non-authoritarian as to structure, and (5) suspicious of church history and traditional expressions. Yet, in a relatively short span, encouraging signs of the evangelical community's coming of age sprouted. In many of these areas evangelicals were outgrowing their adolescence and were creeping back toward the classical. They were rediscovering in large numbers the generations of saints who had gone before and who could now assist as counselors. After many bumps, bruises, and embarrassing skinned knees, these evangelicals loved their Lord enough to learn from their own mistakes. The excesses of Jim Jones, Jim Bakker, and Jim Swaggart drove many to better approaches to ministry. The best theologies of ministry would take these lessons into account and recognize historiaphobia as an ill.

Forsaking the intemperances of the Jones' and with a concern for the name of their Savior, evangelicals sought safe harbor in the channel of classic paleo-orthodoxy. A powerful, albeit older, tradition was unearthed in the process. Many evangelicals rediscovered the "old paths" that J. C. Ryle and Jeremiah had discussed. The Old School approach actually had strength, balance, maturity, stability, and safety, for which many nigh-unto-cultish evangelicals yearned. Some things from our parents and grandparents, we learned, did have value after all. There was safety in the classic turn.

Mark Noll's *Confessions and Catechisms of the Reformation* came out and was a success. Thomas Oden was in demand. Hatch, Marsden and other sympathetic friends were gently critical of the "democratization" of American evangelicalism, a posture that demanded an anti-classic posture. Others became suspicious of the domineering mannerisms of near-papal authoritarianism of some ministers and ministries.

Perhaps the most appropriate analogy for this trend is a comparison of these coming-of-age evangelicals with 1970s teenagers who grew up to become parents in the 1990s. One pundit (Irving Kristol) once asked to provide a definition rhetorically asked, "What is a neo-conservative?" and answered with this astute definition: "It is a liberal with his own sixteen year old daughter." Evangelicals resembled that remark. Something about responsibility does seem to impel us

---

[21] Idem.

toward tradition and the past. Ethics and standards became important, and neo-conservative parents began to sound strangely like classic conservatives, only now with wire-rims and mini-vans. After having rejected and spurned most of the traditions of our parents, we hiked through the drug-infested 60s, the me-centered 80s, and awoke as aging Jesus People with children, with responsibility (horrors!), and the charge to "pass it on to . . . next generation."[22] It was no longer a luxury to indulge in the excesses of earlier decades; nor could a retreat to pietism help. What was needed was a fast course in maturity. Evangelicals, sensing the shallowness and deficiencies of many modern attempts at such, became refugees from modernism by seeking asylum in the classic. As postmodernism was being elegized, this return to the classic was definitely noticeable. Perhaps this "turn" would prove part of the larger "reshaping of American Religion" discussed by sociologist Robert Wuthnow."[23]

Within this analogy, as the parents were growing and maturing they reached for some values that precluded a repetition of the charismatic chaos of an earlier, unstructured day. Evangelicals in the 1990s rediscovered this classic complex of values. Perhaps traditional Christianity did not possess as much flair as some cults, but it offered stability. If that was not the turn, then it was sure overdue. The twenty-first century would verify the direction.

Even creeds staged a small comeback by the close of the 1980s. Symptomatic was the freshly-released British work, *The Making of Creeds* by Frances Young[24] who incidentally appears to be a convert from earlier 'The Myth of God Incarnate' days. Young observes,

> Christianity is the only major religion to set such store by creeds and doctrines. Other religions have scriptures, others have their characteristic ways of worship, others have their own peculiar ethics and lifestyle; other religions also have

---

[22] P. J. O'Rourke explained humorously, "What I believed in the Sixties": "Everything. You name it and I believed it. I believed love was all you need. I believed you should be here now. I believed drugs could make everyone a better person. I believed I could hitchhike to California with thirty-five cents and people would be glad to feed me. I believed Mao was cute. I believed private property was wrong. I believed my girlfriend was a witch. I believed my parents were Nazi space monsters. I believed the university was putting saltpeter in the cafeteria food. I believed stones had souls. I believed the NLF were the good guys in Vietnam. I believed Lyndon Johnson was plotting to murder all the Negroes. I believed Yoko Ono was an artist. I believed Bob Dylan was a musician. I believed I would live forever or until twenty-one, whichever came first. I believed the world was about to end. I believed the Age of Aquarius was about to happen. I believed the *I Ching* said to cut classes and take over the dean's office. I believed wearing my hair long would end poverty and injustice. I believed there was a great throbbing web of psychic mucus and we were all part of it somehow. I managed to believe Gandhi and H. Rap Brown at the same time. With the exception of anything my mom and dad said, I believed everything." P. J. O'Rourke, "Second Thoughts About the 1960s" in *Give War a Chance* (1992), p. 90.

[23] *The Restructuring of American Religion* (Princeton, NJ: Princeton Univ. Press, 1988).

[24] London: SCM, 1991; cf. *The Expository Times*, June 1991, vol. 102, no. 9, p. 257.

philosophical, intellectual or mystical form as well as more popular manifestations. But except in response to Christianity, they have not developed creeds, statements of standard belief to which the orthodox are supposed to adhere. Other religions have hymns and prayers, they have festivals, they have popular myths, stories of saints and heroes, they have art forms, and have moulded whole societies and cultures. But they have no "orthodoxy," a sense of right belief which is doctrinally sound and from which deviation means heresy.[25]

This defense of doctrine *per se* makes the following point:

Every group seeks self-definition, but why did Christianity set the test of membership in terms of correct belief? . . . [T]he issue of truth became paramount because of challenges to the sovereignty, goodness and unity of God, loyalty to the one true God having been inherited from Judaism. It was assumed that truth and morality went together, and most heretics were attacked on moral as well as doctrinal grounds. Thus Christian totalitarianism became complete, with demands for uniformity of practice as well as belief.[26]

Also with the graying of evangelicalism came a renewed commitment to a more conservative socio-economic platform. Whereas the 1970s began with the heralding of socialism, the end of the 1980s would witness a revival of traditional capitalism. Along with the overthrow of Marxism and the fascination with communitarianism came the demise of liberation theology. One consequence was the re-acceptance of democratic capitalism. Capitalism was back in vogue by the end of the 1980s, whereas at the beginning of the decade it had been viewed as an old wineskin. Capitalism was no longer a dirty word.

In one collection of essays, evangelicals finally gave a non-secular explanation for the collapse of communism, providing an inherently religious (not to mention credible) justification for the collapse of communism in our time.[27] Locating a sufficient explanation for the demise of Marxism in its faulty anthropology and theology, the renascent orthodox Christian faith appeared to be responsible for the overthrow of this three-fourths century of misanthropy.

Michael Bauman provided evangelicals not only with the report of the retreat of communism, but further he enunciated five systemic reasons for its inevitable fall. Bauman affirmed that Marxism entails a faulty view of: (1) human nature, (2) cause and effect, (3) justice (reducing such to absolute equality), (4) human property, and (5) the nature of wealth. Bauman commenced his essay with the observation that "Reality is resilient." Related to that stubborn fact, he observed that, "No religion, no political system and no means of production can prosper if it is not firmly rooted in things as they are rather than things as we would like them to

---

[25] Ibid., p. 257.

[26] Ibid., p. 258.

[27] Michael Bauman, ed. *Man and Marxism: Religion and the Communist Retreat* (Hillsdale, MI: Hillsdale College, 1991).

be. Precisely here Marxism fails."[28] Bauman locates the problem of Marxism as residing within the human heart and is quick to posit that Marxism "depends upon altruism where little or none exists."[29] In place of this faulty mechanism, Bauman provides an argument for democratic capitalism, rooted in the observation that we are "an incurably selfish lot."[30] Similarly, by the early 1990s, George Weigel would call communism a "heresy"[31] in the pages of the *National Review*.

It was Leonard Sweet in "Straddling Modernism and Postmodernism" who observed:

> The only more blatant irrelevance that comes to mind is the march toward Marxism-Leninism by the darlings of the Western church (liberation theologians) and the academic darlings of the Western university (Marxist scholars). This procession is unforgettable. For crossing the bridge going the other way was another liberation march—the whole geopolitical world of communism in stampede from Marxism-Leninism, led by members of the Eastern church. Marxism has been moribund for years. The last to know it were the Western church and academy.[32]

By the end of the 1980s, evangelicals had been provided with the removal of Marxist stumblingblocks that had been rife with economic unreality. With intellectual critiques of communism that coaxed them to forsake the fad of socialism, the way was clear to return to a more classic and orthodox economic philosophy.

The darlings of the 1980s, even among evangelicals, had been liberation theology, contextualization, feminism, inclusivism, and its chief fad was deconstructionism. Yet, by the end of the decade, evangelicals were experiencing a homecoming to the classic. The most noticeable symptoms were the decrease in pietism, the social activism noted above, and the revived commitment to worldview Christianity emphasized by groups such as Inter-Varsity and others. A retreatist, uninvolved pietistic expression of evangelicalism was on the wane.

Most indicative of this evangelical turn was the recommitment to the local church as the primary vehicle of ministry. Indicative of this was the rediscovery of the local church as the most valid ministry forum, with the once-outdated office of pastor resurrected again in its nobility. Along with this came a revival of classic preaching. Richard Wentz observed the earlier protocol:

> Even the most scholarly and reclusive of theologians found themselves in pulpits, or in lecture halls where they were called upon to break open the truth of the Christian faith to cultured despisers. They spoke to preachers and laity, and sought to address the superstitions of modern intellectuals. The Niebuhrs, Richard and

---

[28] Ibid., p. 8.
[29] Ibid., p. 9.
[30] Ibid., p. 7.
[31] *The National Review*, Jan. 20, 1992, p. 42.
[32] *Theology Today*, July 1990, vol. xlvii, no. 2, p. 163.

Reinhold, were preachers, so was Paul Tillich. . . . Creative theology either emerged from the pulpit or it moved from the classroom into the pulpit. Theologians preached in churches, college and university chapels, and before the conventions and councils of denominations. Any attempt to understand the history of theology until very recent times must come to terms with the role of preaching in theological development . . . What was true in the twentieth century until recently was even truer in previous times.[33]

Wentz went further emphasizing the value of tradition:

Much of the theology done within the warrants of Religious Studies is done by people with little or no loyalty to a tradition, most often without ever having the responsibility of preaching to a congregation of people who expect the Word to be present, or wish to be guided into the truth that is necessary to the living of their days. The resultant academic theology is unconcerned with the proclamation of good news. Its discourse may be a form of clear reasoning or an exercise in torturous semantics—no matter which, *'those who can preach; those who can't, find something else to do.'* Without loyalty to a tradition and a community, with no responsibility to communicate to people who want to be nurtured in their faith, the theology is likely to be inept and seldom worthy of the honor of its distinguished heritage.

To hear from one who lived through the shifting sands of the 1980s, consider the comments of Paige Patterson, President of Southeastern Baptist Theological Seminary and Co-Architect of the conservative *coup* within the SBC. Patterson articulates a clarion call for a return to traditional orthodoxy:

Admittedly, the *Zeitgeist*, favors 'topical forays' and 'possibility motifs,' but NT Christianity, while living within a culture, has always rubbed the cat's fur the wrong way. The idea is never just to make the cat miserable but rather to convince the cat to turn around so the fur can be massaged without irritation. . . . Thus to expound the Scriptures means a reversal in the theological direction in colleges and seminaries. Rather than reducing or eliminating the requirements in the biblical languages, these disciplines must receive an increased emphasis. Theology, Old and New Testament studies, hermeneutics, and church history must take precedence over psychology, sociology, and even 'Christian education' as the paramount disciplines of the academy. This does not imply that Baptist colleges and universities curtail other programs of study or diminish the quality of those programs. It does suggest that theology be returned to its proper role as 'queen of the sciences.'[34]

---

[33] Richard Wentz, "Theologian as Preacher," *Anglican Theological Review*, Spring 1989, vol. lxxi, no. 2, pp. 4-7.

[34] Paige Patterson, "My Vision of the Twenty-First Century SBC," *Review and Expositor*, Winter 1991, vol. 88, no. 1, p. 39.

Subconsciously Patterson is advocating discipline, doctrine, and a classical model of theology instead of the experimentation so frequently exhibited. He continues,

> Surely everyone agrees that there must be parameters. Now, as in each generation, we must determine what those parameters will be. If the priesthood of the believers, the autonomy of the local church, and the competency of the soul before God are so construed as to mean, as some have suggested, that Baptists need no confession at all, then Baptists become indistinguishable from the rest of the religious world. Maimonides, Avicenna, and Mao can be welcomed as fellow Baptists . . . Since few, if any, would argue this way logically, historically, or theologically, the point is made; and we must set our minds to determine what it means to be a Baptist both historically and in the modern milieu. We must determine what we will support and what we will not support.[35]

Whether he intended to or not, Paige Patterson was pleading for fixed doctrinal formularies very much like the classical church creeds. As Oden said, the days of "dubious experimentation and fitful wandering"[36] were over.

Evangelicals did have sufficient precedent from church history for such retrogression to orthodoxy. A century earlier, another such classic turn was led by Phillip Schaff and John W. Nevin. It was Nevin who warned against a "spiritual solipsism," even if evangelical. Nevin feared that privatized judgment could be reduced to an ahistorical "utilitarian salvationism . . . fashioned out of what had been partial truth in the history of Christianity, and, [it] like all partial truths elevated to prominence, must be considered a heresy. The Bible and private judgment are valid principles . . . only within the context of the Body of Christ as a living constitution of grace and truth."[37]

Evangelicals in the 1980s were learning just that—to avoid not only spiritual solipsism but also those who "wished to find ultimate authority for their own private insights and claims."[38] Nevin insisted it was only the visible church, rooted in the classic *traditio* of the Scriptures, that "could avoid the caricature of religion which is evident in the twentieth century—when religious life is characterized by the exploitation of 'every wind of doctrine' and the individual's right to 'start a church' or 'new religion.'"[39]

All in all there was an increasing hunger for the classic. Was it merely a retreat from modernity? Or could it have been as Chesterton opined in admiration for the strength of the classic: Every generation must re-apply a fresh coat of paint on the fenceposts. If not—if one merely leaves the fence post alone—it will not remain

---

[35] Ibid., p. 41.

[36] Oden, op. cit., p. 77 *supra*.

[37] Richard Wentz, "John Williamson Nevin as Public Theologian," *American Presbyterians*, Winter 1991, vol. 69, no. 4, p. 297.

[38] Ibid., p. 303.

[39] Idem.

white but it will tarnish. Such may be possible explanations for the rediscovery of the Puritans. As John MacArthur refound them in theology, others mined the classics for sanctification. Still others unearthed the earlier stalwarts of church/state matters; Jerry Falwell and Peter Marshall, Jr., for example, returned to the classics in those fields.

One could also argue that if the construction of local church buildings was any indicator of this transition, this thesis may receive even more corroboration. During the 1980s, an unprecedented number of dollars were spent on new church construction. Church edifices were growing in importance. Evangelicals were moving into the church-house and assuming roles as salt and light, even if in a fashion that was more traditional than two decades earlier.

The family was coming of age. The once-wayward teenagers were again coming home. The house-church may have been enough for the 1960s and 1970s, but after the 1980s a more sturdy structure of the church house would be needed, would provide safety and continuity, and would outlast the excesses of the previous decades. It remained to be seen whether this turn to the classic was itself a short-term fad or correction, or whether it was the beginning of a maturation of a renewed tradition.[40]

The response of many evangelicals in the 1990s to the classic turn was almost a sigh of relief. Their experimentation with the novel—which, in retrospect, was frequently a deviation from the orthodox—would not continue as rapidly in the 1990s as it did in the 1970s. A rediscovery of the classic was proving helpful, and the memories of our spiritual parents did not deserve to be repressed. The old was not necessarily mold. The likes of Jones, Webber, Oden, and others forced or helped us to mature our theologies of ministry in the direction of the classic turn.

---

[40] Of course, there is still much folly among many segments of evangelicalism. Much subjectivism, ill-advised application of Scripture, and at times, outright existentialism prevails. This survey concentrated on many of the more conservative evangelical groups.

A Miscellany of Application

All problems are not soluble by historical analysis, but many are. Recently, several critical social and cultural issues have arisen to challenge Christianity. It appears that only the old Christian faith can expose and meet these challenges.

An admission that there are few genuinely novel concepts aids in the diagnosis of modern issues. Indeed, if a historical perspective is rejected, we are left at a distinct disadvantage. Those who believe that an acquaintance with the past is not worth the trouble or impractical need to recall what British statesman Disraeli surmised: "Practical men are men who practice the blunders of their predecessors." Such advice may be sorely needed in the age of techno-utopia.

The sections below contain various applications of the main theme presented in this book. By these short pieces, the reader can see how valuable history is as an assistant in the evaluation of modern ideas.

Multi-Culturalism: How New is it?

Is the latest smart bomb aimed at education really that new? Just how new is multi-culturalism, really? I recently ran across a 1774 poem that spoke of the sibling of multi-culturalism in the theological arena at that time. In 1774, Archibald Bruce in *The Kirkiad: or the Golden Age of Scotland*[1] poetically spoke of the dangers of multi-wishy-washiness in education and truth. His was a day in which "[m]oderation [did] shine/ with far and ever placid mien!" He, too, seemed haunted with the relativity of the professor.

Bruce was alarmed that epistemological nihilism had led to the exaltation of this nothing-but-every-sideism "In ev'ry place, both near and far,/ In pulpit, bench, and at the bar." If this sounds familiar to the multi-culturalism of late, it may be

---

[1] Reprinted in *The Presbyterian Reformed Magazine*, Summer, 1991, pp. 13-14. Words in brackets are comments by the editor and not part of the original.

because multi-culturalism is a type of recycled relativism. Such non-knowledge was manifest over two hundred years ago:

> . . . from the theologic chair:
> There softens ev'ry harsher feature,
> And dictates nought but pure good-nature.

As the poem continues, Bruce exposes the deficiency of the here-and-now approach so characteristic of modern liberal theology as well as educational multi-smorgasbordism:

> Of *Doctor Quidnunc* (here and now) ev'ry lecture
> Holds up to view the charming picture:
> He shuns the orbit systematic,
> For motions new, and quite eratic.

Bruce correctly diagnosed the underlying ill of this pluralistic approach to be its disdain of truth:

> Systems, and system-mongers, he [the multi-cultural professor]
> Thinks bear too hard on liberty. [Poor devil]
> At heretics he seldom snarls,
> As those who love still to pick quarrels . . .
>
> . . .
> For neither side his blood he'll warm;
> Such trifling points can do no harm.
> Of mongrel brood, nor one t'other,
>
> . . .
> No sentiments he will impose,
> But lets each one his liking chuse.
> He thinks it suits not with the chair
> To tell with a dogmatic air,
> What is the truth, or where it lies,
> While 'tis a dispute 'mong the wise
> To no more certainty he'll rise,
> Than—"This affirms," and "That denies."

He continues to describe the multi-cultural misosopher as follows.

> With a true *academic* spirit,
> To seek for truth, but ne'er come near it. [See Acts 17:21]
> With indefatigable pains
> He takes of evidence the grains,
> And throws them in th'opposing scales
> So nicely, that no side prevails;
> But leaves the case in *status quo*,
> Dangling in *Equilibrio*.
> Or if the beam obliquely sways,
> In the *Probabile* it stays.

Bruce laments that "[d]ivines set free from party views,/ Of ev'ry sort may pick and chuse" from a smorgasbord of doctrines eschewing orthodoxy, as does the multi-cultural dogma in our own times.

His epitaph concludes with this stanza that presages multi-culturalism with the term, "multiformity." Sarcastically, he rebukes our forefathers' education, writing:

> What mighty fools our fathers were,
> To raise such hubbub, din and war,
> And lavish out their blood and treasure,
> Zealous for forms above all treasure!
> To put themselves to so much pains
> To forge their fetters and their chains!
> What beauty could these bigots see,
> In their fam'd uniformity;
> When Nature's works throughout declare, [Thus saith the multi-culturalist]
> *Variety* constitutes the *fair?*
> Such puritanic days departed,
> We've got their system quite inverted:
> To ev'ry faith indulgent be,
> Zealous for *Multiformity.*

This clergyman had it right two centuries ago in Scotland. As instructors continue the search for novelty, they ought to know that multi-culturalism is not new at all. The choice seems to be between on the one hand pluralism, non-knowledge, disdain of consistency, multiformity, and the strict avoidance of the antiquated rigors of the old educational forms or, on the other hand structure in education, discipline in knowledge, and vigorous systematic learning. After all, even Crosby, Stills, and Nash sang in the late '60s, "If ev'rybody's right/ Then nobody's wrong." Such choices were previously diagnosed in 1774, and with Archibald Bruce we hope,

> But soon this relick of our slav'ry, [multi-culturalism]
> Support of priestcraft and of knav'ry,
> Which has maintain'd too long its station,
> In this enlightened age and nation,
> Shall root and branch be shov'd away
> As soon as decently it may.

Indeed, may it, root and branch, be chopped down as soon as possible.

I Hate to say, 'I Told You So'

I normally try to avoid telling people "I told you so." However, I am afraid somebody needs to start doing that very thing. Our culture has blatantly disregarded God's Word on several matters for sustained periods of time. Whenever that has happened, noting that God told us all along, one would think that people would have eventually come to realize that God knows his subject matter. Especially as the consequences became disastrous, one would think that they would have acknowledged that he was right to begin with.

Let me point out three examples of non-repentance in which Christians may have to resume saying, "I told you so." It may take an attack that direct to get the message through.

1.   It was only in 1991 that the American Psychological Association reported a study that demolished the character, method, and possible success of the work of Sigmund Freud. Tragically, nearly all of twentieth century psychotherapy was originally built upon that foundation of sand. Christians knew all along this would not work. The world went its own way. God had already told us so. With the very basis of this modern cult obliterated, what will happen? Most likely, the reality will not be admitted quickly unless somebody reads the obituary of Freudianism.

2.   A short time ago it was reported that scientists had recently concluded that all humans were derived from a common DNA structure or pool, dated approximately 200,000 years ago. They named the first DNA code-bearer, "Eve." Interesting. God had already told us so. As a member in our congregation recently related this to me, I congratulated him saying, "You are a genius on the cutting edge of science." The person was not a scientist at all; simply a student of the Bible. God had told us all along that there was an original Eve and that indeed all humans are descended from that one original parent (Acts 17:26). I hate to say, "I told you so," but somebody has to. For years now, Bible-believers have been trying to dispel an erroneous myth of origins. Finally the labs are even discovering this. Will the theory go away? Probably not, unless we say, "I told you so," or more importantly, "God told you so."

3.   Socialism is another die-hard myth. For years, many have said that it would not work. Now it is clear that the experiment has failed. Gorbachev said it most penitentially when he expressed his sincere regrets over the communist experiment by saying he was sorry that "this tragic experiment had taken place on our soil; I only wish it could have been somewhere else." That is quite a confession. Somehow it doesn't seem to have registered yet in the hearing of much of America's present leadership. We may have to start telling them, "I told you so."

It seems unlikely that we will hear American experts confess that any time soon. Ironically, while Lenin's statue has toppled in the very laboratories where these experiments had been assiduously performed for 74 years, in America there is still a push for socialism. In most university sociology classes, Marxist ideals and redistributionist economics are taught *still*. Despite the frank confession in which the Soviet lab technicians report its failure, American universities persist in advocating an outdated socialism. Meanwhile, the World Council of Churches pushes its monolithically leftist agenda and remains consistently anti-American. They will soon appear quite outmoded—at least if Russian church voices are ever considered. All the while, the campus fashion of political correcticity is still virile on university malls, complete with frightened faculties rushing to mold students to outdated models of collapsed experiments lest they find the truth.

Numerous instances of a creeping statism (by any name), make one shout, "Isn't anyone watching the news? Tell congress, tell the faculty, tell the educators, tell the clergy . . . the Experiment FAILED! It is over, guys. Give it up. The world is not flat anymore either. Neither does ether fill outer space, nor is phlogiston the material cause of fire." We told you so; but you would not listen.

Presaging Gorbachev by over a century, one theologian told 'em so: "Materialism and atheism will never win a permanent victory over the human mind; the most they can do is to betray a multitude of unstable souls to their own perdition, by flattering them with future impunity in sin; and to visit upon Christendom occasional spasms of anarchy and crime" (Robert Lewis Dabney). If the failed Soviet experiment is 'The Emperor's New Clothes,' the only remaining nudist camps may soon be located in Washington or PC-pedigreed American colleges. Instead of dogmatically persisting in error, why not accept the results of the experiment? The statist experiment was carried out with a large sample, scientific control, and spanned three generations. That seems representative enough. There is a time to put to rest all falsified theories. The Bible actually told us so long ago. The truth about statism has already been articulated.

We must instead start saying, "I told you so." That still sounds rather presumptuous or proud. I suggest a new "He told you so" campaign. Regarding these human errors, Christians need to speak before, during, and after the collapse of thought-systems. We have been forewarned. We need to declare, "He told you so."

Chicken Little: Crisis du jour

Perhaps a sign that a person (or this person) is aging is that those old nursery rhymes and Aesop's Fables begin to ring truer. Of course, Robert Fulghum has urged that all we need to know could be learned in kindergarten. Without pleading for quite that much simplicity, I cannot resist a strong urge to compare our society to a children's story from time to time. Although some would quickly think of "The Emperor's New Clothes" as instructive, an even more timely children's tale—with instructional value for policy makers today—might be "Chicken Little."

Most will recall how Chicken Little goes about screaming, "The sky is falling The sky is falling. The sky is falling." At first the animals looked up for pieces of descending debris, but there was none. After a while Chicken Little's cries of panic become less alarming. For the sky, you see, is not really falling. The world is not that crisis prone.

Despite all of the claims by the Chicken Littles of our day, many crises never quite materialize as the designated harbingers of disaster have predicted. After all, even the animals in "Chicken Little" realize that if everything is a crisis, then not quite anything really is. Aren't all the mantras of 'unparalleled' or unrivaled crises really fairly self-inflated instances of arrogance or else ignorance of the past?

Is everything really a crisis? This tendency to "commit sociology" (as George Will says) may have started after Watergate when we had a national crisis of conscience and ethics. Next there was an energy crisis in the Carter years. In the abbreviated Ford administration, we had an inflation crisis, and were then called to "Whip Inflation Now." Of course, at the end of the Carter years, we had a humbling hostage "crisis." Crises are everywhere. In the 80s we were told we had a debt crisis and, of course, the perennial—if not obligatory—crime crisis. Later in the 80s, even William Bennett seemed to succumb to this rhetoric as we had education in crisis, and several NBC White Papers reported "Crisis in the American Family." Finally, we had the AIDS crisis and the homeless crisis.

However, all of the above took place over 20 years. In 1992 alone we nearly matched all the previous levels for crises in a single year. First, we had a leadership crisis, a gridlock crisis, followed by a budget crisis; then came a health care crisis (unbeknownst to some 86% who were pleased with their health care), then the welfare crisis (although Sen. Moynihan argued that there is the one but not the other). In between we had a trade crisis (if NAFTA or GATT failed to pass), a TV violence crisis, not to mention the crises concerning Haiti, Bosnia, the former Soviet Union, and Somalia. Crisis R Us.

Do we really have this many crises in one year? All the calls for novel crises make me want to ask: "Just what is new under the sun?" Rather than having many and novel variables, the basic factors of society—complete with its ills—have been around for a long time. For the past three or four millennia, we have had labor problems (Gen. 3:18); fratricide (Gen. 4:8); homicide (Gen. 4:23—perhaps the earliest evidence of Gangsta Rap); moral wickedness (Gen. 6:5); ecological disaster (Gen. 7-9); sexual sin (Gen. 9:22); competition for income (Gen. 13:8-9); consequences stemming from military conquests (Gen. 14); racial hostility (Gen. 16:12); homosexuality (Gen. 19:5); and family alienation (Gen. 21:8 ff.).

We may want to be a little more careful before pronouncing that we are in a completely new or unique situation. Such claims will have to be subjected to scrutiny, as well as Solomon's principle (Eccl. 1:9-11; 3:15). In that light, the plethora of problems takes on a different cast than when we are led to believe that we must create solutions *de novo*.[2] If the problems and dynamics are largely constant, we are afforded a calmer opportunity to assess solutions with more reason and balance. If all is not in crisis, we may view solutions more rationally, and both problems and solutions will be normatively similar over time.

So how are these putative crises new? The sense of constant crisis may be largely attributable to the numerous Chicken Littles chanting: "The crisis is falling. The crisis is falling." Maybe we ought to postpone using crisis language until the

---

[2] Cf. Thomas Sowell, *The Vision of the Anointed* (New York: Basic Books, 1995), pp. 6-9 for a modern exposé of modern tendencies to manufacture crises. In *An All-Round Ministry* (Edinburgh: Banner of Truth, 1986), Charles Spurgeon commented in 1877: "[S]o far as I can see in history, almost every six months some fervid spirit or another has written about 'the present solemn crisis.' There are persons who always believe in the imminent peril of the universe in general and of the Church of God in particular, and a sort of popularity is sure to be gained by always crying 'Woe! Woe!'"

sky falls. A German sociologist once warned: "Sovereign is he who has the power to declare an emergency." Crises may be useful for declaring emergencies and supplanting rational solutions. Indeed, what seems to be a crisis to one interest group or set of incumbents may not be so critical to everybody else. In fact, "The Little Boy who called Wolf" may be an applicable nursery tale for our times, too.

Heterodoxy or Stupidity: Which is Worse?

I have diminishing sympathy for leaders who commit two particular errors at the same time. It is one thing to be wrong because one holds wrong principles. Yet, it is another to offend needlessly an entire tradition in the process. For example, if a politician claims to be a Christian, while at the same time voting against something harmless like prayer at graduation, or if a politician who professes to be personally opposed to abortion is unwilling to "impose" his morality on others, he deserves to squirm in public as he holds the opposite of what the orthodox have always held.

The same is true for preachers. It is disappointing to see them subscribe to erroneous theological notions as:

- The right program and method will produce church growth (Finneyism).
- Standards of conduct must never be elevated so high that they offend members.
- People are more important than principles.

A minister recently announced from his pulpit that he would be promulgating a perspective on divine election that had never been articulated. Without even hearing his explanation, the listener should quickly unpack his assumptions. *One* of those assumptions is that this minister's theological understanding surpasses that of all previous theologians. So far no one had discovered this deep truth, but we are fortunate to have the Reverend Stubble now articulate a grand synthesis. His insight is nothing short of superior to that of Augustine, Calvin, and Luther. The *second* problem is that it is a grand synthesis, while frequently biblical truth requires antithesis. Our modern age, driven by an epistemological girl-scoutism that hopes to have everyone hold hands in a circle and sing, gravitates toward synthesis. With the elevation of civility as a *summa*, no one can be excluded; so we must find an expression that allows everyone to participate equally. Unfortunately, such affirmative action in epistemology is the voluntary euthanasia of biblical truth.

Had the pastor above taken just a little more time, investigated church history just a bit more, or had he dared to submit his brilliant comprehension to his church's confession, he might have spared eventual embarrassment to himself, disruption in his church, and confusion among numerous weaker young Christians. But no; Pastor Stubble had to be smarter than Augustine, more perceptive than Luther and Calvin, brighter than Spurgeon and Whitfield. Indeed he reached the stunning position earlier held by Pelagius, Amyrauldius, Arminius, and Barth—that which has been condemned by various councils and orthodox theological classics. Pastor Stubble was convinced that he was more clever than all the others, but in reality, he was merely repeating previous error. A little consultation of earlier siblings in the faith would have prevented this error, except this pastor unintentionally held to the epistemology of modernism, i. e., that old truth is probably inferior while new discovery is superior. But this pastor should have (and could have) known better. Like many others, his theology should be better.

At first glance, surely unorthodoxy, or holding to wrong theological positions, is more dangerous than stupidity. But I am not sure. If one is determined to reject the guidance of orthodoxy and liberate himself from truth, one could at least avoid the dual error performance that is often given in such maladroit fashion. For example, if one holds to the views above hoping to curry favor with a constituency, does it not seem reasonable that he would want to appease more people than he offends with such heterodoxy? That is to ask, if one is to go out on a limb and seek change, does it not seem that he would at least want to satisfy the majority if the search for audience approval motivates him to begin with?

Yet, many who opt for heterodoxy also couple that with the worst pragmatic approaches. For example, why veto school prayer (if currying favor is the goal) when there are more Bible-thumpers in the community than rabid atheists? That is being stupid as well as heterodox. One certainly should not be both.

The same application could be made to preachers. Don't be both. If and only if one must have wrong ideas or principles, (yes, Johnny, there are right and wrong ones.) that is bad enough. But for Pete's sake, please don't be heterodox in pursuit of pleasing a minority.

That sounds doubly stupid. So I am not sure which is worse. I think heterodoxy is worse, but the more I am around some preachers and some politicians, the more I wonder if stupidity may not be the crowning gem in the pig's snout. Whatever the case, I am sure that both of these vices combined make for rough going.

Epistemologically, Six of One, Half Dozen of the other: Modernism, Post-Modernism, or Post Post-Modernism

An old friend recently warned me against too much rejoicing over the imminent collapse over post-modernism. A set of essays in a recent issue of our journal did expose and celebrate, after a fashion, the demise of post-modernism. Yet, many Christians remain steadfastly unaware of the distinction between modernism, post-modernism, and post post-modernism. Indeed, I do not claim to know all the intricacies of distinguishing between these various schools or fads of thought.

However, when I read about the collapse of post-modernism my normal response is, "So?" I hate to confess my lack of philosophical sophistication, but is the sinking of the *Good Ship Postmodern* really that different from the submersion of modernism in general? I remain unconvinced that the critical epistemological fault line lies between modernism and post-modernism so that the post-modern cataclysm takes on virtual eschatological status. The epistemological crack may be more like the collapse of socialism following the death of communism. Is that a startling surprise? Will many care a hundred years from now?

David Wells describes how each generation tends to think of itself as *sui generis*. He notes that most also think they are superior to past generations. "Every generation tries to get airborne on the plastic wings of this kind of conceit, and in this atmosphere it is almost inevitable that we become breathless about the present and begin to say and do foolish things, as did the pastor whose morning prayer in church began: 'O Lord, have you seen the *New York Times* today?'"[3] Similarly, hysteria about the collapse of modernism should be avoided.

Throughout history, movements often spawn siblings. Consequently, when the parent dies, so do the descendants. For example, in pre-modern (sic) philosophy, the rapid retirement of the philosophies of Descartes, Hume, and Berkeley is seldom seen as the collapse of three separate movements but as an epistemological revolution overturning a major paradigm. Similarly, we do not think of the demise of Hellenism (Plato), post-Hellenism (Aristotle), and post post-Hellenism (Philo or Augustine); we simply think of the retirement of Greek philosophy. A genetic relationship is noted, and the epistemological wreck of Greek philosophy is merely acknowledged, with the sub-differences between minuscule distinctives remaining to be treated as six of one, or half dozen of the other.

Again I confess, I am not that surprised that the obituaries are beginning to be written for post post-modernism. Nor do I see that movement as categorically different from the grandparent—modernism. What, after all, are the major epistemological differences (other than nuance or degree)? Philosophically, once one adopts the following:

- The invisible is non-existent or trivial;
- Truth is in the mind of the beholder;
- Ethics and truth are relative, if existent at all;
- Perspective is everything;
- Absolutes are a myth of the patriarchal and pre-scientific past;
- "The world is all there is," and linguistic analysis is the key (Wittgenstein, a half century ago);

then what are the epistemological differences between modernism, post-modernism, and post post-modernism. Other than updates (perhaps, post post-modernism is the **Windows '97** of thought.), degree of nuance, or increased boldness in rejecting God's absolutes, the substance has remained the same. It seems to me that once the modernist paradigm is adopted, it is but a generation away from post post-modernism. Accordingly, when the parent paradigm is proven deficient, aren't the others as well? The continental divide in epistemology seems to

---

[3] Cf. David Wells, "This Unique Moment: The Changing of the Guard and What it means for Christians Today," *Modern Reformation*, Sept./Oct. 1995.

lie between modernism and ancientism. That may explain part of the revival of paleo-orthodoxy. If all the "neos" and updates are being repudiated, then the only two major epistemological super-highways seem to be: (1) a continuation of failed modernistic off-shoots, or (2) a return to pre-modernism.

Similarly, in theology when Barth and others announced the death of liberal theology and the invention of neo-orthodoxy, most Bible believers yawned. Many saw an organic connection between liberalism and neo-orthodoxy that is similar to the epistemological relationship between modernism and its prefixed children. Some, therefore, rejected neo-orthodoxy as much as they did liberalism and returned to a more paleo-orthodox paradigm. What we may be witnessing, at most, may be a paradigm shift. If so, we should lead the revolution backwards, rather than seek to continue to prop up a moribund modernism.

Carl Henry recently wrote,

> Among the almost 16 million college and university students . . . many are more prone than their pluralistic and relativistic predecessors of the 1960s to fluster their mentors. Few high-school students are aware of deconstructionists and post-modernists like Jacques Derrida, Richard Rorty, Stanley Fish, and others who shower abuse on all who profess a serious interest in objectivity and truth—but the ideas have trickled down. From the '60s, ideas of truth and objectivity have been rejected by a vocal vanguard of sociologists, historians, literary critics, and multi-culturalists. Postmodernism disavows any transcendent warrant for knowledge. Perspectivists scorn scholars who contend that one culture is superior to another or who hold that humans have access to absolute truth about anything. Now when some trendy professor dogmatizes about the real nature of things . . . a feisty student may raise a hand and comment inquiringly, 'That's your opinion, sir?' Any teacher who claims to utter universal truth while he affirms the culture-conditionedness of all knowledge is playing a shell game. [4]

But what difference is the above from a student in the 60s (modernism) asking the professor who claims that all things are relative, "Is that relatively or absolutely true?" The more things change, the more they stay the same.

J. Gresham Machen spotted this major paradigm decades ago in his book, *Christianity and Liberalism*. He called the primitive church "radically doctrinal" —hardly an attribute for churches dominated by the spirit of either modernism or post-modernism. This ancient church—it is not too much to call it "paleo"— confronted "synchronism and tolerance." Said Machen: "A man . . . could not agree to refrain from proselytizing among men of other faiths, but came forward, no matter what it might cost, with a universal appeal. That is what I mean by saying that the primitive Christian church was radically intolerant."[5] He saw Christianity and modernism as the two primary options; the choice was not between

---

[4] *World*, Sept. 16, 1995, p. 25.

[5] Darryl Hart and John Muether, *Fighting the Good Fight* (Philadelphia: The Committee for the Historian of the Orthodox Presbyterian Church, 1995), pp. 202-203.

Christianity, liberalism, post-liberalism, and post post-liberalism. Epistemologically, there were two major options. The same is true today.

And the currents of the world move on. In light of that, David Wells provides an analysis of the modern era that is worthy of our attention.

> What has now happened . . . is that the postmodernists have turned on the Enlightenment, rightly seeing it as a failed project. The attack has been savage. The intellectual soul of modernity has been eviscerated and replaced by emptiness. Where the Enlightenment spoke of purpose, the postmodernists now have havoc; where the Enlightenment believed that what was true could be rationally discovered, the postmodernists mock the notion of truth as simply nostalgia for the past and believe that reason points to nothing but itself; where the Enlightenment gave itself hope in the thought that life was progressing, the postmodernists have abandoned that hope and plunged into nihilism; and where the Enlightenment had order, the postmodernists have only anarchy. They have, in other words, stripped modernity of the hope and sense of order that, however wishful and even fraudulent they were, had made life a little more bearable. It is the argument of the postmodernists that since there is no truth, all such claims actually mask the lust to power and, therefore, their task is often conceived as exposing this lust, deconstructing the world around them. . . . Those who are drawn into this world are being drawn into a vortex where meaning of every kind perishes. [6]

Because of the collapse of modernism or its various "posts," these essays call thinking Christians back, back to ancientism or paleo-orthodoxy. if we find that essentially we are fighting the same battles (as Machen and Solomon), then ought we not link arms with these great paleo-soldiers who have battled so heroically?

Off Track; Turn Around

However, one common response to the above still misses the mark in our opinion. Several thinkers have alleged that by repudiating post-modernism and returning to paleo-motifs, we are being simplistic or unaware of the infrastructure of modernism. To the contrary, in our celebration of the death of post-modernism we understand how pervasive modernism is. We simply wish to reject modernism as an epistemological base. Are we not free—not to mention, prudent—to do so? We are informed that the saturation of the modern is so prevalent that we cannot escape it even if we wish to repudiate it. But we disagree.

Certainly we do not wish to escape the benefits of certain technological improvements (which do not on balance squelch true humanity) or other humane developments. It is all too obvious that neither do we wish to reject technological advance whenever possible. Rather, we appreciate these modern tools. But that is all they are: tools. Christians may use certain tools without buying into a world view. For example, a Christian may certainly use a hammer crafted by a modernist

---

[6] Wells, op. cit.

pagan. A Christian may also drive a car for evangelistic meetings and not necessarily be infected by the modernism of Detroit. A Christian may use cable TV, the telephone, and on-line services without being an epistemological modernist.

I fail to see why we are not free to reject modernism and its step-children altogether. Does it depend on how flawed the system is? If a world view is so incompatible with the epistemology of revelation—unless Christians have reduced their beliefs to little more than modernism *cum* evangelical bumper stickers and small groups—why is it that a Christian cannot just sit this one out?

Our challenge may be succinctly stated: If Christians did not follow the world in modernism, post-modernism, or post post-modernism, i.e., if all the while we philosophically repudiated that world view and its successive generations, then why may we not simply say, "You're off track; you've been off track, and you were so far off track that the only way to get back on track is to retreat—not continue to follow the rut of errors already dug"?[7]

Permit me an example from childhood. Maybe it was because my dad traveled for a living, but vacations for the Hall family became high adventure. When riding with my dad, we became explorers, for we never knew where the short cut my dad selected would take us. I sense I am not the only directionally challenged child.

Richard E. Hall always knew a shorter, more creative route to a destination than simply following the highway. Perhaps it is a male attribute (as my wife suggests) that somehow makes it impossible for certain males to follow either maps or directions. We think—no, we are sure—that we know a better way. So in the early 1960s before the flowering of interstates, off the track went the Hall's 1961 Chevrolet. The famous saying for Hall family vacations was, "Oh, I know this good little gravel road up ahead that is a great shortcut."

But it is possible to get off the track; in fact, to continue in that off-the-track direction may only take us farther from our destination. We may become hopelessly bogged down with no possibility of cutting back to the main thoroughfare.

---

[7] Sometime after my first draft of this section, I discovered that even in my choice of metaphor, C. S. Lewis had beaten me to the punch by at least a half century. I thought I was so original to employ the metaphor below, but alas Lewis said similarly: "First, as to putting the clock back. Would you think I was joking if I said that you can put a clock back, and that if the clock is wrong it is often a very sensible thing to do? But I would rather get away from that whole idea of clocks. We all want progress. But progress means getting nearer to the place where you want to be. And if you have taken a wrong turning, then to go forward does not get you any nearer. If you are on the wrong road, progress means doing an about-turn and walking back to the right road; and in that case the man who turns back soonest is the most progressive man. We have all seen this when doing arithmetic. When I have started a sum the wrong way, the sooner I admit this and go back and start over again, the faster I shall get on. There is nothing progressive about being pigheaded and refusing to admit a mistake. And I think if you look at the present state of the world, it is pretty plain that humanity has been making some big mistakes. We are on the wrong road. And if that is so, we must go back. Going back is the quickest way on." C. S. Lewis, *Mere Christianity* (Christian Library Edition Westwood, NJ: Barbour and Company, Inc., 1952), pp. 24-25.

Some "good little gravel roads" have only one solution: *Stop, turn around, retrace your path, go back until you get back to the point of deviation.* Our family had to follow that trajectory more than once. It is a course that is quite familiar to us.

A similar trajectory may be required by recovering postmodernists. If indeed, post-modernism is as far off the track as we believe, so is modernism. Neither will ever lead back to the straight and narrow—no matter how much acceleration is applied and regardless of new models. Accordingly, if a person wishes to arrive at the destination of truth, he will have to stop, turn around, and return to the point of deviation before traveling any further.

Epistemologically, that seems to describe where we are at the present moment. Both modernism and post-modernism are so deviant from a Christian worldview that if one holds to either of these epistemological "good little gravel roads," then he will never arrive at truth, certainty, or sufficiency—unless he stops his vehicle, reverses his path (some even need to junk their car and walk back), and returns to the "old paths" (Jer. 6:16).

Instead of modernism (of the worldview sort) having become an essential ingredient of life, it is a key cause of massive confusion. The solution, therefore, is a return to the pre-modern, a return to the point of departure—if we ever wish to move ahead.

Perhaps this will clarify our earlier assertions and also help us to understand what is really at stake. If anyone wishes to take issue with my argument above, as a final verification, I may send him on a vacation chauffeured by Richard Hall. Some "good little gravel roads" lead nowhere and should be abandoned. I will take the interstates, thank you. If that makes me a modernist, at least I am not a post-modernist; and I have yet to hear anyone described as a paleo-modernist.

Conservatives often repeat, "If it ain't broke, don't fix it." However, let me recommend this as well: "If it is hopelessly broke, don't fix it, either."

Along that line, Cal Thomas wrote: "Coleridge said of the past, 'If men could learn from history, what lessons it might teach us! But passion and party blind our eyes, and the light which experience gives is a lantern on the stern, which shines only on the waves behind us!' Sadly, the closest we get to history today is the instant replay. A generation of baby boomers, who mostly discarded the past as morally inferior to the present, has mired us in a cultural goo from which it is extremely difficult to extricate ourselves.[8]

Semper Revisionendum

Watching church bodies redefine themselves and transform themselves into something they have never been is not a pretty sight. In an age in which the Episcopalians would have us believe that they have never condemned homosexuality, and the Southern Baptists were never for slavery, and the mainline Presbyterians were

---

[8] Cal Thomas, Preface, *Fighting for Liberty and Virtue* by Marvin Olasky (Wheaton: Crossway, 1995)

always open to pluralism, it seems that revisionism is as rampant as AIDS was once predicted to become. As I monitor a number of church convocations, it becomes increasingly clear to me that they may be roughly divided into two kinds of assemblies: (1) Those that are infatuated with progressivism and conformity to the latest trends, even if they must redefine themselves and their very origins, and (2) Those that stick to their guns. Pardon my oversimplification, but I am less and less impressed with the first sort.

The Anglican church has a noble heritage. Founded contemporaneously with most of the continental reformed churches, the Church of England once offered strong liturgy coupled with orthodox theology and ethics. Now, however, after a century of modernization, the Episcopal Church can hardly be differentiated from a Unitarian congregation except in its external forms and order. The modern Episcopal church is so busy trying to ordain women and ordain homosexuals—and protect bishops who do—that she appears to be a chief victim of the virus of revisionism. To the naïve observer, she looks like First Church of the *Hic et Nunc* —always changing, always revising. One may transform a church that way, to be sure, but the outcome is not always salutary.

The Southern Baptists, a quite conservative group, are also busy of late seeking to avoid a racist reputation. Certainly, any Christian church should avoid racism or sinful bigotry. To ask forgiveness for past sins is appropriate in many cases. However, amidst all the penance, communions ought to simply confess rather than seek to deny that earlier generations were wrong. We commend the Southern Baptist Convention for their sincere efforts to reconcile with African Americans and to repent of their former sins. Other churches have done the same. What will not work, however, is to rationalize the past or act as if it can be redesigned as easily as Luther's "nose of wax." The past is rather stubborn, even though many moderns seek to resculpt it.

Similarly, the mainline Presbyterian Church sometimes appears to want to be as far away from its old school Calvinistic heritage as possible. In 1996, the PCUSA had before it propositions to ordain homosexuals and to merge into the Church of Christ Uniting (COCU, a mega-ecumenical effort that would have instituted bishops). Fortunately, some of the more conservative positions held the day, even if narrowly in this assembly. We commend that, while we repudiate the attempts to so transform the Presbyterian church into an *ecclesia modernus.*

Revisionism is an equal opportunity disease, one that can afflict conservatives as well as liberals. A few years back, I attended a conference in which a group was trying implicitly to redefine itself. Amidst this conservative group, I was surprised to hear its leaders so readily invoke the *Semper Reformandum* (perpetually being reformed) mantra. Having come out of a liberal denomination as a young man I learned to reach for my wallet to protect what little cash we had left whenever I heard that phrase. In most cases, the phrase "continually reforming" (besides being a poor Latin translation, rendered in the active voice instead of the passive gerundive; it should be "continually being reformed") signaled an attempt to move away from received truth. Of course, we realize that the past contains error and that no tradition is infallible. However, seldom has a church body been improved by the "continually updating" wing. More often than not, the alterations have been departures from the best expressions of orthodoxy. Hence, I developed an instinctive distrust for the continual faddishness of the *Semper* wing.

Thus, I am surprised when I hear conservatives invoke that cant. Of equal interest, at the same conference, not a single speaker showed equal opportunity bias by stressing or citing the first part of the rubric: *Reformatus* ("having been reformed"). If one simply must be a *Semper Reformandum* advocate, then the least one could do to avoid total revisionism is to cite the first half of the motto ("having been reformed") as emphatically as he calls for updating.

Isn't that what the reformers did? Actually, I am not sure they were so open to revisionism. From my reading of Calvin and others, I cannot locate their invocation of *Semper Reformandum*; the reformers seemed to think that the church could simply be reformed to the eternal truths of the Word of God and gave little countenance to modernization dynamics.[9] In fact, I cannot find anywhere that they used the "*Semper*" phrase. Can someone help me? Most likely it is just one of those vacuums in my theological education, but would someone cite for me where Calvin advocated the *Semper Reformandum*? It is abundantly clear that he called for "*Reformatus est*," but I cannot put my finger on a call for "*Semper Reformandum*" by Calvin, Luther or Turretin. I cannot locate it in the great sixteenth and seventeenth century theologians. I see no charge to be "always hip" in the great Confessions. I cannot find this phrase or its paraphrase in Scottish or American Presbyterianism of the eighteenth century. I do not see it in Hodge, Bavinck, Wollebius, Ames, Perkins, Boston, Watson, etc. Perhaps I am just reading the wrong volumes. Or could it be that the "*Semper*" aspect is to theology what "unconditional positive regard" is to psychology: an invention of modernism to justify the *de facto* revisionism? I wonder. This phrase's moment of evolutionary appearance may be as instructive as its discovery.[10]

If, as I suspect, the *Semper Reformandum* addition is of relatively recent origin—and that it is a result of definite modernizing impulses—then perhaps my instinctive flinching from such vocabulary is warranted. Could it be that I was taught correctly in earlier years that *Semper Reformandum* was an inherently liberalizing phrase? B. B. Warfield once warned: "But let us equally loudly assert that progressive orthodoxy and retrogressive heterodoxy can scarcely be convertible terms."

---

[9] The Church of Christ needs more than anything else to grow into conformity to Christ but conformity to Christ is not to be confused with conformity to revised ideas or modern *ethoi*.

[10] Last year *Premise* offered a prize for anyone who could show us an original use of this phrase prior to the year 1800. Still, no one has reported a sighting, possibly making a pre-1800 instance of *Semper Reformandum* less verified than either UFOs or the viability of Social Security in its present economic health. If this strand of *ur*-progressivism was so dominant early on, one wonders why it is so difficult to unearth multiple early instances.

We should have learned from Charles Spurgeon who warned earlier:

Macauley rightly said that theology is immutable; but these men are continually contradicting that opinion in the most practical manner, for their theology is fickle as the winds. Landmarks are laughed at, and fixed teaching is despised. 'Progress' is their watchword, and we hear it repeated *ad nauseam*. Very far are we from denying that men ought to make progress in the knowledge of the truth, for we are aiming at that ourselves . . . we trust that in some humble measure we are gaining it. But the words need interpreting—what is intended by 'progress' in this case? Which way does it go?
It is too often progress *from the truth*, which, being interpreted, is progressing backwards. They talk of higher thought, but it is an ascending downwards. . . . their progress is a going from, not a going to, the place of our desires. Evidently, it is progress *from usefulness*. They invite us to follow them in their advance towards a barren Socinianism, for thither the new theology tends, or to something worse. Now, we know, at the present time, certain ancient chapels shut up, with grass growing in front of them, and over the door of them is the name *Unitarian Baptist Chapel*. . . . we have no desire to empty our pews in order to grow more grass. We have . . . not yet arrived at that consummation where the spiders are dwelling in delightful quietude in which the pews are more numerous than the people . . .[11]

From the Old Wives' Tales Department

A number of myths have been perpetuated by well-meaning but theologically-stunted Christian thought. Let me be clear about what I mean. More often than I wish, I have heard an otherwise reputable Christian attribute something to some other fine theologian. What was attributed sounded totally foreign to what I had read in the *corpus* of that theologian. Note, it is usually only deceased theologians who are subjected to such myth-making, lest living thinkers repudiate the allegation.

For example, when someone says, "John Calvin advocated group sex on Fridays," that raises a little suspicion. Indeed, I am surprised that normally thought-ful Christians have their suspicion raised so *seldom* when equally absurd attri-butions are made. Likewise, if someone says, "Luther was fond of asserting that Pentium Pro chips were superior to 486s," even I might suspect that I was hearing a myth or an old wives' tale.

One must be careful with the attributions he accepts. Maybe myths abound more in days when truth is a stranger and when gullibility is sometimes confused with virtue. To watch some Christians at work, it seems as if there is some hidden obligation to accept any supposed citation, even if it goes against the bulk of a theologian's teaching. I am amazed, for example, how nearly everyone in my particular communion uses Francis Schaeffer's revered name to settle an issue. To hear the debates, Schaeffer (under whom I once studied) doubted the Noahic flood or believed it was universal (depending on the speaker); Schaeffer repudiated

---

[11] Charles Spurgeon, *An All-Round Ministry* (Edinburgh: Banner of Truth, 1986), 94-95.

women's ordination (or embraced it) depending on the speaker; Schaeffer hated church discipline or salivated over it (depending on the argument); Schaeffer was an evidentialist or was a presuppositionalist; Schaeffer advocated group sex on Fridays or Schaeffer advocated group sex on Saturdays. Surely, he did not really say all these things. Maybe we need a little skepticism when we see the various authorities quoted out of context. Is it too much to ask that speakers really check these things out before promulgating them? With ever-expanding data bases and media, maybe Christians will prove to be the epistemologists of integrity.

Three examples of fine Christians being cited against their grain come to mind.

(1) I have often heard Luther invoked as a rationalization for less-than-Christian politics. Supposedly, Luther said, "I'd rather have a wise Turk to govern than a foolish Christian." That aphorism, of course, gives away much of the store. I have heard expert friends from Michael Cromartie to Ralph Reed to Charles Colson to Joel Belz and many others ascribe that to Luther. Every time I heard that, I assumed I was the dummy in the conversation, because: (a) I had never seen (nor could I find) that quote, and (b) it sounded a little incompatible with some of the other material I had read in Luther.

Finally, Richard Neuhaus is trying to put that myth to rest. Of this pseudo-Luther sound bite, he admitted: "I had used it for years in speeches and writing until I was challenged. My curiosity piqued, I launched an inquiry that ended up involving scholars and librarians both here and in Europe, only to discover that Luther never said it. It fit Luther's 'twofold kingdom' approach to civil governance, and he said much of the same purport, but please take this as yet another effort to put it to rest."[12] Neuhaus had earlier noted that this myth was like the cat that has "nine times nine lives." Why don't we join Dr. Neuhaus and take this aphorism out of Luther's mouth (since it never was on his lips), unless someone can show a clear citation? Seems only fair and reasonable to me, unless someone just wants to support a position with illegitimate material. If that is the case, why not just cite this pseudo-Luther attribution as "Old Wives' Tale Number 359"?

(2) Augustine is frequently cited as an adherent, yea verily an advocate, of long days for creation. Cited by those ranging from Hugh Ross to Davis Young (and others), if one does not apply a due skepticism, one will believe that St. Augustine was really a pretty-hip, pro-evolutionary kind of guy. If it strikes you as unusual to think that more than 150 decades ago Augustine would agree with Darwin and post-Darwinian fundamentalists, you may be correct. Orators may want to research what St. Augustine really said on the subject, before they pollute the discussion stream with false or misleading attributions. Let's refer to this one as "Old Wives' Tale Number 666" from now on.

(3) In late 1996, the Pope was reported as releasing a statement that evolution was an acceptable orthodox interpretation. It seems that his much-balleyhooed comments were, alas, a misinterpretation by a liberal press. When first released

---

[12] Richard Neuhaus, *First Things*, January, 1997, number 69, p. 63.

many of the faithful, who had respected Pope John Paul II for his uncompromised moral stands, were shocked and in disbelief. They were right. The Pope never really said such a thing. What he did say—that was not widely reported—in his Address to the Pontifical Academy of Sciences was this: "Consequently, theories of evolution which, in accordance with the philosophies inspiring them, consider the spirit as emerging from the forces of living matter or as a mere epiphenomenon of this matter are incompatible with the truth about man. Nor are they able to ground the dignity of the person. With man, then we find ourselves in the presence of an ontological difference, an ontological leap, one would say."[13] John Paul II continued to raise the question about how such "ontological discontinuity" could fit with evolutionary theory. Thus, we refer to this myth as O. W. T. #756.

Maybe these three above, and no doubt more, are myths that are nearly equivalent to the "old wives' tales" in Timothy's day. Paul told Timothy: "Have nothing to do with godless myths and old wives' tales; rather train yourself to be godly." (1 Tim. 4:7)

Our scholarship would improve if we could have more verification of sources. Indeed, these instances I cite above may be no more credible (although they may have more than nine lives as Neuhaus suggests) than the recurrent reports that Madelene Murray O'Hare is about to take over the FCC, or that the "good times virus" will eat your computer's hard drive, or the paranoia that someone might litigate if you follow the Scriptures.

Yeah, and the sky's falling, and aliens are attacking, and church growth happens like the Pythagorean experts say. Right.

Believe these if you will, but it might be the better part of valor to check some of these out. These may be modern versions of the endless myths and old wives' tales (I agree, old husbands' have tales, too.) that should be laughed at. Right up there with John Boswell's allegation that in early medieval days the church authorized same-sex marriage liturgies.

Then again, maybe that great theologian P. J. O'Rourke is correct. He once said, "Those who fail to learn their lessons of history . . . also failed geometry." There is a definite tendency, once one abandons the lessons of the past, to be quite prolific in mistakes in other areas as well. Forsaking the past may generate more blindness to the truth.

Knowledge of history is certainly helpful for any field of human endeavor.

---

[13] "Theories of Evolution," by John Paul II, *First Things*, March 1997, no. 71, pp. 28-29.

Index

A Gift to our Frequent Readers

If you appreciate the books from *The Covenant Foundation*, we want you to be a frequent reader of our growing stock of excellent literature. If you wish to order any of these titles at a Frequent Reader's Discount please return this as an order form with a check payable to: **The Covenant Foundation**, 190 Manhattan Ave., Oak Ridge, TN (USA). Please include $3.00 for shipping/handling per volume. Sorry, we don't accept credit cards.

The following are available at **20% off retail** while quantities last:

_____*Savior or Servant?: Putting Government in Its Place* by David W. Hall
405 pp., retail, $18.95; Frequent Reader's Discount, $15.15.

Savior or Servant? is a revival of a classic approach to limited government. As nations are beginning to shrink governments, a surprising source commends itself as an able assistant in reform. The biblical view of the state, removed from the varied fads of political science, provides an enduring perspective by which to measure all states. Beginning with a survey of biblical teaching on pressing matters of state today, this study follows the contours of the Old and New Testaments. Savior or Servant? calls all levels of government to a servant posture, rather than allowing officials to dominate. A historical tracing of the best and most pertinent that theology has to offer on the subject is contained in these pages.

> "*Savior or Servant?* is the single best volume of Christian thinking on the issue of the increasingly intrusive state since the halcyon days of the Puritans. Theology at its very best: orthodox, comprehensive, relevant, and provocative." — **George Grant**
> "Hall contributes substantively to our civic education. His work provides an entry way to an intelligent, orthodox, conservative, believing agenda in a society in the death grip of a dying modernity and a nascent postmodernism — **J. Ligon Duncan III**
> "This ambitious and important book introduces a rich and undeservedly neglected tradition of Christian political thought."— **Richard John Neuhaus**
> "Extremely well-written, thoughtful, and comprehensive" — **Ralph Reed**
> "Good policy books by Christians are distressingly rare. An important exception is David Hall's *Savior or Servant?* from the Kuyper Institute." — **Doug Bandow**

_____*Welfare Reformed: A Compassionate Approach*, David W. Hall, ed.
256 pp., retail, $10.95; Frequent Reader's Discount, $8.95.

"A much needed corrective and a bracing tonic for those tired of seeing good intentions produce alarming results." — **Michael Cromartie**
"More important now than ever." — **Joel Belz**

_____*Election Day Sermons*, David W. Hall, ed.
220 pp., retail, $14.95; Frequent Reader's Discount, $11.95.

_____*Leading in Worship* by Terry L. Johnson
Cloth, retail, $17.95: Frequent Reader's Discount, $14.35.

_____*Paradigms in Polity*, David W. Hall/Joseph H. Hall, eds.
616 pp., cloth, retail, $29.95; Frequent Reader's Discount, $23.95.